MW00785899

American City, Southern Place

American City, Southern Place

A CULTURAL HISTORY OF
Antebellum Richmond

Gregg D. Kimball

The University of Georgia Press   Athens and London

© 2000 by the University of Georgia Press
Athens, Georgia 30602
All rights reserved

Designed by Sandra Strother Hudson
Set in Monotype Walbaum by G&S Typesetters, Inc.
Printed and bound by Maple-Vail
The paper in this book meets the guidelines for permanence
and durability of the Committee on Production Guidelines for
Book Longevity of the Council on Library Resources.

Printed in the United States of America
04 03 02 01 00   C   5 4 3 2 1

Library of Congress Cataloging-in-Publication Data
Kimball, Gregg D.
American city, southern place : a cultural history
of antebellum Richmond / Gregg D. Kimball.
p.   cm.
Includes bibliographical references (p.) and index.
ISBN 0-8203-2234-2 (alk. paper)
1. Richmond (Va.)—History—19th century.   2. Richmond
(Va.)—Social conditions—19th century.   3. Richmond
(Va.)—Social life and customs—19th century.   I. Title.
F234.R557 K56   2000
975.5'45103—dc21   99-089013

British Library Cataloging-in-Publication Data available

An early version of chapter 6 appeared in John Saillant, ed.,
Afro-Virginian History and Culture (Garland, 1998).
Used by permission.

For

Gordon and Joan Kimball

and

Cheryl, Elizabeth, Nathaniel, and Virginia

CONTENTS

FIGURES, TABLE, AND MAPS

ACKNOWLEDGMENTS

his book is the culmination of thirteen years of striving to understand my adopted home—Richmond, Virginia. Through research, exhibitions, and articles, often done collaboratively with colleagues in academia and public history, I have poked and prodded much of Richmond's often contradictory past. But no period seemed more interesting to me than the decades before the Civil War.

I had no idea what awaited me when I moved to Richmond in 1986 to join the staff of a small city institution called the Valentine Museum. Founded by and named after one of Richmond's most influential families, the Valentine was a special place at that time. The museum's director, B. Frank Jewell, was creating new programs and exhibitions, based on a rigorous scholarly agenda. It was during the museum's in-house seminars, exhibition meetings, and research forays that many of the central questions of this study arose. We had a tremendous staff who all greatly influenced me. Marie Tyler-McGraw and I worked on an exhibition and publication on antebellum black life and culture that launched my interest in Richmond's African-American history. Jane Webb Smith's work on the Valentine family spurred my own curiosity about the consciousness of Southern merchants. Greg Galer and Richard Love collaborated with me on the research and the recovery of artifacts for an exhibition on Richmond's working class and the restoration of the Tredegar Iron Works. Barbara Batson and I curated an exhibition on the relationship of slaves and masters in Richmond that was tied to the interpretation of the museum's Wickham House; we debated the material culture evidence and the nature of urban households in the South. I pored over images with Teresa Roane, trying to understand the visual record of Richmond's past. Colleen Callahan made me realize the cultural importance of clothing and outward display, especially in the South. Many fine interns helped me with specific research areas. Cynthia Hasley explored the Tredegar Iron Works records, and Anne Hodgson delved into the world of Richmond's German community. Frank Jewell cared enough about the intellectual grounding of the museum's work that he facilitated my return to graduate school; he always cared about the big picture and the broad historical questions. Every major project that I was involved with at the Valentine—five exhibitions and numerous publications—brought me into contact with historians, designers, consultants, and archivists, who further expanded my horizons. I thank them all.

It was through my work at the Valentine that I first met two scholars who most influenced this work. David R. Goldfield helped shape the museum's interpretive agenda from the beginning and remained a stalwart friend. He was kind enough to read an early version of the entire manuscript. I also knew Edward L. Ayers from my work at the Valentine, and he became my advisor when I entered the University of Virginia to pursue the doctorate in history. Besides his incredible energy and support, he allowed me to tackle a very large historical subject for the dissertation. The study long defied organization due to its broad content and unusual approach; Ed helped me conceptualize a way to make the narrative work.

Many people took the time to make useful and substantial comments on various versions of this work. My dissertation committee—Ed Ayers, Cindy Aron, Nelson Lichtenstein, and Richard Handler—raised excellent questions and made numerous suggestions for improvements. Beth Schweiger brought a fresh eye to the manuscript and pushed me to improve my analysis in a number of areas. Mark Greenough used his encyclopedic knowledge of Richmond's antebellum militias to correct errors and suggest changes. Richard Love and Charles Dew both read parts of the book manuscript. The two readers for the University of Georgia Press provided valuable insights and suggestions. My current colleagues at the Library of Virginia, including Brent Tarter, John Kneebone, Julie Campbell, and Stacy Moore, either read parts of the manuscript or were subjected to endless discussions of major and minor points in it. Emily Salmon went the extra mile and read the entire manuscript one last time before it went to the press—and I'm glad she did. Sara Daniels Bowersox designed effective maps and figures with her usual grace. Theresa Roane, Howard McManus, and Mary Beth Corrigan provided invaluable help in locating illustrations.

A great benefit of working in a public research institution is meeting people who are studying various aspects of Virginia's history. Some, like Elsa Barkley Brown, became valued colleagues in research or publishing endeavors. Others have influenced my perspective on Richmond and Virginia more than they probably know in numerous conversations and contacts. They include Michael Bell, Charles Dew, Steve Hoffman, Charlene Lewis, John O'Brien, Peter Rachleff, Nancy Jawish Rives, Phil Schwarz, Phil Troutman, and Tracey Weis.

As a former manuscript curator, I understand the importance of the keepers of records in helping define and shape a scholar's research project. I would especially like to thank the staffs of the Library of Virginia; the Virginia Historical Society; the Special Collections Department at the University of Virginia Library; the Rare Book, Manuscript, and Special Collections Library of Duke University; the Southern Historical Collection at the Wilson Library, University of North Carolina, Chapel Hill; and the Manuscript Division, Library of Congress, for their excellent guidance. The Clements Library at the University of Michigan also provided access to a key collection at a distance. I received exceptional service and sage advice at all of these places no matter with whom I worked—thus I feel somewhat reluctant to include the obligatory recitation of archivists' names. Yet I would be remiss to pass over people I have known both as archival colleagues and as a researcher, for I have especially mined their knowledge. They include Conley Edwards, Michael Plunkett, E. Lee Shepard, and Minor Weisiger. I also cannot fail to mention the late Waverly Winfree, who introduced me to Virginia history as no one else could. Naturally, I accept responsibility for all errors in this work.

I have always believed that the solitary scholar is a myth. When we read the works of previous generations we engage them in a dialogue about the past. I hope that this book will contribute in some small way to that larger conversation and assist future collaborators in the great enterprise of understanding our past.

his work is a study of how different groups of residents of Richmond, Virginia, understood their world in the period from 1840 to the Civil War. Richmonders' ideas about themselves and their society were very much tied to complex concepts of place. Like all cities in the highly mobile society of antebellum America, Richmond was a point of connection for a myriad of far-flung cultural, economic, and social relationships. Richmond's antebellum populace belonged to, and struggled with ideas about, a series of intersecting worlds.

In Richmond's commercial houses, dry-goods merchants fresh from buying trips to New York haggled with visitors from the Virginia countryside; in ironworks and shops, Yankee transplants worked alongside native Virginians; in African-American churches, free blacks discussed going to Northern cities, and enslaved men and women arrived from scattered plantation communities; near the city market, slave traders sold black Virginians to the Cotton South as other slaves from rural plantations hired their services for the coming year; in Capitol Square, German and Irish militias paraded with native white Virginians, celebrating national holidays and state heroes. Richmonders constructed their identities within and in response to this complex web of relationships.

All of these scenes reflect a fluidity of experience impossible to reconstruct through census data, city directories, and tax lists, which is precisely why urban social history has failed to capture the dynamic interplay of people and ideas that characterized American cities and society before the Civil War. The importance of these connections to this study is not so much the raw statistical facts of mobility, labor markets, and commercial links (although these are also important historical topics), but how the identities of different groups of Richmonders were shaped and reshaped in this cauldron of experience and contact. Such an intricate world allows us neither to reduce Richmond to a part of a monolithic South nor to easily assume the attitudes of its people.[1]

The diaries, letters, memoirs, and other private writings of city residents that form the core of this study reflect the complexity of the world of the 1850s, and especially Richmond. Northerners and Southerners, city dwellers and country folk, free people and slaves, those high born and low—all viewed the Upper South city according to the larger cultural worlds they inhabited. They lived on the edge of country and city, the North and South, and liberty and slavery. Not surprisingly, their perceptions of the dangers and constraints, as well as the opportunities and possibilities, of their society differed greatly depending on their positions within these networks. Richmonders often ignored or explained away the contradictions that flowed through their society. Their words and thoughts remind us that human beings have a remarkable capacity to filter their immediate world through personal views and perceptions. I have not corrected the misspellings in the transcription of manuscript sources, but I have silently regularized punctuation in some cases to make the quotes easier to understand. I have also capitalized the words "Southern" and "Northern" throughout. I have done so because these terms carried a great deal of meaning for many of the historical actors in my story.

Part 1 introduces the late antebellum city's politics, economy, and culture. Richmond's role as Virginia's capital made it an important national center of America's civic religion of the Revolution and its leaders, combining the iconography of state and the Union. Moreover, the torchlight parades, barbecues, and rallies of Virginia's parties increasingly mirrored the general form and accents of America's vigorous political street theater. The pilgrims and party hacks from throughout Virginia and the nation who came to venerate Washington and other symbolic figures of the Revolution saw a skyline dominated by church steeples and neoclassical public buildings that spoke to America's fascination with ancient republics. Those coming to worship the almighty dollar were probably more impressed with the city's bustling docks, factories, and markets.[2]

Infrastructure and industrial operations accelerated as city elites tried to push Richmond forward in the race for urban wealth and prominence. As the preeminent industrial city in the Upper South, Richmond solidified intra-urban connections with the North. Richmond and its sister cities in the South stood largely unconnected with each other and became increasingly dependent on Northern factors and trade. A Richmond merchant had a better chance of encountering a Charlestonian in New York than in either man's home city.[3]

Economic resurgence also tightened Richmond's embrace of the Virginia countryside, however, and the city became deeply implicated in the system of slavery by its relationship to its hinterland. Railroads, agricultural improvements, and industrialization only made slavery stronger through the reciprocal relationship between the city and countryside.[4] Internal improvements moved the Virginia tobacco belt into the Piedmont region, while the old Tidewater areas became rejuvenated through agricultural diversification. Urban slave hiring emerged as a labor market for the old Tidewater region's growing African-American population, filling the factories that manufactured tobacco grown by slaves in the expanding Piedmont region and even southwest Virginia. Slavery was hardly dying in Virginia, but it certainly was becoming more varied. Enslaved African Americans used the complexities of the new economy to their advantage, expanding their world and their lives along the canals, railroads, and steamship lines that connected Richmond to the larger world.[5]

Despite its reliance on slavery, Richmond had all the trappings of American urban culture. Visiting its hotels, theaters, and other urban institutions was a familiar experience for middle-class Americans. Many of the reform movements sweeping urban America—temperance, asylums, and education—also took hold in Richmond. Moreover, the working-class and ethnic composition of the city became even more like Northern cities in the 1850s. Some elements of the city's life, such as the development of Hollywood Cemetery, reflected typical American middle-class, bourgeois values. While touring the North, Virginia women visited similar rural cemeteries. Gender relations between men and women seemed remarkably Victorian and conventional.[6]

Yet many people in Richmond looked to the Virginia countryside for their cultural values. For example, the supervision of domestic slaves provided continuity between the countryside and the city. Industrial slavery has long overshadowed domestic service as a topic of historical study in the Upper South, but in Richmond, enslaved domestic workers far outnumbered enslaved factory laborers.[7] While urban bondage has often been characterized as "freer" than plantation slavery, black and white women met in households on very similar terms in both places. The strong connections between urban and rural white slaveholding families reinforced similar attitudes toward slavery and society.[8]

Although Richmond's diverse residents often met in the streets and public spaces of the city, they inhabited inner worlds that transected different parts of the American, urban, and Southern landscapes. The views from the ethnic enclave, urban townhouse, and back-alley slave quarter were decidedly different. Part 2 of this work looks at how Richmonders' connections to the world beyond their immediate environment—Virginia—shaped their perceptions of themselves and their world, examining four specific spheres of culture in late antebellum Richmond: the relationship of merchants and their families to Northern cities through trade and travel; the diaspora of African Americans and its points of connections, especially the church; the world of the Northern- and foreign-born ironworkers who labored at the Tredegar Iron Works; and the politics and culture of antebellum urban militias. These case studies demonstrate that most city leaders, politicians, and merchants shared the assumptions of like men and women in the Virginia countryside to whom they were closely tied by economics, kinship, and slavery, but that they also faced urban working people, slaves, and free blacks who inhabited very different worlds shaped by their own ideas and traditions. Slavery created deep fault lines in the community, and occasionally class and ethnic conflict emerged into public view. White Richmonders struggled to create unity through public rituals and Revolutionary symbols, but these moments of white solidarity only masked the contradictory worldviews of a deeply conflicted antebellum community.

The personal and business letters of merchant families reveal their adherence to Southern values and ideals. Traveling frequently to the North, merchants had the opportunity to see Northern social relations for themselves. The Northern urban society they encountered on their frequent buying trips seemed chaotic, impersonal, and deeply divided between rich and poor. Men and women of the commercial classes argued that Richmond would escape this fate thanks to the organic and happy relationship between masters and slaves. Urban elites defended the idea of the Southern household rooted in slavery and rejected Northern "isms" that seemed to threaten their traditional notions of family and religion. They did not see slavery as an unfortunate legacy that they were powerless to change but as an antidote to the disorder of the North.[9]

Virginians harbored deep fears that the new Richmond of the 1850s would fall prey to the social disorder seen in Northern cities. They were especially alarmed at the penetration of Yankee people, ways, and ideas into Virginia's capital. In mills, militias, counting houses, parlors, and reform societies, Yankees rubbed shoulders with native Virginians. Commercial men noted the increase in "sharp," vaguely unethical trading and other manifestations of Yankee practices. As urban problems such as poverty, gambling, and crime increased, commercial elites pushed the blame for these problems onto a whole cast of others: Jews, slave traders, immigrants, and what Daniel R. Hundley, one of the antebellum South's most perceptive chroniclers, called "Southern Yankees."[10]

Richmond's commercial elites were deeply involved in civic organizations and local politics and realized that their fortunes would rise and fall with the city's fate.[11] In the competitive commercial world of the 1850s, urban leaders saw Northern cities as rivals and dreamed of a Virginia freed from dependence on the North. Many even saw (somewhat prophetically) Virginia as the commercial capital of a Southern confederacy, indulging in commercial conventions that often became venues for prosecession statements. For all the modernity that Richmond seemed to evince in the 1850s as the city marched forward in the market revolution, most members of its merchant class stood resolutely in the social world of Old Virginia and viewed themselves as Southerners. Ingrained social and cultural values trumped commercial connections and market relations in shaping the ideology of the elite.[12]

Those Richmonders with the greatest access to the wider world—the city's commercial elite—became the most parochial in interest and perception. As the city's largest economic stakeholders in the plantation economy and the system of slavery, merchants turned inward and became increasingly strident in their defense of the South against any perceived threat from outsiders. At the same time, Richmonders from the most rural, economically impoverished, and politically repressed sector of Virginia society turned outward to a larger world that seemed to offer possibilities for greater freedom and independence.[13]

James Horton has emphasized the African-American understanding of an interconnected urban black world and the continued engagement of Northern free blacks with their slave brothers and sisters in the South in the 1840s and 1850s. Reaching back to the time of Gabriel's planned rebellion in 1800, African Americans in Virginia were part of an elaborate network that tied together a trans-Atlantic black world. The African-American role in the world of trade as boatmen and draymen and the emerging slave-hiring system linked the black community in the countryside and city in post-Revolutionary Richmond. These systems were in turn connected to larger trade systems by black seamen and émigrés from the West Indies.[14]

By the 1850s African Americans in Richmond belonged to a complex black world that included Africa, the urban North, the western frontier, Canada, and the slave South. The minutes of First African Baptist Church from 1841 to 1859 reveal migration patterns of African Americans to and from Richmond. Many free blacks, especially in the 1850s, left for the North and West, joining escaped slaves in their new homes. Ironically, the modern technologies of steamships and railroads made escaping along trade routes much easier for Richmond slaves, as did the information that flowed surreptitiously through the mail system. The correspondence of the Scott family, who migrated to Ohio and then Canada, legislative petitions of free blacks asking to stay in Virginia, and published runaway accounts also provide evidence of African-American connections to the larger world and the effect of those connections. African Americans carefully weighed the possibilities and dangers of life outside Virginia against the ever-present threats of a slave society that sent thousands of men and women southward in the slave trade. The potential for education and greater freedom inspired many to emigrate, but the thought of leaving

family and friends for an unknown and potentially hostile land kept others
in the Old Dominion. Whether assessing the possibilities of Liberian emigration or residence in a Northern city, black Richmonders drew on a variety of sources to make their decision. Travelers' tales, letters, lecturers, and
the printed word all opened a plethora of possibilities and created a sense
of belonging to a common history. Africa, America, and Virginia were
all part of the varied cultural vision that Richmond's African Americans
shared.

White urban artisans and workers also operated within a larger cultural
framework. As the fastest-growing segment of the antebellum city's working class, Northern- and foreign-born newcomers were an important political and cultural group, and they were also a key segment of Richmond's
labor force. The success of the Tredegar Iron Works, Richmond's most
prominent Southern home industry, would have been impossible without
the Northern- and foreign-born workers who brought essential skills to the
works. Nevertheless, Joseph Reid Anderson, the master of Tredegar, soon
decided his labor costs were too high and decided to employ slave workers
in the mills.[15]

The use of slave workers led to conflict with Northern- and foreign-born
workers. Speaking directly to their laboring brothers in Great Britain and
the American North, Richmond's artisans defended themselves against attacks from the city's conservative leadership, articulating their rights to
control their labor. Anderson quashed a strike in 1847 and has generally
been regarded as the victor in this labor struggle. This conclusion is questionable. His belief that no man had the right to interfere with his use of
slave labor struck a responsive chord in his homeland, but Anderson continued to have difficulty controlling his white workers, when he could recruit them at all, and the output of his rolling mills fell dramatically for
many years. The Northern- and foreign-born workers at Tredegar belonged
to a skilled, itinerant working class that stretched across America and back
to the British Isles and Germany. Learning quickly of the strike, rolling-
mill workers made Anderson pay for his decision, avoiding Richmond
whenever possible.[16]

Never expanding his force of skilled slaves after 1850, Anderson eventually came to an accommodation with the white workmen who dominated

the works by the Civil War. Anderson sought not only industrial peace but also a political truce with his men. A major voting block in the more democratic politics of the 1850s, Tredegar's workers could call politician Anderson to account, just as he tried to enforce discipline at the works. Thus, although many authors assume the hegemony of Southern elites, workers pushed state leaders like Anderson and Governor Henry A. Wise toward a conception of politics that included white workingmen.[17]

Anderson and his men met not only on the shop floor in the 1850s but also in torchlight parades and sumptuous banquets, where both parties articulated their vision of the world. The complex negotiation of culture among white men in Richmond found its purest expression in commemorations of tradition—the creation of a shared past. White Virginians considered themselves heirs to the founders of the American Republic, and even as the state's inordinate influence on early national politics faded, Virginians fashioned an epic national creation story centering on its Revolutionary heroes—America's first great civic religion. The uses of tradition defined the behavior and beliefs of Richmonders in the increasingly partisan 1850s, largely as a way to promote sectional mediation and reconciliation.[18]

Key to the development of Revolutionary tradition, volunteer militia companies brought together the broad middle of Richmond's white male population, emphasizing brotherhood, conviviality, and manliness. Richmond's military and cultural leaders joined these men in civic commemorations and travels to Northern cities, emphasizing in their speeches Virginia's and America's Revolutionary heritage and icons, as well as a remarkably integrated vision of the world built around the twin, but deeply intertwined, ideas of Virginia and Union.[19]

Richmond's militias hosted and entertained men from Philadelphia, New York, and Baltimore in Virginia's capital, and these interchanges illustrate the presence of a pan-urban class of artisans and clerks that were the heart and soul of Richmond's militias and those of other eastern cities. This common experience of militia training and display may have helped shape the central notions of courage and manliness articulated by soldiers, and especially officers, on both sides in the early years of the Civil War. These men were part of a mobile petty bourgeoisie and working class that shared many of the same values and the same culture.[20]

European immigrants, Northerners, and native Virginians, primarily of the artisan, clerking, and petty-merchant classes, assembled to bond in brotherhood through drinking, eating, sport, and military discipline. They paid homage to state and nation through Revolutionary icons and ceremony. When visiting their militia brothers in other East Coast cities to the North, their face-to-face contact told them that the sectional issues of the day were largely the work of fanatics on both sides.

Political and militia leaders were careful to couch state and national allegiances within the context of a confederation of states. By mediating between the ideas of Virginia and Union, often by using symbols like George Washington, militia leaders integrated a heterogeneous mass of men into a coherent military body and public culture. The officers, dignitaries, and statesmen who addressed the militias on public occasions clearly anticipated the preconceptions and beliefs of the men who stood before them. Yankees, immigrants, and other outsiders who made Richmond their home and joined in public commemoration affected public discourse and thus profoundly shaped Richmond's culture.

As the 1850s came to a close, the city celebrated a new statue of Washington and reburied James Monroe in solemn ceremonies attended by Northern militias, harking back to Virginia's glorious political past. But by 1861 even the honoring of dead heroes of Virginia and the Republic could not mask underlying sectional tensions. Harper's Ferry and Lincoln's election had not caused Virginia to leave the Union, but as the events of April 1861 unfolded, Union sentiment withered and secession fever gripped Richmond. Many immigrants and Northern-born men attracted by the city's progressive spirit and thriving economy left, and others decided to sit out a war not of their choosing. Many others enthusiastically responded to the Southern call to arms. The decisive turn southward ended an era in Richmond's social relations with its many exterior worlds.

Part 3 of this study shows how the antebellum views of Richmonders shaped allegiances during and after the Civil War. Richmonders made reasoned choices based on their prewar perceptions. Merchant families quickly came to support secession along with their rural kin and most of the city elite, and against the wishes of their Northern trade partners. More interesting, Northern- and foreign-born people as well as working men and Unionists evinced at best lukewarm support for, and at times outright resistance to, the war and the Confederacy. Moreover, many of these elements of the population joined African Americans in postwar political alliances within the Republican, Readjuster, and Knights of Labor movements.

This account supports Daniel Crofts's analysis that many in the Upper South were reluctant Confederates. Opposition took many forms, including flight from the city, draft resistance, labor strikes, rioting, and espionage for the Union. For example, many German and Irish soldiers initially supported the war but quickly became disenchanted. Allegiance to the Confederacy waned in ethnic companies, and after a revision of the laws that freed the foreign-born from military service, the men left their units while in the field. Length of residence in Richmond was a determining factor in loyalty. German residents of long standing sometimes expressed decidedly pro-Southern beliefs, as did many German Jews, who preferred to fight in established units such as the Richmond Light Infantry Blues, but these men were in the minority.

Active resistance to the Confederacy also grew in the wartime city. F. W. E. Lohman, who had served with the Virginia Rifles, assisted foreign-born men to escape conscription, and also aided Elizabeth Van Lew, a Union spy, in one of her most daring actions during the war. These Germans were part of a Unionist underground that included men and women, the native and foreign-born, Virginians and Yankees. The motivation of these men and women ran the gamut, including antislavery sentiment, Unconditional Unionism, and in some cases, profit.

The antebellum legacy, aided by the forces of war, shaped the postbellum world. A worldly African-American community, drawing on years of organizing and leadership in churches and burial societies, now participated in political, reform, and labor movements on the national level and strengthened the bonds of family and fraternity at home. Likewise, workers pushed forward with the organizing and activism begun in the 1850s, further alienating Richmond's old elite. A new political order emerged, forging links between white working-class and foreign-born voters and newly enfranchised black citizens in the Republican and Readjuster Parties and the Knights of Labor.

City leaders and businessmen looked on with both horror and disbelief as they cast about for a way to reassert control. Maintaining their dream of

Richmond as a major commercial city, merchants and industrialists quickly reestablished economic ties to the North, and through the Lost Cause and sentimental plantation novels, they also reasserted their belief in a paternalistic Southern world. Richmond's old elite would eventually establish a conservative political and social order of one-party rule and Jim Crow that marked much of the twentieth-century South. But for most of the late nineteenth century they faced challenges to their power that had their origins in the years before the Civil War.

PART ONE

Richmond
in the 1850s

CHAPTER ONE

Capital and Commercial City

Richmond at a glance from adjacent high ground, through a dull cloud of
bituminous smoke, upon a lowering winter's day, has a very picturesque
appearance . . . but the moment it is examined at all in detail, there is but one
spot, in the whole picture, upon which the eye is at all attracted to rest. This is
the Capitol, an imposing Grecian edifice, standing alone, and finely placed on
open and elevated ground, in the center of the town.

FREDERICK LAW OLMSTED, 1856

We have a city numbering now nearly fifty thousand inhabitants, including the
immediate suburbs. It is now in a fair way to become one of the most important
cities of the whole South, both as regards manufactures and commerce. With a
waterpower unsurpassed, and a back country abounding in raw material of every
description, it offers to capitalists and business men of all classes, advantages
rarely met with, and a location most favorable to manufacturing purposes.

Richmond Business Directory, 1858

essie Lacy, the daughter of a North Carolina minister, was
crestfallen at her first sight of Richmond in 1848: "I was greatly
disappointed when I looked out on the Railroad bridge & saw
the place. It was a dark misty morning when we went thundering over
James River & the coal dust made the streets & alleys look darker & more
dismal than ever." [1] Her first impression of the city belied the many period
lithographs and engravings that portrayed Richmond as a picturesque river
town and that conformed more with the report of the *Richmond Enquirer*

3

at the bridge's opening ten years earlier. Two railroad cars had crossed the span with passengers "who were willing to try the experiment of passing over the river on this air built Bridge. The cars glided over with the greatest ease—presenting the most beautiful views of the surrounding Landscape to the delighted passengers."[2]

After settling in with her cousin Moses Drury Hoge, minister at Second Presbyterian Church, Bessie Lacy slowly changed her mind about Richmond. She wrote, "I think that Richmond is a beautiful place now that I have walked about the streets a little & have been on the balcony of our house," a fine residence on Fifth Street in one of the city's better quarters. Like most visitors, she was especially interested in Jefferson's capitol and its grounds, comparing it to her state's capitol at Raleigh. She "walked through the Capitol Square & have been so daring as to say that the edifice was no handsomer than ours—though the square is as Eden to a wilderness when you look at our barren area."[3]

Bessie Lacy's perceptions of Richmond reflected the two reasons for the city's growth after the American Revolution and its central role in state life. As the capital of Virginia, the largest, wealthiest, and most populous state at the time of the Revolution, Richmond was heir to the political heritage of the Founding Fathers and quickly assumed the role of a mecca for Virginia's civic religion—the veneration of Revolutionary heroes. On a more practical level, the state government brought with it from Williamsburg those urban middle classes who thrived on life in the capital: the lawyers, artisans, printers, and other functionaries.

Bessie Lacy's railroad trip over the James River amid the coal smoke of the thundering train was emblematic of Richmond's other centralizing role in Virginia: a trading, manufacturing, and transportation center for several overlapping Virginia hinterlands. Tobacco, wheat, corn, and other staples arrived for processing in the city's mills and factories. The diversification of outlying farms and plantations went hand in hand with the growth of the commercial entrepôt, transforming the landscape of both the countryside and the city. By 1861 five railroads and the James River and Kanawha Canal linked Richmond with much of the rest of the state. Many of the locomotives that rolled across the Virginia landscape were built at the Tredegar Iron Works, and numerous other iron mills supported railroads as well as

Richmond's other industries. Just as Richmond's status as state capital drew population to the falls of the James, so did economic activity, creating a dynamic center of urban/rural migration of white and black, slave and free. Hired slaves, planters, country merchants, white workers, and other visitors and migrants traveled the roads, canal, and rails to Richmond.

The two great functions of the city, as commercial center and political stage, said much about the interplay of tradition and modernization in antebellum Virginia. "Old Virginia" was enshrined in Richmond, and its residents both celebrated and struggled with that legacy. Slavery continued to be the backbone of Virginia's labor system. The ever-tightening relationship between countryside and city, including the slave trade, increased Richmond's involvement in the "peculiar institution." In the shadow of Jefferson's capitol, factories expanded on the labor of slave workers. Richmond residents enthusiastically celebrated Virginia's political and intellectual patrimony, but many wanted conveniently to forget the founders' words of warning regarding slavery.

The opening pages of the 1858 *Richmond Business Directory* informed the reader of its main purpose: herein "are classed the principal mercantile houses, extensive manufacturing establishments, and every business contributing to the general welfare of this commercial metropolis." Yet in a section on "Objects of Interest," business took a backseat. For the "first object which attracts the eye of the stranger on his near approach to the city of Richmond, whether from the East, South or the West . . . is the *Capitol,* a plain but noble looking building, situated in the center of the city." The directory's author reproduced the inscription on the Houdon statue of Washington "acknowledged, by all who have seen it, to be one of the finest works of art in this country," and looked forward to the dedication of Thomas Crawford's equestrian statue of Washington later that year. The commanding and picturesque view from the Capitol's portico referred to in the city guide looked out over the commercial riverfront, and for most of the antebellum era politics had stood far above commerce in Virginia.[4]

When state legislators voted in 1779 to move the state capital to Richmond from Williamsburg, the lawmakers decided on the urging of Thomas Jefferson to locate the new government—the capitol, courts, jail buildings, and public market—on a largely unsettled hill on the west side of Shockoe Creek opposite the earlier settlement on Church Hill. Jefferson designed the new capitol, intending it to "improve the taste of my countrymen, to increase their reputation, to reconcile to them the respect of the world and procure them its praise." This neoclassical building, completed in brick in 1792 and stuccoed in 1798, dominated Shockoe Hill and the city both physically and symbolically. Capitol Square remained a wilderness until 1818 when it was fenced and landscaped according to a design by exiled French architect Maximilian Godefroy, a partner of Benjamin Henry Latrobe. Godefroy not only gave Jefferson's Capitol building a proper neoclassical environment but also refurbished the Capitol itself and added to the civic square by completing and improving the design of Richmond's first city hall, a domed Greek Revival building originally designed by renowned architect Robert Mills.[5]

The placement of other public buildings confounded the original intention of Jefferson and his colleagues and created a not-so-subtle hierarchy in the cityscape. Benjamin Henry Latrobe's penitentiary, a tour de force of the new penology, was exiled to the western limits of the city, although positioned high enough to be viewed from a distance. Scots merchant Thomas Rutherfoord discovered that the building was to rise on land purchased from a neighbor; he quickly negotiated a land swap with the state to remove the penitentiary a safe distance. The Enlightenment ideals of reform through solitary reflection and penitence may have inspired men in the abstract but tested civic virtue in the here and now. The city market was set low in Shockoe Valley, huddled near warehouses, shops, and factories in the chaotic jumble of commerce that reached down to the riverfront.[6]

Capitol Square was a center of America's emerging civic religion of the Revolution and its heroes, the first widely held icons of American public memory. Foremost among these icons was George Washington, and the two monuments erected to him within the confines of Capitol Square testify to changes in politics and public memory in the antebellum era. The General Assembly of Virginia commissioned the first (and often copied) sculpture of Washington, Jean-Antoine Houdon's full-length statue. The French sculptor traveled to Mount Vernon to prepare his work, widely regarded as a masterpiece. Houdon's understanding of Washington's preferences for the work is clear. The statue was a reference to the Cincinnatus myth, "the military hero returning to civilian life." Washington holds a cane in one hand, balancing his other hand on a fasces draped with a sword and a cape. Behind him is a plow, a symbol of Washington's return to Mount Vernon as a common citizen. The statue was installed in the capitol building without fanfare or ceremony.[7]

The second major statue of Washington erected in Capitol Square in 1858 projected a different image. An equestrian statue by sculptor Thomas Crawford, it presented Washington as warrior. Michael Kammen believes that this transformation of Washington in art was pervasive: "In a very real sense, Houdon's Washington returning to civilian life (1796) and Greenough's Washington the lawgiver (1841) were supplanted in the American mind by Washington as 'a man on horseback.'" Despite extremely bad weather on the day of the statue's unveiling on Washington's birthday in 1858, "a large number of Military Companies from abroad were present to unite with our own military on the occasion, and there were altogether *Thirty Four* companies in the procession, making the largest and most imposing military pageant ever seen in Richmond. The procession formed on East Main Street and marched along Main, Second & Broad Streets to Eleventh, and thence to the Capitol Square, where the ceremonies took place." Dedicated amid extensive public celebration and martial display, Crawford's Washington symbolized the type of leader many thought the state and country required in the 1850s.[8]

The rise of a coherent Revolutionary iconography could only occur with the waning of the fierce partisan wars of the early Republic, and Virginia was a primary battleground of these conflicts. Even Washington had public detractors during his lifetime, especially those who feared the power of his hold on the popular mind. Jefferson, Madison, Monroe, and the other Virginia Founding Fathers were embroiled in partisan combat on the national and state level along with Virginia's influential newspaper editors. But by the 1820s the Revolutionary generation was passing, and "the decline of Republican and Federalist factionalism and the rise of historical interest in the Revolutionary era led to a more cohesive view of the Declaration of Independence and the celebration on the Fourth." The return of Lafayette to the United States in 1824–25 further integrated the historical memory of the Revolution and its heroes. Richmond entertained "The Nation's Guest" with elaborate ceremonies in Capitol Square, solidifying the centrality of Virginia in the Revolutionary struggle. In anticipation of Lafayette's visit in 1824, the Richmond Light Artillery changed its name to the Fayette Light Artillery, delivering numerous cannonades to mark the occasion.[9]

While the memory of the American Revolution brought white Virginians together, the war's legacy remained far more ambiguous for black Virginians. Events during the Lafayette tour revealed deep contradictions. During the ceremonies at Yorktown, Lafayette glimpsed an old comrade— James, a former slave of William Armistead, who had spied for the Marquis in the camp of Cornwallis. Lafayette had supported James's freedom petition to the Virginia General Assembly, which was granted, and the grateful former slave took the surname of his benefactor. Now, in 1824, the nobleman and James Lafayette embraced at the scene of American victory. Despite the stirring and well-known stories of the few slaves liberated for supporting the American cause (James Lafayette became a central character in an 1828 novel), the reality of black life in Virginia was quite different by 1824. The published "Order of the Day" for Lafayette's visit to Richmond stated that "no intoxicated or colored person will be permitted to enter the [Capitol] Square." Later legal codes completely barred blacks from the square, a primary target of the slave Gabriel's aborted rebellion in 1800. The legacy of Revolution for some black Virginians included Gabriel's attempted insurrection in 1800 and the Haitian Revolution, events that whites did not care to celebrate.[10]

The figures of Revolutionary heroes surrounding the base of Crawford's Virginia Washington Monument testified to the integration of the meaning of the Revolution for whites in antebellum Virginia. The sculptor completed two full-length figures—Patrick Henry and Thomas Jefferson—before the 1858 unveiling. John B. Danforth related the arrival of the bronze statues in August 1855 to his brother in Charleston, South Carolina, and found the two figures "really magnificent." Danforth opined that "the contrast between Henry & Jefferson is exceedingly fine. The one truly representing the most impassioned life & gesture—the other as impressively the most calm & profound thought. The bronze is light in color, entirely free from all anticipated objections & beautiful far, far beyond my conception. The posture, anatomy, & drapery of both statues appear to me faultless." [11]

White Virginians of an earlier generation would probably have been more interested in articulating the ideological differences and similarities between Henry and Jefferson, as well as Washington, rather than comparing their posture. But by the 1850s these icons of a created Revolutionary past could easily coexist, albeit through ceremonies masking a growing sectionalism. Unionists saw these men as the creators of the glorious Union, a major preoccupation of militia events and patriotic celebrations. Southern nationalists just as easily could envision the common ground between the antifederalist Henry, the Jefferson of the Virginia and Kentucky Resolves, and Washington, defender against state tyranny.

Some Virginians complained about the intent behind civic events, reading them through a partisan lens. Dr. William P. Palmer hewed to the thoroughly Whig principles of his father, and reported to him that "we are to have a grand celebration here in honor of the city's being illuminated with gas on the 22nd—and by way of arousing the dormant patriotism of *seceders* I suppose, the intention is to wake up the old spirit of 76 with an occasional cheer to the resolutions of 98 & 9, with sundry hurrahs to the old Dominion 'this proud old mother of us all.' " The veneration of Virginia's past could always be read several ways.[12]

The retreat into the glorious Revolutionary past helped white Virginians ignore or forget the decline of the state's influence on the national political stage. The passing of the giants of the Virginia Dynasty was only the most superficial manifestation of the state's reduced stature. More basic was Virginia's shrinking number of seats in the United States House of Representatives, falling from twenty-three in 1810 to thirteen in 1860, directly reflecting the atrophy of the state's population. The successive waves of Virginians who left the Old Dominion from the Revolution onward took the state's political influence with them.[13]

By the time of the Gold Rush more than 388,000 Virginia-born people lived throughout the United States, in contrast to the Old Dominion's population of 949,000 residents. This migration spread in several waves, as the "leading destinations changed from the Carolinas and Georgia in the eighteenth century, to Kentucky and Tennessee in the early republic, to

Ohio and the Old Northwest in the early nineteenth century, and increasingly to the trans-Mississippi West" in the late antebellum era. Virginians sought new land, fortunes, and freedom in the antebellum exodus, and the 1850s began with the prospect of yet another frontier draining the state of many of its most productive and enterprising young men and women to California.[14]

The draining of Virginia's national preeminence and prestige did not dampen the enthusiasm for popular politics in Virginia and Richmond. Beginning with the partisan struggles of the Jacksonian era, participation in Virginia elections steadily increased. Even before the removal of property qualifications for voting, more than half of the state's white, adult males came to the polls in the presidential contests of 1840 and 1844; with the removal of the property barrier as a result of the new state constitution approved in 1851, 63 percent voted in the campaign of 1852. A vigorous two-party system emerged in Virginia that mirrored the experience in the United States as a whole. Well-organized political parties nominated candidates, staked out ideological positions, and mobilized voters with stump speeches, barbecues, and torchlight parades.[15]

The relative balance between Whigs and Democrats throughout the state makes generalizations about the geography of party affiliation difficult. Ethnoreligious factors, level of slaveholding, and connection to the market all affected partisan affiliation. Virginia's cities and towns generally favored the Whig Party and its message of internal improvements, social reform, and economic advancement. Of the twenty-seven towns with more than one thousand inhabitants in 1850, twenty-one regularly returned majorities for the party of Henry Clay. Also, voters in the counties where these towns were located often followed the Whig persuasion. Residents of Virginia's towns and their hinterlands included many nonagricultural workers, new immigrants, and Scots and Scots-Irish Presbyterians—all groups that responded well to appeals from the Whigs.[16]

Whigs emerged victorious in the mid-1830s on the votes of those eager to connect farms and urban markets in the state. In the 1840s, a newly invigorated Democratic Party again took control of the state, but Richmond usually remained steady in the Whig column despite the support of some Democrats for railroads and canals. Charles Palmer expressed the general

Whig sentiment among Richmond's merchant class, urging his son, "for my sake don't vote for a *Democrat*, especially one who voted against all improvements in Virginia." [17]

As in most other American cities, Richmonders mobilized for political contests in ever-greater numbers in the late antebellum period, carrying the contest beyond the official confines of Capitol Square into the streets of the city. Bessie Lacy stayed home from church on a "dark gloomy night" in 1848 and was treated to "quite an excitement among the rabble." Taking to the streets, "the Whigs formed a torchlight procession and marched with transparent banners." Lacy reported "almost all of the houses illuminated but ours," due to the fact that her cousin, the Reverend Moses Drury Hoge, was "anti-politics of all sorts." The revelries continued, as "cannons were firing & rockets ascending nearly all night," with "bonfires on Shockoe Hill & Church Hill" lighting the city. She mused that "I expect the Taylorites feel rather the worse this morning for their long walk through the mud and mire last night." [18]

The nature of Virginia's electorate and political community changed profoundly in the 1840s and 1850s. While some traditionalists and older, elite members of the community looked askance, certain groups, especially workingmen and white women, became deeply involved in political activity. White women took an active part in the campaigns of the Whig Party, and thereafter were a force to be reckoned with in state politics. Women ran the log cabins erected for party meetings and did other campaign duties. This did not sit well with some men. Jefferson Wallace wrote his brother that "I am heartily tired of hearing politics. nothing but that is spoken of and even the *feminines* are stiring it with shirt poles." Upholding Richmond's position as a Whig stronghold, Richmond women contributed mightily to the campaign by the "Ladies of Virginia" to erect a statue of Henry Clay on Capitol Square. Their contributions culminated in a great public outpouring at the 1860 dedication ceremony, attended by women from throughout the state. The contributors to the Clay statue included many women from merchant families usually found in the Whig camp.[19]

Virginia's white laboring classes also began to exert greater influence on politics. At the insistence of western Virginians and city dwellers, the Virginia Constitution of 1851 opened the polls to nonproperty-holding white males and approved a more equitable balance of representation between the counties beyond the Blue Ridge Mountains and the Black Belt counties of the Piedmont and Tidewater. The next year Richmond voters overwhelmingly passed a new city charter approved by the general assembly, removing property qualifications for voting in local elections and making many appointive offices open to the will of the people. Although Richmond's politics never reached the rough-and-tumble state of Baltimore and other American cities, observers clearly perceived a new style of campaigning and greater use of appeals to the workingman.[20]

The electoral career of Martin Meredith Lipscomb, a bricklayer, demonstrated the new electioneering. Lipscomb first tried to unseat popular mayor Joseph Mayo in 1853; predictably, Mayo drubbed the newcomer. Undaunted, a year later Lipscomb set his sights on the city sergeant John Milton Fergusson, who had held his post for fifteen years. Lipscomb took his campaign directly to the city's working class in the halls and taverns of the city, and chided his opponent for his failure to meet voters "in their republican gatherings — to take the working man by the hand, and to mix and mingle with the bone and sinew of the land." Clearly in his element, Lipscomb mobilized the city's voters like no one before, soundly defeating the incumbent and shaking Richmond's political establishment to its core. Lipscomb would emerge victorious again in 1855 and 1856, but this time on a unified Know-Nothing ticket including many old Whigs, among them Joseph Mayo.[21]

The campaigns of 1855 and 1856 brought a new element to city politics — the explicit identification of candidates for city offices with political parties. Both before and after these campaigns the nominees in local contests eschewed party labels, although city voters usually rewarded Whig candidates for state and national offices. After the governor's race in 1855, Jefferson Wallace reported to his brother in California that "the Ellection of mayor and other city officers take place the 4th of this month and the partys are making their preparations for the contest. Nothing spoken of here now excepting politics and I am sick and tired of it." He was troubled and probably disappointed when reporting the strength of the Know-Nothings in Richmond a few weeks later: "Our ellections passed of the other day for city officials and the Know Nothings carried their ticket. . . . One thing I must say that this new party is in my opinion a very contemptible one."[22]

Most Richmonders of foreign birth, especially Catholics, would have concurred in Jefferson Wallace's disdain for the American Party. Richmond's newest citizens cast votes in increasing numbers, and native Virginians watched closely as those born on European shores entered electoral politics. Jefferson Wallace believed that "nearly all of our foreign born citizens voted the democratic ticket" in the 1855 gubernatorial election. A German-American musician recorded in his diary that on Tuesday, November 4, 1856, he "went to City Hall and cast my vote for Buchanan. Got hissed." Apparently Richmond's Know-Nothings patrolled their voting stations as did those in other cities, and Virginia's retention of viva voce voting meant that the crowds of ward healers and hangers-on who frequented the polls instantly discovered the voter's political preference. Luckily for the unidentified musician, the American Party in Virginia resorted to less physical means of restraining opposition voting behavior than did their peers in Baltimore and Philadelphia.[23]

In the mid-1850s, Democrats increased their totals in city contests, probably on the strength of foreign-born votes coupled with defections of old Whigs from a party in disarray. In 1855, Jefferson Wallace listed some of those who switched parties, noting that "Tom Stevenson voted the democratic ticket—his son Bob is a democrat—a good many whigs here voted the democratic ticket William Anderson, Sam Perrin and some of the old line whigs."[24]

In 1856 a number of prominent Whigs, fearing a Republican victory in a three-way contest, threw their support to James Buchanan in the presidential race. Joseph Reid Anderson was one of those who defected to Buchanan, and the next year he joined the Democratic slate that swept Richmond's general assembly seats. An ironmaster of impeccable Whig lineage, Anderson had strongly supported the internal improvements program of the party of Clay. But the threat to slavery seemed so palpable in 1857 that the American industrialist turned decisively into a Southern nationalist.[25]

Campaigns intensified as races became more competitive, the rhetoric more shrill, and national issues increasingly important. Robert Granniss eagerly attended meetings of both the Whigs and Democrats in Richmond in the 1858 contest, although he clearly hewed to the Whig faith. He duly noted his presence at "a political meeting of the Democracy of Richmond,"

held to select delegates for a meeting in Petersburg to nominate a gubernatorial candidate. He heard "Mr. Roger A. Prior editor of the 'South' speak
also O. Jennings Wise the antagonist of Sherrard Clemens in the late duel
and son of the present Governor." The young man, although new to
Richmond, correctly speculated that John Letcher would get the Democratic nod.[26] Granniss expressed his sincere "hope that Goggin is elected
Governor but of course all is uncertainty until we hear from the other
parts of the State." His hopes were partially fulfilled as "the Whigs . . .
triumphed" in Richmond, although state voters as a whole went for
Letcher. The young clerk reported that "a large crowd assembled in front
of the 'Richmond Whig' office to hear the telegraphic returns. At 10 o'clk
they proceeded en masse accompanied by the Armory Band to serenade the
successful candidates. . . . altogether we had a grand time." [27]

After the meteoric rise and fall of the American Party, Richmond's
Whigs staged a revival in the late antebellum era. Joseph Reid Anderson
felt the sting of defeat in 1859, after at least a decade of continuous service
to Richmond-area voters. Former Whigs and Know-Nothings reclaimed all
three Richmond seats in the House of Delegates.[28]

To most Virginians, the men memorialized in Capitol Square stood far
above the politicians of their own day. Jefferson Wallace attended mass political meetings, but with little fervor. Declaring that the "day of humbug
is passed with the American people," he expressed the deep cynicism of
many with current politics. He heard "Judge Douglas the little Giant"
stumping for Democrat Henry Wise at the First African Baptist Church
during the 1855 gubernatorial contest between Wise and the Know-
Nothing nominee, Thomas S. Flournoy, formerly a states' rights Whig.
Despite his clear Democratic leanings, Wallace "was much disapointed in
him [Douglas], but did not hear him to much advantage as the politics of
the day is almost barren of instruction with bigotry and intolerance on one
side and a threadbare argument of old on tother." Wallace believed that
politics drained too much energy away from commercial activity, noting
that "the great fault of Virginians is their great propensity for politics and
not attending to their business or other pursuits. The State and her people
would have been much better off but for this bugbear." [29]

Yet even Jefferson Wallace wondered at the economic and urban progress
of the capital city in the 1850s. He remarked to a friend that "you would

hardly know Richmond. I meet every day hundred[s] of new faces. The business of the city has also improved much. The town is extending around the suburbs, the connection between the Basin and Dock makes the old Basin have a deserted look. Warwick & Barksdale are building another mill larger then either of the old ones on the site of the old Basin spring. They have made a fortune this year." The *Richmond Business Directory* asserted that "the stranger should by no means omit paying a visit to the extensive *Flour Mills* of Richmond," the Gallego Mills of Warwick and Barksdale being "among the largest in this country." Richmond's millers exploited a lucrative South American trade, and almost all of the flour received at the port of San Francisco in the 1850s came from Richmond's mills.[30]

The *Business Directory* trumpeted Richmond's successes to the world, listing its ironworks, flour mills, tobacco factories, and numerous other industries. By 1860 the value of the city's manufactures ranked it thirteenth in the United States despite standing only twenty-fifth in population, but this progress had been reached in fits and starts. After the state government and its ancillary trades and services filtered into the city following the Revolution, Richmond began to expand its economic base beyond the small fall-line town incorporated in 1742. Richmond had been a trading post since the 1670s, and its first merchants inspected tobacco, bartered in the Indian trade, and sold slaves to an expanding Piedmont region.[31]

Despite the prevalence of tobacco as an overarching symbol of Virginia history, Richmond's emergence as a major entrepôt in the late 1700s was tied to the marketing and milling of grains, especially wheat and corn. In 1701 tobacco stood practically alone as the export for Virginia, but by 1774 it was only about 61 percent of the value of total export. Virginia's exports had diversified into wheat, corn, maize, beef, pork, iron, lumber, and other products, which "prevented the utter collapse of Virginia's money economy." Although usually thought of as a response to soil exhaustion in the older Chesapeake areas, the trade was also a response to a new Northern and worldwide demand that fluctuated greatly due to crop failures and the disruption of trade caused by warfare.[32]

The colonial shift to grains greatly favored Richmond as a trade and milling center, as the Upper James district that formed its immediate hinterland produced ever-larger quantities of corn and wheat. Earlier important as a warehousing and inspection point for tobacco, and as the new capital of Virginia by 1780, Richmond's spectacular growth from 1800 to 1810 was tied to milling. The abundant fall of water available at Richmond, created by the gradual transition from the Piedmont to the Tidewater region, would power mills. The position of Richmond at the head of navigation would fulfill William Byrd II's long-held belief that "these two places [Richmond and Petersburg] being the uppermost Landing of the James and Appamattux Rivers, are naturally intended for Marts, where the Traffick of the Outer Inhabitants must Center. Thus we did not build Castles only, but also Citys in the Air." [33]

Grain processing had a greater multiplier effect on the urban economy than tobacco ever could. Much more so than tobacco, which was long marketed directly from the docks of planters, the bulky and highly perishable grains demanded warehousing, milling, and transportation services. The sheer volume of the grain trade greatly outstripped the tobacco trade, expanding the need for cooperages to produce barrels, tanneries to process leather used for harnesses and wagon construction, and other subsidiary industries. From grinding wheat and corn, Richmond's millers expanded their business interests to naileries, foundries, and cotton and woolen manufactories. Imports of sophisticated machinery needed for efficient milling of grain competed with local foundries to supply the needs of Richmond's mills. [34]

Foreign-born entrepreneurs, especially British merchants, were critical to Richmond's growth after the Revolution. Many of the merchants "were no longer content to be junior partners of mercantile houses in Great Britain, and had begun to trade for themselves, to buy land, to build up their own wealth, and to marry Virginia belles." Experienced in business and aided by access to European capital, these men quickly assumed an active role in the expansion of the iron trade, coal mining, tobacco manufacturing, and milling, often establishing new production facilities in the Richmond area. [35]

The development of the James River and Kanawha Canal further solidified the gains in trade and also provided power sources for new mills. The largest flour mills, Gallego and Haxall, sat near the canal's turning basin, a man-made lake several blocks long. From here the canal ran west, providing a transportation connection to western wheat fields and water power for paper mills, flour mills, and the Tredegar Iron Works, the South's premier producer of iron. The most important canal project of the 1850s was the Tidewater Connection linking the great basin to the city docks, a complicated set of locks that further transformed Richmond's riverfront into a dense industrial maze. Jefferson Wallace nostalgically recounted for his brother "a short ramble amongst the Islands on Mayo's bridge," where "I again fancied myself a boy with fishing rod in hand waiting for a bite! Now commerce with her rude hands have demolished the old hunting & fishing grounds and in their stead have erected improvements by which man is enriched and romance is ended. I can now realize the feeling of the Indian when he sees civilization driving him out from his old familiar haunts and making new homes to be driven forth again, untill worried out, he again returns to some familiar spot and their chants his last lay." [36]

The effect and efficiency of transportation were as hotly debated by contemporaries as they are today by historians. Germain Bréant, a Frenchman who had lived in Richmond, replied to a letter from his friend Charles Palmer: "Speaking of embelishments, I am glad to hear from all sides, that improvements are going on in Richmond; but as long as trade with the great West is shut up to it it will never be what it ought to be. The railroads do not make a large city, and as long as Richmond will not be connected to the Ohio river by the canal, it will hardly be worthy of the State of Virginia for its metropolis, which ought to be at least half as big as New York." [37] Certainly the failure to continue work on the canal in the early 1800s limited Richmond's ability to capture its western hinterlands. By the end of the antebellum era the state had extended the works almost two hundred miles to the town of Buchanan in western Virginia, but the canal never provided the long-desired direct connection with the waters of the Ohio.

Joseph Reid Anderson's Tredegar Iron Works greatly depended on the railroad revolution in Virginia and the South for its survival, but Anderson supported the James River and Kanawha Canal into the 1850s. James S. Woods sought a sympathetic ear when he wrote Anderson from Buchanan in western Virginia urging the abandonment of further extensions of the canal works. Anderson probably surprised Woods by asserting that "on the contrary I am more and more convinced the longer I live of the immense value of the improvement and the importance of carrying it all the way to the Ohio." As a builder of railroads and as a user of the canal for the transportation of his raw materials, Anderson was well aware of the limitations of railroads in an age of iron rails and small hauling-capacities.[38]

As a new technology, railroads were subject to the usual trials that accompanied innovations. Henry L. Cathell, a traveler from New York, stayed a night in Richmond, attending the theater before retiring to his room at the Exchange Hotel. On his trip northward the next day on the Richmond, Fredericksburg, and Potomac Railroad, he encountered a train that had departed Richmond when he first arrived. Cathell sarcastically recorded that the passengers "had the pleasure of 'Camping out' in the storm all night in consequence of running off the track 3 different times." [39]

The experience of modern travel especially challenged older Virginians not used to new modes of transportation. Edward Valentine chuckled to his father that "Ma is thinking about the way she is to get home, whether to cross the 'temporary track' or 'high bridge' or go on the '*horrid canal boats*.' She says she [would] rather walk home than cross the mountain again in the cars." Valentine's mother told her son that "she would do Mr. Ellett the engineer on the road no harm, but she thinks he is a person of unsound mind, and the sooner he is carried to *Staunton* [site of one of the state's mental institutions] the better." [40]

The temporary track carried railroad travelers over the Blue Ridge Mountains while a tunnel was being constructed. One Richmond clerk marveled at a thirty-three-ton locomotive constructed at Tredegar expressly to pull trains up the steep grades, but noted that "some persons think that it will be impossible to draw a train over it." Elizabeth Ann Valentine Gray, Edward Valentine's sister, shared these reservations about the train's ability safely to convey the train on the nerve-racking hour-and-a-half trip over the mountains. While she conceded that "all railroads, and any other kind of travelling [is] very dangerous, yet I think that railroads over mountains are *most dangerous*. . . . I had no idea when I used to admire that high mountain that I should ever find myself in a railroad car *mounted high on it* making curves around it. Oh! It is a dreadful road." [41]

Engineer Claudius Crozet's Blue Ridge Tunnel apparently took some of the thrill out of the mountain crossing. Ann Webster Gordon Christian felt "no sensation of fear or oppression" as she "went *under* the mountain" on a trip to Staunton, and considered it "wonderful what industry, perseverance & *Money* can accomplish." But when her mother took a brief excursion from Richmond to "Belle Isle on the cars" it was "her first trip by railroad which she seemed to dread very much."[42]

Despite problems of reliability, railroads did extend the commercial and cultural sphere of Richmond. The city became the southernmost outpost of a Northern railroad complex in the 1830s. The earliest line from the city, the Richmond, Fredericksburg, and Potomac Railroad, integrated Richmond into the emerging rail system that eventually connected the major eastern cities from Boston to Washington, although it required a steamship connection from Aquia Creek to Washington. Other early lines sent their tentacles into Virginia's hinterland. The Louisa Railroad (soon renamed the Virginia Central) traveled westward toward Gordonsville in the Piedmont region, and the Richmond and Petersburg penetrated Southside Virginia.

In the 1840s the Richmond and Danville further consolidated the connection with Southside Virginia, and the Richmond and York River Railroad reached out to the port of West Point in the late antebellum period. In turn, these railroads linked up with other lines that stretched into neighboring states to the north, south, and west. Virginia ranked sixth among the states in railroad mileage in 1850 with about 515 miles of track. By 1860, about 1,771 miles of track belonging to nineteen Virginia railroads crisscrossed the Old Dominion, the greatest mileage of any Southern state. Virginia remained sixth nationally, passing Georgia and Massachusetts, but was eclipsed by the growth of lines in Indiana and Illinois. Although the southern and western connections were late in coming and less well-integrated than the northeastern rail system, Richmond's improved links to the Virginia countryside further stimulated the city's iron, tobacco, and coal industries.[43]

Several Richmond ironworks took advantage of railroad expansion. The massive Tredegar Iron Works, founded in 1837, produced spikes, car wheels, rail-connecting plates, and many other railroad products on a five-acre site between the James River and the James River and Kanawha Canal. Manufacturing primarily for Virginia and Southern railroad clients, the works employed more than seven hundred white workers in 1860, includ-

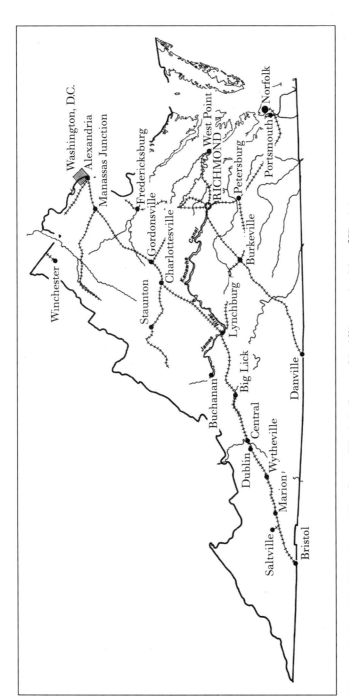

Figure 1. Railroads in Virginia, ca. 1860. *Source:* Virginia Geographic Alliance, *An Atlas of Virginia: Seventeenth, Eighteenth, and Early Nineteenth Centuries* (Dubuque, Iowa: Kendall/Hunt, 1989), 25.

ing many Northern- and foreign-born artisans. Tredegar also employed eighty slave workers, including a small but elite group of skilled rolling-mill hands.[44]

Amid the clanging of hammers and dense clouds of bituminous coal smoke, the Tredegar clerks recorded the fabrication of forty-one locomotives between 1850 and 1855, more than half for Virginia lines, most notably the Virginia and Tennessee Railroad, which purchased ten engines.[45] All but two other engines were for Southern railroads. Joseph Reid Anderson, the principal force behind Tredegar, was anxious to develop his Southern business in the face of cutthroat competition from Northern and British firms.

Eventually, the integration of central Virginia's transportation systems created not only massive iron and flour mills producing for faraway markets, but also farms and plantations using the most advanced agricultural methods and machinery. One such plantation—Hickory Hill—lay just north of Richmond in Hanover County. The farm produced wheat, corn, oats, and various vegetables and fruits. The Wickham family of Hickory Hill employed crop rotation and other soil conservation methods, and fertilized their fields with Peruvian guano, a product that returned on ships carrying Richmond flour to South America. The yearly yields were sent to Richmond on the Virginia Central Railroad from a siding on the plantation. The Wickham family purchased up-to-date machinery including reapers and harvesters, and sent 80 to 90 percent of its produce directly to Richmond markets. What was not sent to Richmond was used on the plantation, which served both to increase self-sufficiency and to isolate the Wickhams' holdings from the rest of the county.[46]

Even as the old tobacco-growing Tidewater area of Virginia was transformed by new crops and forms of production, a resurgent Tobacco Belt emerged west of Richmond, carrying slavery with it into the Piedmont region. The Tobacco Belt was further tied to Richmond in the antebellum era by the growth of an indigenous tobacco manufacturing industry. No longer content simply to ship their raw tobacco for processing elsewhere, Richmond's merchants created an industry that not only expanded the agricultural and industrial production of tobacco but also increased the need for slave labor on plantations and in factories.[47]

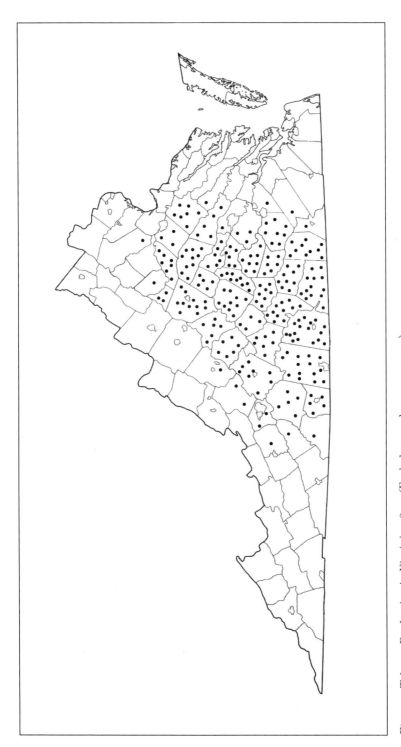

Figure 2. Tobacco Production in Virginia, 1859. (Each dot equals 500,000 tons.)
Source: U.S. Department of Agriculture, Bureau of Agricultural Economics.

The coal smoke from Tredegar and other Richmond foundries mixed with the smell of tobacco during the peak manufacturing season. By 1860 Richmond boasted more than fifty tobacco factories and employed at least 3,404 African-American workers according to the conservative numbers of the census, a gain of almost 1,400 workers over the 1850 federal numbers. A survey done for *Hunt's Merchant's Magazine* in 1858 put the number of factories at fifty-three, and workers, mostly male slaves, at more than 4,000. Manufacturers increasingly relied on hiring, rather than ownership, to secure their enslaved workers. In 1850, Virginia manufacturers owned 58 percent of their enslaved factory workers, but by 1860 more than half were hired. Large establishments employed more than 150 workers. New markets stretched to California and Australia in the late antebellum era, although manufacturers and Southern nationalists still chafed under the control of the trade by factors in Northern cities. By 1850, New York City alone controlled almost half of all the tobacco manufactured in Virginia and North Carolina.[48]

The canal and railroads further tightened Richmond's hold on the Virginia Tobacco Belt and regions beyond. The construction of the Virginia and Tennessee Railroad brought the market economy, tobacco, and slaves to Southwest Virginia in the 1850s. The ties were both economic and ideological, for "not only did southern modernization and slavery go hand in hand . . . but the determination to defend slavery and the broader economic and social system it held on its back joined them. Linked to Richmond's markets, Southwest Virginians also were linked in 1861 to Richmond's cause."[49]

The centralizing influence of transportation on trade made Richmond the clear winner among Virginia's cities. In 1852 tobacco inspections in Richmond were 46 percent of the state total; in 1861 Richmond inspections reached 61 percent.[50] Tobacco Belt planters and farmers were closely tied to the city because of the centralization of the warehousing and manufacturing of tobacco, working with commission merchants and buyers to dispose of their crops. A set of memorials to new governor Joseph Johnson in 1852 revealed the bonds that linked the Tobacco Belt and Richmond. Robert L. Wren and Seldon C. Macon vied for a position as a tobacco inspector in the public warehouse in Richmond, and both garnered support from men across Virginia's Tobacco Belt counties. Seeking to influence the appointment, two memorials from "Planters, commission Merchants and Buyers of Tobacco" recommended the promotion of Robert L. Wren "if your Excellency should remove Mr. S. C. Macon from the office of Second Inspector of Tobacco at the Public Ware House." A group of "Planters and farmers of the county of Albemarle" also threw their support to Wren, considering him "honest, Capable and accommodating in all matters concerning our interest." Macon was not without his supporters, however, and several memorials urged his reappointment. Numerous "Planters of Tobacco" reported that "we have known him for some years and have full confidence in his capacity and integrity for the office." The interests of merchants, planters, and farmers merged when it came to choosing who would run an "institution with whom we chiefly transacted our business."[51]

Relationships between planters and merchants were based on ideas of honor and trust common to Southern society. Thomas J. Macon, the son of a planter, went to work in the city in the early 1850s at the dry-goods house of Parker, Nimmo, and Company. Macon related the story of a Southside Virginia tobacco planter who came to the city twice a year "bringing with him a memorandum for dry goods to be purchased nearly a yard long." He would proceed to the firm of Binford, Mayo, and Blair, and leave the list of supplies to "be filled in the best manner, and with reasonable prices." After receiving payment for his crops from a commission merchant, the planter would return to the store and settle his bill. Thus "the thing went on year after year to the satisfaction of both parties." When the planter died, however, his wife came to town and took another approach to buying. She compared Binford, Mayo, and Blair's prices with those at other stores in Richmond. Mr. Binford voiced his consternation with this procedure to his clerk, and, unwittingly, the planter's wife, who had quietly and unexpectedly returned from her sojourn. Binford had a personal relationship with the planter based on mutual trust, and he resented the implication that he had abused that trust by charging unfair prices.[52]

Economic connections to the countryside were reinforced by personal and family associations, especially important in an antebellum world where buying on credit was gained through the trust of established businessmen. Jonathan Pitts, an Albemarle County resident, wrote to Thomas and Charles Ellis in 1850: "I take the liberty of introducing a young gentleman of my acquaintance who is about to commence business in our village and is desirous of purchasing goods in your line and I have taken it upon myself to recommend him to you believing he can do as well with you as any where else in the City." Crucial to Pitts's recommendation was his judgment that "he will be perfectly good for any thing he may want on time." [53]

Many country merchants had gone directly to Northern cities for goods in the early national period. By the late 1840s, country merchants increasingly turned to urban Virginia merchants for goods rather than making the arduous and expensive trip to a Northern city. Improved transportation networks facilitated the movement of goods from Richmond to surrounding towns and counties, and interurban connections substantially reduced prices in Richmond's dry-goods establishments. New York-born merchant Lewis Ginter advertised his wares in the *Richmond Times* in 1851 directly "To Country Merchants," claiming to "have now in store the most complete stock of Fancy Goods in the State, and purchasers are assured of buying at Northern prices." [54]

Richmond's civic leaders used every opportunity to draw visitors to the city. Richmond boosters began holding the annual Virginia State Agricultural Fair in 1853 as a way for planters, farmers, industrialists, and merchants to share scientific advances, create economic development, and promote the state. Richmonder John B. Danforth wrote to a New York friend that "our State Agricultural Fair has just closed" and reported that "it brought together some 40 or 50,000 persons from almost every section of Virginia & was an affair of much general interest." He condescendingly added, "I wish you could have been with us to enjoy a look at *the people* as well as the *cattle of Virga;*—not to mention numerous other things presenting more or less attraction." [55]

Some agriculturalists saw the event as an exploitation of rural people, for "the trapping of country gulls." Inexperienced rural dwellers gazed "admiringly on the show windows of the stores," and other entrepreneurs lured them to entertainments that made little pretense to economic, intellectual, or moral uplift. One clerk described "a great many booths outside the Fair grounds with fat girls, mustachoed ditto, bears with only two legs &c &c, pick-pockets *were* numerous." [56]

Despite these sometimes tawdry sideshows, Virginians genuinely marveled at the machinery and innovations on display. Philip Whitlock, a Jewish immigrant to Richmond, remembered that he saw "the Great American Inventions that I heard about when I was a child." Trained as a tailor, Whitlock especially recalled the sewing machine, which "was then in its crude state as it was then mounted on a wooden box instead of on iron table, and it was worked with one foot with a wooden pedle." Other visitors were far less impressed. Robert Granniss, a young clerk and a native of Brooklyn, New York, confided to his diary in 1858 that he "went to the Fair of the US Agricultural Society now being held at the Fair Grounds just on the edge of the city. The display is poor and the place terribly dusty. I would not go again." Northerners might have been difficult to please, but Richmond expanded its economic sphere southward through the agricultural fairs. After the first event in 1854, Dr. M. M. Harrison, from the Gaston, North Carolina, area, bought a Tredegar Iron Works sawmill including an "engine, Cross cut fixtures and everything complete that worked at the Fair." [57]

Just as country people flowed into the city for fairs, so did raw recruits for the factories, stores, and counting houses. Richmond was a magnet for white Virginians seeking work and economic advancement. The city provided alternative opportunities for Virginians who might otherwise leave the state as so many had done since the late 1700s. Even the lure of a fortune in gold in California could not hold some Virginians in El Dorado. Three brothers, Charles, Jefferson, and Manson Wallace all trekked to California but returned with many other Virginia Argonauts who partially countered the out-migration that had plagued Virginia for decades. Richmond was full of men who had "seen the Elephant" in California, and Jefferson Wallace reported frequent contacts with returning Virginians. In 1855, he informed his brother Charlie, still in California, about dozens of encounters on the streets with old California hands, including Samuel Drinker, who had been treasurer of the Madison Mining and Trading Company, a Gold Rush consortium launched by Virginians in 1850, and Jimmy Gallagher, a former San Francisco official.[58]

While young white men chose to migrate to the city, slave hiring by masters drove many African Americans into the Richmond markets and into a world of quasi slavery in the city. Virginians, black and white, jostled in the city streets with workingmen from the North and abroad, albeit in very different capacities as citizens and workers.

Slavery took on a new shape as yearly slave hiring from the countryside accelerated, providing an important part of Richmond's economic expansion, as well as creating a geographically far-flung web of family and cultural connections among African Americans. William I. Johnson Jr., a former slave interviewed in the 1930s, described the method of yearly hiring, explaining that "when a slave was hired out, the man would have to sign a contract to pay the owner $250.00 at the end of the year and to give the slave food, shelter, two suits of clothes and the necessary medicine during the year. Whether the slaves stayed with the person who hired him or not, the leassee would have to pay that contract at the end of the year." The hiring was transacted by an agent (sometimes a slave trader), the master, or even the slave, and prices varied depending on skill, age, and gender.[59]

Many variants of hiring emerged. Some masters negotiated directly with those needing labor, though this proved difficult at a distance. Hiring agents specialized in finding a suitable situation, and friends or family often assisted in the search. Frequently slaves hired themselves, thereby saving their masters time and money and providing themselves with some negotiating power and choice of work. Anthony Burns, whose later travels to Boston would severely test the Fugitive Slave Law, first arrived in Richmond under an arrangement that encapsulated the hiring system's strange twists. A Colonel Suttle owned Burns but had entrusted his hire to a William Brent. When Brent moved to Richmond, he called for Burns, and Suttle sent Burns "out for the metropolis of Virginia, having under his charge four other slaves belonging to Col. Suttle, also bound for the hiring-ground." Suttle trusted Burns to hire the other slaves and be responsible for their welfare. Burns succeeded in finding employment for his fellow slaves and found a position for himself at one of the city's flour mills alongside an elder brother.[60]

The geographic patterns of hiring into Richmond reflected the shifts in agriculture and population that had occurred in the late eighteenth and early nineteenth centuries. Where cereals, grains, and truck farming predominated or coexisted with tobacco, masters took advantage of the less

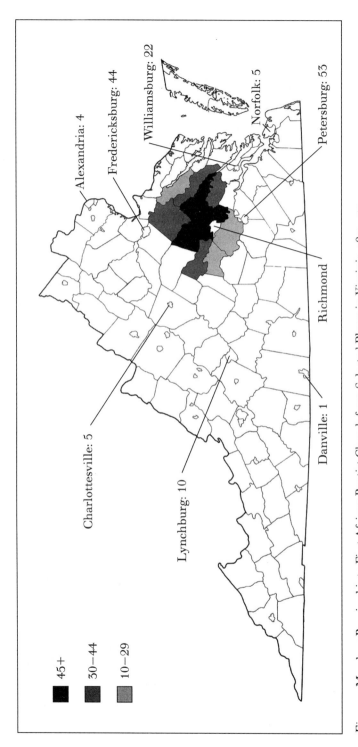

Figure 3. Members Received into First African Baptist Church from Selected Places in Virginia, 1841–59. *Source:* Compiled from church minutes, 1841–59. microfilm, Library of Virginia, Richmond. *Note:* Based only on members received who listed a verifiable place or church of origin.

Alexandria: 4

Fredericksburg: 44

Williamsburg: 22

Norfolk: 5

Petersburg: 53

Richmond

Charlottesville: 5

Lynchburg: 10

Danville: 1

45+

30–44

10–29

labor-intensive or seasonal nature of work by hiring slaves to make cash money. The older eastern areas of the state had a large pool of redundant slave labor. Some masters turned their human property into cash in the slave trade, but others, like former slave William I. Johnson's master, "had more slaves than he could work but . . . preferred to hire them out to selling them." The city offered an excellent opportunity for hiring.[61]

The majority of enslaved newcomers to First African Baptist Church in the two decades before the Civil War came from old Tidewater areas where crop diversification and a large slave population made hiring logical and profitable. New church members came from three general areas: Richmond's immediate hinterland of Henrico, Hanover, and Chesterfield Counties; the Tidewater counties north of the James River; and the other cities and towns of Virginia. At least two hundred and fifty-seven African Americans came to the church from the Tidewater counties north of the James, an area that was dramatically changed by the agricultural revolution but that still held a large African-American population. In contrast, records show only sixty-five congregants arriving from the Tobacco Belt counties of the western Piedmont, and of those, fifty hailed from the agriculturally diverse counties of Powhatan, Goochland, and Amelia, close to Richmond's hiring centers. Not surprisingly, only five people came from the northern Piedmont and three from the Valley region, places where slavery was weak.[62]

Free blacks were more likely to move from city to city than slaves, because of their higher concentration in urban areas and greater relative freedom. Church minutes show that one hundred and sixty-one men and women from other Virginia cities and towns joined First African Baptist Church from 1841 to 1859, around 29 percent of new congregants from other Virginia locations. Slaves from other urban areas made up less than a fourth of the bondsmen and women who joined First African, while almost half of all free blacks entering the church were from other towns and cities.[63]

The ebb and flow of the hiring system peaked during the Christmas season, when thousands of African Americans returned to friends and family in the country for the holidays, returning for the hiring season after the New Year. Manufacturers suspended business, and for the African Americans who remained in or returned to town, it was a time of celebration. This interlude both disturbed and amused whites. A day after Christmas in 1849,

William Palmer invoked his father's memory of the season: "You can well imagine just how the town looks now, by calling to memory the crowds of negroes swarming Main St. and the darkie-dandies promenading the side walks: the whole comunity seems cheerful and busy." [64]

The celebration of the holidays soon gave way to a period of intense business negotiations. The hiring and selling of slaves dominated the month of January in Richmond. John Gault, writing to Samuel Gault in Boston, put it crudely but succinctly: "The city is full of niggers from all parts of the country to let themselves for the coming year & they are selling them at wholesale." [65]

The *Richmond Enquirer* was more businesslike in its analysis of the hiring season, reporting in 1855 that "there was much animation in the hiring business. Prices have become pretty well established, and servants are now going off at a rapid rate, although there are still thousands filling the streets and hiring stations to be disposed of. Farm hands bring from $125 to $150; plough boys $70 to $90; house women $50 to $80, nursing girls from $30 to $40, tobacco factory hands from $100 to $125, for men, and from $30 to $80 for boys, according to size." A few weeks later there were still "crowds of servants, men, women, boys, and girls, for hire . . . to be seen in and around the several hiring stations of this city, although original prices are still maintained." [66]

Richmond's newspapers, as economic and political organs, took careful note of the hiring rates and economic forces driving them. "For tobacco factory hands the demand is now greater than it was two weeks ago, and consequently higher prices are asked and obtained," the *Enquirer* reported. "At the opening of the new year, factory men were hiring for $100 to $125, while farm hands were bringing $140 to $160. This discrepancy has induced some owners to put their factory servants to other duties, and has probably caused a scarcity and a rise in the hire." [67] Demand usually outran supply in Richmond's slave labor market, and hiring became extremely lucrative for masters and middlemen. Railroads, factories, and other labor-intensive enterprises hired most of the enslaved men, while domestic service predominated among the female workers.

Slave labor expanded in the 1850s in Richmond, an era when it was declining in most other Southern cities, but growth in the numbers of the

Table 1. Richmond Population by Race and Nativity, Showing Percentages within the Total Population and the Increase from 1850 to 1860.

Census Year	White			Black and Mulatto			Total
	Native Born	Foreign Born	Total	Slave	Free	Total	
1850	13,172	2,101	15,274	9,927	2,369	12,296	27,570
	(47.8)	(7.6)	(55.4)	(36)	(8.6)	(44.6)	
1860	18,679	4,956	23,635	11,699	2,576	14,275	37,910
	(49.3)	(13)	(62.3)	(30.9)	(6.8)	(37.7)	
Percent Gain from 1850 to 1860	41.8	135.9	54.7	17.85	8.7	16.1	37.5

Source: J. D. B. De Bow, *Statistical View of the United States . . . Being a Compendium of the Seventh Census* (Washington, D.C.: Beverly Tucker, 1854), 398–99; *Population of the United States in 1860; Compiled from the Original Returns of the Eighth Census* (Washington, D.C.: Government Printing Office, 1864), xiii, xxxii.

enslaved did not match the spectacular growth of the foreign-born population. Like the rest of the urban South, Richmond's population grew progressively whiter in the last decade before the Civil War, largely because of new immigrants from Europe. By 1860, the port and river towns of New Orleans, Louisville, and Memphis held percentages of foreign-born men and women that rivaled or exceeded Northern cities such as Philadelphia, Boston, and Providence. Southern ports on the East Coast held smaller but rapidly growing populations of European immigrants. By 1860, the foreign-born made up about 13 percent of Richmond's population and more than one fifth of the white inhabitants.[68]

European immigrants and Northern-born newcomers had an influence on Southern cities far greater than the total numbers would indicate. The foreign-born population in the ten largest Southern cities formed a higher percentage of the adult male population than in most Northern cities by the Civil War, making the newcomers politically important and a source of concern to some Southern leaders. The overwhelmingly young, male newcomers became the principal source of free labor in the urban South. Among Richmond's workingmen, the foreign-born far outstripped all other groups in population growth in the last decade before the Civil War, increasing 166 percent. Likewise, the number of Northern-born white workingmen increased 97 percent, more than double that of free blacks or native whites. Immigrants and Northerners constituted close to half of all free workingmen in the city.[69]

The voices heard shouting above the din of iron forges and rolling mills usually spoke in the accents of Scotland, Wales, and England. Great Britain still dominated the development of iron technology in the early 1800s, and her sons carried their knowledge and skill with them throughout the Atlantic world. Immigrants from the German states, who made up about a third of all the foreign-born in the city, also worked in iron but the majority plied various other trades, making shoes, cutting stone, building houses, and printing newspapers and circulars. Free blacks were already entrenched in some jobs, especially the building trades and shoemaking, and conflict was inevitable. White workingmen often opposed black workers in their trades, not only on the basis of racism but in order to perpetuate their collective ownership of skill, which they passed on to their sons and to favored apprentices.[70]

British and German workers were especially skilled in comparison to Irish and free-black workers. Nine out of ten German and British workers were in skilled trades, while more than six out of ten free blacks worked as laborers. An even greater number of Irish workers—the city's largest immigrant group—dug canals, worked on railroad construction, and toiled on the docks, often working alongside free blacks and slaves. Irish women also bore the stigma of working at a predominantly black occupation in a Southern city. Of the 271 white domestic workers found in the city, almost all were female and Irish.[71]

The white workers who flowed into the city to seek their fortune included not only artisans, tradesmen, and laborers but also clerks and bookkeepers. In a densely packed financial and mercantile district to the west and south of Capitol Square, young men, mostly native-born, worked in the principal dry-goods establishments and retail shops that lined Broad, Grace, Franklin, and Main Streets. In the older dry-goods houses, a single clerk often filled a customer's entire list of purchases, which required considerable familiarity with the various lines of goods. By the 1850s, however, many of the larger houses had instituted a new style of service popular in the North, with clerks stationed in separate departments.[72]

Commercial activity peaked every spring and fall, reacting to a clientele that increasingly demanded new goods for each season. Clerks and bookkeepers labored long hours during these periods, huddling in stockrooms preparing goods, scribbling hurried notes in letterbooks addressed to business associates in the North, and generally facilitating the rush of demand. An eighteen-year-old clerk, recently promoted to head of the print department at Kent, Paine & Company, confessed to his diary that he had been unable to write for over a week, as "Our 'Spring Trade' is fairly inaugurated. Last night the store was open until 2 A.M. but I left at 1." It would be another two months before he again began recording his private thoughts.[73]

The city's commission merchants also handled a glut of business in the spring and fall. Farmers and planters purchased agricultural supplies and negotiated for the sale of their crops, while grocers bought a variety of foodstuffs from the larger firms. William Ludwell Sheppard, a young clerk at John H. Claiborne's mercantile house, frequented the canal basin, where shipping arrived from western Virginia, and the docks at Rocketts Landing on the James River, the gateway to the Atlantic trade. Sheppard, an aspiring artist, complained about the heavy loads of salt and other commodities he handled for the firm with just a few other employees. After returning from a sojourn in the country, he regretted leaving "rural shades & balmy breezes for greasy bacon & odoriferous Guano."[74]

Many young men came to the city to further their fortunes as businessmen. In 1859 dry-goods merchant Mann S. Valentine compiled a list of the "Young Men that have been in my employ since I began business in 1810." Valentine made notes on their business acumen and behavior and also tabulated their place of origin. All but four of thirty-three were from rural Virginia counties. Young men from the country wrote anxiously to city merchants looking for work. John Megginson of Elk Creek informed a Richmond dry-goods and hardware firm that "my friend A. W. Flippin advised me to apply to Mr. Ellis for business saying he saw him during a sale a short time since at Elk Furnace & that he was in want of a young man as a Book Keeper or sales man which business I have followed several years; flatter myself I am capable of filling the office, will however if wanted give you a trial before we bargain." Tobacco manufacturer James Thomas Jr. periodically received requests for employment or assistance. Benjamin Wilkes sent a note to Thomas via his son Corbin, who came to the city "to seek his fortune." Wilkes assured Thomas that "any aid you may give him will be Thankfully received and fondly Reciprocated."[75]

Almost nine hundred clerical workers crowded the city in the late antebellum period, inhabiting boardinghouses and small apartments in the central city. The young diarist of Kent, Paine & Company spent late 1858 looking for a new residence, finally settling on a boardinghouse on Eleventh Street near Main in the heart of Richmond's commercial district. He planned to move in with three other young men in order to share the cost of rent. Most of these clerks and bookkeepers were new to the city but not to the South; more than 80 percent of them had been born in the slave states.[76]

The foreign fabrics and notions handled by the clerks of Richmond rarely came directly to the Virginia capital. One investigator for a New York commercial journal could not "ascertain the value of foreign importations, by our merchants, through New York, but know it to be large." To prove his point he noted that only $75,570 worth of goods arrived in Richmond "under warehouse bonds, and the duties paid in Richmond," while "the remaining paid duties in New York."[77]

Richmond's position in the dry-goods business reflected the general trend of antebellum Atlantic trade—the increasing dominance of New York over all other ports. As early as 1827 Richmond businessman James Rawlings, writing from Boston, had noted that even that city, "notwithstanding the Great, if not redundant capital and the vast industry and enterprize of the people, is confessedly on the decline being within the vortex of *the Great* New York." Although Southerners frequently wrote tracts bemoaning the economic imperialism of Northern ports, men like Rawlings realized that Boston and Philadelphia had suffered a similar fate. In 1821 New York received 37 percent of the total value of all imports, but by 1860 controlled 68.5 percent of the import trade, almost totally at the expense of Boston, Philadelphia, Baltimore, and Charleston. Virginia ports never posted more than a single percent of total imports, highlighting their dependence on the North for most manufactured items and dry goods. New York also ruled exports from American harbors. In 1815 New York claimed around 19 percent of the total value of exports from American ports, with Richmond and Norfolk together capturing a respectable 11.5 percent; by 1860, New York shipping carried more than 36 percent, Norfolk and Richmond a paltry 1.3. The decline was almost as striking for other East Coast cities, including Baltimore, Philadelphia, and Boston, which likewise posted sharp drops in shipping.[78]

The dominance of New York emerged with the rapid tightening of transportation and communication links between the eastern urban centers and the country as a whole. Railroad and steamship connections not only provided daily service to Northern cities from Richmond but also carried newspapers, magazines, and other information quickly to the Virginia capital. Allen and Gentry's Newspaper and Periodical Agency promised to "furnish daily the New York Herald and Tribune; The Philadelphia Ledger, and The Baltimore Sun, and deliver them regularly every afternoon." Richmonders could also receive weeklies from Boston, Philadelphia, New York, and London, ranging from *Ned Buntline* and the *Police Gazette* to *Scientific American* and the *Saturday Post,* as well as monthly magazines such as *Godey's Ladies Book* and *Graham's Magazine* from Philadelphia.[79]

The telegraph further rationalized business dealings with the North. In 1847 the Virginia General Assembly authorized Samuel F. B. Morse and his business partners to erect telegraph lines along the route of the Richmond, Fredericksburg, and Potomac Railroad to Richmond, and from there along the Richmond and Petersburg line into North Carolina. At 1:10 P.M. on July 24, 1847, a company representative relayed the first message from Richmond to Washington, D.C. The line took advantage of railroad rights-of-way through Virginia, but the ultimate goal was the connection of the great center of financial capital and business information—New York—to New Orleans, America's preeminent cotton port, via the country's political center, Washington. By 1849 Richmond physician William P. Palmer marveled that it was "useless to tell" his merchant father in New Orleans "of the election of a Loco to the speaker-ship of Congress when the telegraph whispers the important fact in the twinkling of an eye at the rate of hundreds of miles a wink." [80]

Virginia's planters and commercial men cared more about the price of slaves in the New Orleans market than the going rate for cotton. The telegraph connection to the Crescent City carried orders from slave traders as well as from cotton factors. The large traders in both cities kept in close contact and increasingly replaced the slave coffles that wended their way through the byways of the South with railroad and steamboat shipments of their human cargo. While traveling southward from Richmond, Frederick Law Olmsted commented on two freight cars "occupied by about forty negroes, most of them belonging to traders, who were sending them to the cotton States to be sold. Such kind of evidence of activity in the slave trade of Virginia is to be seen every day." [81]

In the end, slavery in Virginia still paid. As urban slavery declined across the rest of the South, a dynamic, fluid slave system integrating city and country emerged in the one Southern state that combined a modern economy and a conservative social elite. Between 1850 and 1860, Richmond's slave workforce grew from around 10,000 to more than 11,500, and by the eve of the Civil War Virginia had the largest slave population of any state— roughly a half million people in servitude. Hiring preserved slavery in older areas of the state while railroads fueled the expansion of plantation slavery into new areas. The tightening family alliances and commercial connections between planters, merchants, and industrialists made them allies, just as surely as the Cotton Whigs of Massachusetts were allied with Deep South planters. The forces of the advanced, capitalist economy— railroads, factories, and commercialism—were harnessed by a newly unified elite dedicated to forced labor.[82]

CHAPTER TWO

American City in a Southern Place

Yesterday, the 4th of July, the great day of America, was celebrated, as usual,
by speech-making and processions, and drinking of toasts, and publicly reading
of the Declaration of Independence. It was read in the African church of the
city; but why they selected the negro church of all others for the reading of
the declaration of freedom, which is so diametrically opposed to the institution
of slavery, I can not comprehend, when the burlesque of the whole thing
must be so evident to every one.

FREDERIKA BREMER, 1851

*T*he incredulity of the Swedish visitor Frederika Bremer at
the celebration of freedom in First African Baptist Church would
probably have been even greater had she realized that the same
building was used for political conventions, minstrel shows, and every
other sort of meeting and entertainment known to nineteenth-century urban Americans. But the "burlesque of the whole thing" was not evident to
the majority of white Americans or Virginians; regardless of their nativity
or station, most easily reconciled or ignored the contradictions between liberty and slavery. To them, Richmond seemed a typical American city.

Richmond's shops, hotels, and houses of entertainment looked much
like those in other eastern cities, and an urban, bourgeois culture flourished
in the Virginia capital. Likewise, the city's white population became increasingly diverse, offering the German and Irish visitor from Baltimore,
Philadelphia, or New York the sights and sounds of an ethnic, urban culture
typical of antebellum American cities. For artisans and the middle classes,

37

Richmond held the usual opportunities and associations. Members of these classes joined fraternal orders, political clubs, reform organizations, and militias like other urban Americans, and the mobility of clerks and artisans in antebellum America gave them a generally pan-urban perspective on their world. Even the idealization of the rural landscape, as embodied in Richmond's Hollywood Cemetery, was part of a larger American movement.

African Americans also took part in reform and fraternal movements, censuring fellow slaves and free blacks for moral indiscretions, listening to temperance lectures, and forming societies and organizations for relief of the poor and mutual benefit. African-American churches rivaled white congregations in their size and devotion to their religious beliefs. An increasingly sophisticated black population attended urban entertainments and took part in the city's less-respectable amusements along with middle- and working-class whites. Unlike many whites, however, black Richmonders understood the contradictions between liberty and slavery. African Americans borrowed ideas from the larger society's fraternal and reform movements but viewed their organizations, and the city itself, primarily as a vehicle toward greater collective solidarity, autonomy, and freedom.

Beneath the bourgeois facade of urban sameness, slavery deeply influenced the city. Just as commercial ties bound urban and rural Virginians, especially of the mercantile classes, so too did cultural and family ties. Wealthy whites and enslaved blacks moved frequently between city and country, while within affluent urban households whites maintained the social conventions of Virginia plantation life. City leaders struggled to control an increasingly independent urban-slave and free-black community. Visitors and newcomers commented on tobacco factories manned by slave workers and stumbled on the slave auctions and jails of Richmond. Some were only momentarily shaken from their everyday reality, while other more reflective witnesses comprehended the enormity of the institution in the city's life. Just as Frederick Law Olmsted understood the irony of railroads carrying slaves as cargo and passengers, Frederika Bremer grasped the hypocrisy of the gay and happy white, urban society that coexisted with dark and grim slave jails. Having heard "young, beautiful girls declare themselves proud to be Americans, and, above every thing else, proud to be Virginians," she fantasized that she would "like to have taken them to the [slave] jails, and have seen whether, in the face of all this injustice, they could have been proud of being Virginians, proud of the institutions of Virginia." But these young girls, like most white residents of the city, rarely thought about the slave jails that sat within blocks of the theaters, hotels, and concert halls of antebellum Richmond.[1]

The flourishing urban culture of late antebellum Virginia drew much of its life from the Old Dominion's status as the only Southern state that truly developed a system of cities. The linkage of Lynchburg, Petersburg, Fredericksburg, and other cities and towns to the capital fueled overall urban growth. In the period from 1840 to 1860, Virginia's urban population increased 63.3 percent, while the rural population increased only 19 percent, and, by the eve of the Civil War, Virginia's urban population had grown to a substantial 9.5 percent of the total population.[2] Urban dwellers, white and black, increasingly moved between Virginia's cities and towns.

Coming to Richmond became especially easy for residents of other Virginia cities, who frequented the downtown core of the city, where churches, shops, lager beer halls, hotels, and theaters vied for the wide-eyed newcomer's attention. Launcelot Minor Blackford, a student from Lynchburg, recorded periodic trips to Richmond in his diary, making use of the railroads and canal in his travels. The summary of an April 1855 visit, "principally to buy clothes, partly for pleasure," gives a good range of the activities visitors pursued while in the city. The eighteen-year-old Blackford set out "On Saturday last, which was a most beautiful day, went to C.H. and thence by hack to Tomahawk Station, thence by rail to City." After Blackford checked in at the American Hotel, he "knocked around generally." Blackford visited friends and acquaintances, including Charles Dimmock's family at the Virginia State Armory, where Dimmock commanded the state's Public Guard. He attended services at Saint Paul's Episcopal and Second Presbyterian Churches, commenting on the quality of the preaching. He probably counted a drill of the fire companies on Capitol Square as an unexpected highlight of his visit. Late in his stay he "finished . . .

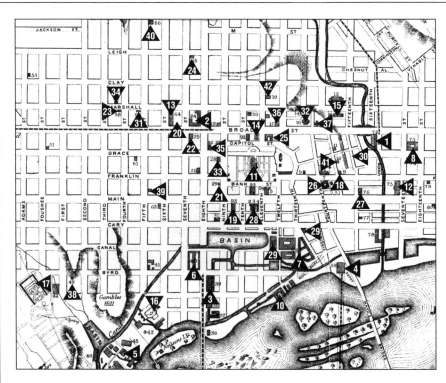

Railroad Depots
1. Virginia Central
2. Richmond, Fredericksburg,
   and Potomac
3. Richmond and Petersburg
4. Richmond and Danville
Industrial Sites
5. Tredegar Iron Works
6. Public Tobacco Warehouses
7. Shockoe Tobacco Warehouses
8. Seabrook's Tobacco Warehouse
9. Gallego Mills
10. Haxall Mills
Public Buildings
11. State Capitol and Square
12. First Market
13. Second Market
14. City Hall
15. City Jail
16. Virginia State Armory
17. Virginia State Penitentiary
Meeting Halls and Theaters
18. Odd Fellows Hall
19. Corinthian Hall
20. Shad's Hall

21. Lafayette Hall
22. Marshall Theatre
Relief Organizations
23. Saint Joseph's Orphan Asylum
24. Richmond Female Orphan Asylum
Hotels
25. Powhatan House
26. Ballard and Exchange Hotel
27. Saint Charles Hotel
28. American Hotel
29. Columbian Hotel
30. Slave Jails (Wall Street)
Churches and Synagogues
31. Saint James' Episcopal
32. Monumental (Episcopal)
33. Saint Paul's Episcopal
34. Saint Mary's German Catholic
35. Saint Peter's Catholic
36. First Baptist
37. First African Baptist
38. Second African Baptist
39. Second Presbyterian
40. Saint John's Evangelical Lutheran
41. Beth Shalome
42. Beth Ahabah

Map 1. Downtown Richmond Sites, ca. 1856. Source: Based on a detail from Moses Ellyson, *Map of the City of Richmond*, 1856.

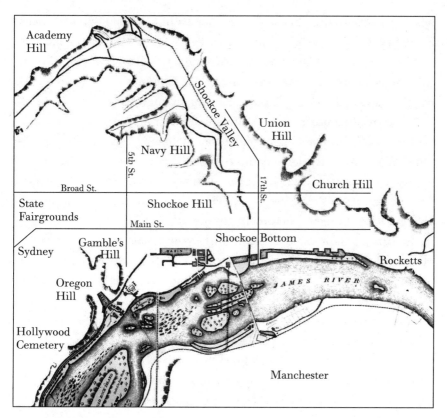

Map 2. Richmond Neighborhoods and Suburbs, ca. 1856. Source: Based on Moses Ellyson, *Map of the City of Richmond*, 1856.

business in the trading line and culminated a bill of about $30 with Keen, Baldwin & Co: Clothiers." He departed "by packet leaving Richmond at 8., to Michaux Ferry. Went then by invitation to 'Hughe's Creek'; Mr. R. Andersons, to dinner where were Mr. & Mrs. Cunningham, and house this Eveg;—have had a snug, pleasant, convenient, useful trip."[3]

Blackford, like other white visitors, may well have consulted a guidebook. Moses Ellyson and other publishers shepherded visitors through the unfamiliar town with their city directories. Ellyson, a printer by trade, considered the "neatly executed copper plate MAP OF THE CITY . . . prepared from actual surveys" that accompanied his 1856 directory a "most acceptable guide to strangers and others, through the streets and thoroughfares of the City." (Maps 1 and 2, based on Ellyson's map, locate many of the places and neighborhoods mentioned in this chapter.) Clearly aimed at the middle-class traveler and businessman, Ellyson's 1856 map listed ninety-five points of interest, dominated by warehouses and factories, churches and synagogues, hotels and meeting halls. Ellyson also warned his readers of the hilly terrain they would encounter. The map's topographical features showed the hillsides that defined the Shockoe Valley, the original center of the city, and the meandering creek that ran north to south along its length into the James River. The map's canals and railroads revealed the hand of man in the city's landscape and Richmond's striving for commercial success.[4]

Middle-class visitors to the city checked into the city's principal hotels, which were clustered in the center city around Capitol Square and the city's First Market. The larger establishments aped the grandeur of the Astor House in New York City and other urban showplaces, emphasizing the increasing sameness of city culture. Slave traders, country and town merchants, entertainment seekers, and those simply passing through filled the lobbies and parlors of the larger establishments. Listings of visitors to the major hotels ran in the local newspapers, providing information for those seeking family, business associates, and old friends. Hotel patrons and visitors craned their necks to see the latest arrivals to the Virginia capital and listened eagerly to the news and gossip provided by weary travelers. A Wilmington, North Carolina, visitor wrote home to "tell Ann Eliza, we were waiting in the Exchange parlor last night, for the lunch, after the

Concert, & who would I find there, but Sally Cooke, & her *betrothed,* Mr. *Bob Duval.*" [5]

Visitors viewed a suitably impressive hotel as the hallmark of a cultivated and prosperous community in urban America. Richmond's Exchange was considered first-rate by most Southerners who visited. Bessie Lacy marveled that "I have seen the famous Exchange & ho! what a splendid building it is & the Powhatan House." Launcelot Minor Blackford first lodged at the Exchange Hotel on a stopover between Edgewood, a rural plantation, and Lynchburg, reporting that "Bye the bye the Exchange is just now the very beau ideal of a fine hotel in my eyes, the most elegant a[nd] complete establishment I ever stopped at, anyhow." [6]

Built by Mr. Boyden, "a northern gentleman," the Exchange was soon purchased by John P. Ballard, who like many of his guests, had followed a familiar route to the state capital. Ballard grew up in "Albemarle county, and commenced business in a country store in that county. Subsequently he removed to Palmyra, where he took charge of a hotel, and there prospered and won a considerable reputation." Soon after purchasing the Exchange, Ballard built a new hotel directly across the street that carried his name. [7]

One of the few differences noted by Northern travelers was the prevalence of African American porters and waiters in Southern hotels. The most economically successful black entrepreneurs in Richmond also worked in or near the city's hotels. Free-black barbers offered haircuts and shaves to a largely white clientele and also advertised their skill at "leeching and cupping"—forms of blood-letting, a common nineteenth-century medical treatment. Robert C. Hobson worked at the American Hotel, and George W. Ruffin and Henry Cousins plied their trade on Thirteenth Street below Main, near the Ballard and Exchange Hotels. Black barbers knew well many of the city's most powerful whites—both Ruffin and barber Lomax B. Smith played clarinet for the band of a prominent white militia company. The trade was also lucrative. Barber John E. Ferguson's 1859 will left three houses and at least nine city lots to his children, as well as a three-acre farm. Barbers did not ignore their own community; they were instrumental in founding the city's first private black cemetery in 1815 and participated in black churches. Ironically, this black economic elite worked in close proximity to the slave jails and auction rooms of Richmond's slave trade. [8]

The guests staying at Richmond's hotels could easily walk to the principal theaters and halls for a night of entertainment or edification. The amusements of Richmond mirrored those found in other American cities. Richmond was part of a performance circuit of major urban centers that brought famous actors like the Booths and the shows of P. T. Barnum to Virginia audiences. Itinerant "professors," lecturers, and hustlers came in a steady stream to amuse and entertain with panorama shows, experiments, and magic acts.[9]

City entertainments opened a new and different world to country visitors, who were both enthralled and revolted by Richmond's lures. Mary Bowen Funsten of Albemarle County reported to a family friend that "Sister Eliza and myself were absent for three months during the winter, on a visit to Richmond and Norfolk. I, of course, enjoyed the gayeties of the city, more than can be expressed, as it was my first taste of a season in town as a young lady." A North Carolina woman visiting relatives in Hanover County bemoaned the dullness of life in the countryside, contrasting this with her visits to Richmond. Writing a friend to give her a "little spice of town life," she explained that Richmond was "Opera mad," and related her internal conflicts over whether to attend a performance: "I *cannot* think it wrong. It appears to me the most innocent & scientific of enjoyments. But my kinsfolk & acquaintance in Hanover imagine if you go to the *Theatre*, you are fit for *purgatory*." [10]

The theater also offended the pious middle-class sensibilities of many Protestant evangelicals. Launcelot Minor Blackford exulted that the Richmond Theatre's presentation of the Batemen children in the "great scene from the 'Merchant of Venice'" was "interesting and really wonderful" but questioned the morality of theater- and party-going in general. He reflected that "Parties Thursday & Friday night and Theatre Saturday was quite a 'round of dissipation' for me." Whatever their feelings about religious propriety, Virginians flocked to the theater. New Yorker Frederick Law Olmsted also attended a benefit given by the Bateman children in Richmond, and, with the legislature in session, he assumed that the audience made up "a fair representation of the Virginians of all parts of the State." Olmsted confessed that he had "rarely seen a finer assemblage of people." [11]

Black evangelicals valued respectability just as much as whites. Congregants learned the hard lesson of censure when the deacons of First African Baptist Church meted out reprimands and expulsions for activities that flourished in the city, including dancing, theatergoing, and gaming. During one meeting in 1842 the church excluded Polly Hardgrove and her daughter Ellen for intemperance, and James Allen lost his membership for gambling.[12]

Members of First African Baptist Church witnessed the state and national debate on alcohol abstinence within their church. In 1844 the church invited John Hartwell Cocke, a prominent Virginia planter and reformer, to speak on temperance to the congregation. When the famed temperance speaker John B. Gough came to Richmond, "no other building could accommodate the crowds that flocked to see and hear him." A later lecture on the evils of drink did not go as well. Minister Robert Ryland added a postscript to his minutes that "the ch. took a recess to hear Judge ONeal of S.C. lecture on Temperance—who gave offence by sundry expressions, to the congregation, as was painfully evident by their murmurs, & by their leaving the house in large numbers.!!" The members' consternation probably derived from the speaker's condescension to his audience, not the message of abstinence.[13]

Ironically, First African Baptist Church's capacious interior and its location across Broad Street from Capitol Square made it a frequent venue for concerts, entertainments, and even political events. Robert Granniss was one of many spectators who crowded into the church during a Whig convention in 1859, listening to numerous stump speeches by local and state figures. Congregation members resented the invasion of their sacred space, especially when indignities were done to the church. In October 1851 the church's choir "complained of their gallery being forcibly entered by some persons at a recent political meeting held in the church & of their books being defaced & removed, besides other injury done, it was agreed after some consultation that the Pastor should publish an article in the City Paper deprecating such proceedings in future." The members' consternation probably heightened when sold-out entertainments were racially segregated in separate showings, as was the 1851 visit of General Tom Thumb. But the performances and conventions brought in needed cash, as in 1848, when the "Committee to let the church" registered more than $160 in profits, primarily from the Whig and Democrat Parties. No doubt the struggles over use of the building and the entertainments it hosted taught the members much about the state of urban America.[14]

Richmond reformers battled the same illicit entertainments found in other American cities. Gambling dens, saloons, and houses of prostitution flourished, although Moses Ellyson omitted them from his map. Thomas J. Macon, a dry-goods clerk in the antebellum city, considered the gaming houses "an important part of the city's life" and remembered the "elegantly furnished" gambling establishments of "Worsham and Brother, the Morgan Brothers, and Nat Reeves," where "every night a sumptuous supper was spread before their patrons, which was greatly enjoyed by many planters coming to town to sell their crops."[15]

As early as 1833 a committee of twenty-four was assembled to investigate gambling in Richmond. The committee's draft report listed the prin cipal gaming houses with their locations and investigated several changes in the law to deal with the situation. They considered the proposition "that it would be expedient to license Gaming Houses, it being the only efficient mode, in the opinion of the advocates of the measure, to diminish the evil complained of," but eventually decided against such a measure after noting the negative examples of Paris and New Orleans where gambling was legal. Seeking counsel from someone with considerably more experience with vice, the members wrote a New York City official. Sadly, the city's district attorney replied that New York made little attempt to keep records on gambling, and "the truth is that New York has been as much demoralized by the practice of gaming as any other city, and I am sorry to say that the means employed to repress this vice have been inefficient to a great degree."[16]

The Richmond committee summarized "individual instances of ruin" from gambling houses, often young merchants, bookkeepers, or clerks corrupted by an insatiable desire to test their luck at the card game faro. According to the committee, the employer's money often found its way to the gambling tables, but Thomas J. Macon related an episode that provided a slight twist to that scenario. The senior member of a prominent dry-goods house called aside a clerk named William Perkins. Although a good employee, Perkins also excelled at cards. When the merchant informed Perkins that he understood that he "play[ed] cards a great deal," the clerk countered by asking if his work for the firm had been satisfactory. The merchant replied in the affirmative and asked Perkins for "any real good pointers in draw-poker." [17]

The former clerk Macon obviously told this story for comic effect many years after the fact; yet some clerks genuinely feared the effects of gambling on their young associates. Jefferson Wallace tried to reform his friend Jack Nowlans, "a regular goer to the Faro Banks for some three years and plays pretty high." While Nowlans had quit wagering at cards at his friend's urging, he informed Wallace that "everyone goes even some of our merchants and nearly every young man in the city—they think no more of being seen in a Faro Bank than in a Bar Room." [18]

The barroom captured just as many men as gambling dens. After his return to Richmond from California, Jefferson Wallace encountered a steady stream of friends and acquaintances who had turned to the bottle. He voiced his dismay to his brother Charlie at "what a sad thing it is when we see men who once was highly respectable now not fit companions for the worst of free negroes." In another letter, he recounted seeing "Old Mountjoy the stone mason . . . a complete drunkard and reels about the streets like a confirmed loafer." One of Charlie's old friends, Billy Allen, "got whipped twice" while "in liquor" on the street. He insulted a dentist and received a caning and then offended Roger Pryor, an editor of the *Enquirer*, who "pitched into Billy and pounded him severely." Wallace concluded that "our city has gotten to be quite pugnacious." [19]

Middle-class reformers easily grasped the dangers of drink to clerks and bookkeepers, just as industrialists saw the inefficiencies of intoxicated workmen. Joseph Reid Anderson considered intemperance a serious problem among the white workingmen at the Tredegar Iron Works. Apologizing for a bad shipment of iron to a Boston firm in 1846, Anderson reasoned that "I suppose it has been over heated and burnt which will sometimes happen until temperance is more prevalent among workman." Anderson discharged roller David Jones in 1848 for "repeatedly absenting yourself from the mill and by dissipation," although the ironmaster regretted losing a worker who had made high wages through his exertions. Workers themselves, no doubt with management's blessing, formed the Armory and Tredegar Total Abstinence Society connected to a Sons of Temperance division. The city boasted eleven divisions of the organization by 1852.[20]

The efforts of national and state temperance organizations notwithstanding, public drinking remained a feature of political events and other occasions. Philadelphian Jacob Bechtel attended the 1858 dedication of the Virginia Washington Monument on Capitol Square in a "driving sleet all day." "Such was the Excitement," he exclaimed to his brother, "that you would have supposed it was the most sunshiny day in the World & due as much by the way to the free distribution of Toddy as to Patriotism." A visiting friend remained "abstemious to the utmost degree, yet he did not escape as well as many who imbibed more freely, as he fell against the fence, and nearly tore his Coat off his back."[21]

Richmond's city fathers were most concerned with the proliferation of grog shops, tippling houses, gambling establishments, and houses of prostitution that flourished in the city's poorer sections. Officials feared the mixing of working-class whites, free blacks, and slaves in such neighborhoods more than the problem of drunkenness and public order. Legal codes barred blacks from operating a "cook shop or eating house" without a license and punished whites and free blacks for serving alcohol to slaves. The police stepped up raids on establishments in infamous districts such as Pink Alley, "as notorious in the police annals of Richmond as are the Five Points in those of New York." After a sweep in August 1853, four women stood accused in the city courts of running houses of ill fame in Shockoe Bottom. Apparently not satisfied with the city's vigilance, a group of young men from Jefferson Ward in 1856 formed the Rocketts Regulators to warn and punish those committing sexual indiscretions in the city's dock neighborhood. The men descended on the homes of two interracial couples, subjecting them to various indignities including dunkings in the James River.[22]

The raucous nature of the city streets and its dangers, as well as the prevailing gender relations of Victorian America, prescribed that a respectable young woman should be accompanied in public by a male, greatly complicating her ability to travel. Robert Granniss received a note from his erstwhile girlfriend Emma Kent: "Mr. Granniss—Having no brother whom I can call upon, I waive all ceremony and invite you to a party at Dr. Deane's tomorrow evening." The stiff formality of the note itself indicates the Victorian sensibilities that informed Richmond's middle classes. Granniss accompanied Emma Kent and her sisters to countless lectures, church services, and parties.[23]

Women violated this code only at their peril, and sometimes took unusual steps to go forth alone. A small note affectionately addressed to "My dear Bob" pleaded "I must speak out. Will you meet me alone on tomorrow evening by moon light on the French Garden. Where I will be in the dress of a man. When you get there & if you see a figure in black it will be your love—and then but whistle & Ill come to get my lad. Farewell awhile My dear Bobby." The French Garden, once a popular entertainment spot, seemed a romantic enough spot for two lovers to meet.[24]

Despite the perception of the city as a place of banal display, spectacle, and vice, the city also provided spiritual rewards to those who traveled to Richmond, and houses of worship vied with secular pursuits in the bustling urban core. Richmond's antebellum skyline bristled with the steeples and domes of its many denominations, testifying to approaching travelers the importance of urban religious life. The men who led these churches and synagogues were thought to be just as impressive as their substantial congregations and church buildings. Seeing both was essential for the religious traveler to Richmond.

The city's African-American congregations, ethnic churches, and synagogues held the majority of the city's religious practitioners, but directories and guidebooks pointed visitors to the established Episcopal and Presbyterian edifices of the city. Bessie Lacy, a Presbyterian minister's daughter from North Carolina, provided her father with her impressions of the major churches: "The Monumental Church . . . is a beautiful church with arched roof and a skylight, St. Pauls church is a very pretty church too—but I like ours [Second Presbyterian] the best. It is so purely Gothic. All the others combine several different styles of Architecture." These churches were certainly the most architecturally significant in the city, and all were

extremely desirable pulpits. Saint Paul's and Monumental stood close by
Capitol Square, and Second Presbyterian adorned South Fifth Street, a
fashionable address. New York-born resident Robert Granniss admired
Saint Paul's as the "most aristocratic in the city. The congregation appeared
to be all highly respectable."[25]

The diaries of middle-class visitors to Richmond testify to the importance of religious expression and sustenance. Episcopalian Launcelot Minor
Blackford spent Christmas in the Richmond area in 1854 and attended services at a number of different congregations. On New Year's Eve he heard
the Reverend George B. Cummins, rector of Saint James Episcopal Church,
"in a very fine sermon." That afternoon he had journeyed to Second Presbyterian Church to hear the renowned Moses Drury Hoge, but left disappointed when Hoge did not preach. That evening Blackford returned to
Saint James and received the "*chef d'oeuvre,*" from Cummins. "The crowd
was immense . . . the church 'chocked full,'" he wrote,

> And of the *sermon* what shall I say! In a word, at least, I think I might call it
> the finest effort ever heard from the pulpit, and methinks I could have sat
> down last night and written it off almost, for I hardly lost a word. . . . The
> text was Habakkuk II.1. He confined himself to the "Death of the year." He
> was grand and pathetic, but with what ever sentiment he introduced there
> was so much practical application as to be just right. The sermon was the
> kind to do good, and good I believe it will do—it *must* do. . . . I was delighted
> beyond measure as were the people generally I think.[26]

The "grand and pathetic" manner that Blackford appreciated left
William Ludwell Sheppard cold. The young clerk flatly stated that "I don't
like his manner in the pulpit at all, he speaks too much with his hands &
features, altogether his delivery & gesture is very theatrical." Sheppard also
visited Second Presbyterian Church and found "a great want of reverence"
during prayers when many people stood "looking about the church, even
members." Sheppard attributed his reaction to his upbringing in the
Episcopal Church, "where, kneeling is the attitude of prayer, & it seems to
me the proper one." Visitors attended churches in Richmond on an ecu-
menical basis, trying to hear the best ministers, but were not shy about expressing their opinions of the quality of the minister or congregation.[27]

White visitors often attended First African Baptist Church, curious to see the rituals and hear the singing of the congregation. Mary Virginia Hawes Terhune remembered that "what were known as the 'Amen benches,' at the left of the pulpit, were reserved for white auditors. They were always full." One member of the congregation, a former slave who had purchased his freedom, complained to a Northern visitor that white Richmonders often implored strangers to visit First African Baptist Church. He feared—correctly—that some Northern and foreign visitors would mistake the religious enthusiasm and Sunday dress of the congregation as proof of the happy condition of the city's slaves. European visitors often made the pilgrimage to the church, and some came away surprised at the independence given church members in leading spontaneous songs and the role of a few prominent black "exhorters." White and black Virginians did not come to hear Robert Ryland, who himself realized the prudence of allowing storied black ministers like Joseph Abrams to lead the congregation. Contrary to the letter of the law, but in the spirit of church comity and peace, Ryland condoned the continuation of the tradition of black ministers as leaders.[28]

Saint Peter's, Richmond's oldest Catholic church building, stood within a block of Saint Paul's Episcopal Church on Grace Street near Capitol Square, but later Catholic, Lutheran, and Methodist churches anchored immigrant populations in areas such as Navy Hill, located just northwest of the central commercial district. Intersected by an area of free-black settlement farther west around Leigh and Jackson Streets, a visitor to the Navy Hill neighborhood in 1858 could begin his or her tour on Fifth Street above Jackson, at the "German Lutheran" Church, known to congregants as Saint John's. Proceeding just a few blocks to the southwest, the visitor would soon see the humble brick building of Bethlehem Lutheran, whose members had recently broken away from Saint John's. Saint Mary's German Catholic Church would be the next stop, just south on Fourth Street. All of these congregations ran their own schools and created church-based welfare organizations.[29] Although hardly enough of a walk to build up a thirst, our visitor might find the saloon of Johann Gottfried Lange a natural stopping point, being only half a block away. As a prominent member of St. John's and a founding member of many of the German societies in Richmond, he would no doubt regale the visitor with some of the recent happenings in the German community.[30]

Richmond's Germans founded organizations similar to those in other urban communities throughout the United States, such as the *Gesangverein* (singing society), *Krankenverein* (a sick benefit society), and the *Turnverein* (a sports organization). Following the pattern of Germans in other parts of America, the schools, organizations, and churches reinforced the use of the German language, as did the German press. Burghardt Hassel, the publisher of Richmond's German-language newspaper, the *Richmonder Anzeiger*, also published a German reading text. Richmonders walking through Union Hill, Navy Hill, and other neighborhoods where Germans clustered could hear the regional dialects of Saxony, Hesse, and Hanover, among others. Charles Hennighausen remembered that he and his fellow German soldiers were still "conspicuous by our German speech" at the outbreak of the Civil War.[31]

Most Germans came to Richmond after 1850, and each new set of immigrants caused problems for the already established population. Johann Gottfried Lange, a shoemaker born in the Prussian city of Erfurt, signed a contract with an agent of the James River and Kanawha Canal Company in Bremen, providing him with passage to Richmond in exchange for six months' work on the canal and twenty Thaler in pay. Lange remembered that when the ship carrying the workers docked on September 16, 1837, a large, curious crowd turned out to see its arrival. He and fourteen other men moved into a house together, their sense of isolation heightened by the fact that no one could understand them and that "only about 24 German families were living in Richmond, most of them merchants who shied away from speaking to the new immigrants and kept their noses in the air higher than necessary."[32]

Many of these merchants were German Jews who had been early settlers in Richmond. Richmond's Jewish community was made up of both Sephardic Jews, whose origins were in Portugal and Spain, and Ashkenazic Jews from the German States and Eastern Europe. Both attended Beth Shalome, Richmond's first synagogue, but soon the growing German population founded Beth Ahabah. The established Jewish families "acted rather condescendingly towards the recently arrived immigrants," even of their own faith. In one case a marriage proposal from a recently arrived German Jew to a member of an established family became a family joke. Family members mocked the new immigrant's accent, and the proposal was, of course, rejected.³³

Despite the treatment he had received, Lange complained about those who arrived after he did, including a group of Germans who had taken part in a *"Freie Gemeinde"* (Free Society). A young Social Democrat from Baden, Carl Steinmetz, arrived in Richmond in late 1850 and led the organization. Lange excoriated the society's leaders for hoisting the red flag over their meeting house and advocating labor and land reform, slave emancipation, and universal suffrage. Lange and other conservative Germans suppressed the group, advising Steinmetz to leave the city. The young radical complied. An old newspaper report about the group from the *Baltimore Wecker* resurfaced in 1854 in the *Richmond Whig,* just in time to aid the Know-Nothing campaign. The flap over the organization probably said more about the anxiousness of city leaders than the radicalism of Richmond's Germans.³⁴

Many immigrants of Lange's generation also took the step of becoming naturalized as American citizens. Thomas Ruppert had, like Lange, wandered throughout the German states and kingdoms as a journeyman shoemaker before embarking for America. His *Wanderbuch* records his travel to Würzburg, Nürnberg, and many other German cities. On April 13, 1847, he took the oath to become a citizen of the United States based on five years' residence in the country and his good moral character. Testifying to his character were August Schad and Casper Wendlinger, both already naturalized, and both members of Saint John's Evangelical Lutheran Church. The vast majority of Richmond's Germans, however, still owed no direct political allegiance to the United States.³⁵

Most immigrants developed a set of overlapping allegiances and associations that mediated between the local community, American identity, and ethnic heritage. They took part in national celebrations as militia men, celebrated in German and Irish festivals, and participated in community-wide events. The complexity of these associations is seen in the 1856 diary of an unidentified German musician who traveled between the worlds of public Richmond and the German community. The musician himself had adapted well to American society, recording in clear English his performances for militia parades, the Richmond theater, and private events. He received three dollars for two parades of the National Guard, a militia company, and played for "Major Harvie's funeral for the Regiment." On one memorable night at the theater, he recalled that the audience threw onions at a performer named Lewis. He later backed up "Christys Great New York Minstrels (Humbug) and received $2.50 cts. for it."[36]

The musician had obviously become quite familiar with American slang, but his connections to the German community remained deep. He played for many German charity events, including a concert at Schad's Hall "given for the benefit of the poor" and a fair for Saint Mary's German Catholic Church held at Corinthian Hall. He remained connected to German societies and fraternal orders, attending a "turner festival at the Ramelsburg" and gathering with his fellow Germans at a mass meeting at Schad's Hall to plan a festival. He spent his few odd hours of leisure in typical German conviviality, drinking lager beer and playing cards and tenpins at various German establishments throughout the city, as well as attending German celebrations.[37]

Fluent in the ways of both the American and German world, the musician often assisted less-experienced countrymen. He wrote several letters for his friend E. Loebman to John Ford, the manager of the Richmond Theatre, and another to a Colonel Smith in Lexington. He accompanied several fellow *landsman* to the office of "Abel Mayo, Clerk of the United States Court," or deposited papers for them, and also inquired about documents at the Richmond Hustings Court. There is little doubt he attempted to assist them in obtaining papers related to their citizenship status. While some in the German community sought citizenship, the vast majority were relative newcomers and probably had little interest in becoming naturalized.[38]

Like the Germans, most of Richmond's Irish community arrived in the 1850s, growing from fewer than five hundred to more than two thousand residents in just a decade. The Irish also mediated between their Old World allegiances and American institutions. Richmond's Hibernians celebrated ties to the mother country while an all-Irish militia company, the Montgomery Guard, celebrated American national holidays on Capitol Square.[39]

Family ties and the ethnic communities in American ports of entry smoothed the way for immigrants to Richmond in the 1850s. Jewish immigrant Philip Whitlock arrived in America after an arduous trip across eastern Europe to Berlin, on to Bremen, and then sailing to Bremerhaven and finally to New York. After visiting relatives in New York, he boarded a steamship to City Point, Virginia, meeting family members and arriving in Richmond on August 4, 1854. Whitlock went to live in his brother's home on Main Street between Fifteenth and Sixteenth Streets, just across from the city's First Market. Whitlock, a tailor, worked for his sister-in-law's uncle, Prussian-born Ellis Morris, who ran a clothing store next door to the family home and served as the patriarch of the whole clan.[40]

Northern-born Richmonders had few problems assimilating themselves into the city's fabric. The diary of Robert A. Granniss reveals how similar the urban culture of Richmond had become to that of other East Coast cities. Born and raised in Brooklyn, Granniss moved to Richmond in September 1858 and began his diary on September 12 while at sea en route to Richmond. His father apparently had business connections with one of the principals of Kent, Paine and Company, and Granniss was immediately employed by this firm on his arrival. His diary betrays very few adjustment problems for a Northern-born man in Richmond, and most of the entries record observations and social events typical of a middle-class clerk in urban America in the 1850s. Granniss courted Mr. Kent's daughter Emma, accompanying her to church activities and social occasions, took flute lessons, and joined a volunteer militia. Along with throngs of other Richmonders, he enjoyed a day of celebration and merriment on the Fourth of July 1859 with his young friends. They observed the "evolutions" of the militia, partook of "Lager Schwitzer Cheese & Rye bread followed by segars & Claret" at Schad's Hall, a German beer garden and hall, where they also rolled tenpins. Later they rented a barouche to visit James Monroe's recently erected tomb at Hollywood Cemetery in the western suburbs of the city. Returning to town they went to Pizzini's confectionary for "cream" and capped the day by again traveling to the western edge of the city to attend the fireworks at the state fairgrounds.[41]

Granniss's visits to the fairgrounds and Hollywood Cemetery demonstrate the yearning of nineteenth-century urban dwellers for rural landscapes. The easy retreat of city streets into the well-worn paths of country roads and byways helped merge country and city in the minds of its residents. The suburbs of Richmond offered a variety of leisurely pursuits

for the population of the city. Forming a ring around the city that made
the metropolis fade almost imperceptibly into the countryside, a series of
springs, pleasure gardens, racetracks, and other rural retreats welcomed
pedestrians from Virginia's metropolis.

The militia musters, barbecues, and picnics held in the countryside were
not the exclusive domains of the elite and middle classes. Richmond's immigrant population also favored Richmond's immediate hinterland as a
place of recreation. Like most other people from a rapidly industrializing
society, Germans idealized the rural world of their forefathers through
shooting clubs, beer gardens, and the preservation of country folkways.
August Schad, a prominent German leader and the proprietor of Schad's
Hall in Richmond, owned a farm outside the city where the German
community staged celebrations, militia drills, and other events. While
German men often went for a drink at Schad's beer garden without their
families, Schad's farm hosted events for families and the extended ethnic
community.[42]

Hollywood Cemetery became the most famous site in the western suburbs by the end of the antebellum era, but it had a most inauspicious beginning. Richmond businessmen Joshua Jefferson Fry and William Henry
Haxall chanced to meet in Boston in 1847, and, like many middle-class
travelers, decided to visit the renowned Mount Auburn Cemetery, the first
of the planned, parklike cemeteries in America, dedicated in 1831. Inspired
by the experience, the two men began planning a Richmond cemetery that
would embody the same rustic, rural ideals. Interesting other city leaders,
including New Englanders James Henry Gardner, Horace Kent, and Isaac
Davenport Sr., they organized a board of directors and proposed a cemetery
on a tract called Harvie's Woods. The location bordered several sites already popular with those escaping the bustle of the city, including Clarke's
Springs, the grounds of Major John Clarke's estate, and Belvidere, the former home of William Byrd III. Just beyond the developing industrial suburbs of Oregon Hill (supposedly so named because of its remoteness from
the city) and Sydney, and above the city waterworks, Hollywood would provide much-needed relief for the city's overcrowded cemeteries.[43]

Initial plans for the cemetery ran into unexpected political opposition.
Although complaints about the cemetery's location above the city waterworks prompted some concern, most of these early problems came from

partisan enmities between the president of the Hollywood Association and his political enemies. These finally resolved, the cemetery developed into a premier attraction by the late 1850s, its fame greatly enhanced by the re-burial of President James Monroe in 1858.[44]

Women walked the wandering paths and haunting beauty of the rural cemetery both as recreation and to mourn. Ann Webster Gordon Christian visited Hollywood one afternoon in 1860 with her cousin. Christian had "not walked there . . . for years. Had a very pleasant time. Was very glad to have it in my power to lay even a few evergreens on Cousin h's grave." Departing, she reflected on the combination of man-made art and nature: "As we were leaving the cemetery & would look back the clouds & sky looked beautiful, & I hope they lead me to think of the still greater beauty, brightness & glory of that happy place where I am sure my dear cousin is." The rural cemetery invoked powerful religious and romantic themes important to Victorian men and women.[45]

The transcendent appeal of the rural cemetery in Victorian America comes through in the travel diaries of Virginians. Maria Watts Gwathmey, a Hanover County native, set off with a party of seventeen in 1853, following the usual path to Niagara Falls. In Philadelphia, she found Laurel Hill Cemetery "an interesting place, a kind of Gothic structure & a sleeping child were among the sublimest tombstones — old mortality with his white horse at the gate attracted my attention more than anything else." Images of death, tinged with sentimentality and sublime reflection, impressed themselves on Virginia's women, reinforcing their crucial religious and social role in mourning.[46]

The integration of man's art and God's nature made Fairmont Waterworks in Philadelphia another major destination for tourists. Virginian Samuella Hart Curd considered Fairmont Water Works to be "truly beautiful and from the grounds the view of the city is very fine," and Maria Watts Gwathmey found it "a most romantic beautiful place." Gwathmey described an impressive fountain with a child riding a dolphin spouting water thirty feet in the air and concluded that the "whole place was one of romantic beauty." [47]

Middle-class Northerners and Southerners alike could appreciate picturesque cemeteries and parklike grounds, a self-conscious adaptation of nature to the demands of city life. Southerners rarely failed to visit them on their frequent trips northward. But Richmond's elite retained an allegiance to another countryside, a rural world of plantations and farms where their ideas about society, family, and slavery were formed. The connection between city and plantation was easily seen in Richmond's early cityscape.

Charles Dickens outraged Richmonders with his unflattering comments on the city in his *American Notes,* leaving no doubt that he believed slavery blighted both country and city. Approaching the city on a southbound train from Fredericksburg in 1842, Dickens perceived that "in this district as in all others where slavery sits brooding . . . there is an air of ruin and decay abroad which is inseparable from the system." Dickens cataloged the "log-cabins . . . squalid in the last degree," "miserable stations by the railway side," and "negro children rolling on the ground before the cabin doors, with dogs and pigs"—"gloom and dejection are upon them all."[48]

During his stay in Richmond, Dickens toured the city and visited the state legislature as well as a tobacco factory. He concluded that the "same decay and gloom that overhang the way by which it is approached hover above the town of Richmond." Dickens freely admitted that "there are pretty villas and cheerful houses in its streets, and Nature smiles upon the country round; but jostling its handsome residences, like slavery itself going hand in hand with many lofty virtues, are deplorable tenements, fences unrepaired, walls crumbling into ruinous heaps. Hinting gloomily at things below the surface, these and many other tokens of the same description force themselves upon the notice, and are remembered, with depressing influence, when livelier features are forgotten." Dickens clearly understood the connection between the rural outbuildings he witnessed in the Virginia countryside and the wooden houses and slave quarters that stood throughout the city.[49]

Richmonders of the 1850s would have surely protested that the city had made substantial gains in the decade since Dickens's visit, but, despite the fine new hotels, halls, and theaters, the city's alleys and bottoms still teamed with outbuildings and cabins housing much of Richmond's African-American population. Most important, elite masters still maintained an understanding of their society based on the social relations of the countryside. City elites believed deeply in slavery, as evinced by their high levels of ownership of bondsmen and -women. More than 80 percent of urban leaders owned slaves by 1850, and the elite classes of the city owned or hired 80 percent of the city's slaves by 1860.[50]

Urban merchants, professionals, and manufacturers shared more than just slaveholding with planters; they often had strong family and cultural connections to the rural elite. As one historian, herself a descendant of a powerful Virginia ironmaster, explained, planters and men of commerce were "linked by a thousand ties of blood kin," and "for all his superiority to 'trade,' the planter when with his family he visited the capital, whether to attend the races or to govern the commonwealth, mingled with the bankers, the tobacco manufacturers, the flour millers, the ironmasters, the colliers, and their families with all the hospitable fellowship and grace and ease for which the commonwealth was famed."[51]

Richmonders owned considerable property in the surrounding counties throughout the mid-1800s, holding thirty thousand acres in adjacent Henrico County by 1860. As always, Richmond's elite speculated in land, betting on the future expansion of the city and a corresponding rise in the value of real estate. Others owned outlying plantations and farms that had come down to them through their families, which served as rural retreats or were operated for additional income. Still others found the business of market gardening profitable with easy access to Richmond markets. Thirty-one Richmonders invested in market gardening by the Civil War, cultivating almost two-thirds of the more than six thousand acres they owned.[52]

Ownership of a country estate facilitated the diverse interests of Richmond's elite families. Nicholas Mills purchased a substantial house on Leigh Street in the Shockoe Hill neighborhood in 1828. A major investor in the extensive coal mines southwest of Richmond in Chesterfield County, Mills retained a country home nearby. He traveled northward over the James from his Chesterfield estate to Richmond in a fine carriage drawn by a team of four horses.[53]

For elite city dwellers, having a country estate was a mark of distinction. A German musician recorded his frequent trips to play at parties on rural estates on the city's periphery. For one performance he traveled "on a canal boat 13 miles in the country to Mr. Jo. Allen's farm a beautiful place. Had very much to play, but got treated very well." Another private affair at

"Mr. Mayo's Farm" drew the busy musician into the countryside. The same musician spent late July and most of August and early September entertaining at the ballroom of the Amelia Springs. Much closer than the springs of western Virginia, it was a popular retreat, as was "Slash Cottage" north of the city.[54]

Affluent members of the community often traveled to the more remote country estates of relatives. Emma and Louise Kent, the daughters of prominent Richmond merchant Horace L. Kent, made trips to their uncle's farm in Virginia's Piedmont. While in the country, the children were exposed to another life, the life of farm and countryside. Slavery flourished there just as it did in the beautiful mansion on fashionable Franklin Street that the Kent sisters inhabited.

Apparently, one of the Kent daughters became more Southern than her father, a native of Connecticut, wished. A firm Union man, he left the daughter "Confederate bonds, emancipated slaves, and other such unrealizable assets," in his will after the Civil War, commenting that "I could continue the list to the extent of more than half a million dollars, but the above will suffice—she will see what the effect of secession has been."[55]

Kinship defined much of elite and middle-class women's sphere in antebellum Virginia and provided one of the most profound connections between country and city. Whether traveling to family-held plantations to visit or summer with relatives or attending a season at one of Virginia's springs, white women moved within an extended family network. Their own households replicated the plantation "big house," and their ideas about their slaves were not markedly different from those of their country cousins. The reform activities they advocated, such as the religious education of slaves, could be controversial but generally served only to reinforce, rather than erode, the regime of slavery.

Mary Virginia Hawes Terhune, known to nineteenth-century novel readers as Marion Harland, grew up moving between city and county, absorbing both bourgeois tastes rooted in American middle-class society and the dominant domestic values of a slaveholding society. The daughter of a Northern-born merchant, Terhune actively cultivated a self-image more in line with the Southern plantation mistress. Her father, Samuel Pierce

Hawes, arrived in Richmond from his native Massachusetts in the early nineteenth century. Terhune's mother, Judith Anna Smith, grew up at Olney, a plantation five miles east of Richmond on the Chickahominy River. Soon after their marriage, Samuel Hawes's business fortunes in Richmond turned sour when his partner defaulted, and the family moved to Amelia County to begin anew. The growing family moved in quick secession to various rural addresses, including Montrose, a plantation owned by a branch of Judith Anna Smith Hawes's family. They finally settled in Powhatan County, where Samuel Hawes's mercantile business met with success. Becoming "the confidential advisor of the embarrassed planter and the struggling mechanic," he also participated in the political and religious life of the community. The recovering fortunes of the family allowed the children to live more on a par with their Virginia cousins. Terhune reported that they "had . . . carriage and horses, my sister and I a riding-horse apiece, abundance of delicacies for the table, and new clothes of excellent quality whenever we wanted them." [56]

The family moved back to Richmond in 1845, much to everyone's relief. In 1851 Samuel Hawes's mother, Ann Clapp, bought the family a house in Richmond on Leigh Street at the corner of Fifth. As Terhune remembered it, "the locality was then quietly, but eminently, aristocratic. There were few new houses, and the old had a rural, rather than an urban, air." The brick Federal-style house dated to the glory years of Richmond's architecture and reflected the transplanted Yankee patriarch's respectable position in the city's business circles and society, serving as a deacon at Second Presbyterian Church. The Massachusetts-born Hawes also emulated his well-to-do neighbors by holding five slaves in bondage by 1850.[57]

Returning to the city at about the age of fifteen, Terhune took full advantage of the city's lectures, entertainments, fairs, and other cultural attractions. Previously taught by tutors at home, she now attended a Presbyterian seminary for girls. Like many other middle-class women of the antebellum era, however, Terhune also maintained contact with her rural upbringing after her family returned to Richmond. She traveled to see friends and family in Powhatan County during Christmas and sometimes spent a month's vacation in her old stomping grounds.[58]

Surrounded by servants during her early life, Terhune absorbed the lessons of household management in her various homes and through the example of her mother's family. Terhune's mother related vivid stories of Terhune's grandmother at Olney, and Terhune imagined her moving "about the modest homestead, directing and overseeing servants, key-basket on arm, keeping, as she did, a daily record of provisions 'given out' from storeroom and smoke-house." Terhune commented that "'looking after the servants' was no idle figure of speech with" women like her grandmother and that "eternal vigilance was the price of home comfort." Thoroughly middle class in many ways, Terhune idealized the Southern values of her mother's people, drawing sharp contrasts between Northern and Southern social relations.[59]

Virginia Sarah Tucker Brooke, the wife of lawyer and railroad entrepreneur Henry L. Brooke, made yearly trips with her children to Fort Hill, the Tucker home in Winchester, Virginia. Her mother entertained many children and grandchildren during the summer months on the Tucker estate. Usually the family embarked on the Richmond, Fredericksburg, and Potomac Railroad, traveling to Aquia Creek, where the steamboat carried them to Washington. The next day they clambered on board the cars of the Baltimore and Ohio Railroad, changing trains at the "Relay" (a station) to reach Winchester.[60]

Travel exposed Richmond families to new sights and sounds, but they were not always appreciated. On one return trip home the Brooke family waited an hour and a half for the cars to Washington at the Relay with several drunken men, who luckily remained outside the station house. The family encountered another difficulty when the train was "very much crowded with several companies of Firemen from Baltimore coming over here [Washington] to some celebration."[61]

The web of relations that connected slaves and masters in city and county could be exceedingly complex. The Brooke family and their slaves inhabited numerous plantations across Virginia belonging to both the Tucker and Brooke sides of the family. The family visited Millvale, Henry L. Brooke's boyhood home in Stafford County, managed by his brother, Samuel Selden Brooke. Only about three miles south stood New Salvington, a plantation Henry L. Brooke had inherited from his mother and where he had learned "the three cardinal virtues of a gentleman of that time—'to ride, to shoot and to tell the truth.'" Virginia S. Brooke encountered several family slaves while in the neighborhood in 1852, reporting to her mother that "I found black Nanny at the farm having come up to *visit* Neil. . . . I saw Henry and he looks perfectly well and told me to give his love to his Mammy & tell her he was 'well and doing well, and liked this part of the country very well.' Dave too came grinning up to enquire after 'Old Mistress & Mammy.' His wife and children too are well and send their love to her." The letter indicates the scattering of black family members among the Tucker and Brooke families' properties in Winchester, Stafford County, and Richmond.[62]

Elite Richmonders and their slaves experienced the rural world in another way, traveling to the mountain springs during the hot, humid Virginia summers. Trips to the Virginia springs presented white women with the excitement of meeting new acquaintances and some relief from daily cares, but basic conventions of gender and race still applied. Older women and men took the cure while chaperoning younger visitors who danced, played, and courted with fellow Southerners. African Americans still did the work of cooking, laundering, and cleaning, although personal servants sometimes were given more latitude than in their masters' homes.

Margaret, one of the slaves of merchant Mann S. Valentine Sr., played a major role in several letters written home by Elizabeth Ann Valentine Gray, the businessman's daughter. Gray told her husband that "Margaret had a severe attack of her heart last night. I think it was as much caused by indigestion as any thing else." The worried women applied a mustard plaster to Margaret's back and considered calling for a doctor. Margaret "had been out most of the afternoon," Gray reported, "and we inquired what she had been eating. Would you believe it, she had been at quite an elaborate *dinner party*, at which they had *champagne*—what we have not seen since we have been here—of which she said that she only took one *glass*. But she was not accustomed to such a convivial scene and drinking at all."[63]

Elizabeth Ann Valentine Gray clearly took some amusement in the idea that her slave attended a dinner party, although she obviously knew that people who routinely provided the food and drink for the table of those of her class knew how to throw a respectable affair. The situation positioned her slave as an elite within her caste. Indeed, Gray claimed that "I never saw a *greater belle.* You scarcely ever see her without an escort, they all seem to vie with each other which shall pay her the most attention. . . . from her account, she lives much better than we do." A period oil painting of a kitchen ball among African-American slaves at White Sulphur Springs reflects the belief that the springs hosted the cream of Virginia's slave population. The participants are all dressed in fashionable clothes as they celebrate the marriage of two servants, seen dressed in white.[64]

Margaret further confirmed her status as a belle when she "caught the 'head dining room servant,' quite an elegant looking gentleman." Gray surmised that "through his devotion to her we may probably be treated quite well." The Valentine women assisted Margaret in wooing her catch. Margaret had been "very busy, hemming handkerchiefs for the 'head dining room servant,' and marking them with her *hair.* She asked Mary Martha to write the name for her, and then she marked it with her hair." The Valentine women delighted in this very Victorian present, concluding that Margaret "is decidedly a great belle, and whatever requests she makes among the servants are sure to be granted, and catching the 'head dining room servant' is decidedly considered the *greatest catch of the Springs for the colored gentry.*"[65]

The amusement of the Valentine family with Margaret's romance and coquettish behavior might seem at first blush to be remarkably liberal and indulgent, but the family's reaction actually confirmed their conservative views of Virginia's social relations. Richmond's elites fancied their house servants as a "colored gentry," who adopted the refinements of white society and stood at the top of black society, looking down on laborers, field hands, and factory slaves. Just as the Valentines met Richmond-area peers at the springs, Margaret entertained "many *gentlemen acquaintances from Richmond, Brown DuPriest Robert* &c &c I cannot tell how many, she is constantly being recognized by some acquaintance."[66] In the mind of her mistress, Margaret's behavior did not challenge the social or racial order of Virginia society; rather, it confirmed the natural ascendancy of those brought up within the civilizing influence of genteel white culture.

Elites reasoned that slaves themselves recognized the necessity of a social order based on social hierarchy and good breeding, so important to the white Virginian's own idea of Southern culture. Samuel Mordecai, Richmond's first chronicler, entitled a chapter in his history "The Colored Aristocracy." Describing a group of elite slaves belonging to the finest families, Mordecai emphasized both their pretensions and real gentility. Mordecai retold the anecdote of a longtime servant who was asked by his mistress why he had ceased to attend church. He replied "that when he could sit by Mr. Wickham's Bob and Judge Marshall's Jack, he liked to join *siety*, but now he never knew who he *sot* by, and he stayed at home." [67]

Slavery within the household provided a continuity of experience between country and city for black and white women. While the mostly male force of African-American factory workers in Richmond lived throughout the city in a variety of arrangements, the majority of enslaved women lived in outbuildings behind Richmond's town houses, or in the "big house" itself. Richmond's prosperous neighborhoods—Church Hill below Broad Street, Shockoe Hill, and West Franklin and Grace Streets—presented an impressive facade of Federal and Greek Revival townhouses, but a cluster of outbuildings supported each household. Slaves in domestic service typically lived in two-story, multipen dwellings with exterior porches, amid smokehouses, necessaries, carriage houses, and other dependencies. The first floor of the quarters quite often housed the laundry and main kitchen, thus removing a fire hazard and unpleasant smells from the main house. The layout and structure of these quarters closely resembled the slave quarters near the plantation houses that dotted the Virginia countryside. [68]

Antebellum visitors made it a point to visit Richmond's tobacco factories, drawn by the unusual sight of black industrial workers coordinating their repetitive motions through collective song. Historians have also emphasized industrial slavery as the hallmark of Richmond's system of bondage. But the more than eight thousand workers who labored in Richmond's households made up the vast majority of the city's labor force, and these workers were overwhelmingly enslaved African Americans. Domestic slaves in Richmond's elite households encountered a situation very unlike the lives of most factory slaves. Almost one hundred slaves labored in just fifteen households along Franklin Street west of Capitol Square. Among the African Americans in these households, women outnumbered men, living in the outbuildings of the main house where they labored. Owned by their employers rather than hired, their situation contrasted sharply with the many hired, overwhelmingly male, factory slaves who walked the city streets. Most elite Richmond women stood in essentially the same position vis-à-vis their slaves as their country relatives, owning bondsmen and women who lived within their domain—the domestic household.[69]

Relations between slaves and mistresses in the city could be far from cordial. During the slave-hiring season in 1851, Virginia S. Brooke wrote her mother that in Richmond "nothing is talked of now but trouble with servants—making changes &c. &c. with which I have nothing to do fortunately as mine all do very well indeed—except poor Neil who was born to be a trouble to every body and gives me a great deal. But you have enough of that sort of trouble yourself, without my adding to it by telling you mine." [70]

Brooke ranted against her slaves in 1852. She informed her mother that on returning to Richmond "I found my coloured friends as usual. Lucy perfectly self satisfied—Pat humble & penitent—Isaiah *fierce*—*Bene* stupid & Eliza hateful—the dear little *bantlings* who have arrived since I left, I have neither seen nor enquired after." Her troubles with her African-American chattel reveal the tensions that flowed just below the surface of race relations in the urban "big house." [71]

Conflict between white and black women exploded into public view in July 1852, when slave Jane Williams and her husband were accused and convicted of murdering the Winston family in their beds. Sarah Benetta Valentine, another daughter of merchant Mann S. Valentine Sr., reported the chilling details to her brother, how "the whole of this awful deed was done with a hatchet," and that "Mrs. Winston's face and neck were so mangled that they could not be recognized by her friends." The mother and a small child died soon after the attack, but the father survived. "Such excitement was never seen in Richmond before," Sarah wrote, reporting that "on Monday morning the street was filled with men whose faces were pale with sorrow and indignation. Persons of the highest respectability spoke openly of the Lynch Law, as the only just one in such an aggravated case of murder. Jane and her husband have to be closely watched to keep them from being torn to pieces." The crowds did not have to wait long, as Jane Williams and her husband quickly reached the gallows.[72]

Sarah Benetta Valentine comforted herself after the Winston murders by insisting that she had "not seen even a colored person that does not think they ought to be hung without being allowed a trial," but others had no such illusions. Mary Virginia Hawes Terhune saw the murders as part of a pattern of growing conflict, writing a friend that "it is well understood here by both negroes and whites that a struggle for supremacy is near at hand— this is but the beginning of trouble." Chilled by the murders, which took place within two blocks of her home, Terhune related that "a murder, a case of poisoning, and one of incendiarism, all clearly proved, have taken place in our midst within a very short time—in each the coloured race the aggressors, the whites the victims." Terhune's life in Richmond had already been disturbed by periodic scares of "that worst of bugbears to a Southerner—an insurrection." Now the threat of race war and its horrors loomed just below the surface of her waking thoughts.[73]

Both Jane Williams and her husband belonged to First African Baptist Church, and the practice of religious instruction in the church came under severe scrutiny. Such instruction might produce yet more murderers. Robert Ryland, the church's white minister, objected to the unfair condemnation of his entire flock because of the actions of one or two persons (he was unsure of Jane Williams's husband's guilt), and insisted, as did Valentine, that "the whole mass of her own color" condemned Jane Williams. This hardly satisfied the church's critics, who took to the public presses to voice their condemnation of the church as a "cradle of crime." The furor continued into October, when a mass meeting of the three white Baptist churches of the city adopted resolutions in favor of continuing religious instruction of African Americans, defended Ryland, and condemned the unfair attacks on the church for the actions of a few.[74]

The religious education of slaves was part of the myriad antebellum reforms advanced in Richmond. By the 1850s, Richmond's citizens supported numerous orphan asylums, poor relief organizations, and other charitable works that mirrored developments throughout the United States. Christian evangelicals used churches and other organizations to promote education and reform. Likewise, the Catholic Church and German and Irish organizations formed benevolent institutions. Despite these good works, no comprehensive plan of public education existed in Virginia before the Civil War, and some movements linked to reform in the antebellum North, especially slavery abolition and woman's rights, were clearly beyond the pale.[75]

The movement for the religious education of slaves and the development of educational opportunities for white women both illustrate the accomplishments and limits of antebellum reform in Richmond. Self-conscious about criticism of slavery and deeply committed to religious reform, some white women sought to save the souls of slaves by providing religious instruction in Sunday schools throughout the city. Ann Webster Gordon Christian taught a Sunday school for African Americans at the United Presbyterian Church, noting the names of the fifteen scholars and their masters in the back of her diary. Sarah Benetta Valentine also later taught religious lessons to slaves, combining Christian duty and traditional Virginia paternalism. Fearing she had bored her brother in a lengthy letter about saving black souls, she asked, "have I not talked enough to you of 'Africa in America?' But it is a subject of the deepest interest to me, and I am sure your interest would be much increased if you could attend the meetings held Sunday evening in the lecture room. The colored people are first taught and then Mr. Dashiel preaches to them. The room is usually crowded. I have a class which is sometimes composed of twenty-six scholars. There are not only children but gray-haired men and women, who seem deeply interested." She expressed profound misgivings about her ability to give "instructions for a journey heavenward" in her Sunday school, but felt that God would guide her to proper teaching.[76]

White ministers provided texts for the instruction of slaves. First African Baptist Church's Robert Ryland published a popular work in 1848 entitled *Scripture Catechism, for Coloured People.* Joseph Mayo, Richmond's mayor, complained about the possible use of the work to teach reading and writing to slaves. No doubt some African Americans used it for precisely that purpose, but the book's lessons, reflecting Ryland's conservative views, emphasized moral behavior and submission to authority.[77]

By the 1850s, the education of slaves in Virginia was limited by both law and custom. The Old Dominion was one of only four Southern states that restricted slave instruction by law during the entire period from the 1830s to 1865. Virginia legislators criminalized assemblies for the instruction of bondsmen and women and the teaching of slaves for pay, although slave owners reserved the right to educate their own slaves. Probably more significant than legal sanctions was the unrelenting weight of social pressure brought to bear against black education. As early as 1811 Richmond whites quashed a night school for African Americans established by the prominent free black Christopher McPherson, hauling him into court for operating a "nuisance." In Fredericksburg, a group of free blacks migrated to Detroit after their request for a school was denied by the general assembly in 1838.[78]

Among Southern cities, Virginia's capital seems to have been particularly hostile to black schools. While African Americans in Washington, D.C., Nashville, Savannah, and Charleston managed to operate schools in the late antebellum era, Richmond's slaves and free blacks learned only through clandestine private instruction or laborious self-education using spellers and the Bible. Some whites saw the need for instruction to ensure the saving of black souls, but most were not prepared to allow blacks to achieve literacy and in turn educate themselves. Even those who felt that reading the Bible was essential to the Christian experience were discouraged by the legal and social environment of the community.[79]

City and state leaders were just as concerned about controlling the education of their daughters, but for very different reasons. Southern elites understood the importance of women as the arbiters of culture and sought to ensure that the education young women received comported with acceptable Southern views. By the late antebellum period, private academies and institutes for women had sprung up across the South. In Richmond, these institutions touted themselves as "*Southern in every feature*," aimed at the "instruction of Southern young ladies." The Southern Female Institute, housed in stately new row houses on Franklin Street, left no doubt about its allegiances. The principals of the school reassured the planters, farmers, and industrialists who received the *Southern Planter* that they were "Virginians, and were educated in Va. . . . Relying upon the support of the Southern people they established, six years ago, this Institution, Southern in every feature and in all its teachings." If any gentry reader remained skeptical, he could peruse the list of "patrons who have now or have had daughters in the institution," including Virginia governor Henry A. Wise, oceanographer and Southern nationalist Matthew Fontaine Maury, and Secretary of the Commonwealth George Wythe Munford.[80]

Lists of students confirm the Southern makeup of Richmond's private women's schools. A group of Baptists in Richmond received a charter from the legislature in 1853 to establish Richmond's first institution of higher learning for women, the Richmond Female Institute. In 1856, the founders credited "the patriotism of the citizen, and . . . the zeal and sympathies of the Christian" for the school's opening. The patriotism entailed no tribute to the nation, but to the South, for "as Southerners, the originators of this effort desired that the daughters of the South should be educated at the South, and under the refining influences of Southern society."[81]

True to the school's stated mission, Southerners completely dominated the 1856 class. Not surprisingly, 179 Richmond women made up a large majority of the total enrollment of about 250, and 26 Henrico County natives also attended. Thirty-seven women came from across Virginia to attend, and 15 Southerners from eight states filled out the enrollment, with the exception of a Hoosier, a Washington, D.C., student, and a scholar from Maine.[82]

The battles over education in Richmond reflected the anxiousness of urban leaders throughout the South, who bitterly complained about the penetration of Yankee ideas into and the increased autonomy of African Americans in the antebellum city. Ironically, African-American religious and reform efforts and organizations heightened the anxiety of whites. African Americans created a multitude of institutions and associations to support themselves, combining knowledge of the secret societies and fraternal organizations that flourished in American cities with ideas of mutualism that had roots in African traditions. Burial societies flourished, providing a service and decent interment for the dead. At least two black-run cemeteries occupied lots just outside the city's northwestern boundary on Academy Hill. The requirement that white ministers attend all religious services for slaves caused difficulties even with burials. African Americans formed five churches before the Civil War, providing poor relief for their own members and assistance to other needy congregations.[83]

The coherence of Richmond's black community grew as many hired, urban slaves managed to remain in Richmond over a long period of time. The First African Baptist Church at its founding numbered almost one thousand congregants. The church received more than four hundred slave migrants—those whose place of origin is known—from other Virginia counties, towns, and cities from 1841 to 1859, but only recorded the loss of thirty-one slave members going back to churches in the rest of Virginia. These facts, coupled with abundant anecdotal evidence of the long-term hiring of slaves in the city, suggest that Richmond's slave population had the time and experience in the city truly to become "urban slaves," especially in the sense of being "urbane"—having a wide knowledge of the greater world.[84]

The existence of a system of cities in Virginia facilitated contact among African-American communities. First African Baptist reached out to other urban congregations in the state, assisting with building projects. During a deacons' meeting in 1851, "Bro. Clopton's letter asking . . . to build a house of worship in Lynchbg for the African Ch." was brought up, and "it was resolved to give him a collection on the 3d Sunday in May"; in 1855 the church took up a collection for the "colored" church in Williamsburg. These contacts facilitated a sense of fellowship with and belonging to a larger world of African-American life and culture.[85]

Ever suspicious of black aspirations, especially when slaves and free blacks united in a cause, whites kept a watchful eye on African-American activities, imposing white ministers on black churches and opening mail from Northern climes. They especially feared secret societies, which they believed were hotbeds of Underground Railroad activity. In 1858 the *Dispatch* claimed that "there are some ten or twelve of these societies in existence in Richmond." Although created ostensibly to provide "charity . . . it is known to the Mayor and police, that a negro man, belonging to James H. Grant, received money from one of these societies to take him to the North."[86]

Whites continually tightened legal restrictions on African Americans in the antebellum era, resulting in a city code that by 1859 prescribed whippings for a myriad of offenses. Many elements of the code expressly limited the freedom of movement of slaves and free blacks and dictated public conduct. The law required slaves to carry passes from masters or employers two hours after sunset; a free black could be asked for an "attested copy of his register" at any time. African Americans—slave or free—could not walk in Capitol Square, in a white cemetery, or in the "grounds adjacent to the

City Spring or City Hall" without written permission from whites. Blacks were totally forbidden to form secret societies, smoke tobacco in public, carry weapons, or congregate outside a church or "side-walk at or near the corner of a street or public alley" in groups larger than five. Owners and employers were enjoined from letting slaves hire their own time or make arrangements for their own lodging. Many elements of the code served mainly to assert white supremacy in everyday life, dictating that African Americans yield the sidewalk to any and all whites and that virtually any word or gesture found offensive by a white person could result in a black's public whipping.[87]

Control of slaves by public means proved difficult. Some provisions, such as the pass system and the curb on self-hire, cut against the interests of busy masters and employers. Manufacturers and absentee masters had little time to monitor the actions of slaves, and most were not enthusiastic about the use of government force against their workers or property.[88]

Slaves often flouted laws that restricted their movement. The city sergeant imprisoned many slaves who ran away from rural plantations hoping to blend into the anonymous urban culture. In February 1846 John Pearce apprehended William, a slave belonging to William F. Wickham of the Hickory Hill plantation in Hanover County. Pearce received five dollars for his efforts. By the 1840s, the officers of the Richmond Police Guard spent much of their time looking out for runaways from the counties. Most were thought to be visiting relatives in the city. Phil ran away from John H. Smith, of Dinwiddie, possibly to reach his mother, Hannah, a nurse at the Richmond Cotton Factory, although he also had "relation at Mr. Moncures & Robt C. Nicholas"; William, known in Richmond as Bill Allen, ran away from Robert West, and might be seen with his wife, a free mulatto named Nancy Harris who lived on Cary Street below the Columbian Hotel; Jane from King William County was thought to be going to Richmond to see relatives, for "she once lived with her aunt in Richmond" and "she has hired herself for many years." Reconstructing family, even for a short time, became a principal aim of black Richmond.[89]

Boatmen appeared frequently in the police guard's accounts. Officers kept a watchful eye out for Jackson, a "bright mulatto man," known to be "well acquainted from Buchanan to Richmond has been a waterman on the River. Ran from John Dillard." Experienced at negotiating the canals and rivers of the commonwealth, boatmen transmitted information throughout a widely dispersed African-American community.[90]

Legal codes especially circumscribed the movements of free blacks. Considered by whites to be at best an anomaly and at worst a danger to a well-ordered slave society, free blacks lived in a legal limbo between citizenship and slavery. The law required free blacks to be registered in their home communities and carry papers to prove their status. Further restricting movement, the city code required that a free black from another jurisdiction who stayed in Richmond more than two months had to register in the city. Similar laws created problems for free blacks like Henry Mason, who had been apprenticed to Charles Jennings for seven years as a brick mason and emancipated by Joseph W. Mason. He had the permission of the Petersburg Hustings Court to remain there but asked the state legislature for permission to reside anywhere in the state, wherever his services would be needed.[91]

Free blacks faced serious consequences if caught without a pass, especially those unable to pay jail fees. On September 6, 1843, Richmond's city sergeant arrested Jacob Pittman on a warrant from the mayor for "want of a true copy of his register." Late that month the jailor carried the free black to the city's First Market in Shockoe Bottom and auctioned Pittman to a white bidder to cover his jail fees. The seven-dollar penalty cost Pittman ten years of servitude.[92]

Despite legal restrictions, African-American migrants to the city stayed in contact with relatives and friends in the countryside through carried messages as well as through the mail. Free blacks Lucy and William Scott wrote their kin in New Kent County apologizing for their inability to visit due to illness in the family. Peter Lennard, a free artisan born in Charles City County, wrote a poignant letter from his new home in Richmond to Eliza Pearman, of New Kent County, in 1843, confessing that "I have not enjoyed an hours happiness since I saw you last neither do I expect to until I see you and hear frome you." Lennard sadly admitted to Pearman that "you have not given me any caus to beleive that you have any special regard for me," yet "I flatter myself that you may have, if I am too bold I beg to be excused for my love for you makes me so." Lennard sent his love letter in hopes that "as soon as you receive this . . . you will favour me with an answer." Apparently Pearman did not reciprocate Lennard's feelings; by 1850 he lived in Richmond with his wife, Harriet, and a son, Robert, less than a year old.[93]

A failed romance led Fields Cook, a slave living in the countryside, to seek the greater possibilities of the city. Cook became engaged to a girl, "but for some circomstance which happened we were disappointed of our exspectations which disappointment was so hertful to me that I concluded to remove from the country where I could never see her: so I askds my owners to let me go to Richmond to live which request they granted forthwith and I lift that place in tree daies after." [94]

Slaves like Fields Cook encountered a jumble of living arrangements in the city. Most tobacco manufacturers did not care to provide housing to enslaved workers but merely paid a small sum for "boarding out." Slaves negotiated a hundred different domestic arrangements, living in outbuildings, attics, and cellars, or with free blacks in clusters throughout the city, a situation considered especially dangerous by Richmond's authorities. A large concentration of free blacks and slaves centered around Third African Baptist Church (soon renamed Ebenezer), in the city's northwestern sector. The solid houses of free-black artisans, such as the homes of plasterer John Adams and seamstress Catherine Harris on West Leigh Street, shared the streets with the homes of white craftsmen and mechanics in a neighborhood bordering Navy Hill.[95]

Industrial or low-lying areas supported the homes of working-class black and white families and those on the margins of society. Oregon Hill stood above the Tredegar Iron Works in the western suburbs, covered in a pall of bituminous coal smoke produced by the labors of its denizens, many from the British Isles. The east end of town supported the dock area of Rocketts and the neighborhoods of Fulton, Port Mayo, and the auspiciously named Mount Erin. Here a mix of white foreign-born and native workers lived alongside small clusters of African Americans, often residing in narrow alley dwellings. A sugar refinery and brickworks also operated in the area.

Large segments of the city's eastern and western suburbs grew outside the city's corporate limits, receiving no city services and little respect from middle-class residents; Moses Ellyson did not even consider most of the eastern neighborhoods worthy of inclusion on his map.[96]

The valleys were typically the most noxious and crowded areas, where poorer whites and blacks lived in the small cottages that ambled up and down the slopes formed by Richmond's hilly terrain. The entire length of the Shockoe Valley was an uneven mixture of housing, industry, and shops. Officials of the Central Railroad realized the advantages of the valley as an access to the city and laid rail along the valley bottom terminating near Broad Street. Jewish immigrant Philip Whitlock embarked on his first commercial venture in a Shockoe Valley neighborhood called Butcher-town, opening a small store. The neighborhood "was not of the best in the City the inhabitants, especially the younger class were inclined to row-dism." One night, after Whitlock threw a boy out of his store, a group of young toughs followed Whitlock "in order to whip me. I saw that they were getting close to me I backed up against a Fence on cor 17th & Grace St and drew my weapon a long dagger (as I allways carried that with me at night for self protection)." With no chance of police intervention, the frightened Whitlock dared them to come on, but, after many oaths "not fit for publi-cation" the boys retired.[97]

Whitlock also recalled his first face-to-face confrontation with slavery stripped bare of its paternal veneer. A Jewish immigrant from eastern Europe trained as a tailor, he remembered and recorded many scenes of Richmond life from an immigrant's perspective. Whitlock lived and la-bored within a few blocks of the center of the slave trade in his early years in Richmond and carefully recounted his first (and last) witnessing of a slave sale.

One Saturday morning Whitlock happened to be walking down Wall Street, the location of numerous slave jails and auction rooms, and "heard some loud talking inside a store or an office." Curious, he "looked in and saw a crowd of men standing around and one man on an Elevated platform Crying going, going, 'going' gone." Momentarily, he "saw a door in the rear opening and a white man leading a collored woman and two children about two and 5 years old and placed on the Elevated platform. The Cryer said how much am I offered for that woman twenty three years old and two children one boy and one girl. Twelve Hundred Dollars I heard and so it went on and sold for $1350.00." He then witnessed the sale of "a great big man" for $2,300.00. With trousers and sleeves rolled up, "some of the buyers examined him by feeling his legs and arms."[98]

Whitlock reported that "I left after that and never had any desire to go there again—Although it was novel to me still my feeling of humanity was such, that I did not approve of that traffic although there were a good many people who were then looked upon as respectfull and in good standing that were engaged in that business." Whitlock tempered his bad memories of the trade by recalling that slave trading was a legitimate business in antebellum Richmond. He specifically noted fellow Jews of some social standing who took part in the trade, although non-Jews clearly dominated slave trading generally.[99]

New Yorker Robert Granniss also witnessed a slave sale, recording it in his diary. Granniss's account contained many of the same details as Whitlock's, especially those calculated to provoke an emotional response, such as the physical examination of slaves like animals and the sale of children. As Granniss passed through the central commercial area of the city, near the city market and Richmond's finest hotels, he "passed a negro auction and stepping in I behold a fellow being *sold*. A fine negro boy was standing on the platform and waiting to be knocked down to the highest bidder." The scene may have been in the Saint Charles Hotel or the Odd Fellows Hall, both equipped with auction rooms, and Granniss undoubtedly stood within a few blocks of Wall Street, also known as Lumpkin's Alley, where the grim holding pens of Richmond's slave trade faced the streets with barred windows.

The careful inspection of the human merchandise on sale both fascinated and appalled Granniss. He wrote that the slave's "trousers were rolled up to his knees to better display his legs and his shirt sleeves rolled up in order to show him to more advantage. He was ordered to step down on the floor and a space being cleared he walked from the stand to the door about 20 feet and back. Like a horse his 'action' was then shown. He was then or-

dered to stand still and his teeth were examined and his chest and head."
The young clerk recorded that the fourteen-year-old slave, only a few years
his junior, "was sold for $1100 & odd," considered a high price by Granniss.
He "left the scene thoroughly disgusted with the 'peculiar institution.'" [100]
Granniss, from a society where selling was a way of life, was not prepared
to confront the inspection of a human being for sale as a commodity.

There was clearly a generational difference in attitudes expressed by
immigrants and Northerners regarding America, Southern life, and issues
such as slavery. Older leaders often espoused the ideology of the larger society. Longtime residents, such as Johann Gottfried Lange, felt perfectly
comfortable with the institution of slavery. Writing after the Civil War,
Lange could not understand why Germans "who never in their life had
seen a Negro" had fought in the conflict for the North. Sounding very much
like Southern defenders of slavery, Lange skewered New Englanders for
their hypocritical participation in the slave trade, and went on to assert that
in the antebellum days, "as long as they [slaves] behaved well, were honest
and industrious they were rewarded and had many advantages. But when a
Negro was lazy and didn't conduct himself well he was punished and sold
again. This trading of slaves on Franklin Street one could always watch." [101]

Philadelphian Jacob Bechtel, a clerk at Adolphus Morris's bookstore,
stood strongly for preservation of the Union but mouthed sentiments regarding slavery in concert with most white Virginians' views. Decrying the
increasingly acrimonious sectional debate, he denounced the appeals of
Northern abolitionists, while "poor Sambo, over whose *Miserable estate*
they have been shedding many pious drops, enjoys his Christmas turkey
and fried bacon within his Comfortable Cabin, before a roaring fire, while
the banjo and fiddle keep time to the singing of the kettle—or the music
of the frying pan." A resident of Virginia since the 1840s, he implicitly
compared the plight of the Northern poor with that of the Southern slave:
"No cares of a starving family disturb his repose. No shivering barefooted
children are sent by him on a weary tramp to sell matches or beg a six-
pence to keep a poor Mamma from starving.—O most perverted philanthropy!—when will people have Common Sense!" Bechtel agonized about
the tendency of Southerners to treat abolitionism as indicative of Northern

thought, and his own comments reflect the abiding conservatism and racism of many Yankees.[102]

Even as European immigrants and Northerners became inured to the sights and sounds of slavery, a few Virginians still clung to the fleeting hope of eventual emancipation. The ideas of the Revolutionary generation could still be heard in the slavery debates that echoed in the halls of the Capitol during the legislative session of 1831–32, when the dream of eventual emancipation and the ending of the curse of slavery was again articulated. But the late antebellum period saw a hardening of the official, public position on slavery among Richmond's leaders. The city's critical position as a nexus of slavery made its white residents increasingly sensitive about criticism of the institution and drove most of those whites who were sympathetic to the plight of enslaved African Americans into colonization schemes and other reforms. The intellectual tradition of slavery as an evil fell to the much longer tradition of slavery as a profitable enterprise. It was never more profitable than in the economy of the 1850s.

The auction rooms and slave jails of Richmond were a focal point not only of the routinized violence of family separation but also of tense confrontations over the system of slavery. Richmond experienced a different kind of public tumult than its antebellum counterparts of Baltimore, Philadelphia, and New Orleans, where anti-Catholicism, political violence, and labor riots took a terrible toll. White Richmonders saved their fiercest responses for those who transgressed against the ideal of slavery, although they usually clenched their teeth and let the law take its course, lest a Northern newspaperman be watching. Just as the Winston murders filled the streets with "Persons of the highest respectability" calling loudly for the "Lynch Law" and threatening to tear the accused murderers to pieces, other cases involving slaves provoked public anger in the 1850s.

When slave catchers returned the fugitive slave Anthony Burns from Boston amid widespread public outrage in the North, he was placed in Robert Lumpkin's Richmond slave jail. After a four-month imprisonment, Burns came up for sale to the South. As he mounted the auction block, the crowd gave vent to "an explosion of wrathful feeling. Angry speeches were made about him and he was personally insulted. The violence of one encouraged that of another, and the tumult, momently increasing, threatened to burst over all bounds." With Burns in imminent danger of harm, calmer heads interceded and allowed the sale to proceed. Sold for $905 to a North Carolina planter, Burns and his new master waited until three o'clock in the morning to leave for the train station for fear of an angry mob.[103]

Eyre Crowe, an English artist, found that even the drawing of an image of slave trading created suspicion and fear among Virginians in the 1850s. While traveling through Richmond with William Thackeray on his lecture tour of America, Crowe read of a slave auction in the local paper and decided to attend. He proceeded to Wall Street, entered the slave auction, and began sketching the scene. He was threatened and eventually forced to leave the room. The assembled planters, traders, and speculators had good reason to suspect Crowe would cast them in an unfavorable light. Crowe did numerous sketches and paintings of the slave trade in the South, and in 1856 a group of engravings based on his studies appeared in the *Illustrated London News*. The central image shows a black family being sold by an auctioneer before a group of Virginia "gentlemen." [104]

Crowe began the written description accompanying his illustrations with this caveat: "As no pen, we think, can adequately delineate the choking sense of horror which overcomes one on first witnessing these degrading spectacles, we prefer limiting ourselves to mere description of what we saw." Crowe's feelings about the participants in the sale are very clear. He described the auctioneer as "an eye-bepatched and ruffianly-looking fellow in check trousers, and grimy in every part of his person." The buyers received no better treatment from Crowe: "Their features are callous; and one gentleman we particularly noticed, who had a cowhide-looking weapon, which dangled between his legs in such a way as to make one wonder whether his feet were cloven or not." [105]

Such descriptions were common fare in abolitionist literature and in English popular works, although American journals such as *Harper's* avoided such inflammatory statements in deference to their large Southern readership. White Richmond's "respectable" classes reacted violently against criticism in the Northern and English presses of their "peculiar institution" but were at the same time restrained by the knowledge that the eyes of outsiders were on them. Outbreaks of open conflict were quickly suppressed. Slavery's centrality to Richmond—literally and symbolically—silently influenced every social relation in the city, even as the clicks of telegraphic transactions and the roars of theater crowds masked its importance within the mundane daily rituals of urban America.

PART TWO

Connections
and Consciousness

CHAPTER THREE

The World of Goods

I am well, and striving to meet these yankees at least half way in shrewdness—
a matter difficult indeed.

MANN S. VALENTINE JR., New York, to his wife, 1857

Richmond, if my family were not living in it, would see me off tomorrow, it has
lost all charms to me. It is getting to be too much of a Yankee town.

JEFFERSON WALLACE to CHARLES BLAIR, 1855

Mann Satterwhite Valentine Jr.'s father had written hundreds of letters to his family after long, hectic days buying dry goods in New York. Now the son followed reluctantly in the father's footsteps. A frustrated scientist and author, Valentine had studied for a year at the College of William and Mary, taking a special interest in chemistry. He had dabbled in various artistic projects, stimulated by the artist James Hubard, whom his father generously patronized.[1]

In the 1850s the eldest son finally bent to his father's will, becoming a partner in the family firm. Traveling by rail and steamboat to the Northern marts, the Virginian walked Broadway, bought at Stewart's Palace, and lodged at the Astor Hotel. Much of what he saw disgusted him. Scathing descriptions of Yankee behavior and society flowed from his pen and made their way by mail packet to family and friends in Richmond.

Southern merchants like Mann Valentine Jr. did not need to construct a defense of their society by reading proslavery tracts or the Bible; the legitimacy of Richmond and Southern society was borne out by comparisons to

Northern cities. The superiority of slavery over free labor was clear from the treatment accorded bondsmen and free workers in their respective societies, and the cold, impersonal nature of Yankee cities bespoke a society barren of the organic social and family ties so important to Southerners. A business ethic that emphasized honesty and forthrightness increasingly conflicted with a notion of secretive, manipulative "sharp trading" supposedly characteristic of the Yankee.

Jefferson Wallace was also the son of a merchant. His father, William Manson Wallace, arrived in America around 1815 from Scotland and, after a few years in Pennsylvania, settled in Richmond as a merchant of groceries, wine, and liquors. Jefferson's mother, Irish-born Catherine Leighey, raised nine children in Virginia's capital. Jefferson followed his brother Charles Montriou Wallace to the California goldfields in 1851. Because of their father's declining health, Jefferson Wallace returned to Richmond on November 9, 1854, to help run the family business.[2]

Writing to his brother and friends in California, Wallace expressed dismay at the Richmond he found on his return. Reminiscing about the natural, orderly city he had left, Wallace denounced the penetration of Yankee people, goods, ideas, and behaviors into the city during the 1850s. Bourgeois striving, Northern dress, and free-labor ideas offended him, but he also expressed a desire to rise in the world and become as wealthy and prosperous as the new Richmond. Jefferson Wallace, like the Southern commercial class to which he belonged, shared the American enthusiasm for railroads, steamships, and other trappings of modernity but continued to question the social order created under Northern capitalism. He and his peers often pointed to the influx of European immigrants, Northerners, and "Southern Yankees" (unscrupulous followers of Mammon who happened to be born in the South), as the cause of Richmond's problems.[3] Thus, the merchant class reconciled its Old Virginia values within a Northern world of commerce.

Richmond's substantial trade with the North and its increasing dominance of the Virginia countryside was reflected in both the composition and viewpoint of its commercial community. Most of the city's merchants hailed from Virginia, building on connections to the countryside. Nevertheless, significant numbers of Northern businessmen could be found in certain sectors of the economy that were tied to Northern trade.[4]

In businesses where manufacturing know-how, skill, or understanding of the trade played a key role, Yankee businessmen played a significant role. Robert Rankin of Maine worked as one of Richmond's handful of ships' chandlers along with fellow down-easter Luther Libby, whose warehouse would become infamous as a Civil War prison. William H. Hubbard, who arrived in Richmond in 1809, "learned tanning and shoemaking in his native Connecticut, and always maintained his New England connections, especially with the great shoe center of Lynn, Massachusetts." Hubbard's clerk and later partner James Henry Gardner, a native of Lynn, arrived in 1812, and both men retained more than commercial connections to the North; long after their arrival in Richmond they married sisters Phebe and Ann Phillips, the daughters of a Lynn family. Yankee ingenuity was also evident in the metal trades. Hiram M. Smith of Vermont had been producing agricultural implements in Richmond since 1829 and eventually expanded his business to include machinery for tobacco manufacturing. Likewise, men from Connecticut, Massachusetts, Pennsylvania, New York, and Ohio ran firms listed as tinners, gas fitters, and sheet metal works.[5]

Despite these pockets of Yankee influence, Virginians made up the majority of the city's commission and dry-goods merchants. Men from the Old Dominion controlled the commission trade, a business built on confidence and credit, requiring a mutual familiarity between merchants, planters, and farmers. Such relationships took years to establish and usually required long-standing family and business connections. Dry-goods merchants encountered country customers as well as Yankees. Because of rapidly changing tastes, fluctuations in prices, and wide variations in product quality, success in dry goods required merchants to go to Northern cities to buy, coming face-to-face with Northern traders and merchants. Among thirty-four of Richmond's principal dry-goods merchants in 1852, five were Northern-born and six foreign-born. Northerners entered the Richmond dry-goods business with an excellent knowledge of the trade and renewed confidence in the inter-urban connections with, and possibilities of, the Southern market. Three of the Yankee dry-goods merchants also married Virginians, as did several of the foreign-born entrepreneurs.

Although small in numbers, a few Northern-born dry-goods merchants were extremely successful and important members of the community, particularly Horace Kent from Connecticut and Samuel P. Lathrop of Christian & Lathrop, a native of New York. Kent built "the splendid store of Kent, Paine & Co., the first specimen in Richmond of the Broadway style of dry goods palaces," no doubt mimicking the grandeur of Stewart's Palace in New York. One of the most prominent businessman in Richmond and a slaveholder, he was elected the first president of the Richmond Board of Trade by his peers. Not surprisingly, Kent consistently defended the city's economic interests. He apparently felt little anxiety over his New England background in his role as a Southern entrepreneur. Richmond merchants liked and respected Kent. Virginian Charles Palmer fondly recalled Kent as "natures *Nobleman,*" and Mann Valentine visited him at the Irvine House in New York during a sudden illness.[6]

Whether born above or below the Mason-Dixon Line, Richmond's dry-goods merchants spent long periods every spring and fall conducting a rush of buying in Northern cities. Virginia-born merchant Thomas R. Price spoke of the difficult schedule kept by the Southern merchant in the Northern marts. "I have been for the most part employed in the ordinary routine of my duties," the tired Price related to his wife, "and to day so much so that I did not get up to my dinner at all, and in consequence do not feel as comfortable tonight as usual." Price speculated that he might seek other lodgings where he could "dine at 5 OC as it is impossible for me to get to the Hotel by the dinner hour," which seems to have been 3:00 P.M. Other problems faced Price at his lodging besides the dinner hour. He usually went out in the evening "after the duties of the day," complaining that "there is no comfort in staying at the Hotel to be smoked and almost spitted to death." Price mentioned the odd dinner with merchant friends and relatives in New York, but spent most of his time in pursuit of goods.[7]

Mann Satterwhite Valentine Sr. bought goods in all the major Northern cities during a career that spanned the four decades before the Civil War. Valentine was born in King William County, Virginia, in 1786, the son of a planter, and he came to Richmond in 1806 to read law. Because of debts, his father could no longer afford his legal training, and, after a brief period of duty in the Public Guard, Valentine received an appointment as storekeeper at the Virginia State Penitentiary in 1810. "Influenced perhaps by the discovery that he possessed superior business qualifications," Valentine "drifted into the general merchandise business and was one of the first native Virginians to successfully compete with the British merchants, who had hitherto practically controlled the commerce of the State." Valentine thrived in the dry-goods trade, building several partnerships with other Virginians.[8]

Valentine used his wealth to become a prominent patron of the arts, and his success also allowed his large family to enjoy the material benefits of the life of the Virginia elite, including fine clothes, trips to the springs, and ownership of slaves. Valentine purchased individual slaves and a family group from the estate of his father-in-law, owning seven or eight bondspeople throughout the 1840s.[9]

Like many of his fellow Virginians, Valentine was unimpressed by the entertainments and lures of Northern cities and disapproved of the cold and relentless pursuit of gain in the North. In an 1850 letter from New York to his wife he related that "I keep pretty much at my boarding house after business is over." Noting that two fellow merchants had gone to Niblos Garden, a popular New York entertainment house, he confessed that "I have no relish for such places and during the 25 years that I have been visiting this City I have never been a dozen times to places of amusement." He decried the tumultuous crowds of strangers "bolting along like it was the last day they had to live . . . eating, drinking, and smoking in the great NY game for which I should think they can beat the World." Valentine conceded that New York was "a great place and still it seems to me there are but few who are really contented and happy. Money making casts in the shade all other considerations and those that have the most seem the most eager after it." [10]

Mann Valentine felt that New York was "a place made up of show and outward appearances, for judging from what is every day expended or rather thrown away, in high living, at theatres, gardens, etc. one would conclude that there was money here without end." Nevertheless, he did not shrink from the world, nor from allowing his family to experience its lures and dangers. Although "neither pleasure nor any rational enjoyment can be found at such a place, still I am desirous that my children should see the world in all its variety and let me live to have the proof that they have virtue and understanding enough to resist the follies and frivolities of this life, and follow in the footsteps of those who have been distinguished for their learning, prudence, industry and general intelligence." [11]

Despite the temptations and dangers, most men of commerce accepted the idea that seeing the world and being involved in public life were as essential to a young man's education as learning to read and write. Valentine and other merchants sometimes took their children on business trips, possibly as training for their future partnership in the family business. Valentine's sons William Winston, Edward Virginius, and Mann S. Valentine Jr. traveled with their father and other family members to the metropolis. Mann Valentine asked his daughter in an 1842 letter from New York to "tell your mother that Mann is very regular in his habits and employs his time of nights in reading and is never in the streets. Young Binford, Drewry & Eloquence is his regular companions. I find them frequently taking a hit at backgammon which seems to be a favorite amusement with the boarders." [12]

The female members of Valentine's large family also experienced Northern cities. Daughters Elizabeth Ann, Mary Martha, and Sarah Benetta Valentine all visited him periodically in the North. During a trip to New York in early August 1851 Valentine wrote to Mann Valentine Jr. reporting the visit of other members of the family. He noted that "the City is very full of strangers which prevented our getting in at the Astor House and had to take lodging at the American on the next square above. Yesterday Mr. Gray . . . & the girls were driving about the city. Last night we were all at the Opera at Castle Garden, with which they seemed to be delighted. These late hours rather interfere with my business and I expect they will rid me the trouble of attending to them by leaving this evening." A program from Castle Garden, dated August 12, 1851, in Valentine's papers indicates that the merchant was forced to entertain somewhat longer than he hoped. [13]

Virginia merchants created their own domestic world within the Northern metropolis. Mann Valentine had always stayed in close contact with other Richmond merchants in New York, and several Virginians boarded at various times in the same hotel with Valentine from the early 1840s into the 1850s. An 1850s letter reported that "we have a great many Richmond people in the City and a large number [torn] this house Brooks, Binford, Frey, Cr[torn], Mr. Quarles, Mitchell and others." Valentine had a few Northern friends in New York, but spent most of his time furiously buying at the various commercial houses and returning at night to his lodgings and Richmond friends.[14]

Mann Valentine Jr., like his father, lodged with other Virginians in New York but felt far more isolated in the Northern city. In 1856 he wished that "my little wife should only see me in my present lodgings—escaped from the odious Astor. I am quietly spending my sleeping hours and dining days at 125 Chamber Street—otherwise known among the Virginians as the Emigrants Hotel. Eight dollars per week.—as good lodging & rest as ever St. Nicholas afforded.—But not . . . our home.—not brightened by a wifes smile.—or visited by her unending attentions." [15] His wife's letter probably crossed paths with his, as Ann Maria Gray Valentine informed Mann that "Mr. Brooks told Pa he had taken you from the Astor and carried you to a nicer and more comfortable place; Taylor has arrived at the Emigrants Hotel by this time and you and he are enjoying yourselves like you used to, when you were an old Bachelor." [16]

The solidarity of the "Emigrants Hotel" underscored the sense of being alone in a large, unfriendly city. One young man in New York wrote his Richmond friend Charles Wallace in care of the latter's father, merchant William Wallace, about his yearning for companionship during the holidays: "I wish you happy New Year Oh! Charly I wish I was in Richmond on Christmas day I know that I would have had some fine fun we would have had some eagnoge we would have got drunk, Smoke some of Fishers best Segars. Well it is no use to talk about it I was not there I did not have any fun here on Christmas in a city like ours we know no body and don't want to know any one." [17]

Richmonders sensed that the omnipresent anonymity of the Northern city was really only the outward sign of a cold, heartless culture. Connecticut-born James S. Kent had followed his uncle Horace Kent to Richmond while a youth. Like his elder relative, he dealt in dry goods and became a slaveholder. Kent apologized to a female acquaintance—Mann Valentine's daughter Elizabeth Ann—for trying her patience with a long letter written in pencil, "yet it is a pleasure for me to write, (I mean pencil) I feel quite lonely—even here in this far famed 'Astor House' with hundreds of people within its walls of brick and stone—finding so little fellowship amongst them I can only pencil to you and wish myself in Richmond. My trip has been irksome beyond measure and I am heartily tired of this vile City. to remain here long would be to dry up the fountain of goodness within me—there is so much here to sicken human nature." [18]

The feeling of social isolation in a world that cared only for commerce permeated many of Mann Valentine Jr.'s letters to his wife from New York, a place where "the streets [are] filled with clouds of dust and the roaring omnibus is heard only" and where as "you are hustled from the pavement your toes are trampled and your head nearly unsettled by a bucket of oranges." Valentine could not understand how "such crowds of human pratlers and jabblers can move so noiselessly and speechlessly along these everlasting streets.—and not turn to say how do you do? or pass one word of any sort." New Yorkers' loss of any sense of community or social values stripped them of their humanity; indeed, it placed them below other animals, Valentine believed. He had "seen a thousand busy ants eternally moving to & fro business like, as human beings, yet they stop to exchange a passing word.—to know the way—or make the usual inquiry of their friends. I have seen horses along our streets nose each other & make acquaintance, but N. York people, are beasts of burthen without courtesy, animals destitute of all the beautiful instincts of Eden." New Yorkers, in Valentine's eyes, had become both antisocial and ungodly. He felt that "so prime [is] the neglect of social virtue, even friendly suavity, that I look upon them as the Christian looks upon the heathen before the Gospel call." [19]

Valentine believed that the destruction of social virtue and godliness in Northern cities had its roots in the lack of a proper domestic sphere. He felt almost sorry for the New Yorkers, who have "not the advantages of Domestic life, but hurled out into the stormy New York in their infancy, to weather it—to rise or fall and it is one unending struggle to compass it—all other things being forgotten [in] the restless, lifelong, daily service of the onset." In contrast Valentine extolled the virtues of hearth and home, which he "would not exchange . . . with my daily labors and sweet nightly return to wife and child for Stewarts marble palace, with Stewarts anxious look, crisped hair, and his marble mind & heart, building yet other marble palaces on which to enthrone a name, & in which to increase his poor ambition." The reluctant merchant Mann Valentine Jr. repudiated Stewart's marble palace, the great New York symbol of consumerism and material wealth, for although "Stewart might have his palaces, mine should be a prouder and holier one—the altar of my home—with the sweet benediction of my parents, and the lovely virtues of my wife the crown, and my childs encircling arms the vine clinging to me for protection while its growing strength shall build, & strengthen me. . . . In all honesty, & sincerity I acknowledge, the day of my domestic bliss was my best." [20]

Northern capitalists not only lacked proper regard for domestic relations but also built their palaces on the backs of the urban poor. The widening gap between the rich and poor manifest on the city's streets was a testimony to the sickness of Northern society as well as an affirmation of Southern superiority, according to men like the Valentines. Charles Wallace, the son of Richmond merchant William Wallace, wrote his sister Isabella in 1845 from New York: "You think perhaps that I am unsafe or unhappy abroad. My own insecurity and unhappiness when contrasted with those of many thousands of wretches beneath me make me ashamed of repining or complaining." Wallace related that "in passing through the country you see the people singing merrily over their work," but "in this city how different." Wallace asked, "How can I be happy when I am in the midst of degradation," lamenting that "if I look at pleasing things and smile at them the next moment there is thrust into my sight this or that remnant of a man, and I am made in truth to weep. The faces of the old men here are pitiful and dejected and even those engaged in a petty trafficking of small wares and unripe fruit are never seen to smile." [21]

Wallace related many affecting scenes, including a blind man led by his small son, "and though the noise and bustle of the scene rose high in the air, yet the sound of his flute was too sweet to be mistaken." He believed "that where words are powerless music, and that alone can arrest the attention of every passenger in a hard hearted multitude." He also encountered an old man huddled in a ruined building, racked by fevers from "rheumatic pains." Wallace gave him money and literally the shirt off his back. [22]

The Northern poor and destitute were certainly to be pitied, and Richmond's commercial men laid the blame for their plight squarely on the Northern class system. In 1856, Mann Valentine Jr. witnessed a powerful scene in New York that epitomized the Southern understanding of Yankee class relations: "Here yesterday I saw a grand and pompous funeral in which the hearse all covered in glass disclosed a magnificently wrought coffin, & Broadway for half a mile was lined with elegant coaches making a show of pageantry that only New York could afford—& in contrast not less than one thousand ragged, meagre men, women & children—'the lame, the halt & the blind' of this great city, made another train, irregular it was—this last train of beggars—sometimes beneath the feet of the omnibus horses, sometimes thrust into the gutters of the police of the Great, the Rich, & the Powerful—for the police belong to these & the poor are the inheritance of the slaves, of the police." Valentine saw poverty not as an unfortunate condition but as a state created by "the Great, the Rich, & the Powerful," who used the police to enforce their social order. He waxed philosophical on "what it is to be Rich . . . what it is to be poor" in such a society: "To be Rich is to ravish the eye of the world, to be envied, to be revered & honored;—to be poor is to be uncomely to the eye, foul to the breathing, to be discarded, dishonored—and given to the Yellow Fever. It is a great wonder that we have not seen all the poor sent down to Fort Hamilton for the disease to feed upon." [23]

Valentine explicitly recognized the emergence of a new middle class defined by the cold, calculating nature of its social striving. He reported to his wife that "there is another & the largest class of this place . . . he who has limited means, & intends by 'hook or by crook' to have more. They are masters of plausability, adept in effrontery, and born with the multiplication table in their heads—& the 'rule of one' in their hearts—and the devil incites them to practice both. There may be exceptions here—God knows there ought to be if our master in heaven intends any redemption in this place." [24]

White Richmonders were anxious to condemn the Northern social order as cruel and coercive, using their observations as a condemnation of free labor and as a foil for the supposedly mild system of slavery in their own society. James H. Stanard, a free black emancipated in Richmond around

1847, wrote from Philadelphia in 1857 to George D. Fisher, an agent for the Haxall mills, one of Richmond's major flour concerns, inquiring about friends and family. Although Stanard's letter does not survive, Fisher's reply indicates that Stanard commented on the bad state of affairs in Philadelphia in the depths of the national economic depression. Fisher wrote Stanard that "I have been reading in the newspapers the same sort of account which you give of the Condition of things among the poor and labouring people in Philadelphia as well as in the other large northern Cities, and it is very much to be deplored indeed, but I hope there will be no riots growing out of it, for so far from making things better, such a state of affairs will make them worse. The only plan for everybody to pursue is to spend not one cent more than is actually necessary to live upon, and to do all the work they can to earn a little." Fisher admitted that "there is suffering here also among the poor and daily laborers, but not as much as in the Northern Cities, for our servants have owners to take care of them, and they are all free from the cares which others have who provide for themselves." [25]

The acceptance of the superiority of slavery over free labor was not restricted to native Virginians. Many longtime residents of foreign birth who had made it into the middle and upper ranks of Richmond society accepted it readily. Commission merchant William Wallace, a native of Scotland, wrote to his sister in Great Britain regarding some "Ladies of England, who have addressed the Ladies of America, on a most delicate subject; One which will produce much recrimination, and opening of wounds, which had been rapidly healing up between this country and Great Britain." Wallace referred to an address to American women delivered to Harriet Beecher Stowe by the Duchess of Sutherland on behalf of some half-million British women. Prompted by the enormous popularity of *Uncle Tom's Cabin* in England, the petitioners called on their American sisters to assist in ending slavery. The address drew sharp responses from Southern novelist Maria McIntosh and Julia Gardiner Tyler, the widow of former president John Tyler. Wallace maintained that "from a long residence in a Slave State, and considerable experience as regards the management of the negroe, and the treatment they generally receive, I do not hesitate a moment, in pronouncing their actual condition to be much more happy, and comfortable, than the one forth part of the population, who fill up our cities, and manufacturing towns, who are in the possession of free suffrage." [26]

Wallace did not simply endorse the beneficial effects of slavery but posed it as a superior social system to democratic societies that had liberally extended the franchise. He proclaimed that "the wisest and the best men in the U.S. and in your own country, entertain strong doubts whether the Universal Suffrage, is likely to be so beneficial to the human family, as a well regulated State of Slavery." Wallace was obviously unimpressed with Northern and British philanthropy aimed at the urban poor. Following a familiar script, Wallace claimed that under slavery "the laws, oblige those who have Slaves, that they shall be humanely treated, well clothed, and fed, as well in sickness, as in old age," but under unrestrained capitalism "the poor and improvident have no one to administer to their wants, excepting what flows from cold and calculating, Pharisitical professors of charity, and humanity, such as Dickens Mrs. Jellyby." [27]

Wallace's comparison of the English women with Mrs. Jellyby, a character from Charles Dickens's *Bleak House,* probably had several meanings. Mrs. Jellyby, like the English petitioners, indulged in "telescopic philanthropy." She spent all of her waking hours, as well as her daughter's, on a scheme to colonize families to cultivate coffee in Africa and educate the "natives of Borrioboola-Gha, on the left bank of the Niger." While Dickens implicitly censures this misguided reform, the novel is most biting regarding Mrs. Jellyby's complete dereliction of her domestic role and duties. Her home is in shambles; her children roam dirty and unsupervised through the house and streets; and her husband silently sits, ignored and broken by his wife's obsession.[28]

Southerners were especially sensitive to proper domestic relations, which they considered the foundation of slavery's success. Wallace and his peers believed that the Duchess of Sutherland and her supporters ignored their proper role by indulging in explicit political action and meddling in the affairs of a society they did not understand, instead of solving their own society's considerable social problems.

Mann Valentine Jr. also took exception to foreign interference in American slavery. In a letter to his brother Edward V. Valentine in Europe, Valentine disparaged English abolitionism, boasting that "we are ready at any time to teach insolent Lord Broughm that an idiotic old man shall not malign our institutions, in his preference for negro blood & color." He exulted that "we have slavery—we will have slavery, & none of your white slaves either, but a rich & glossy black, greasy with good living—none of your half starved outcasts of creation." England, with its "Lords of the Loom" and its "wage slaves," had no moral ground to criticize slavery, Valentine averred; neither did the North.[29]

Sarah Benetta Valentine, a daughter of merchant Mann Valentine Sr., had also visited the great metropolises of the North. Her experiences and her Christian convictions shaped her view of slavery, slaves, and abolitionists. Valentine believed slaves to be "uniformly the most pious set of persons to be found in any state, or rank of life. I believe no one acquainted with them will deny. This is the more remarkable from the fact of their leading lives of almost *unalloyed happiness.*—a circumstance which in other cases almost invariably tends to an opposite effect." She warned that the happiness of slaves would be ruined by "*distant weepers,*" who "work against the comfort of this exiled race" by trying to liberate them.

Valentine insisted that "God rules the soul of Southern men as well as those of others who despise them." As long as masters remembered their Christian duty to slaves, God's judgment could not fall against slaveholders, for "God hath in a mysterious union forever united the master and the slave. Man may not, *man cannot put them asunder.*" Reading in the *New York Herald* of the English abolitionists, she expressed her contempt for men whose own fortunes expanded with the growth of the Cotton South, "*not by need,* but *lowest avarice,*" and whose "efforts unwearied to enhance the value of those southern products, the very greatness of whose demand, (if their eyes were not so filled with sympathetic tears), they might easily perceive could *only tend to add* more labor to the slave." She sarcastically sighed, "Alas poor African, these are they whose souls, filled with an unchecked love of gain, are weeping far away at thought of Thee.—of all thy anguish and endurance."[30]

Women like Sarah Benetta Valentine filtered the reality of slavery through the personal relationships of their own hearth and home, removed from the slave jails and squalid cabins observed by foreign visitors. The urban households of middle-class professionals and merchants were neither primarily dependent on slaves for their financial success nor as impersonal as the plantation. By accepting the ideal but ignoring the larger reality of American slavery, Southern urban women created a space within which they could issue their trenchant critiques of Northern and British hypocrisy without confronting their own.

Women of the commercial classes explicitly contrasted slave and free workers, often couching their analysis within domestic and religious ideals. They buttressed their opinions with firsthand knowledge of servant relations in the North and Europe, which they compared unfavorably to the master-slave relationship. Mann Valentine Jr.'s wife, Ann Maria Gray Valentine, wrote to her brother-in-law William Winston Valentine in Paris regarding the reaction of servants in Europe to Southerners, stating her belief that "the southern people are so much better and have kinder hearts than other people, and servants are surprised at being treated even with civility by persons who are their superiors. I know how domestics are treated in Yankee land, and conclude a similar course is pursued where ever white labour exists." [31]

Virginia women frequently expressed their disdain for Northern domestic relations. A Petersburg housekeeper graciously received a Northern woman selling books door-to-door but took the opportunity to deliver a "dissertation upon the manners, character, and mode of living at the North." The itinerant bookseller related that the Virginian matron "pronounced us cold-hearted, cruel — in fact quite devoid of heart and conscience; our servants poor, and not cared for; our ladies indolent, poor housekeepers, and without half the responsibility of their Southern sisters." [32]

Mary Virginia Hawes Terhune, author and the daughter of a Richmond merchant, visited Massachusetts and New York during the antebellum period. With that perspective, she related the unique role of the mid-nineteenth-century Virginia housewife, especially in contrast with Northern mistresses. "The Virginian matron of *antebellum* days never wielded broom or duster. She did not make beds or stand at wash-tub or ironing-table. Yet she was as busy in her line of housewifely duty as her 'Yankee' sister." Terhune described the day of the typical housewife, from the morning trip to the storeroom to dole out ingredients to the cook, to the supervision of the cleaning of glass and china. Most of all, "surveillance was exercised over each branch of housework" by the Virginia mistress, although sewing "was her own especial task." The rural connections of many Southern women informed their ideas of domestic and family relations, which they viewed as fundamentally different from the North.[33]

Terhune made explicit her contrast between Southern and Northern domestic relations in her third novel, *Moss-side* (1857). Terhune had attended the precursor of Moses Hoge's school and thoroughly absorbed the precepts of Southern society, despite her father's Yankee heritage. Written after her first visit to New York City, *Moss-side* centers on Grace, a daughter of the Virginia aristocracy and a thinly veiled stand-in for Terhune. Grace visits her school friend Louise Wynne in New York to attend her wedding and accompanies the wedding party to the White Mountains and Niagara Falls. Seduced by the intellectual stimulation of Louise and her freethinking friends, as well as the glitter of the big city, Grace returns to her plantation home deeply troubled. Frustrated at the apparent backwardness and plainness of her Virginia life in contrast to her Northern experience, Grace ignores her duties to her family, destroying the harmony of the plantation. Later, she reads a book Louise has published that advocates the dreaded "isms" of Northern reform, the most extreme being woman's rights. Grace is carried back from the abyss of cynical, freethinking feminism by her sister-in-law May, who restores her faith in the sacred duties of hearth and home.[34]

Moss-side reflected Terhune's misgivings about Northern society, which she had seen personally in trips to visit her father's family in the Boston area and to the great metropolis of New York. In letters to friends in Virginia, she recounted a familiar litany of Yankee failings. While visiting the Boston area in 1851, Terhune waxed poetic about the beauty of the small New England villages she visited but criticized the lack of religious belief and feeling she found there. "Were I disposed to prophecy," she opined, "I would predict that in fifty years this will become a community of materialists or infidels." Terhune, herself the daughter of a Northern-born merchant, noted the "calculating spirit" of her hosts and felt "that if they possess as much genuine warmth of heart as we Southerners, it is harder to get through the outer crust."[35]

Terhune visited New York in 1855 after the publication of her first novel and expressed her fascination and revulsion at the excessive wealth and display of the commercial entrepôt. Writing to a friend, she exposed the pretensions of parties filled with clever chatter and denounced the emptiness of Unitarianism, Spiritualism, and the many other "isms" that occupied the minds of Northern elites.[36]

Next to abolitionism, perhaps no other "ism" frightened Southerners more than the movement for woman's rights. An incident that occurred during Virginian Samuella Hart Curd's stay in New York illustrates the divergence of perceptions regarding women's proper roles. Samuella Hart married Thomas Curd on May 3, 1860, in Richmond, and left that night with a wedding party of nine, including another pair of newlyweds, Fanny Gaines and Seaton Linsley of Hanover County. The fathers of both grooms accompanied the group on their trip. The party traveled a path blazed by thousands of other Southern tourists in the antebellum era. They first journeyed to Washington, then continued on to Baltimore, Philadelphia, and New York, finally reaching Niagara Falls.[37]

For the most part, the wedding party enjoyed typical amusements and entertainments, especially the rural cemeteries of the East Coast cities. While in Philadelphia, Curd visited Fairmont Water Works, Stephen Girard College, and Laurel Hill Cemetery, "a lovely spot [with] some very handsome Tomb Stones, have a fine view of the Shuylkill [River] from several points." In New York, Curd and her party attended an opera at the Academy of Music, saw Barnum's Museum, and toured Brooklyn's Greenwood Cemetery, "truly an enchanting spot, Nature & Art have contributed largely to its beauty, Many of the Tomb Stones are splendid and the view of the bay from many points is very fine."[38]

In New York, the joyous proceedings took a more serious turn. Two male chaperones took the ladies in the party to "Cousin Eliza's" and the women then decided to attend the "Woman's Rights Convention." They "dismissed the gentlemen after getting there and off we started to the Convention. It was raining; but the Hall was well filled, I was shocked to see Negro men and women take seats in the white congregation but nothing is too disgusting for them; the proceedings were contemptable." Curd's city cousin apparently got cold feet during the affair, fearing what family members might think of their actions. "Afraid Fanny and myself would be called to account for our conduct," Eliza and the girls "left quite soon." [39]

Not all travel experiences confirmed the negative view of Northern social and race relations presented by the merchant elite. Northerners pointed to their charity organizations and societies to counter such views. While in Philadelphia in 1855, the Richmond Light Infantry Blues were invited to a ceremony at Stephen Girard College, where an orphan addressed the company. Northerners were well aware of Southern criticism of their class relations, and these staged events were intentional displays of philanthropy toward the needy, the restoration of societal ties that commercial development had seemingly eroded.[40]

Some Richmond leaders appreciated the Northern concern for the growing ranks of the poor. Captain Charles H. Dimmock, of the Virginia Public Guard, a unit permanently stationed at the Virginia State Armory, traveled with the Richmond Grays to New York in 1859 and accompanied them to a boys' orphanage on Randall's Island. After a greeting from Master Ryan, the head of the institution, Dimmock responded on behalf of the Grays: "GENTLEMEN AND BOYS: I have read in the newspapers from time to time for years past that New York was governed by a set of nothing but political speculators and swindlers; that they had not a heart to feel for the widow and the orphan; that theirs was merely a life of trickery and corruption." Dimmock could easily have been referring to several Richmond newspapers that routinely skewered Northern class relations. Then Dimmock exclaimed, "My God! how I have been mistaken! I wish I had the power of speech and eloquence this day. There are one thousand human beings here possessed of souls, who, but for the city authorities of the city of New York, would now be wandering about the streets, lost, degraded, ignorant, fitted only for institutions of punishment; and now here they are cared for— intellectually cared for, physically cared for, morally cared for, and, I suppose I may say, cared for religiously." Dimmock went on to say that any of the children present could grow up to be president, offering a classic paean to America as a meritocracy of social and class mobility.[41]

Dimmock was a prominent urban leader in Richmond and held an important state office, but his championing of Northern reform was probably influenced by his Massachusetts upbringing. A graduate of West Point,

Dimmock served in the United States Army until 1836. Dimmock's engineering and organizational talents brought him to Virginia, where he contributed to a flurry of development, serving as president of the Portsmouth and Roanoke Railroad from 1841 to 1843 and as a director of the James River and Kanawha Canal Company from 1843 to 1847.[42] Like most Northern industrialists and entrepreneurs, Dimmock accepted the social cost of free-labor policies, expecting philanthropy to play an ongoing role in society. The majority of Richmond's elite, by contrast, felt that such policies produced ruin, breaking down the organic family bonds that were the bedrock of social relationships in the South. Although Southerners created relief organizations when needed, the emphasis was on temporary aid to individuals usually by private means, rather than systematic aid to a permanent class of needy recipients.

Southern criticism of the consequences of Yankee capitalism was not the only attack on the Northern world of goods made by Virginians in the 1850s. Trade itself became embroiled in the politics of sectionalism. Public calls for the nonimportation of goods as a weapon against the North became shrill after the fallout from the Compromise of 1850. In December 1850 a meeting was called in Richmond's Bosher's Hall "to devise some active and efficient measures to guard against Northern aggression." Commission merchant William Wallace called Daniel London to the chair. London, a thirty-two-year-old dry-goods merchant, charged the convention with the creation of an organization that "seeks the vindication of Southern rights, and the equal administration of the laws." After the election of officers, a constitution was introduced for the Central Southern Rights Society of Virginia, calling for the enforcement of the Fugitive Slave Law, condemning the abolition of the slave trade in Washington, D.C., and deploring the admission of California into the Union as a free state and the "dismemberment" of Texas. The proposed constitution asserted the "great doctrine of secession" as an "unqualified right" reserved to the states.[43]

Despite the overblown political rhetoric, the main weapon of the organization was to be economic. The members of the association would pledge to "use every exertion to have enacted by the Legislature of the State, such laws as shall prevent the sale or the introduction of Northern goods into the State of Virginia, particularly the productions of the States of Massachusetts and Vermont," the two states that had recently challenged the Fugitive Slave Law. Members would "in all cases desist from the purchase of anything produced in the Northern non-slaveholding States, provided the article can be obtained of Southern manufacture or direct importation." [44]

Lawyer Robert G. Scott then rose and offered a substantially different set of resolutions. Scott condemned the specific acts of citizens of Boston and the Vermont legislature in interfering with the Fugitive Slave Law but believed that if the situation was rectified, normal trade relations could resume. Scott said nothing of California or Texas, nor a word about secession. The meeting referred both constitutions to a committee of thirteen, as well as a detailed set of resolutions proposed by the Prince George Association, apparently a county affiliate. These resolutions barred members from buying a wide range of Northern-made articles, including "coarse cottons or woolens, or brogues of negro wear," ready-made clothing, carriages, saddles, plows, and axes. The Prince George Association took Southern chauvinism to new heights, pledging members to "employ no Northern teachers, male or female, to patronize no school in which such are employed; and, under no circumstances, to send a child to the North to be educated." Northern preachers would be persona non grata, unless associated "with some Southern religious Society and pledged to become a citizen of the South." Workmen and merchants should be avoided unless "fully identified in interest and feeling with the South" and any Northern newspaper strictly boycotted "unless it unequivocally advocates justice to the South." Pleasure trips to the North, especially to "any watering place," were unacceptable, and members should "extend the rights of hospitality to no itinerant book or newspaper agent, pedlar, preacher or land hunter, who is not by letter, or otherwise, introduced as trustworthy." [45]

Robert G. Scott's version of the constitution prevailed, and the members of the Central Southern Rights Association of Virginia resolved to "give a preference to all articles of merchandise or manufacture offered for sale among us, coming from what quarter they may, over such as may be brought into the Commonwealth from any State whose people or whose laws throw obstructions in the way of the execution of the Fugitive Slave Law." [46] In the concluding debate, merchant William Wallace, a member of the committee, claimed to have "tacitly acquiesced in the report," although not considering it strong enough. Wallace railed against the entry of the western free states and denounced Northern attacks on slavery, declaring himself "almost ready for secession, and thought it must surely come. The North would never give up the sceptre, but would insist upon taking away all our rights." Others declared that there was really no practical way to carry out "non-intercourse" with the North. Some also felt compelled to assert that the movement was not secessionist but truly Unionist, "aiming to preserve the Constitution in its original purity by claiming for the South equal rights and privileges." [47]

The constitution was perfected at a later meeting, using economic language closer to the original proposal, pledging members "in all cases, [to] desist from the purchase of any thing produced in the non-slaveholding States, provided the article can be obtained of *Southern* manufacture or of direct importation." Mirroring the concerns of other merchants, Daniel London and William Wallace clearly would have preferred stronger measures. [48]

The rhetoric of the Central Southern Rights Society of Virginia echoed across the South in the 1850s. Delegates to Southern commercial conventions, the Southern press, and prominent individuals as different as William G. Brownlow and William Gilmore Simms inveighed against Yankee goods, religion, education, and ideas, even imploring Southerners to cease their extensive tourist trips to the North. Yet many Southerners, like Richmonders, failed to live up to that challenge, continuing to buy, travel, and learn in the North. Even the outspoken Southern chauvinist James D. B. De Bow owned land in the North, printed most issues of his famed *Review* on Yankee soil, and spent much of his 1860 honeymoon with his second wife sampling the sights and goods of Philadelphia and New York. [49]

The Central Southern Rights Association of Virginia was similarly ineffective. London corresponded with individuals in Europe and the South advocating direct trade, attempting to muster support, and gathering information, but he made little headway. By February 1851, amid reports of continued trade with the North, the organization appointed a committee "to procure pledges from manufacturers, in and about Richmond, that they will give to Virginia merchants and consumers a preference on the same terms for the sale of their productions." Petitions to the General Assembly urging the organization's economic program failed to garner support among legislators. After an initial surge in membership the organization quickly became moribund. Its minutes record no meetings between October 28, 1851, and March 25, 1854, when an upsurge in sectional tensions over the Kansas-Nebraska debacle briefly rallied the membership. The next gathering did not occur until after the Harper's Ferry incident electrified Virginia and the South and sparked renewed calls for nonintercourse with the North.[50]

The economic nationalism and political views of pro-Southern men were met with unqualified scorn from some Unionists in Richmond's merchant community. The irony of fire-eaters, especially politicians, dressing in Northern garb irked merchant Charles Palmer. Just a few months before the Richmond meeting of the Central Southern Rights Association of Virginia, Palmer, lecturing his son on solid Whig principles, asserted that "Of States Rights I have the same respect as I have for an old Rotten 'Nest Egg' it just serves to lie there. These boasting dashing Southern War Hawks generally get their pants & Breast pins from the Yankees whom they pretend to abuse." [51]

Jefferson Wallace also perceived the irony of Southerners outfitted in Northern styles but saw it as an unwelcome invasion of Yankee ways. After returning in 1854 from several years in California, he wrote to his friend Charles Blair that "Yankee notions are all the go here from tight pantaloons stub toed boots short tail coats to stove pipes. I have been much amused in seeing some of our exquisites cutting monkey shines and fancy to myself what amusement it would give you and the boys in our part of the country to meet in with some of them on the plains of the San Juaquin." [52]

The association of Yankee ways with new styles of dress should have been especially troubling to Richmond's economic elite, for the clothing described by Jefferson Wallace flowed southward in the dry-goods trade that increased the wealth of Richmond's commercial class. Merchants and their families were in the vanguard of bringing Yankee notions to Richmond even as some of them grew to deplore ever more strongly the society they directly encountered in the North. Advertisements in Richmond newspapers were full of references to New York goods, a sign of quality to the buyer, and every new form of dress, social custom, and piece of sheet music that traveled southward diminished the outward differences between urban Americans.

Women contributed greatly to the demand for Northern goods. The women of the South took part in the development of the North as an arbiter of fashion and refinement through their demands for Yankee wares and their reading material, which included Northern magazines such as *Godey's Ladies Book,* published in Philadelphia. The novelist Mary Virginia Hawes Terhune recalled that her mother was "one of the earliest subscribers" to *Godey's,* and her nearby cousin Mary "took *Graham's Magazine— Godey's* only rival." Family members exchanged numerous other publications published in Philadelphia and New York, including the *Saturday Evening Post* and *Parley's Magazine.*[53]

Southern women ignored the advice of Southern nationalists and visited the great dry-goods palaces, hotels, and homes of Northern cities, further shaping their sense of taste, and taste for consuming goods. Women traveled to the North under various circumstances. Some accompanied male relatives on business trips northward, as did members of the Valentine family on occasion. Wedding tours often wended their way through the principal Eastern cities before culminating in a visit to Niagara Falls. Merchant Thomas R. Price, in New York on business, revealed to his wife, with some surprise, that "in passing thru Broadway last Friday I saw Maria Manly who told me she was just from Richmd with a Bridal party which after some questioning I found was Frank Smith & Ms. Crump!" Smith, a fifty-two-year-old hotelkeeper, and the thirty-nine-year-old Martha Crump had been married on April 28 in Richmond, and then made their way to New York.[54] Still others simply went as part of a "grand tour." Maria Watts Gwathmey, of Hanover County, just outside Richmond, set off with a party of seventeen for a tour of the American North and Canada that took them to all the major American East Coast cities, Niagara Falls, and Montreal.[55]

Interestingly, the travel diaries of middle-class and elite women rarely commented negatively on what they saw in the North, for their experience was fundamentally different from that of male merchants. Women of the classes that could afford to travel rarely moved about alone. In fact, they typically traveled with a party made up of family and friends, and the group usually included men and women. Thus the loneliness expressed by merchants rarely occurred. For the women the emphasis was on amusements and viewing sites of interest that conveyed a sense of the romantic and sublime. Moreover, women visited cousins and acquaintances while in the North far more frequently than men, who were usually caught up in the crush of business.

While Southern women enjoyed the amusements of the city, their visits to the North were just as commercial as those of their merchant fathers and brothers. Women educated their eyes and their tastes on the world of goods available and on display in the great metropolises. Shopping was always a major feature of their tours. Samuella Hart Curd reported that in New York they "went to the millinors. Matt, Fanny & myself, each got an immense bonnet, mine and F's alike, Matt's purple; they were the tip of fashion." [56] Anne Eliza Pleasants Gordon went on a bridal tour in 1857 with her husband that included an extensive European tour, but only after the usual tour of Eastern cities and Niagara Falls. In Fredericksburg they were joined by their cousin, Virginia Soutter Knox, who had accompanied her own brother on his honeymoon in 1832. Among their shopping adventures was a morning spent "examining the bronzes, plate, etc., at Tiffany's" in New York.[57]

Elizabeth Ann Valentine Gray found Stewart's Palace a "splendid establishment," reporting that she had been reliably informed that "their receipts amount to three million a year." She hastily scribbled across the top of a letter to her brother to "tell Lucy we are looking all about for her dress—and tell Mary Martha and Nettie [Sarah Benetta] that Pa has bought them some beautiful dresses." [58] Elizabeth's parents bought her a wedding trousseau at Stewart's on this same visit to the great city, a veritable cornucopia of the world of goods. A list from this buying spree records sixty-nine entries, often with multiple purchases ("muslin dresses" and "bonnets"). Clothing and jewelry topped the list, including everything from "pretty night gowns and caps" to satin slippers.[59]

Women and men learned new tastes not only at shops but also at museums, hotels, and tourist attractions. Maria Watts Gwathmey recounted one day's activities in New York when "Mr. Lee called to see me & took me to

Duseldorf's picture gallery & to the St. Nicholas & Metropolitan hotels which exceed in magnificence any I ever saw. We afterwards went to Taylor's soloon, the most beautiful establishment of the kind by far I ever saw." She viewed rooms the "walls of which are made up almost entirely of mirrors & chandeliers & when lighted up at night, it is indeed a most dazlingly bright & beautiful place." Later she went to the Crystal Palace Exposition, and she confessed to her diary that she "could not tell one tenth of all I saw," describing paintings, silver services, statuary, and other treasures. At the Saint Nicholas Hotel the Virginian gawked at "the beautiful bridal chamber which is so celebrated, it is the most splendid folly I ever saw." She marveled at the walls of fluted satin and white silk curtains, in a room that reportedly cost $150 to $200 per day.[60]

The great Crystal Palace Exposition of 1853 in New York attracted large numbers of Southerners. The editor of Richmond's *Southern Literary Messenger* visited the exposition and recommended the marvels of the event to his readership. The exhibits not only shaped tastes but also promoted consumerism by offering many of the displayed items for sale. Alfred and Ellen Mordecai of Richmond both wrote letters home imploring their other siblings to attend the great event and describing the available wares.[61]

Women and men who had seen the glories of New York's dry-goods palaces, hotels, and amusements would not easily settle for lesser goods at home. Mann Valentine and his compatriots made sure to return with the best the Yankee mercantile capital had to offer.

Indeed, Virginia merchants and their wives and daughters seem to have cut a most impressive figure. What New Yorker Frederick Law Olmsted, certainly inured to the sight of ostentatious display, found "most remarkable in the appearance of the people of the better class" in Richmond was "their invariably *high-dressed* condition; look down the opposite side of the table, even at breakfast, and you will probably see thirty men drinking coffee, all in full funeral dress, not an easy coat amongst them." The same standard applied on the street, where "silk and satin, under umbrellas, rustle along the side-walk, or skip across it between carriages and the shops, as if they were going to a dinner-party, at eleven o'clock in the morning." Olmsted sniffed that the dress of the ladies was "only New York repeated, to be sure, but the gentlemen carry it further than in New York, and seem never to indulge in undress." [62]

The high degree of dress commented on by Olmsted was paralleled by a certain overreaching in social behavior. A Northern woman commented especially on the conduct of "professional men" in Richmond, finding them "possessing what we at the North usually ascribe to Southern gentlemen— polish of manner, generosity, and a gallant bearing. But for the last, it strikes me some of the younger gentlemen have been too often told of the latter characteristic, and make it too prominent." Unlike the easy, natural gallantry of the old aristocracy, Richmond's urban bourgeoisie strained to be even more Southern in manners than their country cousins. Perhaps this exaggeration of gentry manners and formality of dress served to counter the sameness of urban life and the Yankeefication of Southern society.[63]

Although the city's elite certainly favored Northern and European fashions, their censure of Yankee modes of dress probably referred to clothing of a more dandyish variety. Upper- and middle-class Americans generally associated certain kinds of dress with the excess and corruption of the lower orders, especially of the urban North. The Bowery B'hoy and the Broadway Swell became comedic staples of American popular culture, prompting laughter by their foppish dress and exaggerated mannerisms. Richmond merchants would have instantly recognized such a Northern stereotype and nodded their heads approvingly at the stock minstrel-show character Zip Coon, the epitome of the free-black dandy. These characters fit neatly into Richmonder's assumptions about the Northern lower classes and free blacks. Mann Valentine commented that in New York "the young men dress extravagantly and foppishly. Many of the poor things drink and sit up untill their faces are double the natural size, and their legs are not larger than the Walking Cane of my old friend Michael Garber." [64]

The streets of Richmond increasingly became a showplace for finery from the North. Such display was not reserved to the promenades of white clerks and bookkeepers but also became a trademark of African-American dress. Frederick Law Olmsted recounted his observation of black "dandies" in Richmond "dressed with laughably foppish extravagance and a great many in clothing of the most expensive material and in the latest style of fashion. In . . . the fashionable streets, there were many more well-dressed and highly-dressed colored people than white, and among this dandy gentry the finest French cloths, embroidered waistcoats, patent leather shoes, resplendent brooches, silk hats, kid gloves, and *eau de mille fleurs,* were quite as common as among the New York 'dry goods clerks,' in their Sunday promenades, in Broadway." Olmsted complimented the "colored ladies," who were "dressed not only expensively, but with good taste and effect, after the latest Parisian mode. Many of them were quite attractive in appearance, and some would have produced a decided sensation in any European drawing-room."[65]

Encountering slaves and free blacks dressed in the latest fashions must have greatly disturbed masters, whose own emphasis on high dress undoubtedly sprang from a desire to create class distinctions based on appearance. To be sure, many black factory workers and laborers bore the mark of slavery by their coarse, ill-fitting attire of "negro cloth." But others wore Northern and European finery courtesy of the merchant class and challenged the prevailing codes of deference simply through their sense of fashion. Like the Bowery B'hoys and Broadway Swells, African Americans challenged upper-crust society's class and caste system through expressions of style.

Yet Northern dress and conspicuous display simply augured a deeper malady: the spread of Yankee ideas. The merchant class itself seemed particularly susceptible to the lure of money and class status. A Northern woman found considerable amusement in the remark of an older resident of Richmond "who, in speaking of the money-getting spirit that has found its way here, and of the moneyed aristocracy, that it seems is supplanting the older and better, said, it was now the height of the ambition of the citizens to get a 'place' on Shokkoe Hill, which, I suppose from this, is *the* hill, and belongs exclusively to 'upper-tendom.'" The Yankee visitor found numerous residents who lamented the passing of "the golden age of this modern seven-hilled city," but she believed that it was symptomatic of a more general transformation of American city life, where "the hurry of business, and a luxurious gaudy display in material things, is taking the place of the plainer but more elegant and chaste of former days." The Yankee visitor echoed a critique of American urban society advanced by Northern intellectuals, such as James Fenimore Cooper and Herman Melville.[66]

While Northerners saw such changes as part of a national pattern, Southerners explicitly viewed the transformation as Yankee-inspired. Jefferson Wallace, after several years in the gold fields of California, perceived the quickening of speculation and greed among most merchants in his native town. He reported with surprise to his brother in California that "you could hardly realize the change that has taken place, money here is everything, its influence everywhere. The first question on meeting any friend or acquaintance is have you made plenty of Gold & wo to the poor devil who answers in the negative." No sooner had Wallace set foot in his father's store when "Jno Maben & old Mordecai the Jew accosted me and the first word without any salutation was did you bring your Specie with you or leave it in New York. I answered that we had left it where I had made it and better employed than loaning it out to speculators to opperate on." [67]

Wallace was deeply offended by, yet envious of, the mania for money and power that he encountered on his arrival in Richmond. Just weeks after his return he wrote to his brother Charles that "when I was in Cala a dollar was nothing now it is the almighty dollar. Richmond people now are Yankee nothing for the man and every thing for the money. . . . we in Cal do not know the value of Gold, with 50,000 in gold I could control all the Banks in this city and the Big ones of the town would fawn & tremble . . . Gold is *power*." Wallace spoke with both admiration and disquiet of the changes wrought in social position brought about by advancing capitalism, informing Charles that "people in Richmond who when we left there [were] poor, are now independent, young men at that time employed as small clerks have now their large establishments & doing a heavy business." He implored his brother that "*now* is the time for us to make a fortune." [68]

But just a few months later during a momentary economic downturn, Wallace bemoaned the results of living in a capitalist world. He noted that "times are very hard here and have been so for months, money exceedingly scarce and great distress among all classes and more especially among our mercantile community." Pointing out the consequences of avarice and display, he wrote to his friend Charles Blair that "classes here as elsewhere having been living too extravagantly much above their income trying no doubt to imitate the merchant princes such as Flemming James and a host of others, who have gotten rich by breakages & stoppages." The specter of dependency loomed over him and his family, for "this city might do to live in if a person has plenty of the worlds wealth, but without it and dependant on the favors of others you had better be a slave, for a man without money here is a mere nothing, but if you have the rhino you can do almost anything with the folks here, for they love money more than they love their Bible." [69]

Wallace exploited both the love of gold and the reputation of California as a treasure trove of wealth to promote the family's business. He quickly realized that "the credit of the [family] concern had been doubted by nearly every business house in the city and elsewhere . . . but it is now growing stronger and my arrival of course will hasten it, as all here have heard of our steady business habits in Cal, and believe us to be well off."

Nevertheless, Wallace struggled with this image of success. The belief among Richmond friends and business associates that the Wallace brothers had made a competence in the California goldfields greatly enhanced their access to capital but forced them to be coy about their actual circumstances, which were considerably more modest. A former acquaintance from California, Jimmy Gallagher, particularly annoyed Jefferson Wallace by telling "everyone that we are worth from a hundred to hundred and fifty thousand." He worried that "Jimmy is a great Gasser and the people here are not such fools as they are taken for, they must have visible proof before they will believe." Yet Wallace did nothing to discourage such talk and led one creditor to "understand that we have made money, and doing a thriving business letting them place their own construction as to what we are worth, which I supose they put a most liberal construction on it." [70]

Yankee behavior was simply the cost of doing business in a more commercial age, and even the most conservative of Richmond's old guard could not escape the reality of economic facts. Merchants often found that their business ethics were at variance with the beliefs of planters and farmers. In an 1857 report to the Richmond Board of Trade, a standing committee pursuing the repeal of the usury laws, which held interest to 6 percent, reported that they had "made no positive progress." They further noted that "a change in public sentiment is the only avenue by which this end can be attained, and an agricultural people are naturally slow in comprehending necessities which bear with such force upon those engaged in the enterprises of commerce." The Board sought total repeal, but at least wanted to exclude "negotiable paper" from the law. Such debates tested their allegiance to their country clients and friends while competing in an increasingly aggressive capitalist economy.[71]

Equally troubling to Richmonders as an example of Yankee behavior was the slave trade, the Achilles heel of the proslavery argument. Old-school Virginians were acutely aware of how vulnerable were their claims of benevolence toward slaves in the face of the expanding domestic trade. Samuel Mordecai probably felt a twinge of guilt when a New York firm requested that he assist them in gathering statistics on the slave trade. After thanking Mordecai for the information he had previously sent on Richmond's trade, Maury Brothers asked him if he could "have similar inquiries made at Petersburg (which used to be another great 'head quarters of Negro-traders.') We do not ask you to go & talk with any of these gentry— as the writer well remembers your feelings of repugnance towards them." The data collected certainly contradicted the idyllic world of Virginia compiled by Mordecai in his history of Richmond.[72]

Southerners generally deflected the issue of the slave trade through resort to myths of outsiders. Southern authors of proslavery novels written in response to Harriet Beecher Stowe's *Uncle Tom's Cabin* indulged in blatant scapegoating when discussing the slave trade. In typical plotlines, Northerner speculators and merchants drove planters into financial straits, resulting in the "forced" sale of slaves; abolitionists fueled the trade by inspiring slaves to run away, thus forcing their sale; emigrant Yankee planters in the South ruthlessly sold slaves, taking the lead in breaking up families; and Yankees even came to dominate the slave-trading profession in the Southern mind. Even when not born in the North, traders were transformed into "Southern Yankees," "the oily speculator in all his repellent features and with all his characteristic vices," including greed, sharp trading, and lying.[73] Richmonders indulged in similar scapegoating when attempting to explain the economic or social behavior they found distasteful in their own community.

Many Southerners saw slave traders simply as part of a larger class of speculators. Charles Palmer had been a merchant in Richmond for many years when debts caused the failure of his business. He left for New Orleans, attempting to regain his fortunes, and wrote frequently to his son in Richmond, Dr. William P. Palmer. He asked his son to "look at the patronage recd business given to strangers & I am unnoticed. . . . look farther for corruption . . . in your councils & courts made up of vulgarity Swindlers Gamblers Negro traders & Shavers." Palmer's linking of "Negro traders" and "councils" held some truth. Several Richmond city councilmen in the antebellum period bought, sold, and hired slaves for their livelihood. Bacon Tait operated a private slave jail on Fifteenth Street in Shockoe Bottom in 1850 and also served on the city's common council. Nathaniel Boush Hill, born in King and Queen County, served on city council from 1852 to 1854, and then nine consecutive years from 1857 through the Civil War. He eventually entered into the partnership of Dickinson, Hill, and Company, one of the city's largest slave-trading operations.[74]

Charles Palmer despised the actions of many businessmen in Richmond, even attributing their behavior to religion. He railed against "Shavers as Edmund & Davenport, Dabney Miller & Divers others Methodists & Baptists Shavers & *Suckers.*" He lamented the fate of good men like his friend "*Chittenden* with all his *goodness* & cleverness" who had "run through a fortune in a few years without any *vice* but foolery," at the mercy of "shavers" and "vultures." The Episcopalian Palmer did not reserve his invective only for Baptists and Methodists. Palmer warned against "Christians men & women honoring fostering associating & *teaching German Jews* to denounce *Jesus Christ* as an imposter, whom they abuse and call *false*," and reported that he had "read the flourishes of the late *Jew Ball* for the 'Education of the Jews' whom I regard as pirates to the rest of mankind, Gus. Myers inclusive altho president of the *common* council." The inclusion of Gustavus Myers, one of Richmond's most prominent citizens, in Palmer's rogues' gallery of speculators demonstrates the fissures caused by religion and nativity within Richmond's merchant community.[75]

Sculptor Edward V. Valentine, the brother of Mann Valentine Jr., recounted the social visits of Jewish merchant Samuel Mordecai to the Valentine household, and his comments reflect a disturbing undercurrent of hostility towards Jews. One of the first busts the young artist made was of Mordecai, and the older gentleman took an active interest in the budding sculptor's work. Obviously, the urbanity and wit of Mordecai, Richmond's first chronicler, impressed Valentine, for he wrote that "Mr. Mordecai had none of those repulsive qualities attributed by so many to the Jews. He was retiring." The Mordecais had lived in Richmond since its formative years, as had many other Jewish families.[76]

Ironically, Samuel Mordecai spoke for the city's leaders and merchants in censuring the groups most often identified as the cause of the urban problems that beset Richmond—Northerners and immigrants. In the second edition of his history of Richmond he deplored the growth of destitution in Richmond. Mordecai laid the blame on an influx of foreign-born "paupers" from the North, while affirming the supposedly happy condition of slaves. During the extreme cold and snow during the winter of 1855–56, Mordecai observed that "the black servants and slaves are provided with food, fuel and clothing, while our poor-houses and other receptacles for the destitute or dissipated whites, are crowded to overflowing, chiefly with foreign paupers; contributions are raised in every mode that can be devised for the relief of the destitute whites, for many of whom we are indebted to our philanthropic brethren of the North, who seek to entice our slaves to the same destitute condition there—perhaps, on the principle of reciprocity." [77]

Many native Virginians looked with fear and loathing on the Northerners who came to their city. Clerk William Ludwell Sheppard frequently walked to the docks at Rocketts Landing while conducting business for his commercial house, and there he met many Yankees firsthand. He committed to his diary a recollection of a schooner's mate, "an uncouth Down-Easter, a sort of a Long Tom Coffin, [who] told me that he was a Tom Paine man, that is a believer in the scepticism of that miserable Atheist." Sheppard also certainly knew a few stories of Yankee ships' captains carrying human cargo to Northern ports. A few years after Sheppard's encounter with the Yankee mate, Virginia lawmakers passed new regulations for the inspection of ships in search of runaway slaves.[78]

Richmond's leaders were quick to push the blame for slavery's failures onto immigrants and Yankees. In 1850 agents involved in slave hiring complained to the general assembly of a recent change in the state law requiring masters, rather than hirers, to pay the cost of recovering runaway slaves, unless mistreatment by the hirer could be shown. Stating that "We, the undersigned, have had much and long experience in the negro hiring business," the hiring agents contended "that with the respectable portion of our community there is hardly ever a difficulty, whilst with the lower classes there are continually difficulties." The agents claimed that "a large portion of those who hire negroes, especially in our cities, consists of Foreigners and of poor and ignorant persons, who have no other idea of right and wrong than that which conforms exactly to their interests." Bereft of the proper regard for paternalism, working people and the foreign-born would abuse slaves despite the letter of the law, the hirers maintained, because in "Ninety Nine cases out of one hundred" the master "will have to depend on the bare statement of the negro which will amount to nothing." The agents maintained that if a poor or foreign-born hirer no longer needed the slave, he or she would allow or compel the slave to run away.[79]

The petitioners probably considered the hiring of domestic slaves, the largest group of slave workers in the city, the greatest part of the difficulty. Four out of ten slaves within households in Richmond's Madison Ward in 1860 were hired. Middle- and working-class whites presumably found the hiring of servants both a relief from the drudgery of housework and a less expensive, more flexible alternative than purchasing slaves during a period of high prices. Immigrant and Northern-born women certainly understood the implications of their neighbors' almost exclusive use of slave women as domestic workers, despite the presence of a small percentage of free-black and white women in domestic service. "Mastering" slaves, even as a hirer, may have conferred status and legitimacy in a society built on bondage. While hiring slaves might be an emulation of upper-class views of labor, the practice also suggests a change from the paternalism of ownership toward the cash nexus, an evolution that disturbed some.[80]

Proslavery Richmonders found easy scapegoats in foreigners, Northerners, and other outsiders, thereby salving their conscience and explaining away contradictions in the Southern social order. Nevertheless, the commercial class rightly perceived that slavery remained an open issue on which even some native Virginians held dangerously unorthodox views. The abolition of slavery in Virginia had been seriously debated by the general assembly in 1831–32, when respectable men could still lament the burden of slavery on Virginia, at least in theory. James Rawlings, writing from Boston in 1827, expressed a typical sentiment of the Revolutionary-era generation: "Everything in this Country [the North] demonstrates the benefits of free labour and shews the injuries our blessed old mother country has entracted upon her sons and daughters by the curse of slavery." Charles Palmer, a merchant of Richmond who had moved to New Orleans, wrote his son Dr. William P. Palmer, a Colonization Society manager, that "I agree with you . . . about *Abolition*, it must come in spite of the volcanic spirits of the South & in the right way if left to its own course." Palmer and Rawlings, like many older Virginians, may have still subscribed to the generally held Jeffersonian view that the eventual abolition of slavery would be a blessing to Virginia, provided that a place of migration could be found for African Americans.[81]

Despite such sentiments, in the atmosphere of the 1850s anyone suspected of abolition was subjected to distrust and possible censure in the South. The New York firm of Chittenden and Bliss bore the onus of association with abolitionists, and in 1850 one of its agents was asked to leave Montgomery, Alabama. Mann Valentine noted in 1851 that "we have not been to see our abolition friends though called on and solicited by Chittenden and his young men. The Prophet I think has been among them looking for something cheap. The tale will likely be told upon him & not much to their advantage. There are more of the negro friend class here than dare show themselves. It is quite amusing to see how hard it goes with them to deny and suppress it." The "Prophet" had apparently been working in Richmond, although his identity is a mystery.[82]

A great deal of circumstantial evidence suggests that some Northern-born merchants in Richmond were indeed part of the "negro friend class," although they were usually careful about how openly they expressed themselves. Many came to their beliefs on black education and uplift by way of their religious conviction. James C. Crane and his brother William were both important figures in the Baptist church in Richmond and also did a great deal of religious and educational work among African Americans. Born in Newark, New Jersey, the Cranes followed their brother Jonas to Richmond, William arriving in 1811 and James sometime before 1820, to clerk for their brother. William, trained as a shoemaker, first sold shoes on commission from a Newark merchant, and was later established as a shoe dealer by the "Mr. Evans, of Newark, [who] not only trusted him with two thousand dollars in shoes, but loaned him fifty dollars for his traveling expenses."[83]

William Crane taught in a night school established within First Baptist Church for African Americans around 1810. The school "continued about three years" and included among its students several founders of Liberia, including Lott Cary and Collin and Hillary Teage. In 1813, William Crane was a founder of the Richmond African Baptist Missionary Society, and James Crane also assisted with this work. Both brothers were founding members of Second Baptist Church and were instrumental in creating and publishing the *Religious Herald.* William Crane traveled frequently to Baltimore; seeing a need to promote religious work there, he purchased a church in the city and moved his family northward in 1835. James Crane, by now a full partner, continued the shoe business in Richmond. William Crane continued his work among black Baptists, funding the Saratoga Street African Baptist Church in Baltimore and speaking to First African Baptist Church in Richmond during occasional visits. James Crane maintained his membership in the American Colonization Society and the Virginia Colonization Society, serving as a manager in 1849.[84]

William Crane, like many other white men and women of Christian conviction, took a personally liberal but publicly conservative view of slave emancipation. His biographer eulogized Crane, saying that he was "ever friendly to a proper legal abolition of slavery" and "in his judgment, as in his conscience, he disapproved" of human bondage. Nevertheless, Crane felt the only proper way to administer such a change was through "State action." Accordingly "there probably never was a time when, as a citizen, he would not have voted to abolish the institution entirely," yet he passionately disapproved of Northern abolitionism.[85] Proslavery Southerners saw little distinction between Northern abolitionism and those who favored the state-sponsored abolition of slavery. Men like William Crane still posed a threat to the Southern social order.

Elizabeth Van Lew and her brother John N. Van Lew were decidedly antislavery in their beliefs. Elizabeth and John were the children of John Van Lew, a New Yorker of "good old Dutch descent," and Elizabeth Baker, the daughter of a former mayor of Philadelphia. John Van Lew was "one of the leading hardware merchants of Richmond" and established a good reputation as "an excellent man, and an old Whig." [86] His son soon came into his father's firm and the family flourished, owning one of the most prominent houses in Richmond's Church Hill neighborhood. Elizabeth Van Lew was sent to school in Philadelphia, and there "she developed that interest in the negro which shaped her life." When the Swedish author Frederika Bremer, "a pronounced abolitionist," traveled to Richmond in the early 1850s, she stayed with the Van Lews. Bremer described Van Lew as a "pleasing, pale blonde," who "expressed so much compassion for the sufferings of the slave, that I was immediately attracted to her." During her sojourn in Richmond, Bremer and Van Lew visited a tobacco factory to see the labors of the enslaved tobacco hands, and Bremer reported that "Good Miss Van L. could not refrain from weeping" at the conditions of their bondage.[87]

Northern-born men and women of the merchant class made up a significant segment of the colonization movement in Virginia. The dream of Jefferson and others of the eventual emancipation and colonization of African-American slaves was central to the slavery debate in Richmond and Virginia from the 1780s onward. The American Colonization Society began in 1817, and several Virginia auxiliaries were organized soon thereafter. The Society's most active and illustrious auxiliary met in Richmond, including as members such Virginia luminaries as John Marshall. The colonization movement brought Africa prominently into the African-American and white consciousness, and Virginians were the most prominent leaders of the movement, black and white. In the 1840s and 1850s many Northern-born men and women of the merchant class appear in records of the American Colonization Society, such as the Cranes, shoe merchants James H. Gardner and Samuel Putney, dry-goods merchant Samuel Lathrop, and Elizabeth Van Lew.

Northerners could have argued that they were simply expressing long-held sentiments on slavery and colonization, voiced by most of Virginia's prominent statesmen of the past. The slavery debates in the Virginia General Assembly of 1831–32 concluded with majority agreement that the ending of slavery was desirable and necessary. Colonization seemed the most practicable way to implement the eventual end of slavery.

Colonization increasingly came under attack in the late antebellum period, however, not only from African Americans who viewed the removal
of free blacks as a plot to strengthen slavery but also from proslavery whites
who felt that masters might fulfill the Jeffersonian vision by emancipating
and sending former slaves to Africa, eventually transforming the upper
South into a Free-Soil bastion.

The politics surrounding the Richmond-based Virginia Colonization
Society illuminate the divergent opinions on slavery current in the increasingly diverse Richmond community. Transplanted Northerners, religious
reformers, and native slaveholders formed an uneasy alliance to reorganize
the moribund Virginia Colonization Society in 1849. The Society carefully
worded its mission in hopes it could stand above the sectional and slavery
debates, but it faced suspicion from all sides. Some antislavery Richmonders sidestepped the Virginia society because of its perceived proslavery
views, dealing directly with its parent, the American Colonization Society.
Acrimony between the state and national organizations also reflected the
differing motives of white colonizationists. The Virginia society publicly
stressed free black removal, while correspondents with the American
Colonization Society, including Virginians, emphasized the eventual and
peaceful creation of a white, free-labor society in America and a black republic in Africa. This position seemed eminently consistent with conservative principles to many Virginians, a rebuke to both fire-eaters and abolitionists alike.

White colonizationists defended themselves against proslavery attacks
by resorting to tradition. In an 1851 meeting, Tazewell Taylor proposed a
resolution, unanimously adopted, that colonization, having been promoted
by Jefferson, Madison, Monroe, and Marshall, was "entitled to be regarded
as a measure of Virginia policy, having high claims to the confidence of all
Virginians."[88] At the same meeting, J. B. Dorman moved for the adoption
of a resolution "considering the principle of African Colonization as best responding to the demands of Southern patriotism and benevolence, and as
offering to the temperate wisdom of all parties and every section a common
ground of resistance against the mischievous and reckless enterprises of
Abolitionists." John Janney of Loudoun County in northern Virginia was
then asked to speak. The prominent Whig leader deftly sidestepped any di-

rect reference to abolition and sectionalism, proposing instead a resolution "that the colonization of the free people of colour in Virginia on the coast of Africa, or elsewhere, is a political and social necessity." The resolution carried unanimously.[89]

Although Richmond harbored some merchants and their families who did not subscribe to the view that slavery was a positive good, the city was overwhelmingly controlled by men who believed precisely that and who would brook little dissent on the issue. It would take the coming of the Civil War to open to public view the cracks in the veneer of consensus, but occasionally events occurred that reminded Virginians of the complexity of the slavery problem. The debate surrounding Jordan Hatcher, a slave convicted of murdering his overseer in 1852, was just such an event, demonstrating the political price of taking a position that could be construed as antislavery. The case also revealed, however, the broad consensus of Richmond's elite on maintaining paternalism in the slave-master relationship, despite the growth of free-labor ideas among some in Richmond's working and manufacturing classes.

Hatcher, in his late teens, was a hired slave from Chesterfield County employed as a stemmer in the Walker and Harris tobacco factory. The factory's overseer, nineteen-year-old William P. Jackson, complained about Hatcher's work and began to whip him. The punishment ended when Hatcher killed Jackson with a single blow from a stove poker. Convicted by the Richmond Hustings Court and sentenced to death, Hatcher received support in the form of a clemency petition to the governor from sixty prominent Richmond citizens. More than a quarter were lawyers, including John M. Patton Jr., the captain of the Richmond Light Infantry Blues, and Wyatt Mosely Elliott, captain of the Richmond Grays and editor of the *Richmond Whig*. Many distinguished ministers also signed the petition, including Moses Drury Hoge of Second Presbyterian Church. Nearly half of the signers were commercial men. Longtime merchants lent their support, among them Samuel Mordecai and Thomas H. Ellis. Industrialists Joseph Reid Anderson of the Tredegar Iron Works and Bolling W. Haxall of the Haxall Flour Mills signed the petition, as did clerks and salesmen such as George D. Fisher of the Haxall firm. Commission merchants, grocers, tobacco buyers, and warehouse managers connected to the country trade im-

plored the governor to spare Hatcher's life. Twenty-eight Richmonders petitioned against clemency, primarily tobacco manufacturers and managers
concerned over maintaining order in their industry.[90]

The governor commuted Hatcher's sentence to transportation, provok-
ing a firestorm of criticism and political debate. A crowd formed outside the governor's mansion, loudly denouncing the decision. Politicians
traded accusations, filling the House of Delegates with acrimony and party
wrangling. The newly elected governor, Democrat Joseph Johnson, hailed
from western Virginia, and some interpreted his leniency toward Jordan
Hatcher as a sign of his region's softness on slavery. Partisan conflict led to
bitter recriminations, with attacks on the petitioners and proposals that the
state capital be moved westward from Richmond. One western Democrat
who defended Johnson by turning the tables on the Richmond "mob" proclaimed that "hybrid" Richmond, "overrun with *Yankees* and German
Societies," was "not to be trusted on the slavery question"; outraged residents of the city replied by assaulting the legislator on his way back to his
hotel.[91]

While historians have been most interested in the politics of the affair,
the status of the petitioners tells us something about the enduring paternalism of many in Richmond's leadership class, including commercial men.
Requesting the commutation of Hatcher's sentence was an act of noblesse
oblige worthy of the best sort of Virginia planter. It proclaimed to the world
the justice available to the lowliest in the Southern order, a far cry from the
helplessness of Northern proletarians. Tobacco manufacturers were among
the few commercial men in Richmond who had come to understand slavery as simply a form of labor, and not surprisingly, white Southern proletarians were not amused by the killing of one of their own without recom-
pense. But neither tobacco lords nor urban workers ran Richmond.

City and state leaders generally succeeded in keeping discussion of the
slavery question aligned on a North-South axis. In their travels, merchants
sometimes tested the statements made by Virginia's politicians and newspapers about Northern political beliefs. Mann Valentine Jr. used the railroad routes northward to satisfy his father-in-law's curiosity about the 1856
presidential contest. In an aside in a letter to his wife, he recorded "a word

to your father in a matter I take no interest in myself—politics—he said to me some days ago that the race for the Presidency would be between Buck & Fremont. I verily believe he is correct." Mann Valentine Jr. found that "Fremont men are not silent—every train of cars from Richmond to New York was canvassed to try the thing—between Balt & Phila Buck 71 Fill 49 Fremont 16. Then every train after Fremont increased & Fillmore fell off & it has been tried thru the East & Fremont runs far better." The result signaled support for the Republican candidate, a dismal, even frightening, prospect for almost any young white Southerner.[92]

Valentine's brother-in-law, merchant William Gray, made his own inquiries among his Northern business associates. After the John Brown Raid, Gray wrote a letter to his New York commercial house inquiring about Northern attitudes. The reply would have only reinforced the view of Northern society shared by pro-Southern merchants:

> The Writer not being a Citizen of this Country has no intercourse with its politicians, but in daily intercourse with business men has heard very little indeed said about the Brown affair, and not a word prejudicial to the South. Some think the old man was a "Christian maniac"and too good for the Gallows per se, but all acknowledge his deep guilt, & the right of Va to hang him, & many consider it also expedient as an Example. After 16 years residence in this City we are satisfied that the South entirely misapprehends the *mind* of the people regarding them. *Theoretically* it may be opposed to slavery and desire its removal. *Practically* it is perfectly indifferent, desires peace with all its neighbors, not we apprehend from any philanthropic or commendable motive, but simply that trade may be uninterrupted. The "almighty dollar" is *the* topic of a New Yorkers dreams, thoughts & conversation. In this Estimate we except a very few fanatics & a great many selfish Politicians.[93]

Mann Valentine Jr., like most other members of Richmond's merchant class, would not have been reassured by such an answer to Gray's inquiry. The avarice of New Yorkers was apparent enough to him, but he hardly felt that it would keep slave society safe. Yet Valentine and other pro-Southern merchants took few steps to remove themselves from the New York trade and were largely unaware of its corrosive power within Richmond itself. His critique of the world of goods was strictly separated from his own storehouse of wares.

One incident, however, may have made Mann Valentine Sr. think twice about his role as a conduit of the commercial world and brought into question his characterizations of the relations between slaves and masters in his beloved South. Washington Winston, a trusted family servant, apparently found the "world of goods" in his master's shop too tempting, appropriating large quantities over a period of time. He had passed many items to a free black, Nancy Redcross, "with whom he was on intimate terms." A search of her house revealed around sixty dollars' worth of property as well as "letters of a questionable character . . . and books and papers belonging to a secret society" kept by Winston, a clear suggestion that authorities suspected him of aiding the escape of slaves.[94]

Because Winston was the secretary of the secret society as well as "a high churchman and a Sabbath school teacher," the *Richmond Daily Dispatch* used the incident to brand such societies "nurseries of mischief" and to rail against the too-close association of free blacks and slaves. Other Richmonders consistently mocked the pretensions of slaves wearing the latest fashions and laughed at the parades of black fraternal orders. Mann S. Valentine worried that a trusted servant in whom he had "always entertained the highest opinion of his honesty and faithfulness" would steal from him. For slaves living in an increasingly commercial world within which they were both unpaid producers as well as products, such an appropriation might have seemed minor if not mundane. These differences in viewpoint were characteristic of the contradictions flowing through a society built on the slavery of bondsmen and -women but growing through the freedom of the market.[95]

Mayor Joseph Mayo sat in judgment of Washington Winston and Nancy Redcross, quickly finding them guilty. Redcross received "corporal punishment." The *Dispatch* did not report Winston's penalty, but approvingly noted that Mann Valentine "intends sending him South, where he will probably get clear of the corrupting influence of bad free negroes." Free blacks always made convenient scapegoats when slaves behaved in a way antithetical to their master's wishes, and Valentine also considered the power of a woman's wiles. He pondered Winston's culpability in light of "the arts of a vile woman with her smiles and blandishments, . . . many a greater man than he has been undone in a similar manner." [96]

Valentine agonized about the situation, which had "come upon me like an attack of life destroying paralysis from which there is no escaping." Torn between his paternal role as head of his household—slave and free—and the pressures of public attitudes, Valentine wrote of his feelings in a private note. He weighed the possible censure of public opinion if he should fail to send Winston south: "I know it will be said in this I am the apologist for error and dishonesty, not so, for if his [Winston's] feelings alone were to have been consulted he might have gone to the outermost end of the Earth, though his life might pay the forfeit of his folly I should think nothing but justice had been done." Valentine instead considered the disruption of long-standing family relationships. "How can I disregard the mothers servants & wife and childrens feelings in such a case," he moaned. Valentine lamented that Winston's mother China had "raised and watched over the existence and wants of every child we have had" and regretted the harm that would come to Winston's family. Valentine believed that "too much vindictiveness and too little feeling has been displayed" in the affair. Obliquely blaming public pressures for the result, Valentine speculated that "it might have been managed so as to have given me less pain & concern of mind [but] the whole thing was managed so that I had no agency in it." [97]

A cryptic receipt in Mann Valentine's papers recorded payment for Washington Winston's imprisonment for more than a month in the "Cary Street Jail" and a commission of five dollars to Sednum Grady for assisting in the slave's sale. Mann Valentine's paternalism did not prevent him from selling Winston, and it was not the first such sale. In fact, the slave members of Valentine's household had several relatives relegated to other parts of the South. Valentine traveled in a Northern world of commerce not of his choosing; his bondsmen and -women traveled in a Southern world of slavery not of theirs. Washington Winston's suspected dreams of freedom in the North or West and his exile to the South defined the poles of African-American life in Richmond. [98]

CHAPTER FOUR

Liberty and Slavery

Imagine the joy of a father's heart on receiving a letter from a son whom he had
never expected to hear from again. . . . I am glad you are with a kind master and
doing well. . . . Give my love to my dear grandchildren and tell them their
grand-father hopes he may yet live to see them all. Give my love also to your
dear wife and tell her though I have never seen her, I have still a fatherly
feeling for her, and tell her not to let her children forget that they have a
grand-father in "Old Virginia."

HENRY PAGE, enslaved servant of Mann S. Valentine Sr., to his son, 1856

I am in good hopes that this may find you all well an making up you minds to
leave old virginia my marthrs home. My hart morn with sorry to think that I
had to seek a home in a strange land among strangers for the sack of my children. It was hard for me to part with some of my good frends in virginia, an so it
will be with you all but for the sack of you children you all mus part from you
good friends also an come to a land whar you children can be men an women.

LUCY JARVIS PEARMAN SCOTT, Brantford, Canada West,
to "My Dear Children," 1854

O n a Sunday in 1848, Robert Ryland, the white minister of First
African Baptist Church, Richmond, sat down with the African-
American Board of Deacons and conducted the church's business.
During the meeting they made decisions affecting many members of the
church's extended Baptist family. They discussed several former members
now living in the Deep South. The board took up the matter of a debt owed

by Cornelius White, presently a member of a church in New Orleans. A letter was read from the clerk of Jackson Church, Mississippi, asking for a letter of dismissal for Frank Rickman, which was denied because he had been excluded from First African's fellowship and was not a member in good standing. Ryland and the board also dismissed Hannah Julius to an uncertain fate in New Orleans; the minutes of the Richmond congregation do not reveal her attendance at a church in that city.

The board granted letters of dismissal to free blacks Maria Starke, Lucy Philips, and Albert Mathews, possibly headed to, or already in, the North or West, following hundreds of other free people who had migrated before them. Former members used those letters in their new homes as testimony to their membership in good standing of the Baptist Church. Luckily, the church was constantly reinvigorated by new migrants from the Virginia countryside. The board received faithful Christians from the Fredericksburg, Hopeful, and Salem churches into the fold of First African Baptist Church.[1]

The church business transacted that day in 1848 represented just a small number of the varied connections the African-American community had with both near and faraway places. First African Baptist Church was a center of African-American life in Richmond and Virginia, but it was also a node on a much larger network of religion, family, and memory in the African diaspora. The network stretched back to Africa and northward to Canada. It was a fragile link to home and family for some sent to the Deep South through Richmond's infamous slave markets. It followed a path to a tenuous freedom in Northern and Western cities, and connected through these cities to other places. Comprehending the scale of that system expands our notions of the worldview of First African's members and makes more understandable their ready grasp of freedom after the Civil War. Richmond's African-American community created its identity from the spheres of kinship that were essential to its definition of "Virginia" and from contact with kindred communities and institutions throughout the Atlantic world.

The ability of church members to learn about their world and, for some, to gain freedom, was greatly facilitated by the railroads, steamboats, and mail systems that carried the goods of Richmond's merchants. Urban masters could not completely control, or fully comprehend, the sophisticated black community to which their enslaved workers belonged, nor could they fully restrain men and women who gained a concrete understanding of liberty and slavery through a complex community that stretched between both.

In 1841 the white and black members of First Baptist Church parted ways. African Americans had previously petitioned for their own house of worship, citing the crowded condition of the city's churches, which often caused them to be excluded. The white members of First Baptist, a distinct minority of worshipers, felt uneasy, as "some very fastidious people did not like to resort to a church, where so many colored folks congregated." Both sides probably well understood that their forms of worship differed markedly. The white members built a new church only a few blocks away and sold the old church to the African American congregation for "$3,500, with interest to the time of payment."[2]

A white minister was required by law, a provision inspired by the memories of slave revolutionaries Nat Turner and Gabriel. The Reverend Robert Ryland was called to the office. Energetic and well known in the Baptist community, Ryland had only a year before been installed as the first president of the newly formed Richmond College. Born in 1805 at Farmington in King and Queen County, Ryland received a good education, attending Columbian College in Washington. After graduating, Ryland entered the ministry, but by his late twenties he was already running Virginia Baptist Seminary in Richmond, the predecessor of Richmond College. Perhaps his obvious organizational and administrative talents made him the most logical choice for First African's pulpit, or perhaps it was his educational background; Ryland himself embraced his appointment like a good Baptist progressive. Ryland, both a slaveholder and an American Colonization Society officer, viewed the church as an educational and moral mission.[3]

As Ryland cryptically noted, the church's governance was "rather more presbyterial than congregational," but this clearly had nothing to do with questions of denominational doctrine. Instead of all members voting, "*thirty deacons*, chosen by the church, from its most experienced members," governed the church with the pastor, a structure that was "deemed essential to the judicious control of so large a mass of persons, many of whom could scarcely be judged competent to the task of government." The deacons were "scattered over the city, and . . . expected to exercise a general supervision in their respective districts." In cases where the First African Baptist Church could not resolve a dispute, the ultimate authority rested with a white "committee of 24" appointed by the First Baptist Church whose decisions were final. Despite the occasional flaring of tempers and minor disagreements, Ryland and the deacons usually kept the church members' business within its walls.[4]

Ryland faithfully recorded the minutes of First African's business meetings, inscribing baptisms, deaths, the restoration of members, and others' exclusion from fellowship in a large ledger. Ryland also noted the members received into and dismissed from the church by letter, often including their place of origin or destination, creating a picture of his church's relative position in a world of faith that largely overlapped with Richmond's place in the African diaspora. The church minutes also provide glimpses of members' contacts with churches, organizations, and individuals from distant cities and regions. Combined with other records, the minutes offer a remarkable view of the world and identity of Richmond's African-American community. Two major spheres defined black Richmond's place in the antebellum world. Freedom beckoned free blacks and escaped slaves in an exodus to the Northwest, Northeast, and Africa; economic and social forces pulled enslaved African Americans into Richmond from its rural hinterland and sent others to the cotton South.

Robert Ryland presided over a congregation made up largely of enslaved men and women, with a significant minority of free blacks, who, because of their legal and economic status, were often leaders in the church. Ryland recognized that his Sunday audiences were largely bondsmen and -women, especially among those received or converted since the church's founding in 1841. Ryland wrote in the church minute book that "of the baptized to . . . 1851 *sixty six* are free & 720 slaves" and that "the slaves are to the free as 2 to 1 nearly" in the overall church membership. The draining of many free-black congregants in the 1850s would accelerate this process.[5]

From 1841 to 1859, 269 free blacks left First African Baptist Church, making up a significant part of the church's overall dismissals. The minutes of the church reveal destinations for 93 men and women. Of the 85 who left the state, more than 60 percent went to the Northeast, usually to cities. Philadelphia received twenty migrants, the largest single destination. Most of the others went to Canada, the West (especially Ohio), or Liberia. Those going to cities may have then used these locations as jumping-off points to other areas.[6]

The Scott family came to the Virginia capital in the 1840s from New Kent County, but then migrated to Ohio, and finally to Brantford, Canada West. Writing to relatives back home, the patriarch of the family stated, "I [k]now now I wood of saved 150 Dollars by comin to new york and than to Buffalo and from thar to Brantford."[7]

New York, as the major Eastern seaport, led to many other places. Emmanuel Quivers and his wife, Frances, originally were dismissed in 1852 to New York, but they eventually settled in Gold Rush California. Many of the other 269 free people dismissed from First African Baptist traveled similarly complicated paths.[8]

In Northern and Western cities Richmond migrants joined escaped slaves and free-black migrants from other parts of the South and Virginia. More than half of the black population in Midwestern cities such as Detroit was Southern-born by the mid-nineteenth century. Although receiving smaller numbers of Southern blacks than Midwestern cities did, Eastern cities such as Boston and New York saw significant migration from eastern Virginia, Maryland, and North Carolina. Philadelphia remained the exception in the East with almost half its adult black population born in the slave states. Periodic repression, especially in the 1830s, sent many Virginia African Americans north and westward. A lawless campaign against free blacks on the Eastern Shore of Virginia in 1830s drove "many of the best element of the Northampton free Negroes . . . to Philadelphia, where they found a safe place as efficient cooks, caterers, and operators of shops of various kinds." The failure of a petition to the legislature for a school in Fredericksburg in 1838 prompted the "progressive free Negroes" of that city to leave immediately for "Detroit, Michigan, and to other centers."[9]

The migration of free blacks from Richmond was chronologically as well as geographically focused. Of the 269 free blacks who left the church, 69 left in the 1840s and 200 in the 1850s, and the out-migration was particu-

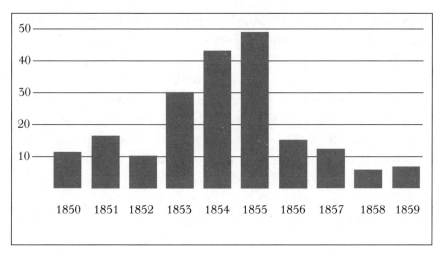

Figure 4. Free-Black Dismissals from First African Baptist Church, 1850–59. *Source:* Compiled from church minutes, 1841–59, microfilm, Library of Virginia, Richmond.

larly intense from 1853 to 1855, when 122 free members left. Leaving was partially related to increasing oppression. During the antebellum period white authorities periodically tightened the legal and social restraints on free blacks, especially reacting to Gabriel's attempted revolution in 1800 and Nat Turner's revolt in 1831.

The federal population statistics for Richmond's free-black community suggest a relationship to increased white oppression. In 1806 a new Virginia law required that emancipated slaves leave the state within six months, unless given express permission to stay by the legislature. Despite this statute, Richmond's free-black population grew almost 60 percent in the 1820s, fueled by post-Revolutionary emancipations and migration to the city, only to fall slightly in actual numbers during the 1830s following Nat Turner's insurrection. In the 1840s the free-black population increased a modest 23 percent, but in the 1850s growth slowed to about 9 percent as some whites renewed calls for reenslavement and further legal restrictions.[10]

Localities registered free blacks and attempted to restrict their movement. Remaining free depended on the possession of a register of freedom attesting to the bearer's status. Free blacks detained without them could be sold for a period of time to defray their jail expenses, and the inability to prove their freedom sometimes brought reenslavement. As early as 1844 the Society of Friends in Richmond complained to the legislature that free people without papers had been imprisoned, resold, and taken from the state.[11]

In a conversation with abolitionist editor James Redpath in 1854, a free-black confectioner and his wife in Richmond could easily reiterate a list of "oppressive laws and ordinances" that substantially matched the city code. The free blacks then explained to Redpath the consequences of the laws—how the lack of freedom papers could ultimately lead to reenslavement, or how any questioning of a white person's words or conduct, no matter how legitimate, could result in being hauled before the mayor's court on charges of being insolent. The confectioner pointed out the increase in slave runaways as a sign of the heightened legal repression suffered by African Americans.[12]

A former slave, the confectioner had hired his own time, working as a porter at a prominent city hotel. After saving enough money to buy his own freedom, he not only established a retail business but also purchased the freedom of seven other slaves, including his wife. Redpath found on a return visit to Richmond in 1857 that his informant had sold his business after the death of his wife and moved to Philadelphia. He apparently could no longer bear the indignities and apprehensions of living in a world defined by slavery.[13]

Despite the very real threat of white restrictions and laws, the exodus of the 1850s, and perhaps earlier migrations, cannot simply be explained by increased oppression. A greater knowledge of the larger world and an ardent desire for freedom came together in the 1850s to fuel the out-migration of free blacks. In fact, the tightly focused out-migration of free blacks in a few years at mid-decade suggests an understanding of the overall American economic climate. Modest prosperity enhanced the ability of Richmond's blacks to improve their economic lot and also may have prompted movement to the urban North or West. With the downturn of the late 1850s, Richmond's free blacks probably chose the security of family and familiar surroundings in the face of competition for jobs in other urban centers.

Those who departed were often established community leaders, who were the best able economically, and most disposed philosophically, to leave

Virginia. The list of dismissals from First African Baptist Church includes many men and women of standing in the church. At least four deacons left during the height of the free-black migration out of Richmond in the 1850s. William C. and Lucy P. Scott migrated first to Ohio and then to Canada with other family members. The church dismissed deacon Wilson Price and his wife, Mary, to Canada in 1854, and three months later recorded the migration of Isham Ellis, a shoemaker and church deacon for many years, and a large group including several family members. A year later church leader John Kinney migrated to Michigan. The leadership exodus continued with the departure of deacon James Oliver, his wife, Maria, and their daughter Catherine for Ohio in 1857.[14]

Like the confectioner interviewed by James Redpath, some migrating free blacks had recently liberated themselves from bondage. Slaves exploited the economic vitality of the revived Richmond economy to earn overwork pay, and hundreds emancipated themselves by self-purchase. While instances of slave self-purchase, or the purchase of another family or community member by slaves or free blacks, were not everyday events, they occurred frequently enough that every slave and free black in Richmond would have known of numerous cases. In fact, slave manumissions were more prevalent in Virginia cities from 1831 to 1860 than in the supposedly more liberal period from 1782 to 1830. Richmond courts recorded 352 manumissions in the later period, a time when only a handful of rural slaves gained their freedom. Most of these manumissions were not owing to the benevolence of masters or to notions of human equality, as in the period of the American Revolution, but directly to the self-purchase of slaves, itself a product of the "system of slave hiring and freedom of movement which grew out of it" and the slave's "increased ability to earn."[15] The number of manumissions may appear to be small, but the desire to emancipate can only be appreciated when the high cost of black emancipations and self-purchases are considered against the small amount of capital available to the black community.

The case of Emmanuel and Frances Quivers and their children illustrates both the difficulty of attaining freedom and the complex networks that African Americans developed. Quivers labored at the Tredegar Iron Works as a hired slave for ironmaster Joseph Reid Anderson, who hoped to increase the number of slaves at Tredegar to counter the high cost and troublesome nature of white workers. For Quivers, Tredegar offered skilled work and a chance to associate with other black workingmen within a thriving African-American community. He and his wife, Frances, soon joined the First African Baptist Church.

In late 1845, Anderson negotiated with Henry Harrison regarding the purchase of Quivers. Anderson bluntly pointed out that "I have not exactly proposed to advance Manuel money to purchase himself, but have expressed a willingness to purchase him." Harrison seems to have suggested the self-purchase idea, but Anderson stated that "I would not purchase Manuel unless at his request and wish, and if I do purchase him it is my own intention to place it in his power to redeem himself within a reasonable time provided he does his duty." Anderson paid the substantial sum of $1,100 for Quivers—evidence of the latter's considerable skill. Emmanuel Quivers would remain enslaved for another seven years.[16]

Quivers labored for many years as a slave at the Tredegar Iron Works, building his skill and capital in order to buy his freedom. His wages went into an account set up by Anderson eventually to allow Quivers to liberate himself and his family. At the beginning of 1847, Anderson deducted $40 a year for the family's fuel and rent of a house. While other slave artisans occupied tenements on the Tredegar site, the Quivers family resided within the community. Frances Quivers contributed to the family income by occasionally making clothing for Tredegar ironworkers.[17]

Emmanuel Quivers sojourned in New York in 1849, finding work and sending a check to Anderson to be placed in his account. A number of free members from Quivers's church, First African Baptist, had already gone to try their luck in the North, and many more would go in the next decade. In early 1850 the slave ironworker returned to Richmond and resumed his job at Tredegar punching iron.[18]

Anderson called on Quivers for one final arduous labor before he would grant him his freedom. In June 1850 Anderson left a deed of emancipation for Quivers with the lawyer Henry L. Brooke, which he should "hold subject to the following conditions and stipulations": Quivers was "to go to California with Mr. Jno. J. Werth & to remain with him subject to his orders & directions in all respects until the 31st of December, 1853. . . . If he

shall have served the said Werth faithfully & done all in his power to forward the objects of his enterprise he is to be entitled to his freedom & to all
the benefit of the contract I have made with the said Werth." The contract
called for Quivers to receive $2.50 a day as well as a small share of the
profits.[19]

Like most California adventures, however, Werth's enterprise faltered,
leaving all parties dissatisfied. In March 1851 Anderson voiced his concern
"at the unfavorable prospect of your enterprise, as gathered from the general tenor of your recent letters," hoping that "if your worst anticipations
should be realized that you may still be able to save the capital invested."
Anderson still believed that "there is doubtless gold in abundance in California but whether you can adopt a successfull means of obtaining it by
vein or surface mining or otherwise you must be the best judge." A month
later Anderson sold an engine built for the California scheme, attempting
to recoup some of his debts, and advised Werth to free Quivers and "let him
work his way home or undertake whatever he chooses." Anderson based
this advice "on account of your dissatisfaction with him & I have since
heard he is restless & dissatisfied & under these circumstances I cannot
think it is either the Interest of the Compy or his that he should remain."[20]

Frances Quivers purchased herself and her five children from Tredegar
Iron Works manager John F. Tanner in October 1852. Emmanuel Quivers
returned to Richmond, and on November 7, 1852, "Emanuel Quivis" and
his wife, Frances, received a letter of dismissal from Richmond's First
African Baptist Church to New York. How long they stayed in that city,
which Emmanuel Quivers had previously visited, is not known, but by
1855 the First African Baptist Church "recvd a letter from J. B. Saxton
of Stockton, Cal. asking for a copy of the letter sent Nov. 7, 1852 . . . to
Emanuel Quivers," dismissing him from the church. In the meantime,
Quivers finally received his freedom, recorded in the Richmond Hustings
Court on December 31, 1853. Werth would eventually return to the Old
Dominion, as would many other disillusioned Virginians, but Quivers saw
a better life in Eldorado that he could pass on to his children, including his
three-year-old son Joseph Reid Quivers.[21]

While Quivers honored his former master in naming his son, he, like
many other African Americans, left Richmond for good in the 1850s. Along

with hundreds of other free blacks and runaway or emancipated slaves from Richmond's First African Baptist Church, Quivers staked his claim in the African-American diaspora. The church provided a network of information for African Americans wishing to leave. The entry of California into the Union in 1850 as a free state probably confirmed Quivers's decision to stay. The Quivers family remained and flourished. Joseph Reid Quivers, born in Richmond while his father labored for his namesake at Tredegar, became a skilled mechanic in Stockton. The "foreman of the Matteson & Williamson firm of agricultural builders" for seventeen years, he worked another twenty for the John Caine Company, "his last big job . . . the John Caine building on El Dorado Street." [22]

Self-emancipation was not limited to skilled workers. Factory laborers were also integrated into the cash economy, and this held out at least the prospect of emancipation by purchase even for these slaves. Richmond's to-bacco factories hired thousands of slaves each year from the countryside, and overpay for extra work was common. Although it took years for factory hands and slave artisans to earn enough to self-emancipate, there is no doubt that some did purchase their freedom, and still more dreamed of the day they could do so. [23]

The exodus of many free blacks and newly emancipated slaves stunted the growth of Richmond's free-black population in the 1850s, but it is prob-able that a significant number of those emancipated chose and were al-lowed to stay, even though "public utterances and state and local laws con-demned them as a class." The pull of family, home, and a familiar land was powerful, even when juxtaposed with dreams of freedom, and many chose to remain in Virginia. The level of contact with and knowledge of the North and West might have inhibited as well as promoted migration, be-cause the Richmond newspapers and even some migrants knew all too well that the urban North and West were hardly paradises. [24]

The First African Baptist Church Minutes record the significant minor-ity who left almost immediately after grasping their freedom. Henry Walker purchased his freedom from former Quaker Cornelius Crew in 1847 and was dismissed that same year; Cornelius Turner bought himself from Sarah Munford in 1851, and by July 20 was dismissed, bound for New Bedford; John Hopes purchased his son Walter Hopes from Dr. James D. McCaw in 1853, and Walter received his dismissal on February 6, leaving for an unrecorded destination. These men and women manifested their desire for freedom by self-purchase, and capitalized on it by leaving the Old Dominion for what they hoped would be freedom in the form of education and greater opportunities in the North.[25] Skill and capital greatly aided the most successful migrants in adjusting to their new homes. Robert Gordon "while still a slave had been allowed to operate a coal yard in Richmond and to keep for himself all the money received for the sale of slack in this business." After purchasing his freedom, he went to Cincinnati and became a successful coal operator.[26]

The letters of one family eloquently attest to the concrete benefits and freedoms that African Americans anticipated in their new homes, as well as the nostalgia for family and fireside in the Old Dominion. Lucy Jarvis was freeborn in York County, Virginia, around 1800, and later bore a number of children while known as Lucy Pearman. After living for a time in New Kent County she moved to the Richmond area with William C. Scott. In 1848 Lucy Jarvis Pearman Scott and several of her teenage children regis-

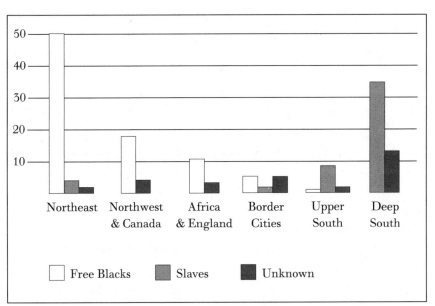

Figure 5. Destinations of Members Dismissed to Places Outside Virginia from First African Baptist Church, 1841–59. *Source:* Compiled from church minutes, 1841–59, microfilm, Library of Virginia, Richmond.
(About seventy-five percent of slave dismissals and about two-thirds of free black dismissals list no destination.)

tered with the Henrico County Court. The clerk recorded her height as
five feet and two inches and described her as "a mulatto woman, with long
straight hair." Both Lucy P. and William C. Scott were in their late for-
ties, and their Richmond neighbors included other members of the Scott
and Pearman families, most in their twenties and all listed as mulattoes.
William Scott was a deacon and Lucy Scott a member of First African
Baptist Church.[27]

Along with a group of relatives, including several of Lucy Jarvis Pearman Scott's children, the Scotts moved first to Ohio and then to Brantford,
Canada West. In a series of letters back to Virginia the Scotts implored
other relatives to join them, discussing the possibilities of life in a new
place. Naturally, good land and employment were topics of discussion.
George Pearman found work as a wheelwright, and McFarlane Pearman
and Thomas King were working together as carpenters. Shoeing a horse
paid $1.50, "carpenters wages 1.50 to 2 dollars per day, whelrite as much."
The family also stressed the importance of education. The Scotts reported
to their other children that "your sisters elizabeth can right as [?] a hand
as any of our ladys in old virginia." The Scotts promised to bring them to
the West, or to send a "conductur," if any of the children were willing to
come.[28]

These letters of family news were infused with a larger theme, the
theme of freedom. William Scott wrote that he "do bless the god of all
mercy for his mercies and goodness towards us, that our lot was cast in a
land where we can set under our own vine & fig tree and none dare to make
us afraid and oh my dear Children what a great blessing it is to have the
freedom of Speech and to be where we can send our little Children to
School together all taught together and that for love instead of hating each
other and calling each other names to hard to be borne."[29]

Education was a powerful symbol of freedom, and although some slaves
had learned to read in Virginia by themselves, in churches, or through their
masters, restrictions on literacy increased in the late antebellum period.
Fields Cook, who wrote a rare personal narrative while still a slave in the
1840s, recorded that he "most always have my book in my hat and many
and many a time have knelt down and beged god to teach me my book
and I beleave that he heard my prayers for it looked to me as if I could get

any lesson that was given me without any troble what ever and all my crave was just to know how to read the bible." Cook's aspirations were severely limited, for he

> had many things to contend with at this undertaken for when I was a boy about the time of nat Turners insurection who had better never been born than to have left such a curse upon his nation I say that he had better never been born: for at that time I was living in the country and we poor colored people could not sleep at nights for the guns and swords being stuck in at our windows and doors to know who was here and what their business was and if they had a pass port and so forth and at that time a colored person was not to be seen with a book in his hand: but all the Books I had had been given to me by my owners and therefore I kept them though many a poor fellow burned his books for fear.[30]

Fields Cook and other slaves clearly understood the relationship between the Nat Turner episode and the increased opposition of whites to black learning and autonomy. Turner, a literate and religious slave, epitomized for whites the consequences of black education. White fears were well founded. Literacy was not only a symbol of freedom but also a powerful tool in the slave's struggle for greater independence of movement and thought.

Richmond tobacco worker Thomas Johnson was inspired to pursue literacy because of his religious conviction to become a preacher and his desire for freedom. He learned the alphabet from his mother and received about a month of instruction from a free black. But most of his literacy skills were gleaned from listening to his young master read Bible chapters and spellers, which he then memorized and correlated with the written text. Johnson saw a path to escape when his master mentioned the fugitive slave Anthony Burns, who had been recently captured in Boston and returned to face sale in a Richmond slave market. When his master stated that Burns's flight had been facilitated by a forged pass, Johnson began learning cursive writing. Although the Civil War came before Johnson perfected his reading and writing skills, he spent the war years holding Bible classes with other African Americans. They especially enjoyed reading Daniel 11, which they interpreted as predicting the victory of the Northern armies.[31]

Despite the possibilities of freedom and education in the North and Canada that inspired both free blacks and slaves, African Americans carefully weighed these benefits against the reality of leaving a familiar home and friends for a strange land. The Scotts sometimes felt isolated, lamenting that "thar is very few blacks in this city [Brantford] in deed to look hear an in some other citys that I have bin in since I left Old Virginia thar is such a few that some times I think I left them all behind in old virginia." Understanding the difficulty of leaving familiar faces and family, Lucy Jarvis Pearman Scott enticed her children to migrate with the "butiful schools hear you can school you child for 25 cent per mont an mak him a man up to bisness. I lick this place better than I do Ohio tho you do not pay anything thar for schooling but you can mack a better livin in this place than in Ohio." [32]

The use of the term "old Virginia" carried with it the ties of family and home that tore at newly emancipated African Americans required by law to leave the state within six months. Peter Strange, formerly enslaved by G. H. Bacchus, stated that "your petitioner is a black smith by trade which he considers a useful one where he is——; that by industry it furnishes him an humble support, but that he is now about 50 years of age & in precarious health so that if he were forced into a strange land without money or friends & severed from his wife & children, who are slaves & to whom he is sincerely attached he could foresee nothing but suffering & distress." Walter D. Blair supported Strange's petition, writing that Strange "for about twenty years past . . . has been the husband of a woman in my family," further noting that "I think he comes up to the standard of character (and the Blacks have their standards of character) that would be useful as an example to those of his colour around him, if permitted to remain in the Commonwealth." [33]

Clara Robinson, an elderly free woman of color, also wished to stay in the state of Virginia after her emancipation by her owner, Elizabeth Gibson. Robinson was of "advanced age (60 years) and bound to the city of Richmond by the strongest ties—all of her children being slaves living in the said city—and holding associations of the kindliest character with many of the families of white citizens here resident." Robinson supported her petition by noting that "she has been for several years professionally employed in the City as an accoucheur or midwife and given satisfaction generally in that capacity—in evidence whereof she tenders the certificate of the Honorable James A. Seddon drawn up in his own hand and signed by a large number of the medical faculty of Richmond who in the course of their obstetrical practice have had occasion to employ her and kindly given this testimonial of their valuation." Skilled free blacks often counted on the support and protection of powerful white patrons in weighing the decision to stay in the state.[34]

Ties between slave and free-black men and women complicated the decision to migrate. A population survey of the wards in Richmond in 1854 showed that there were "152 slaves owned by free persons of color" in the city, many by family members to prevent their resale outside the state.[35] Women sometimes owned their husbands, freeing them to pursue a new life elsewhere. In one church case, "Rebecca Bowser (formerly Cook)" wished to remarry, but testimony revealed "that Rebecca's former husband had been absent in Ohio for nearly four years, and that he had abandoned her, after having been purchased by her and set free." It was decided "after considerable discussion, that the case from its peculiar nature, receive the forbearance of the church." Others freed their spouses later. Anna Thacker, "otherwise called Anna Herman or Hermant a free woman of color," asked in her will to "sell my lot and house thereon on what is called Poplar Street in the Valley of Shockoe Creek . . . also my Household and Kitchen furniture and to apply the proceeds thereof to the benefit of my husband Frank [whom] I purchased by conveyance of Susan, Rachel and Polly Wyatt of the County of Caroline in this State and who at my death or shortly thereafter will leave the State of Virginia." Thacker's purchase and continued ownership of her husband shielded him from the laws that required newly emancipated slaves to leave the state unless granted specific permission to stay by the legislature or local courts. Frank had apparently determined to seek a new life beyond the boundaries of the Old Dominion after the death of his wife, and she aided him with a freedom gained by the sale of her worldly possessions.[36]

The Richmond press took notice when former slaves returned to Virginia, viewing it as validation of their beliefs about the horrors of Northern class society and the benevolence and justness of their own. In a notice entitled "Something for Abolitionists to Reflect Upon," the *Richmond Daily*

Dispatch reported that "some time ago two negro women, Caroline Banks and Mary Francis, emancipated by the will of Mrs. Sarah Branch, of Chesterfield, were taken to New York by the executor of the estate, and there left, with a supply of money sufficient, it was supposed, to last them until they could procure employment." Sometime later, Caroline Banks called on William H. Hardgrove of Richmond while he was in Boston, requesting that he take her children back to Virginia, stating that she would follow. According to the paper, Hardgrove turned down her request, but the sisters soon returned to Richmond and appeared before the mayor, saying they preferred slavery to freedom. While the *Dispatch*'s reporter thought that the incident "affords a fair illustration of the actual benefits of bondage to the negro race," it probably better reflected the economic marginality of free-black women in the North and South and the pains of family separation.[37]

Robert Ryland, the white minister of First African Baptist Church, related a similar story in the *American Baptist Memorial.* In a lengthy biography of one of his parishioners, Brother Nicholas Scott, Ryland related that

> about the time that the Northern people began to display their new-born zeal in behalf of the African race, "Uncle Nick," or as he sometimes facetiously called himself, "Old Nick," went to some of the Northern cities to reside, expecting to find an easier life and greater privileges among the philanthropists of the age. He was sadly disappointed. On his return to Richmond, after an absence of a year or two, he was met in the street by a distinguished gentleman, who gave him a cordial shake of the hand, and inquired why he had come back to the South, "Ah, Sir," said he, "Virginia is my home. The North is no place for a *gentleman* to live at." [38]

Ryland penned these words in 1855; almost every Sunday of that year he recorded dismissals to the North in his own hand on the pages of the First African Baptist Church's minute book.

Literate slaves certainly took white publications with a grain of salt, especially the Richmond newspapers. Abolitionist William Still reported that escaped slave Samuel W. Johnson had worked at the *Dispatch* office "as a carrier of that thoroughly pro-slavery sheet." The *Dispatch* was one of Richmond's first "penny posts," cheaper than other newspapers and widely available throughout the city. Johnson could read the paper he delivered, for he "had possessed himself somehow of a knowledge of reading and writing a little, and for the news of the day he had quite an itching ear." Johnson read more than the *Dispatch*, however, and he "luckily [had] come across a copy of *Uncle Tom's Cabin*, and in perusing it, all his notions with regard to 'Masters and Servants,' soon underwent an entire change." He resolved to escape and soon landed in Philadelphia via steamship.[39]

Positive descriptions from escaped slaves, relatives, and Northern publications of the North and Canada provided a contrast to the stories told by the Southern press and masters who emphasized the cold, forbidding nature of Northern society. When asked by Philadelphia abolitionists whether "many of the slaves are anxious about their Freedom," Richmonder Charles Thompson replied that "the third part of them ain't anxious about it, because the white people have *blinded* them, telling about the North,—they *can't live here;* telling them that the people are worse off than they are there; they say that the 'niggers' in the North have no houses to live in, stand about freezing, dirty, no clothes to wear."[40]

African Americans were the objects of, and participants in, a propaganda war between North and South that tried to influence black behavior and thinking. A Richmond free-black confectioner told abolitionist James Redpath that slaveowners depicted the North as "a place of punishment—a terrestrial hell—where negroes are abused, starved, and kicked about for the amusement of the white race." The former slave then questioned Redpath about the "true character of the people of the North," and the abolitionist responded "as an admirer of her [the North's] character, principles and institutions might be expected to reply." Apparently not satisfied with such generalities, the confectioner inquired if there was "any disrespect shown to people of color." Redpath did not publish his actual response. Obliquely stating that "I love the North, but I worship truth," he wrote an aside that chided Northerners for their "disgraceful and relentless prejudices."[41]

Redpath decided not to articulate to his readers the full truth of black life in the North, but the facts spoke for themselves. Segregated public facilities and schools and denial of political rights faced free blacks in much of the North. The workplace was equally hostile. Discrimination existed everywhere, but in 1850 the greatest percentages of free blacks following entrepreneurial and skilled professions in urban America were in the Lower South cities of New Orleans and Charleston. Free-black skill and success was lower, but not negligible, in Upper South cities like Richmond, where free people perpetuated their skill in the building trades and other professions. Job opportunities for free blacks were bleakest in the urban North, especially New England. Workplace conflict and violence sometimes went hand in hand. Race riots racked numerous Northern cities throughout the antebellum era; Philadelphia, one of the most popular destinations for Richmond's free blacks, had at least five between 1829 and 1849.[42]

Yet for most Southern migrants to the urban North a segregated school promised more than no school at all; the opportunity to associate in churches and societies outside the gaze of whites trumped the impositions of the Southern codes; and the ability to walk down the street without free papers or passes stood in sharp contrast to the Southern system. The North had its prejudices, but African-American communities struggled against them in full public view, an impossibility in the South. For many, it was simply a matter of going where the system of slavery was dead—and many went.

The abolitionist view of the North was no doubt overly positive, and some former slaves and freemen and -women became disenchanted with life above the Mason-Dixon line. Such disillusionment, however, did not usually result in a return trip southward. James Stanard, emancipated in 1847 by his owner's will, went to Philadelphia, reporting to acquaintances in Richmond the difficult economic conditions facing working people in the North. Stanard's descendant Susie Sharper wrote the Virginia Historical Society that "there was a movement on foot for the colored people to go to Haiti to establish a home for themselves" and the disillusioned Stanard decided to leave Philadelphia and never returned, forsaking his wife and children. Stanard may have been part of a late 1850s resettlement effort to Haiti promoted by James Redpath, the Scottish abolitionist who had visited Richmond several times in his earlier trips to interview Southern slaves. Northern blacks investigated colonization schemes to Trinidad, Jamaica, Central America, and other parts of Africa. Some former slaves and free blacks also chose to resettle in states with fewer legal restrictions, such as Massachusetts, or to make the trek to Canada.[43]

The return to Africa was another option for free people and some emancipated slaves. The impulses that led African Americans back to Africa were varied. Many went as missionaries fueled by a desire to redeem the continent for Christ. Others spoke of "civilizing" Africa and, not surprisingly, believed that the creation of a commercial economy was essential to that enterprise. There is also no doubt that some viewed the return to the west coast of Africa, the departure point only years before of European slave ships, as a return to a black homeland. Virginian and Liberian immigrant James Skipwith proclaimed Africa "the Best Country for the Black man that is to Be found on the face of the Earth. God intended Africa for the Black Race."[44]

Africa played a major role in the identities of black Richmonders, free and slave, in the antebellum era. In 1823 "a number of persons of colour residing in the City of Richmond" petitioned the state legislature for a church, noting "that from the rapid increase of population in this City the number of free persons of colour and slaves has become very considerable" and "it has been the misfortune of your petitioners to be excluded from the churches, meeting houses, and other places of public devotion which are used by white persons in consequence of no appropriate places being assigned for them, except in a few houses." The petitioners requested "a law authorizing them to cause to be erected within this city, a house of public worship which may be called the Baptist African Church." It would be another eighteen years before the first African church was allowed to form in Richmond, followed by three other Baptist churches founded in the late antebellum era that described themselves as African.[45]

Although many African Americans did take an interest in the Liberian experiment, especially in its early years, by the early 1830s it was often denounced by Northern blacks and white abolitionists as a proslavery plot. Many African Americans in Richmond were aware of the abolitionist critique of colonization, and many heard the firsthand accounts of returning colonists such as Gilbert Hunt. Hunt was one of the most celebrated figures in antebellum Richmond. He became a local hero by saving many lives from the raging fire that engulfed the Richmond Theatre on Christmas Day, 1811. Despite his brave act, Hunt remained a slave until 1829, when he purchased his own freedom for $850 and left for Liberia on the ship *Harriet*. He returned the next year disillusioned with Liberia. Colonization officials complained that Hunt's negative account of Liberia discouraged others from making the journey to West Africa. As a recognized community leader and deacon of First African Baptist Church, he was in a position to influence others weighing the decision to migrate. He was an eyewitness to the attrition rate of new immigrants and other problems in the new African country. Contact with Northern migrants also carried word of the general disapproval of colonization among Northern free-black communities.[46]

The Virginia Colonization Society was well aware of the bad publicity that the Liberian experiment had received. At an 1851 meeting, Tazewell Taylor, "referring to the ignorance and prejudice of the free coloured people in regard to Liberia, alluded to in the annual report as one of the greatest obstacles to Colonization, moved 'that the friends of this society be earnestly solicited to use all prudent efforts in their power to inform the free colored population of the great benefits which emigration to Liberia offers them.' "[47]

Both the state and national colonization movements found it difficult to convince free blacks to immigrate to Liberia. Colonization forces did receive a boost from the renewed interest of states as disparate as Indiana and New Jersey in promoting and funding the removal of free blacks in the 1850s. The American Colonization Society sent only 1,815 people to Liberia in the 1840s, but 4,677 went in the 1850s. The Virginia General Assembly granted considerable funds to the colonization effort in the 1850s, but reports of high mortality rates and poor economic prospects in Africa still inhibited immigration to Africa. Virginia's free blacks perceived better opportunities for freedom and independence in the American North and West.[48]

A bare trickle of migrants made their way to the west coast of Africa from Virginia in the 1840s and 1850s. On November 13, 1855, the Virginia Colonization Society received $500 "for transportation of 10 free negroes" from the state of Virginia, apparently reflecting the yearly tally, which was paid to the American Colonization Society for services rendered. That same year the ACS sent a total of 207 migrants to Liberia. Only seven immigrants left First African Baptist Church for Africa in the 1840s and six in the 1850s, a minuscule part of Richmond's out-migration of free blacks in the late antebellum period.[49]

Despite the relatively small number of migrants to Liberia, free blacks still identified on a broad symbolic level with their African heritage; the degree of this association with Africa cannot be properly assessed simply by looking at the decision to migrate.[50] African Americans made individual choices based on what they knew of the conditions in Africa and weighed their prospects against the many other possible points of migration. No matter how strongly African Americans felt about the black republic, they knew the reality of mortality, squabbling, and warfare that characterized African settlements. There were also cases where some found white racism and economic competition in Northern cities so harrowing that they later went to Africa from the North. No matter what decision they made, they were still moving within a larger black diaspora within which identity was fundamentally shaped by being of African descent.

The conversion of Africa to Christianity, a primary motivation of earlier Liberian migrants, remained a powerful force in the late antebellum church. First African Baptist assisted several men who professed a desire to go to Africa and preach the gospel. In 1843 Thomas U. Allen came before the First African Baptist Church and stated "his ardent desire to devote himself to the work of preaching the gospel to the heathen, and whereas this church having long observed his upright deportment and his christian spirit, and having now heard from his own lips a relation of his exercises in regard to his contemplated work therefore, Resolved that we cordially approve his design to offer himself to the American Bap. Board in Boston as a foreign missionary, and that we will exert ourselves to sustain him in whatever field the Board may designate."[51]

Sustaining Brother Allen would require more than words; he was a slave, the "property of an orphan child whose guardian has obtained leave of the Court to dispose of him for the sum of $600." The church resolved to "contribute according to our ability to assist him to raise that amount," and requested that Allen visit Manchester, Petersburg, Norfolk, Williamsburg, and Fredericksburg "for the purpose of soliciting from the friends at those places funds to meet this demand." Allen ultimately gained his freedom.[52]

Several years later Thomas U. Allen again appeared before the church and "resigned his office of deacon and his resignation was accepted." All was not well as the Board of Deacons pondered his dismissal from the church: "Bro Allen having been assisted by the brethren generally to purchase his freedom with the expectation of going as a missionary to Africa and it now appearing that he will not probably go, some dissatisfaction was felt among the members, whereupon he stated that he had in good faith offered his services to the Board in Boston & that they for want of funds & in the hope of his becoming better qualified, had declined his proposal at least for the present, and that he had found employment as a pastor in New Bedford Mass and would try to improve his mind and follow the leadings of Divine Providence in regard to his future efforts. The brethren being satisfied granted a cordial dismission." [53]

Despite the dissatisfaction that attended the Thomas Allen case, a few years later First African members again endorsed a missionary who sought passage to Liberia. Boston Drayton "having presented himself before the church on Lords day May 30 was examined by the pastor as to his christian experience, call to the ministry & doctrinal views. The brethren being satisfied with his answers, and he representing to the church that he had made arrangements to sail for Liberia in a few weeks, it was resolved that he be ordained." At the next week's service "Bro. Drayton was this day solemnly set apart by the imposition of hands to the work of the ministry. The exercises were conducted in the presence of a crowded and deeply affected audience." [54]

Other African Americans went to Liberia after living in the North. Elizabeth Van Lew sent one of her slaves to Philadelphia to be educated, and then freed the young woman and paid her way to Liberia as a missionary. Van Lew continued to provide support to the woman in the 1850s through the American Colonization Society.[55]

A few African Americans in Richmond subscribed to the American Colonization Society's journal, the *African Repository*, indicating at least a curiosity about the black republic in West Africa. James B. Burrell, William B. Ballendine, James W. Thompson, and William Williamson all subscribed. Ballendine and Williamson both operated barber shops that catered to whites and plied one of the most lucrative black occupations in Richmond. Ballendine embarked from Baltimore for Liberia on a packet boat on February 24, 1849, but by 1852 he again plied his trade in Richmond. He continued to read about the fortunes of the black republic in the late 1850s. Richard Forrester, an African-American leader in Richmond after the Civil War, also subscribed, although he is not designated as an African American in the subscription book. Another subscriber was Robert Ryland, the white minister of First African Baptist Church.[56]

African Americans must have looked with justifiable confusion at the bizarre politics of colonization in Virginia and America. Whites supported African colonization for a variety of reasons, ranging from a sincere belief that blacks could only flourish outside the restrictions of racist America, to a cynical desire to rid the United States of an inferior race. Ironically, the ideological confusion among colonizationists invited stinging criticism from both proslavery advocates and abolitionists. The Virginia Colonization Society, reorganized in 1849 after a five-year hiatus, constantly stressed its nonpartisan position to avoid controversy. Consequently they strictly limited their discussion of principles to the colonization of free people.[57] Tensions between the Virginia society and the American Colonization Society also added to the confusion. The national organization was considered too liberal by proslavery Virginians but served as a refuge for those more sympathetic with the plight of people of African heritage in America. Elizabeth Van Lew used the national organization as a conduit for money to slaves she had emancipated and sent to Liberia.[58]

No matter where migrants went, separation from family and friends could be harsh. Institutions like First African Baptist Church helped African Americans retain ties to their former homes and to the larger black community. Although most dismissed members never returned from the North, the few free blacks and slaves who did certainly brought news of friends and family as well as more general information. In 1852 the church received "a letter from Elder Richd Vaughan of Phila. inquiring into the deportment of Wm Fisher now of Richmond, but an excluded member of the 1st Af. Bap. Ch. of Phila.—& an applicant for restoration." Fisher, a free black, was finally received formally into the Richmond church on March 6, 1853, and no doubt gave an account of Philadelphia to eager listeners. News was also gained through travelers to the North. In 1855 "Bro Wm Crane of

Balt. came in & made a few remarks in regard to a colored church in that city." Crane was a white man long active in Baptist affairs in Richmond. A member of the Virginia and American Colonization Societies, he vigorously promoted the education of African Americans during his many years in Richmond and later in Baltimore where he funded the establishment of a black Baptist church. His brother James C. Crane remained in Richmond and continued the family shoe business. Through these networks members could stay in contact with family and friends who might later aid them in moving northward.[59]

As members migrated, they often called on the home church for financial support. During a meeting in April 1853 the deacons resolved to take up a collection on the third Sunday of that month for the Buxton Church in Canada. On the same day in 1857 that two free blacks were dismissed to Detroit, "the Pastor read a letter from the Bap. Ch. Detroit, Michigan, asking aid to pay $2,000, on a house lately purchased—theirs having been burned and it was voted to take up a collection for their benefit on the 4th Sabbath in May." The collection amounted to the tidy sum of $71.29. Assistance was also given to churches in Philadelphia and Washington. On some occasions the church had to turn down a needy church. During the construction of Third African Baptist Church (later renamed Ebenezer) in Richmond, First African received a letter from William C. Burke, pastor of a Baptist church in Clayashland, Liberia, requesting aid in building a "House of worship," but "it was resolved to decline it on the ground of our being pressed with a similar enterprise." [60]

Whites were suspicious of Northern contacts, because free blacks were not the only travelers northward. Slaves escaping to Northern ports used information passed by word of mouth and the public mails. The most dramatic illustration of this connection occurred in 1848 when slaveholders became aware that two escaped slaves had used a mail system at First African Baptist Church to write "to their former comrades . . . detailing the manner of their escape, and proposing to them facilities and information for the same experiment." [61]

Robert Ryland routinely received and distributed mail to his congregants, as hundreds of letters of dismissal and "testimonials of membership" from afar passed through his hands. Ryland, "not knowing the parties oftentimes, and having no other method of distribution, . . . announced them from the pulpit on Sunday at the close of worship, and the respective parties came up and received them." Ryland, shocked at the novel use the church's communications had been put to, "felt impelled by a sense of propriety to announce to the congregation that I should not in future deliver any letters from the North without a personal acquaintance with and full confidence in the recipients. The letters were suffered to remain in the post office, and I was released from a great annoyance and from unjust suspicions." Some outraged citizens pressed Ryland to read the letters and report on the contents, but Ryland angrily refused. He "*had* not the least intention, *should* have had none, when I became the pastor of the colored people, to degrade my office to a police to detect and to apprehend *runaways!*" [62]

Ryland's refusal to break trust with his congregation came under intense community suspicion and recrimination. Jeremiah B. Jeter, the minister of First Baptist Church, felt compelled to defend Ryland against rumors of the latter's involvement in the escape attempt in a letter to the *Religious Herald*. Jeter asserted that "on the first suspicion that he had been made subservient to a design in which he has no sympathy, and which he sincerely disapproved, he handed the letters which had come into his possession to the Mayor of the City." Ryland might be faulted for "taking such letters as came from the North from the post office," but Jeter declared that as one "born and bred in Virginia, and himself an owner of slaves," Ryland "surely needs no vindication from the charges of being an abolitionist." Apparently, in Virginia in 1848 he did.[63]

Ryland's ultimate solution to the mail problem generally squared with the usual handling of Northern mail to slaves in the South. A contemporary source reported that at Southern post offices, when a "post-mark indicates a northern origin, the postmaster withholds it from the claimant, inquires his master's name, and then deposits it in the latter's box." African Americans in the South risked stripes or worse from angry slaveholders if discovered to be in league with Northern compatriots through the mails; runaways risked their very freedom. Anthony Burns carefully disguised a letter to his brother in Richmond with a Canadian postmark, but he dated the letter with his true location, Boston. His brother's master read the letter, and reported Burns's whereabouts to his master, setting in motion what would become the most celebrated legal test of the Fugitive Slave Law in the antebellum era.[64]

Burns had lived for many years as a hired slave in Richmond, and he was returned to his former place of residence in chains. Thrown into the jail of slave trader Robert Lumpkin, Burns languished under brutal conditions while awaiting sale. But even this confinement did not stop him from communicating secretly with the other inmates; through a hole in the floor he told them of "his escape from bondage, his free and happy life at the North." Amazingly, he also wrote and had delivered six letters under Robert Lumpkin's nose. Burns managed to avoid confiscation of writing materials hidden on his person. Attaching the letters to a brick, he watched "at his window until he saw some negro passing outside the jail fence," and "contrived by signs to attract his attention and throw to him the letter." Burns knew the Richmond community; he "trusted, not unreasonably, that his wishes would be rightly interpreted, and that his letters would reach the post-office." The U.S. mails did the rest, and two letters reached friends in Boston.[65]

Anthony Burns had originally escaped using his knowledge of the polyglot world along Richmond's riverfront. Hiring his own time, he found hard work at the docks, loading and unloading ships carrying coal, guano, and other goods. A friendly sailor assisted him in stowing away on a ship bound for Norfolk and ultimately Boston. Fugitive slaves and free-black migrants both followed the trading routes of Richmond's commercial base to Northern port cities, and black and white seamen were often suspected or accused of aiding slaves in escaping. Showing an appreciation for these men, many of them African Americans, the First African Baptist Church heard an appeal for funds from the Reverend Joseph Stockbridge, "agent for the Seamens Society of N.Y.," and "took up a collection of $20.58 for that object." [66]

William Still exulted that "no one city furnished a larger number of brave wideawake, and likely-looking Underground Railroad passengers than the city of Richmond." The reasons for the prominence of Richmond on the "railroad" were in fact the new technologies of communication and transportation that provided both the information and the means necessary to escape. Modernity in this sense did materially erode the "peculiar institution." Still's famous work, *The Underground Railroad*, told the story of many Richmond "passengers." Jeremiah W. and Julia Smith had "berths . . . procured for them on one of the Richmond steamers (berths not known to the officers of the boat)." John Henry Hill occupied a "private berth . . . on the Steamship *City of Richmond*, for the amount of $125," while John William Dungy stowed away in the storeroom of the steamer *Pennsylvania*, "containing a lot of rubbish and furniture." [67]

Richmond slaveholders tried to stem the flow of runaways northward. A Richmond society known as the Society for the Prevention of the Absconding and Abduction of Slaves "resolved that the Treasurer be authorized to procure to be printed 1500 copies of 'the act to amend the several acts concerning Slaves, free negroes and mulattoes' passed 11th March 1834, in handbill form to be distributed by the Harbour Masters among the Captains of Vessels and Steam Boats trading and coming to this port, and in such other manner as the Treasurer may think best." [68]

Besides circulating tracts to shipmasters, the society paid a few people who succeeded in carrying out their designs in the 1830s. Thomas Blount and William W. Pearce, "the two Watchmen who detected nine slaves on board the Schooner Chariot on 21st February last," were paid $25 each. Daniel Matthews received $50 "for very important services rendered by him in taking up in New York and bringing to this state a slave belonging to a member of this society." William B. Chamberlayne made $150 by visiting "New York & rendered important services to the slave owners in Virga by causing arrests, and by controverting & aiding in causing to be invalidated certain state Laws of New York which were extremely adverse to the rights and interests of Virginia slave owners." Despite these apparent early successes, the Society seems to have become moribund rather quickly, and many runaways kept the dream of escape by sea alive.[69]

Lawmakers also attempted to halt the exodus to the North by punishing those who assisted fugitives. Lott Mundy, a free black from New York, received a fifteen-year sentence for stowing two slaves, Martin and Thomas, in a chain box in the ship's galley. The slaves had approached Mundy while his ship, the schooner *Danville*, stood at the Richmond docks in late July 1856. Neither of the slaves knew Mundy, the ship's cook, before the incident. Captain William Bayliss, skipper of the ship *Keziah*, seems to have been involved in a much more organized effort to transport slaves out of Virginia by sea, and he received a forty-year sentence in the state penitentiary—eight years for each slave he assisted—in 1858. Both Munday and Bayliss fell under the provisions of a new state law passed in 1856 that increased sentences for those convicted of aiding runaways and also boosted rewards for the arrest of fleeing slaves. Recognizing the bustling, anonymous docks as a favored path toward freedom, legislators also provided for the appointment of special inspection commissioners with the power to board and search vessels for fugitive slaves and their abettors.[70]

Railroads offered another method of fleeing slavery. The most spectacular and widely reported escape was of Henry "Box" Brown. After the cruel sale of his wife and children, Henry Brown resolved to escape from slavery. He intentionally injured his hand to receive a leave from work, and plotted various means of escape with a white friend. Finally, a novel method of escape was revealed to Brown. "At length, after praying earnestly to Him, who seeth afar off, for assistance, in my difficulty, suddenly, as if from above, there darted into my mind these words, 'Go and get a box, and put yourself in it.'" After this revelation, Brown "went to the depot, and there noticed the size of the largest boxes, which commonly were sent by the cars, and returned with their dimensions. I then repaired to a carpenter, and induced him to make me a box of such a description as I wished, informing him of the use I intended to make of it. He assured me I could not live in it; but as it was dear liberty I was in pursuit of, I thought it best to make the trial." [71]

The artisan whom Brown approached was Samuel Smith, a white man who would do time in the Virginia State Penitentiary for assisting Brown and for attempting to send another slave to freedom. Smith was actively in contact with Philadelphia abolitionists and truly represented the "enemy within" that many Southerners feared. Smith was skeptical of the plan, and he only relented when Brown "insisted upon his placing me in it, and nailing me up." After numerous harrowing experiences while being shipped in the box, including spending several hours on his head in an upside down box, Brown arrived in Philadelphia and was carried to an abolitionist's

house where he was uncrated. Henry Box Brown went on to become a staple of the abolitionist lecture circuit in America and England.[72]

The way toward freedom ran counter to the other major place of dismissal for First African Baptist Church members, the slave South. Unlike
the move northward, this was a forced exile fueled by Richmond's important position in the domestic slave trade. Although some entries for Southern ports and states, most notably New Orleans, appear in the minute books,
as well as a few simply noting "To the South," Ryland did not record the
destinations of most enslaved African Americans leaving First African
Baptist Church. In many cases, he probably had no idea where the slave's
travels would ultimately end. Of a total of approximately 318 slave dismissals (excluding those to other Richmond churches), only 81 entries
noted a specific place, or about 25 percent, in contrast to about a third
of free blacks.[73] Despite this lack of specificity, the existing entries point
toward the Deep South. Thirty-two of the 50 recorded dismissals to places
outside Virginia were to Georgia, Alabama, Mississippi, Florida, Texas,
Charleston, and New Orleans, the largest American slave market.

New Orleans, like New York, was a great hub of America's commercial world, but it dealt in cotton and slaves, not dry goods. The slaves dismissed to this location might end up in many other areas of the Deep
South. A fairly large number of dismissals went to Charleston, South
Carolina, another slave-trading center, although some slaves did become
residents of that city. A letter received by the church from Joseph Whilden,
of Charleston, asked for the dismissal of Daniel Carrington, "now of that
place." [74]

The anecdotal evidence in the minute books suggests that the Deep
South was the destination of most of the dismissed slaves from the church.
In 1851, "a letter having been recvd. from J. B. Stiteler, stating that Frank
Rickman—an excluded member—is now residing in Jackson, Mississippi
& is of consistent deportment, it was ordered that the Pastor write to him
stating the facts of the case & authorizing the ch. there to restore him to fellowship if satisfied of his penitence & reformation." In another case, the
church received a letter from Natchez requesting the dismissal of a slave
named Frank, but the deacons and Ryland had to answer with a request

for further information on his identity. The sale of longtime members must have been especially painful. Ryland recorded that Philip Johnson, "once servant of P. B. Jones," was dismissed to Georgia. In a note below, Ryland referred to Johnson's baptism on June 12, 1842, recorded on page twenty-three of the minute book.[75]

The interchange between churches and members created a connection between the worlds of slavery and freedom. Some members returned from the Deep South, such as "Sister Maria Logan, having taken from us to the New Orleans First Bap. Ch. among whom she had sojourned, a letter of commendation, brought over in like manner from that church to us on her recent return." Urban churches further south also solicited funds from First African Baptist in Richmond. In 1856 the congregation welcomed Andrew C. Marshall from Savannah, Georgia. The one-hundred-year-old Marshall had led a remarkable life. Born a slave on a South Carolina plantation in 1755, Marshall had five masters—including a governor of Georgia—before he purchased his own freedom for two hundred dollars. He built a successful drayage business and became one of the wealthiest and most prominent free men of color in Savannah. Called to the ministry, he built First African Baptist Church in Savannah into a 2,417-member congregation by 1830. Like the Richmond church, it was visited frequently by Northern and foreign travelers such as Frederika Bremer. Marshall had traveled northward soliciting funds to repair his church, and the collection plates in Richmond yielded "$ 8.12 in the morning & $ 7.60 in the afternoon" for the project. Sadly, Marshall became ill and died during his stay in the Virginia capital. A Richmond church member accompanied his body on part of the return journey to Georgia.[76]

Communicating by letter with enslaved relatives in the South posed far more difficulty than writing to Northern migrants. The location of a relative or friend sold south might not even be known, and masters on rural plantations and farms could more easily control communication with their slaves than urban masters. A rare letter from Henry Page, a slave coachman owned by Mann Valentine, in reply to an unexpected letter from his son, illustrates the problem of slave communication in the South. Page could neither read nor write; based on similarities in the handwriting, the letter appears to have been physically written by Mann Valentine's daughter

Sarah Benetta, who was still living in her father's household. Page asked his son to "imagine the joy of a father's heart on receiving a letter from a son whom he had never expected to hear from again, or whom he thought if perhaps living had forgotten his affectionate father." Page's son obviously wrote after years of separation, and Page's reply is full of discussions and news of family. Page sent his love to his grandchildren and relayed his "fatherly feeling" for his son's wife, "though I have never seen her." He implored his son's wife to "not to let her children forget that they have a grand-father in 'Old Virginia.'" Page praised his son for his having "so far cherished your Mother's memory as to name your oldest child after her." His granddaughter Sarah was not the only family member with a family name that had been passed down. Page related that his son's sister Kitty was well and that Aunt Kitty "says she intends writing you herself." [77]

Page related messages from others in the Richmond community. He had been to "Mr. Taylor's to see Edward's mother who is very well and sends her love to him." Although Page thought his son might not remember her, he passed on a message from Sally Gladman, formerly Sally Boles, a nurse in the Valentine household: "She says you know her husband who used to belong to Mr. Randolph, Sam Boles was his name. She says if you ever hear of her two sons Stephen and James you will please let me hear in your letters." Mann S. Valentine had purchased Sally Boles Gladman and her four children for $900 in 1831 from the estate of his wife's father, Benjamin Mosby. Page asked his son to confirm his address and told him to send his letters to "M. S. Valentine, esqr." [78]

Page's letter teeters uneasily between the pain of family separations and pious niceties about the duties of servants and masters, as well as entreaties against bad company, gambling, and drink. The letter contains a "postscript not for the sake of praising my master, but because I think sometimes that the pain of absence is partly relieved by knowing that those from whom we are separated are well taken care of. I have one of the kindest masters that a servant ever had." The postscript recites a litany of physical comforts Page enjoyed, including clothing "that many a white gentleman would boast of," food in "greatest plenty" direct from the master's table and "very light" labor. The postscript seems a strained attempt to compensate for the implicit message about slavery carried by the letter itself.[79]

African Americans in Richmond witnessed family separation at the auction block on a massive scale. Between 1846 and 1849 the firm of R. H. Dickinson & Brother sold about two thousand human beings per year, but the Richmond market had yet to experience its peak years. Dickinson, Hill and Company reported doing more than $2 million in sales in 1857, as market prices and demand accelerated. Prices for the most desirable male slaves found in trade circulars and reports for the Richmond markets did not top $860 before 1850; during 1860 traders and others reported prices as high as $1650 for "No. 1 men." The trade in Richmond was fed by smaller traders who collected slaves from the outlying counties and towns (although some came a considerable distance) to be sold to the larger Richmond houses. The major Richmond dealers would then resell the enslaved men, women, and children, primarily to traders from other major markets. Richmond carried on a particularly important trade with New Orleans.[80]

Silas Omohundro, one of the largest Richmond traders, facilitated the trade through his slave jail on Wall Street, sometimes called Lumpkin's Alley after another slave trader, Robert Lumpkin. Within a few blocks of the city's major hotels, Omohundro fed and housed traders, masters, and their human chattel. Despite the powerful pull of the New Orleans market, men, women, and children left Richmond's Wall Street for every Southern state. In 1857, Handy Dean carried Jane to Mississippi; J. McComb took Anderson, a boy, to Tennessee; George Williamson transported Mary, a girl, to North Carolina; and Colonel A. E. Thompson brought another Jane to Georgia.[81]

White visitors and immigrants to Richmond captured the inhumanity of the slave trade particularly in their detailed descriptions of the inspection of slaves—simply as goods to be coldly examined and priced. This inverted white Southerner's typical portrayal of race relations, which was supposedly based on familial affections and loyalty. African Americans felt the inhumanity of the slave trade as no white person ever could—as a desecration of the family bond—and struck even more profoundly at masters' hypocrisy. Patience Martin Avery lived in Petersburg when she was interviewed by Works Progress Administration workers in the 1930s but recounted her experience in Richmond before the Civil War. Her story includes a gripping account of the sale of slaves in Richmond's great slave market and the breaking up of families. Her own parentage was an indictment of the power relationships embedded in the slave system, for her "Mother b'long to Thomas Hatcher, in Chesterfield County, Virginia, an' my daddy was de young master. He was name directly after his daddy, Thomas Hatcher, Junior. Some o' de descendants is still in Richmond. Rev. Hatcher who was connected wid de first Church is a descendant." Avery then recounted her African-American family's situation, testifying that "All o' my folks b'longed to de same master—mommer, gra'ma, an' Uncle Robert Richardson," who "was heid man an' hired hisself to Smelling, de proprietor o' dis sportin' house. Dis house was on Franklin Street near de Ballard House in Richmond. Dis was de las' place dat I, Patience Martin Avery, saw my gra'ma an' mommer." Robert Richardson's "sportin' house" was close to the slave jails and auction houses of Shockoe Bottom, and Patience Avery recalled for her interviewer that "Yes, 'tis plenty o' places dey use to sell slaves," and described the operation of the business:

Well, de way dey did was to bring slaves in groups, tied an' chained together. Den dey would put 'em in pens lak cattle. You seen horses an' cows in a pen havencha? Well, dat's de way humans was treated. Chile, it gives you de creeps up yo' spine to think 'bout it. Sometimes dese po' slaves has walk miles an' miles. De ole masters didn't keer. Dere was a block dey would stan' you on. Firs' dey 'xamine you a bit, den dey start off sellin' lak a auction sale o' property. You know how dey do. Say, "$50.00, $50.00, $50.00, etc., $100.00, $100.00, $100.00, Fine young wench! Who will buy? Who will buy? She got little niggers, good an' healthy. De higes' bidder would get de slave. Um! Um! Um! All de time de sale is goin' on you here de mos' pitiful cries o' mothers bein' part from dey chillun. Sometimes de same master would buy de mother an' her chillun. Seldom you'd find dat, 'cause dey say de chillun was too much trouble. Richmond was a great slave market.[82]

Patience Avery would have given little credence to claims that masters tried to prevent the breaking up of families, and the best historical studies now agree. The economic needs of masters and market overrode whatever paternalism masters harbored.

The slave narrative of Henry "Box" Brown also emphasized the cruel effect of the slave trade on families. Before he shipped himself north, Brown worked as an industrial slave in a tobacco factory in Richmond, along with thousands of other slaves hired from the countryside. Brown's narrative demonstrates the strange world of the hired slave, who could rent a house and even pay a master not to sell his wife, Nancy, who had been owned by several men before their marriage. Brown went on to tell how "on a pleas- ant morning, in the month of August, 1848 . . . I left my wife and three chil- dren safely at our little home, and proceeded to my allotted labor." Brown toiled through the day, until "the hour for the laborers to turn from their tasks . . . was fast approaching." He remembered that then "there burst upon me a sound so dreadful, and so sudden, that the shock well nigh over- whelmed me. . . . And what was it? 'Your wife and smiling babes are gone; in prison they are locked, and to-morrow's sun will see them far away from you, on their way to the distant South!' " [83]

> The next day, I stationed myself by the side of the road, along which the slaves, amounting to three hundred and fifty, were to pass. The purchaser of my wife was a *Methodist* minister, who was about starting for North Carolina. Pretty soon five waggon-loads of little children passed, and look- ing at the foremost one, what should I see but a little child, pointing its tiny hand towards me, exclaiming, "There's my father; I knew he would come and bid me good-bye." It was my eldest child! Soon the gang approached in which my wife was chained. . . . She passed, and came near to where I stood. I seized hold of her hand, *intending* to bid her farewell; but words failed me; the gift of utterance had fled, and I remained speechless. I followed her for some distance, with her hand grasped in mine, as if to save her from her fate, but I could not speak, and I was obliged to turn away in silence.[84]

The fact that many African Americans lived and worked within a few blocks of Richmond's slave pens and auction rooms made them thoroughly familiar with the operations of the slave trade. Just as certain was the fact that contacts with friends, family, and institutions in the North, West, and Africa gave Richmond's African-American community an understanding of freedom, a freedom most would not realize until after the Civil War. One of the first acts after liberation would be the search for lost family members.

CHAPTER FIVE

Strangers, Slaves, & Southern Iron

These works cover several acres, and form almost a town in themselves. Nearly seven hundred men are constantly employed in the various branches of manufacture here carried on. We doubt whether at many points in this Union so busy a scene can be witnessed. The clang of hammers, the roar of hundreds of fires, and of all varieties of machinery, boring, turning, cutting, rolling, planing, and performing all the thousand processes which iron, the King of metals, must undergo to be fitted for human use, was almost deafening; but it had a music of its own, to the ear of one who loves old Virginia, and rejoices in every token of her onward and upward progress. It was eloquent of "a good time coming," and of the beginning of a new era in the history of the South—and we exult in it as affording a grand and worthy specimen of what can be done in this latitude through the skill and enterprise of our own citizens.

"Southern Enterprise," *Richmond Daily Dispatch,* July 13, 1853

he *Richmond Daily Dispatch*'s description of the Tredegar Iron Works in 1853 invoked the heightened sense of industry and power wished for by Southern boosters. "We believe that not one half of our own citizens are aware of the magnitude of these works, or of many others of a similar character in Richmond," the *Dispatch* intoned, and "it will therefore be always a pleasant task for us to spread before the public anything connected with their condition and progress, which will aid in convincing the Rip Van Winkles of the age that better days are in store for us. Wait five years, and see what the Old Dominion in general, and Richmond in particular, will have accomplished in arts, manufactures,

agriculture and commerce."[1] Richmond's antebellum iron industry was
the city's only major business with a substantial market in the American
South, save one—the trade in human beings. Ironically, the growth and
prosperity of the iron trade would be predicated not on the labor of slaves
but of Northern- and foreign-born whites.

Joseph Reid Anderson, the owner of the Tredegar Iron Works, initially
planned to use slaves as the primary workforce in his ironworks. He shared
the fears of the foreign-born held by other city leaders and viewed slavery
as the proper labor relationship for a Southern industry. The use of slave
workers, however, led to conflict with Northern- and foreign-born workers,
whose skills were essential to the initial success of the works. Anderson
turned back a strike in 1847 and placed slave artisans in the Tredegar rolling mills. His belief that no one had the right to interfere with his use
of slave labor struck a responsive chord among his peers in Richmond. To
most observers, Anderson had conquered his troublesome white workers.
Later developments would expose this judgment as premature. Through
continued workplace resistance, solidarity with fellow artisans, and political activism, white ironworkers maintained a hold on most of Tredegar's
best jobs and forced the master of Tredegar to learn the language and traditions of labor.[2]

The economic growth dreamed of by the *Dispatch* had begun haltingly in
the 1830s. In that decade several iron operations began to take shape along
the banks of the James River in Richmond. The beginnings of railroad development in the capital and the growth of the iron needs of manufactures
spurred this development, as did the James River and Kanawha Canal,
which provided both power and access to western Virginia pig iron. Responding to the quickening of industrial progress, the state legislature
passed acts of incorporation for a number of companies. One of these was
the Tredegar Iron Company, incorporated in 1837. Frank B. Deane Jr., the
company's founder, honored engineer and superintendent Rhys Davies by
naming the works after the Welsh ironworks where Davies had received his
training. The next year the company merged with the contiguous Virginia
Foundry Company, and thus was born the Tredegar Iron Works.[3]

The founders soon turned to a West Point graduate from Botetourt
County, Virginia, to run the struggling firm. Joseph Reid Anderson be-

came the company's agent in 1841. Anderson was a trained engineer and a veteran of turnpike-construction projects in western Virginia. Young and ambitious, he later leased the works from the directors and then in 1848 purchased the ironworks, which continued to operate under various partnerships throughout the remainder of the antebellum period.[4] The Anderson name would be associated with the ironworks for three generations and for more than one hundred years.

Making high-quality wrought and cast iron in large quantities in nineteenth-century America was a complex business requiring a multitude of connections to other places. The northeastern United States, from roughly Pennsylvania northward, contained the best raw materials, the most skilled labor, the greatest capital, and the most active markets. All these factors put the Tredegar Iron Works in Richmond at a distinct disadvantage. Competing with Northern ironworks, as well as established companies in Great Britain, Tredegar's officers found it difficult to make their ledgers balance.

Upon taking full control of the Tredegar Iron Works in 1848, Joseph Reid Anderson set out to conquer the Southern markets for iron, thereby increasing sales and fulfilling the dreams of boosters of Southern industry. Tredegar would not only be a great American ironworks but also a flagship of Southern industry producing for a Southern market. The late 1840s were a time of change for Tredegar's markets. Although Anderson's West Point connections yielded important federal contracts for arms and other iron products, he also saw the fading of his Northern markets with the increased competition from Northern and British manufacturers. Accordingly, Anderson kept a watchful eye on the nascent Southern market. An agent for *De Bow's Review* left several issues at the Tredegar office in 1847 and, anticipating a sale, sent several numbers to Anderson. The somewhat embarrassed ironmaster wrote to the *Review* in mid-1848 apologizing for his tardiness and requested missing back issues and a subscription "as I was much pleased with it." Anderson obviously appreciated the aggressive championing of Southern manufacturers in the journal, and he requested an advertisement be placed for his company. Anderson supported "home industry" whenever possible and began attending Southern commercial meetings as early as 1838, eventually sitting on a committee with James D. B. De Bow, the editor of *De Bow's Review*.[5]

As Anderson attempted to expand into the Southern market, he often used blatant appeals to sectional solidarity. In 1850, Anderson penned a letter to James Gadsden of Charleston, South Carolina, asking him to place a weekly advertisement for Tredegar in the city newspaper with the greatest circulation. Anderson apologized to Gadsden for this imposition, confessing that he wrote "knowing the great interest you always take in Southern Manufactures of every description." Anderson also requested that the paper's editor call attention to the advertisement, if possible, and that "he might venture to say it was a Southern Iron Works & Employed Slave Labor."[6]

"Home manufactures" received vigorous support from Richmond's newspapers, and Anderson's ironworks became the darling of the press in matters of Southern economic independence. Whereas dry goods merchants fumed about Northern hegemony, and then shuffled off to New York for their goods, Tredegar became the rare example of a Richmond business substantially supported by Southern customers. The *Richmond Daily Dispatch*, whose editor strongly advocated Southern manufactures, summarized an article on Tredegar by observing, "the railroad spirit recently manifested in the South, has created here a great demand for locomotives, and it must be a matter of congratulation that they can now be obtained so readily and conveniently. The trouble and cost of going to the distant Northern towns to obtain articles so heavy and difficult of transportation has been a matter of serious consideration. The establishments in the South are now, or soon will be, fully equal to the demand; and we hope our railroad companies, and all who require engine work, will patronise and sustain our own home manufactures."[7]

Anderson especially coveted the belatedly expanding railroad market in Virginia and the South, playing the Southern card in business letters when he thought it prudent. Perusing the *Rail Road Journal*, Anderson eyed approvingly a request for proposals to provide rail to the Alabama and Tennessee River Rail Road, which stipulated the use of rail made in the railroad's home state. Anderson praised the decision in a letter to the line's president, J. W. Lapsley, finding it "gratifying to see that the Southern people are looking into the subject of their own resources and are affording indications that they will not prolong their vassalage to the Northern

States by purchasing from them every article demanded by their increasing importance." Anderson understood that Selma stood many miles from Richmond but probably reasoned correctly that few local firms would rise to meet the challenge of rolling rail.[8]

Likewise, Anderson wrote to a Georgia railroad touting his iron by claiming that "the Richmond & Danville Compy whose rails we have contracted for have subjected our iron to trial since my last to you and find it more than twice the strength of the best English rail." In case high quality did not impress this potential customer, he urged that "we offer our Southern Friends there Iron as low as they can buy at the North. All the advantage we ask is the preference at the same price for a similar article."[9]

Anderson enjoyed considerable success in his campaign to conquer the Southern railroad market. A reporter for the *Dispatch*, touring the Tredegar Iron Works in 1853, found twenty-five locomotives under construction, all for Southern railroads. He observed "every species of iron work necessary for railroads and bridges. In this branch of work we understand that this establishment is doing an immense and rapidly increasing amount of business." While Anderson could not in fact meet the price of Northern and British competitors, he accepted payment in the securities offered by Southern railroads on favorable terms and extended them liberal credit.[10]

Southern railroads offered Tredegar a consistent outlet in the 1850s, but other forays into the Southern market succeeded as well. Tredegar began to make sugar mills in the 1840s, erecting numerous mills and engines in Louisiana. In 1846, Anderson told Judge Joshua Baker of Franklin, Louisiana, that "I was pleased to see from the Planters Banner that my sugar mill erected for Mr. Sparks was so well thought of and trust I shall have further opportunity to exhibit Richmond Manufactures in your section."[11]

A steady flow of "Richmond Manufactures" made their way to the sugar plantations of the Deep South in the 1850s, as the Tredegar Iron Works built and installed sugar mills and engines for many masters, including Bishop Leonidas Polk. Anderson proudly referred to his more prominent Louisiana clients in a letter to a planter in Natchez, Mississippi, and proclaimed, "My entire reliance is upon the Southern people for support and I have reason to thank many of them for their preference." In 1860 he opened an agency in New Orleans to expand further his sugar and lumber mill business in that great commercial capital of the Gulf Coast.[12]

Anderson actively sought intelligence on business opportunities in the developing Southern markets. Scotsman Charles Campbell, Anderson's chief engineer and foundry manager, traveled to Savannah to inquire about the construction of the city gasworks and also planned to "stop in Charleston to visit the Rice Mills." Anderson had written in confidence to his contact in Savannah, Dr. William C. Daniel, revealing his suspicions that a competitor for the Savannah project was also Anderson's rival for construction of the Richmond Gas Works. Anderson implored his Southern associate to keep secret his "*name* or *residence* . . . as I do not know what sort of Yankees exactly I have to deal with nor what means they may adopt to carry their point." [13]

In 1852, Anderson requested R. A. Talley, a former roller at Tredegar, to visit Atlanta, New Orleans, and Chattanooga in pursuit of contracts. Talley provided more than a link to contracts in the South. Anderson recommended him to take charge of a new rolling mill in Georgia, despite his youth. In his letter of recommendation for Talley, Anderson informed the Georgia ironmaster that "if I can aid you by teaching Slaves for you it will afford me pleasure." Anderson's open invitation to a potential competitor reaffirmed his ideological position that "eventually all iron establishments in a slave state must come to the employment of slaves." His successful use of slave workers on turnpike projects and his knowledge of the widespread employment of slaves in blast furnaces and forges near his home in the Blue Ridge region buttressed his belief in the desirability and economy of slave labor. Ironically, it was the pressure that the Cotton South exerted on slave prices that helped limit slave use at Tredegar, even as the master of Tredegar reaffirmed his ideological commitment to the institution in his dealings with Southern planters.[14]

The fate of a slave named Solomon owned by Anderson served to illustrate Anderson's behavior as a typical slaveholder and the difficulties of controlling slaves in an urban, industrial environment. Anderson told Judge Joshua Baker, a long-standing customer and sugar planter in Franklin County, Louisiana, about "a very superior smith (Solomon) very humble and obedient, but drawn off in town as he is, I have determined to sell him."

Anderson apparently thought that Solomon would do better further re- moved from the corrupting influence of a major town, a point also empha- sized by manager John Tanner, who told Baker that "you will find him a most valuable man, but will required to be [']reigned up tight.'" [15]

The Virginia ironmaster already planned to send a sugar mill to Baker's district and proposed to send human capital as well. Anderson informed Baker that "if you want him I will sell him at $1000 and send him out by this vessel or if any one else wants him and will make arrangements for the payment I will send him." Anderson gladly accepted the role of slave trader for the judge, emphasizing again that "it seems to me a good oppor- tunity will be afforded by this vessel to send out Negroes direct." Indeed, manager John F. Tanner later told the judge that "a trader called to see him [Solomon] the day before he left with a view of purchasing him for another party & regretted that he was sold, stating that he thought $1200 could be easily had for him." [16]

Anderson played the dutiful slaveholder at home, holding a typically paternalistic view of his black workers. Most African Americans hired or owned by the company lived in company housing. Unlike the vast major- ity of manufacturers in the city of Richmond, especially the tobacco com- panies, Anderson did not allow the "boarding out" of slaves, except in a few rare instances. Operating very much on the model of the iron plantations of western Virginia near Anderson's family home in Botetourt County, Tredegar resembled an urban plantation.

Likewise, Anderson attempted to address the concerns of masters re- garding hired slaves. He often took the families of hired workers at the re- quest of owners. To one owner he wrote that "it will be a great burden for me to take Henry['s] family and as there are to be 5 children, I don't think the services of the mother will pay the expense of keeping them, by thirty dollars. Yet if you are not willing to make this allowance, I suppose to grat- ify Henry I must take Patty and her children for their victuals & clothes, but will not be willing to pay medical or accouchment expenses. These of course are charges on the owner." [17]

Anderson's attempts to control slaves within the Tredegar compound ran afoul of the urban culture that surrounded the ironworks. Slaves easily slipped into the city's streets and highways, joining thousands of other hired men and women at large in the city. Just a few years after the beginning of operations at the ironworks, the Richmond Police Guard hunted for Woodley, a "runaway [who] belongs to the Tredegar iron company eighteen years old dark mulato." [18]

In 1848 John Tanner posted a missive to P. H. Price of Hanover County, relating that he had "hired of Mr. Richd Hill in Jan last a negro man named George who I learn belongs to you." Tanner informed Price that George had "left these Works more than a month ago without any provocation whatever & has not been scince heard from. I understood that he told the Negroes when he left that he was sick but made no complaint whatever to the manager." Tanner made the reasonable assumption that George had returned to his master's "neighborhood" and asked Price to look for him and, if he was found, "take steps to have him sent home." [19]

George's desire to leave, possibly for a brief furlough to visit family and friends or to see the sights of Richmond, was not unique among Tredegar's slave population. It was easy to be "drawn off into town" like Solomon the blacksmith. A thriving community of African Americans, free and enslaved, beckoned ironworkers and their families, opening to them a world well beyond the confines of the laborers' quarters owned by the master of Tredegar.

Anderson's ardent Southern nationalism and his strong belief in slavery were typical of Richmond's leadership class. Initially, his attitude toward free labor also reflected a strongly Southern orientation. In 1842 Joseph Reid Anderson came before his board of directors with a plan to require skilled white workers to sign five-year contracts and, in turn, train slave workers. Anderson eventually settled on yearly contracts to control his mobile and troublesome white workmen. In an 1845 letter to Pittsburgh manager S. H. Hartman, Anderson sought workmen of various types, including puddlers, but complained that "I would never employ a Pittsburg puddler again—I think unless he is willing to make an agreement under a penalty to work for me one year—say to reserve 10 per cent as you know is now my custom." Despite his reservations, Anderson told Hartman, "If these men are willing to come on these terms I think I may employ them," setting his rate at four dollars per ton.[20]

Anderson continued to use such contracts as a means of employing skilled Northern workers throughout the antebellum era. He wrote to New Yorker Evan Hopkins early in 1847 imploring him to come south, "if you are willing to sign a contract for 12 months that you will be steady &c and to reserve 10% from your pay which you will forfeit and your place in the event of breaking your contract." Anderson assured Hopkins that the money withheld would be "paid to you at the end of the time" and also promised the Yankee ironworker that "if you know another good steady puddler and bring him with you I will give him a furnace." [21]

The withholding of pay until the completion of the yearly contract clarifies Anderson's initial position vis-à-vis his white rolling-mill workers and illuminates a dimension of the conflict that resulted in the 1847 strike. Anderson faced a mobile, rebellious group of craft workers whose primary community was not Richmond or Virginia but a series of interconnected iron-making communities stretching across the American North and West and Great Britain. The worker's skill meant that he held the last resort of worker control—the ability simply to leave with a reasonable assurance of work elsewhere. Anderson battled that control-by-mobility with contracts and the withholding of pay.[22]

Both Anderson's inability to control white labor and his disdain for foreign workmen fueled his desire to replace free workers with slaves. Anderson confessed to John Y. Mason that "from the difficulty of controlling in a slave state the white labor employed at high wages in the manufacture of iron I have come to the determination to introduce slave to a great extent." Anderson echoed other Richmond city leaders and capitalists when he disparaged European-born workers, proclaiming that "I must in self defence take steps to sustain my business against foreign pauper labour and I view it as at the same time philanthropic for the slave owner in the south." [23]

When white workers defiantly went on strike in 1847 over the use of slave workers in skilled positions in the recently opened Armory rolling mill, they drew on their broad knowledge of rights in mills in the North and across the Atlantic. The use of slave workers was not just an affront racially; it contradicted accepted practice in Northern and European establishments that allowed skilled workers to select their helpers. Usually they chose their own children or friends, perpetuating their skill. The workers issued an edict to Anderson demanding the removal of black workers from the Armory rolling mill and the positions in the Tredegar rolling mill that they already held. In addition they demanded a raise in the per-ton rate of pay.[24]

Anderson responded with an address "to my late workmen at the Tredegar Iron Works," informing the strikers that they had discharged themselves. Anderson, who had attempted (and would attempt in the future) to control the movements of his workers through strict contracts, rather disingenuously asserted that "I fully recognized the right of any individual to leave my employment at any time." The city's papers backed Anderson completely, elaborating on his contention that no one could dictate the use of slaves to an employer in a slave state, or, for that matter, in a republic that implicitly and explicitly sanctioned slavery. The work stoppage lasted several months, but eventually the dismissed workers left, and production began again, this time with a considerably greater number of slave artisans.[25]

Anderson's battle with white workers made him even more suspicious of foreign-born workers, highlighting the international dimensions of the labor struggles at Tredegar. Desperate to fill the positions of the striking workers, Anderson attempted to entice a Massachusetts puddler to Tredegar and asked him to look for "one or two more good men," with the proviso that "Americans are preferred." In his address to his striking workmen, Anderson specifically identified the puddlers as Welsh, a fact probably not lost on Anderson after the conflict. Despite his preference for American-born workmen, Anderson would employ many more foreigners because they made up such a large element of the workers in the iron trades.[26]

Anderson may have won the battle, but he did not win the war. In the immediate aftermath of the strike, Tredegar suffered economically as the rolling-mill output fell dramatically. In October 1847, John F. Tanner informed a customer that "every effort has been used to have your orders executed as promptly as practicably; but with an accumulation of orders the result of 2 months stoppage I am hardly able to say when an order of late date is received at what moment it can be executed."[27]

The strike had an immediate and devastating effect on rolling-mill production, falling from 2,543 tons in 1846 to 1,978 tons in 1847, and yearly profits plunged from $57,769 to $19,034. Tredegar's management explained that in 1847 and 1848 operations "were almost totally lost in consequence of a strike by the expert operatives in the Rolling Mill against the introduction of coloured labor in that department." Indeed, in 1848 profits fell further to $9,107 and production bottomed out at 1,885 tons.[28]

Other factors also conspired to reduce the sales of Tredegar's rolling-mill products. British rails and bar iron flooded American markets with the slowing of the rapid railway expansion in England, while a minor economic depression affected business generally. But Tredegar's managers bluntly stated on many occasions that the strike and its aftermath caused the majority of the problem. Officers admitted that "for three years thereafter, 1849, 1850 & 1851, our operations were seriously interrupted in the Rolling Mill by the introduction of such unskilled labor, as we could obtain, and our inability to obtain skilled labor at all, because negroes were employed." Although production finally exceeded 1846 levels in 1852, Tredegar's rolling mills never matched the earlier level of profitability during the antebellum era.[29]

In 1855, the rolling-mill management, while touting its productive capacity to a prospective Northern superintendent, contended that they had averaged 2,795 tons per year "including 2 years that we were almost entirely stopped by the 'strike.'" This statement could only be made because 1853 and 1854 were excellent years. From 1844 to 1852 Tredegar only averaged an anemic 2,295, well below its 1846 production.[30]

Northern antislavery and commercial newspapers carried stories on the Tredegar strike that painted the conflict as an attempt by slave masters to degrade white workmen and reduce them to the status of bondsmen. The stories also highlighted the inherent dichotomy between slavery and industrial progress through free labor. Through published reports and their own informal networks of communication, white rolling-mill workers in the North quickly heard about the Tredegar strike. They did not forget it.[31]

In the years following the strike, Anderson struggled to recruit Northern workers willing to train and work alongside slave workers. In a letter to a Fall River, Massachusetts, puddler, Anderson laid out his plan to use "almost exclusively slave labor except as to the Boss men," believing that "this enables me of course to compete with other manufacturers." In the same letter, Anderson casually assumed that puddler Harrison Row was "no doubt well acquainted with the circumstances of the turn out here last May" and sought to apprise him of "all the facts." Anderson understood that the closeness of the ironworking fraternity and the generally negative coverage in Northern newspapers would create problems for him in recruiting white workers.[32]

The company actively sought new men through their Northern contacts, and Anderson traveled north in the fall of 1847 to talk with customers and potential employees. Manager John F. Tanner wrote roller Michael Lynch in October, at the suggestion of a Mr. Norris, who had also told the Tredegar managers about Harrison Row, the Massachusetts puddler. Norris told the Tredegar management that Lynch "would be disposed to come on to Richmond if [he] could get a good situation" and if the company required a "first-rate Merchant & Guide Mill Roller." Tanner urged Lynch to "call on Mr. Joseph R. Anderson the proprietor of the Works who will be at the Astor House in New York on Thursday Friday & Saturday next who will give you the information you need on the subject." Tanner noted that Norris also wrote to Jersey City, "thinking you might be there."[33]

Throughout 1848 and 1849 Tredegar remained short of skilled white labor. Anderson solicited the services of a roller in Boston through a customer and wrote directly to William Dove at "Ellicotts Rolling Mill" in Baltimore. John F. Tanner wrote in 1849 to John Hays of Lancaster, Pennsylvania, stating that "a good pudler can find employment at the Works at any time nearly, and if you were here now I could give you a job."[34]

The rolling-mill workers who did "come on" to Richmond after the strike often turned out to be less than satisfactory. Heater John W. Starke signed a contract to work for Anderson on August 16, 1847. By March 1848 Anderson had asked James W. Churchill to inform Starke that his contract was terminated "in consequence of repeated violations of his contract." W. L. Sherwood's contract had already been terminated in October 1847, but, more than three months later, Anderson instructed Churchill to tell him "that he will be discharged as soon as a hand is hired to take his place, for absenting himself from his work on the night of the 13 inst [the same night as Starke] & general in attention." The full force of Anderson's contracts only held up when a worker was there to replace a discharged iron-worker, and even in Starke's case Anderson allowed Churchill the discretion of giving Starke "any employment you choose until a hand be employed to take his place—*but not under said contract.*"[35]

In some cases, Northern artisans rejected work at Tredegar even before they started their employment. A frustrated Anderson wrote the proprietor of the Columbian Hotel in 1848 complaining that "Wm Tumey, Michael Spencer, Andrew White, & Patrick Hollohan who made an agreement to work for me and were brought to this city from the north at my expense and were quartered at your hotel at my responsibility on Friday evening last have positively refused to comply with their engagements." The iron-master disavowed any responsibility "for their board & lodging after this date & notice."[36]

Anderson's attempts to discipline his white rolling-mill workers met with continued resistance. Anderson informed John Morgan, a roller, that "it has been brought to my notice that you are intentionally spoiling iron on various occasions. I have directed it to be charged to you and give you warning for fear your wages may be all consumed in that way. I call your attention to your contract." Morgan defied Anderson's control by his intentional sabotage of production, and also through nonperformance of work. Anderson complained in an addendum below his signature that Morgan "refused to work last night without any cause."[37]

While Anderson struggled to control the workplace after the strike, he gave up other aspects of control over his white workers. He had housed many white employees on the Tredegar grounds before the work stoppage. Company housing existed as early as 1839, and by the time of the strike included four multiunit tenements within the confines of the works.[38] The added surveillance provided by these quarters certainly contributed to the good order and discipline of the Tredegar works. A bell rang to call the workers to their labors, and Anderson's night watchman was to "be at the Rolling Mill every evening by five oclock" and "assist in getting the hands regulated . . . for the night turn and go to the Foundry when the bell rings at 6 O Clock to close it up."[39]

After the strike of 1847, Anderson evicted fired white workers from Tredegar housing and most likely used the on-site housing for slave work-ers. The homes of white ironworkers rose quickly on Oregon Hill, the hillside just beyond the canal and ironworks. Modest frame dwellings also spread across Belvidere Street into a neighborhood known as Sydney. When Anderson established the Tredegar Free School, he placed it in Oregon Hill. Workers now created their own community on their own terms, even as Anderson tried to influence them from afar.[40]

In the same period the treatment of white apprentices at Tredegar underwent a similar transformation away from paternalism and toward a more businesslike approach. Anderson no doubt hoped that by apprenticing young Virginians in the iron trade he could eventually mold a Southern-born workforce more amenable to the idea of slave workers and the politics of proslavery. In the 1840s, the Tredegar management worked and trained white boys in the same manner as traditional craft apprentices. For example, Anderson informed John Lindsay that his son Loftus would receive a month's trial, and if he passed muster he would be taken as an apprentice finisher "in the usual form." Loftus would be given winter clothes and "board with some one employed at the works and it is always my wish for the parents to select the boarding house. Should you not make a selection your son will board with Mr. Adam Turner, Head Smith & a very respectable man." The apprentice was protected in a familial relationship within the household of the senior workingman, and Anderson assumed responsibility for the necessities of life.[41]

When the Reverend M. L. Chevers wrote Anderson regarding the employment of his son Richard in 1850, he got a very different response. Anderson replied that he had "made some changes in the terms upon which Boys will be taken at these works in the future. One is that their time will be kept and they will be paid only for their time like all other persons in short I do not take them as apprentices & incur no responsibility for doctors or anything else." Anderson believed that an "industrious & economical" boy "will be able to make some" out of the wages received but recommended that Chevers provide his son with money to buy clothes for the first year. Anderson took no responsibility for housing new apprentices, informing parents that their sons should "through your advice get Boarding in a suitable family." [42]

Anderson's new policy may have also been shaped by his inability to control his apprentices. In 1848 he wrote H. D. Bird in Petersburg informing him that "two of my apprentices have absconded just as they have become qualified to repay me in some manner for instruction recd & support Viz Amon Brown & Jesse Clarke. I have understood Brown is in your employment & I am satisfied it is only necessary for you to know he is my apprentice to discharge him & Clarke too if he is with you. I have postponed advertising them till I hear from you, in hopes they would come home to their work in which event I would now overlook this misconduct." In a postscript, Anderson added that "another of my boys, John Burns, being in all probability advised to it by the two boys concerning whom I have written, has to day gone off. I have very little doubt that he will apply for work in Petersburg and therefore call your attention to him." [43]

Apprenticing young Virginians probably seemed more trouble than it was worth, especially since so few came to the Tredegar Iron Works. Only a handful of apprenticeships appear in the early records, and from January 1859 until the outbreak of the Civil War only eighteen young men entered the business. The white sons of Virginia seem to have had little taste for the hard work of forging iron. Anderson continued to recruit Yankees and the foreign-born from the North. Northern white labor, not slave workers or native whites, would come to dominate the Tredegar Iron Works before the Civil War. [44]

Anderson's boastful claim in 1848 to a Northern puddler that he used "almost exclusively slave labor except as to the Boss men" in his rolling mills greatly exaggerated the number of skilled slave workers he actually employed. Anderson may have forced white workers in the rolling mills to work alongside slaves, but even he and his managers seem to have lost their enthusiasm for skilled slave labor during the 1850s. The opposition of white workmen, as well as the steadily increasing cost of hiring and buying slaves generated by the pull of the Cotton South, made the use of slaves expensive and troublesome. Anderson may have also realized that the marginal savings he achieved with slave labor did not justify antagonizing his white workers. [45]

The number of black skilled workers employed by Anderson in the rolling mills stagnated or fell during the 1850s, even as these departments expanded. In 1850 Anderson pessimistically contemplated selling the skilled slaves he owned, telling a Georgian that "I have not fully determined to sell mine, but if I decline the manufacture of iron as I probably shall at the end of the year I would probably sell all my hands . . . puddlers, heaters rollers &c a choice set of young men & boys about thirty five of them." Using an extremely conservative estimate of the number of men required to run the mill, this workforce was sufficient to fill a significant portion of the skilled positions in the Tredegar rolling mill, but certainly not all.[46] In 1855, Anderson hired his force of slaves to a new partnership running the Tredegar rolling mill and listed twenty-four adult male workers, who could barely fill half the skilled jobs required for the day and night turns. Obviously whites laboring in the mill were not exclusively "Boss men," and Anderson did not attempt to expand his slave workforce after the strike.[47]

In the Armory rolling mill, where the imposition of black workers touched off the 1847 strike, the number of slave workers fell even more dramatically. The total number of African Americans in the Armory Works, skilled and unskilled, stood at a high of forty-two in 1849, and dwindled to twenty by 1858. Dr. Robert Archer only owned four slaves by 1860, which probably accounts for all of the skilled workers in the rolling mill. By the eve of the Civil War the majority of the puddlers appear to have been Irish.[48]

Anderson never challenged the dominance of white skilled workers in Tredegar's locomotive shop, machine shops, and foundries, which grew enormously in the 1850s. These shops became critical to Anderson's business as they began production of locomotives, steam engines, and other complicated machine work, including in the 1850s the engines and boilers for two navy frigates. Anderson erected a new locomotive shop in 1852 on the site of a failed cotton mill adjacent to the Tredegar foundry. A newspaperman wondered at the scale of the operation amid the whirling belts and shafting, watching "many operatives" run lathes, planers, punches, and hammers, and "a casual glance at the aggregate number in the several departments, makes us estimate the whole number at more than a hundred." The visitor also noted that "they were selected for their experience and skill, at the best locomotive establishments of the North, and have all recently become citizens of our city. This number, together with their families, forms an important item in our population, and must of course contribute to the business and prosperity of the city."[49]

Anderson became dependent not only on the skilled workmen in these shops but also on a few highly skilled managers of Northern or foreign birth. For most of its antebellum history the Tredegar Iron Works existed as a series of separate companies and partnerships operating on the same physical site, and Anderson formed several partnerships to operate his machine and locomotive shops in the 1850s. Bostonian John Souther and Scotsman Matthew Delaney became artisan-partners in Anderson's locomotive works.[50]

Delaney, listed as a blacksmith or boiler manufacturer in the Richmond city directories, first immigrated to New England, marrying Connecticut-born Charity Lyman Clapp. Delaney, still a young man at thirty, resided in Virginia by 1850. He became a partner in Anderson, Delaney and Company in 1854, bringing much-needed credibility to a locomotive-building operation in trouble as a consequence of two disastrous boiler explosions in Tredegar engines. As a British-trained craftsman, he doubtless shared the values of manliness and worker control common to machinists, boiler-makers, and molders across the Anglo-American industrial world. Such a man understood how to maintain workplace peace and certainly would not have condoned the imposition of slave artisans into his shops.[51]

Anderson became more adept at dealing with skilled white artisans, perhaps under the tutelage of his artisan-managers. He played a significant role in an elaborate celebration on the first anniversary of the Tredegar Locomotive Works, which included a colorful procession and a grand supper in the upper floor of the new engine shops. Tredegar workers held sway in a torchlight parade worthy of a political campaign, beginning at the ironworks and proceeding through the principal streets to the martial strains of the Armory Brass Band. Carrying "various banners and transparencies," the workers celebrated their trades—"paintings embraced engines, and representations of workmen engaged in various departments of their construction." The workmen held aloft familiar mottoes of labor and industry, including "United to Support, but not combined to Injure," "Support Home Industry," and "Competition, but not Rivalry."[52]

Returning to the works, they stopped at Anderson's house, giving him a "complimentary salutation," and then proceeded to the Virginia State Armory to do the same for Captain Charles Dimmock. At the Armory, the

Massachusetts-born Dimmock spoke to the assembled workmen, as did
Mayor Joseph Mayo and Samuel D. Denoon, a brass founder, city councilman, and Democratic Party activist. Denoon himself had risen from the artisan ranks to own a brass foundry and represented many of the assembled
workers as a councilman for Monroe Ward. The artisans then returned to
the locomotive works for their repast. More than three hundred people sat
down at two long tables running the length of the 150-foot room for the
"war of knives and forks," followed by the drinking of "wine and other in-
vigorating beverages." Anderson presided over the supper from his commanding position at the head of the table, and Virginian William Steptoe,
a Tredegar manager, sat at the foot of the table serving "as Vice President
of the evening." [53]

Toasts and speeches continued until midnight, dominated by politicians
and businessmen. Both Mayor Mayo and Councilman Denoon reprised their
earlier performances. Whig activist A. Judson Crane spoke, as did Oliver P.
Baldwin, the editor of the *Richmond Republican* and holder of Richmond's
state Senate seat from 1853 to 1856. Born in New York, Baldwin strongly
supported Richmond's industrial development. Anderson and Dr. Robert
Archer, Anderson's partner and father-in-law, spoke to the assembled workmen, as did former Tredegar manager Charles Campbell, now the superintendent of the city's gas works. The assembly also called on William H.
Macfarland, a prominent Richmond banker who had assisted Anderson in
his purchase of Tredegar, and listened to Edward Robinson, president of
the Richmond, Fredericksburg, and Potomac Railroad.[54]

Although the report did not include accounts of the speeches, the event
clearly combined the style and form of mass political street action so popular
with Richmond's growing working class, and the more traditional colla-
tions familiar to militia musters and other fraternal groups. The politicians
present, including Anderson, acknowledged the power of the working-class
vote after the loosening of voting restrictions by the state and city in 1851
and 1852.[55]

An event almost a year later gives a better idea of the participation of
workmen in these events. Rolling-mill superintendent Henry McCarty retired because of illness, and his fellow workers feted him at the Mount
Vernon Hotel. Joshua Carey, a Tredegar nail cutter, presented McCarty
with a silver pitcher inscribed to him "by the Artizans of the Armory and

Tredegar Rolling Mills, as a testimony of his skill as a Mechanic, and his capacity as a Superintendent." After Carey delivered a speech of appreciation and MacCarty gratefully accept the tribute, the assembled workmen ate dinner. At the meal's conclusion, Joseph R. Anderson assumed the chair and delivered a short address. The ironmaster expressed the hope that McCarty would recover his health and urged "the mechanics to educate their children, and to improve themselves for the higher position they were to assume in government and society," explicitly recognizing the newfound influence of urban workers on electoral politics.[56]

Next Anderson and others gave a series of toasts, each subtly reflecting the politics of the speakers and audience. Industrialists neatly tied the fortunes of industry and workmen together. Anderson praised "all the establishments and all the mechanics of Richmond—we wish them prosperity." Workmen paid tribute to their own, the producers of society, as when roller Edward Wade honored "the Farmers and Mechanics, the wheelhorses of Virginia." James A. Cowardin, the editor of the *Dispatch*, whose newspaper reported the event, paid tribute to "the Mechanics of Richmond—the right arm of the city, on whom she must rely in her struggle for independence," elevating white workmen to defenders of Southern industry. Workmen, by contrast, emphasized unity rather than a struggle for independence. Mechanic John Bradley, a member of the committee of invitation, invoked "the bonds of our Union—the North and the South—Inseparable now and forever" and later sang "that beautiful national ode, 'The Red, White, and Blue.'" Likewise, Charles Campbell, a native of Scotland, proclaimed that "the North and the South cannot be separated while bound together by Railroad iron."[57]

Anderson probably preferred Cowardin's sentiments to those of his workmen, but he increasingly understood the requirements of forging amity and white solidarity. Moreover, as a frequent candidate for office, Anderson had to moderate his public, if not his private, views. He first served on Richmond City Council in 1847 and entered the state legislature in a special election in 1852. He stood for reelection in 1853, emerging victorious on the Whig ticket.[58]

Anderson felt the wrath of angry working-class voters within a few months of taking his seat in his first legislative session. He signed a petition of clemency to commute the death sentence of a slave, Jordan Hatcher, who had killed his overseer in a tobacco factory. An angry mob of whites, mainly of the working classes, surrounded the governor's mansion demanding Hatcher's execution, and denunciations of the petition signers soon followed, both inside and outside the legislature. This bruising political battle introduced Anderson to a new, more democratic period in Virginia politics. The mobilization of Richmond's working class at the polls after 1852 might have made Anderson even more cautious in his actions and less anxious to become embroiled in open conflict with white workers.[59]

Soon an event occurred that tested the industrial peace at Tredegar. Late in December 1854, Tredegar workers placed a "Notice to Machinists and Boiler Makers" in the *Richmond Daily Dispatch*, alerting "the Mechanics of other cities that we had struck in consequence of our wages being reduced twice in one pay to $1.50 per week less than formerly." They asked their fellow artisans for "assistance in sustaining our rights, and not to let misrepresentations induce you to come to this city, for you will be thereby deceived, as we have been." In just a few days, the workers reported "to the Public . . . a reconciliation . . . between the employers and employees" and retracted the charge of deception. While the details of the resolution of the strike remain unknown, Anderson obviously chose not to challenge his workers directly; accommodation replaced confrontation. The Virginia ironmaster thus avoided the disruption of his Northern labor supply, clearly threatened in the workers' memorial to their fellow artisans. Just as important, he did not alienate a very large group of potential voters.[60]

James A. Cowardin, the editor of the *Dispatch*, assisted in the negotiated settlement of the strike. He had previously been embroiled in a labor dispute at his own newspaper in 1852. Cowardin's views were typical of those city leaders who dreamed of Richmond as a great Southern industrial center, and he understood the importance of working-class whites to that dream. Cowardin himself had entered working life as a thirteen-year-old apprentice in the offices of the *Roanoke Sentinel* in Danville, Virginia. After a stint as foreman at a Lynchburg paper, he traveled to Richmond and became chief clerk to the venerable Thomas Ritchie, the dean of Southern newspaper editors and proprietor of the *Richmond Enquirer*. The Whiggish views of the Westerner Cowardin were directly counter to those of the Democrat Ritchie, but they apparently admired each other greatly. After a

short editorship of the *Times and Compiler,* Cowardin took a hiatus from
the newspaper business before founding Richmond's first penny press, the
Dispatch, in 1850.[61]

Although nonpartisan, the *Dispatch*'s editorials clearly argued for a
strong prodevelopment program characteristic of the old "American system" propounded by Henry Clay and his followers. Cowardin became politically active, serving on the city's board of aldermen in 1852 and in the
state House of Delegates in 1853–54. As a former artisan and industrial
booster, Cowardin understood the need to develop a political consensus
that included white workers. He also knew that his own political career
might be threatened if he challenged working-class voters too vigorously.
Cowardin endured a strike of his own workmen in 1852. The Richmond
Typographical Association petitioned the city's newspapers to abolish Sunday work and all agreed except the *Dispatch.* Presented with a list of grievances, Cowardin and his business partner refused, especially censuring the
attempt of white workers to interfere with slavery by asserting rights over
labor in the pressroom. The Typographical Association denied that they
sought to interfere with slavery, and the strike was finally settled when
Cowardin conceded that typesetters and compositors could remain out of
work until midnight on Sundays.[62]

City leaders seemed less willing to concede to combinations of workers pressing broad pay demands. In 1850 a grand jury of the Richmond
Hustings Court and the city's aldermen brought a presentment against the
Society of Journeymen Cordwainers for its attempt to standardize members' fees. The resolution of the conflict is unknown. In 1859 the city also
rejected the demands of Richmond's hackmen for higher rates and a loosening of work rules proscribed by statute. The strike apparently petered out
as cash-strapped hackmen trickled back to work.[63]

Despite occasional setbacks, city artisans clearly became emboldened in
the 1850s. The city newspapers published the complaints of the Journeymen Granite Stonecutters in 1852. The city's undertakers had reduced their
pay for carving headstones and pressured the white workmen to employ
slaves to reduce costs. The workmen threatened to go elsewhere if their demands were not met. Unlike the Tredegar strike, no ringing defenses of
the right to employ slave labor appeared in response to the demands of the

stonecutters, although the resolution of the work dispute is not known. In fact, white stonecutters in Richmond had proclaimed their control of the trade in a pamphlet published years earlier and sent to fellow artisans in other East Coast cities. The *Constitution, By-Laws, and Bill of Prices of the Association of Journeyman Stone-Cutters of the City of Richmond* established day rates and prices for various types of piecework. The rules strictly forbade working with nonunion artisans and penalized scabs $1.50 per day. Further, the members dictated that "no member of this Association shall work in any shop or yard with a Negro Stone-Cutter, until taken into consideration by this Association." Widely circulated among urban workingmen, such union guides informed itinerant workmen of the conditions, organizational rules, and wages in cities throughout the United States and assisted in the standardization of the artisans' workplaces. Workers' publications also put employers on notice regarding fair labor practices.[64]

Workers' attitudes in Richmond toward employers, control of work, and African Americans sprang from sources that cut across the American landscape. The widely held republican beliefs shared by many American artisans drove them to the conclusion that working at the same professions as slaves demeaned them and their free status. When one group of Richmond artisans sought to oust blacks from the mechanical professions, they declared that "we do not aim to conflict with the interests of slave owners, but to elevate ourselves as a class from the degrading positions which competition with those who are not citizens of the commonwealth entails upon us." Skilled workers believed that free labor and citizenship went hand in hand, and both were "degraded" by contact with slavery and slaves. In addition, the pervasive racial stereotypes carried across American popular culture by minstrel shows, newspapers, and cartoons further defined the racial thinking of the white working class.[65]

White artisans and laborers across the United States acted on these beliefs, and in the North they sometimes did so with tremendous ferocity. The 1841 rampage of white workers through Cincinnati's black neighborhood and antebellum race riots in Philadelphia, Washington, D.C., and other Northern cities clearly had roots in economic competition between whites and blacks. Working-class whites in Southern cities rarely took such violent action because it would have been a direct attack on slaveholders' property.

The political and legal war waged against slave and free-black workers in late antebellum Charleston, one of the few American cities that still maintained a large, skilled, black labor force, was more typical, suggesting that white workers in the South tended to see their newfound muscle at the polls as the means of achieving their goals.[66]

The mobilization of white workers in Richmond during the Jordan Hatcher affair and the strikes launched in the 1850s carried an undertone of racial antagonism common to worker activism throughout antebellum urban America. But these actions also suggested an increasing confrontation with slaveholders, a problem not faced directly by white workers in the North. The Tredegar rolling-mill hands not only protested the use of slave workers but also fought against employers to defend their basic work right to choose their own assistants, thus perpetuating their skill and family fortunes. White workers feared, with some justification, that slaveholders would use slaves to control their wages and labor or to eliminate their jobs outright.

The fears of working-class radicalism held by slaveholders and industrialists also raised the possibility that at least some white workers blamed the system of slavery and not the slave for their condition. The master class certainly exaggerated the threat posed by workers and the foreign-born, but city leaders were essentially correct that the sources of potential radicalism were the same in Richmond as in the rest of urban America. German newspapers in cities as close as Baltimore took radical stands for universal suffrage and the emancipation of slaves. While the evidence is elusive, there does seem to have been a small group of Richmond Germans with similarly radical views. Likewise, at the lowest end of the economic scale, blacks and immigrant whites mixed all-too-freely in neighborhoods, tippling houses, and unskilled occupations. Such racial mixing alarmed city leaders. While Virginia's elite often accused immigrants and Northerners of fomenting trouble with slaves, most of the whites incarcerated in the Virginia State Penitentiary in the 1850s for aiding fugitive slaves were Southern-born artisans.[67]

Whatever the source of workers' discontent, the increasing tendency of city politicians and employers to accommodate white artisans suggests that city leaders saw the day coming when power would have to be shared with the white working class. Politicians of all parties spoke increasingly to the concerns of working-class voters, and they understood that the stirrings of labor activism in the 1850s among ironworkers, printers, and stonecutters would eventually have to be addressed. Despite ideological commitments to Southern nationalism and slavery as a core institution defining their society, even powerful elites could envisage a white man's democracy that included skilled white workers, despite their fears about the dangerous tendencies of foreign-born and Northern workers. Anderson negotiated with his workers on the shop floor, banquet halls, polling places, and streets of the city, learning the language of solidarity and fraternalism. Many other civic leaders in Virginia would come to understand the usefulness of meeting the common man in celebration and commemoration.[68]

After the Sale: Slaves Going South From Richmond, ca. 1853. Eyre Crowe, artist. Oil on canvas. Chicago Historical Society.

British artist Eyre Crowe toured America with William Makepeace Thackeray, visiting Richmond in 1853. He captured the contradictory nature of Richmond's landscape. Slaves begin the trip southward from Richmond's slave jails on a cart but are being transferred to a train. In the background, Jefferson's capitol, a symbol of Republicanism, stands above the factories and smokestacks of Richmond's industrial landscape.

Richmond, Va., from Hollywood Cemetery, 1854. William MacLeod, artist. Lithograph by Endicott and Co., New York. Valentine Museum, Richmond, Virginia.

Hollywood Cemetery beckoned strollers to the western suburbs of the city, offering an experience similar to that of Boston's Mount Auburn and Brooklyn's

Greenwood. The grounds took advantage of a commanding view of the James River and the city. McLeod's view of Richmond typified the urban panoramas produced in the nineteenth century, integrating symbols of industrial progress—trains, factories, and canals—into a bucolic setting.

Fair Grounds of the Virginia State Agricultural Society, 1854. Lithograph by Ritchie and Dunnavant, Richmond. Valentine Museum, Richmond, Virginia.

The city of Richmond purchased an area west of the city in 1851 to serve as a recreational park for urban dwellers. The Virginia State Agricultural Society soon petitioned to use Western Square, as it was originally known, for its annual fair. The society constructed animal stalls around the periphery of the eight-acre fairgrounds and a horse track. Planters, industrialists, and curious city dwellers flocked to the annual fair first held in 1853, and the grounds also hosted a national agricultural fair in 1858. The fair moved to a new site in 1860.

Farmer with beans and corn, n.d. Sixth plate daguerreotype. Valentine Museum, Richmond, Virginia. 34.40.12.

A proud agriculturalist holds the fruits of the harvest. Farmers and planters came to Richmond to sell their produce, buy provisions, and enjoy the entertainments of the capital city.

Installation of the Virginia Washington Monument, 1858. Salt print. Prints and Photographs Division, Library of Congress, Washington, D.C.

Thomas Crawford's Virginia Washington Monument memorialized the state's Revolutionary heroes and eventually included six figures around its base— statues of Thomas Jefferson and Patrick Henry had arrived in 1855 and were installed for the 1858 dedication. Thousands of citizens from across Virginia attended the event despite sleet and rain.

Interment of the Remains of President Monroe in Hollywood Cemetery, Richmond, 1858. Wood engraving from *Frank Leslie's Illustrated Newspaper* 6, no. 139 (July 31, 1858): 135. Valentine Museum, Richmond, Virginia.

Richmonders hosted dignitaries and militiamen from New York during the reburial of James Monroe in 1858. Widely hailed for its promotion of sectional harmony, the event included banquets, parades, and a speech by Governor Henry A. Wise.

Slave Auction at Richmond Virginia, 1856. Eyre Crowe, artist. *The Illustrated London News,* Sept. 27, 1856. Valentine Museum, Richmond, Virginia.

The white men present at the slave auction threatened British artist Eyre Crowe as he sketched this scene. His portrayal of the proceedings justified their fears. Published in *The Illustrated London News,* the image and text conveyed the horror of the scene for British readers.

Advertisement for Pulliam and Betts, Slave Traders, 1858. Wood engraving from E. M. Coffield and Co., comp., *Richmond Business Directory, and Merchants and Manufacturers' Advertiser* (Richmond: John W. Randolph, 1858). Valentine Museum, Richmond, Virginia.

The auctions held at the Odd Fellows Hall demonstrated the centrality of the sale of human beings to Richmond's commercial and civic life. Located near popular hotels and other public halls, the building was within a block of Wall Street, where several traders maintained their slave jails. Wall Street was also known as "Lumpkin's Alley" after Robert Lumpkin, one of the city's most active slave traders.

African-American Nurse with Emily and Ann Glasgow, ca. 1858. Photograph. Valentine Museum, Richmond, Virginia. Urban slavery was overwhelmingly a domestic institution, even in an industrial city like Richmond. Thousands of slaves served in upper-class households, often traveling between country and city. This unidentified nurse of the Glasgow family may have worked at both Green Forest, the family plantation in Rockbridge County, and the Richmond residence of Francis T. Glasgow, who was a manager at the Tredegar Iron Works in the mid-1850s.

Sally Boles Gladman, ca. 1852. Sixth plate daguerreotype. Valentine Museum, Richmond, Virginia. V.87.26.

Sally Boles Gladman experienced many of the harsh realities faced by slave women. Her first husband, Sam Boles, belonged to a Mr. Randolph. Mann S. Valentine Sr. purchased Sally Boles and her four children for nine hundred dollars in 1831 from the estate of his father-in-law. She raised several Valentine children and by the 1850s was known as Sally Gladman. Her son Henry Boles also served the Valentines, but sons James and Stephen Boles were either sold or taken to another part of the South by the 1850s. The fate of her daughter, Milley Ann Boles, is unknown.

Mann Satterwhite Valentine Sr., ca. 1852. Half plate daguerreotype by Montgomery P. Simons, Richmond. Valentine Museum, Richmond, Virginia. X53.1.45.

Mann Satterwhite Valentine Jr., ca. 1855. Sixteenth plate daguerreotype. Valentine Museum, Richmond, Virginia. X53.1.69.

The son of a planter, Mann Satterwhite Valentine Sr. came to Richmond in 1807 and rose from a guard in the penitentiary to become one of the city's most prominent dry-goods merchants. Every year he made several trips to the North to purchase goods. His namesake son reluctantly followed in his footsteps, and Mann Valentine Jr.'s experiences buying in the great Yankee metropolises increased his belief in the South's moral superiority.

Elizabeth Ann Valentine and Philip Elliott, 1844. Quarter plate daguerreotype.
Valentine Museum, Richmond, Virginia. L.68.80.7.

The daughters of Mann S. Valentine Sr. visited the North with their father and
shared the general disdain for Yankee ways. Elizabeth Ann Valentine wrote several
letters describing a buying spree at Stewart's Palace in 1850. On the same visit her
merchant father bought her an extensive trousseau for her wedding to William
Frederick Gray.

First African Baptist Church, 1865.
Prints and Photographs Division,
Library of Congress, Washington, D.C.

Founded in 1841, First African Baptist
Church served the needs of nearly three
thousand black congregants by the Civil
War. The church was also one of the
largest public meeting halls in the city,
hosting political conventions and popular entertainments.

Robert Ryland, n.d. Photograph by
Charles R. Rees and Company,
Richmond. Virginia Baptist Historical
Society, Richmond.

For more than twenty-five years
Robert Ryland preached at First African
Baptist Church and attended meetings
with the African-American Board of
Deacons. Ryland often walked a fine
line with the white community, facing
criticism for passing out mail to black
congregants and for the church's
modest educational activities.
Ryland also served as president
of Richmond College and
penned a catechism for
black Christians.

Gilbert Hunt, ca. 1860. Photograph by Smith and Vannerson, Richmond. Valentine Museum, Richmond, Virginia.

First African Baptist Church deacon Gilbert Hunt lived one of the most remarkable lives of any antebellum Richmonder. A slave blacksmith who saved numerous lives in the 1811 theater fire, Hunt bought his freedom in 1829 and removed to Liberia in 1830. He returned quickly, disillusioned with the African colony. He angered colonizationists when he discouraged other free blacks from going to Liberia. Hunt's church activities also showed him to be unafraid of controversy or white authority.

View from Gamble's Hill, ca. 1856. Edward Beyer, artist. Tinted lithograph with additional hand-coloring by Anst v. W. Loelliot, Berlin. Plate 18 from *Album of Virginia; or, Illustrations of the Old Dominion.* Richmond, 1858. Valentine Museum, Richmond, Virginia.

German-born artist Edward Beyer created his *Album of Virginia* "to illustrate the natural curiosities, the favorite resorts of pleasure and health, and the many triumphs of art and skill, as developed by the improvements in the State." The view looking south from Gamble's Hill highlights both natural and man-made features in Richmond's landscape. A train crosses the James River on the Richmond and Petersburg Railroad Bridge (1838) while strollers look down on the industrial complex drawing power from the James River and Kanawha Canal, including (*left to right*) the Virginia State Armory (formerly the Virginia Manufactory of Arms), the Armory rolling mill, the Tredegar Iron Works, and the Crenshaw Flour Mill.

Joseph Reid Anderson, 1865. Photograph by Matthew Brady. Prints and Photographs Division, Library of Congress, Washington, D.C.

Anderson, a West Point graduate, posed after the Civil War in his Confederate uniform. A former Whig turned Southern nationalist, Anderson built the Tredegar Iron Works into the most dynamic ironmaker in the South. During the Civil War Anderson struggled to produce Confederate ordnance while losing many of his Northern- and foreign-born workers, turning instead to enslaved African Americans.

Matthew Delaney and son, ca. 1845–48. Ambrotype by Wells and Kneeland, Northampton, Mass. Valentine Museum, Richmond, Virginia. P.77.28.4b.

Charity Lyman Clapp, ca. 1845–48. Ambrotype by Wells and Kneeland, Northampton, Mass. Valentine Museum, Richmond, Virginia. P.77.28.4a.

Matthew Delaney, his wife, and his son posed for photographs in Northampton, Massachusetts. The Scots ironworker first settled in New England, marrying Connecticut-born Charity Lyman Clapp. The family moved to Richmond before 1850. One of the thousands of British ironworkers who found ready employment in American shops, Delaney became a partner with Joseph Reid Anderson in the Tredegar Locomotive Works in 1854.

*To the Richmond Light
Infantry Blues,* 1841.
John B. Danforth,
artist. Hand-colored
lithograph by P. S.
Duval, Philadelphia.
Published by Huddy
and Duval. Valentine
Museum, Richmond,
Virginia. 47.100.

The Richmond
Light Infantry Blues
soldier stands in his
military splendor
while his company
musters on Richmond's
Capitol Square. Be-
hind the soldier is the
Executive Mansion; the
United States flag flies
over Jefferson's classi-
cally inspired Capitol.

George Wythe Munford, 1855.
Half plate daguerreotype by
William A. Pratt, Richmond.
Private Collection.

William Pratt's camera
captured George Wythe
Munford's noble bearing and
the tool of his trade—the pen.
Legal scholar, author, and clerk
of the House of Delegates for
twenty-six years, Munford was
the secretary of the commonwealth when this image was
taken. A former captain of the
Richmond Light Infantry
Blues, Colonel Munford often
attended militia events.

Militiamen of the First Virginia Regiment, Charles Town, Virginia, 1859. Ambrotype, probably by Lewis Dinkle, Charles Town. Valentine Museum, Richmond, Virginia.

Members of companies of the First Virginia Regiment mug for the camera at Charles Town, Virginia, the site of the trial and execution of John Brown. Most of the men probably belonged to the Richmond Grays, who had recently returned from a fraternal visit with fellow militiamen in New York. A member of the Virginia Rifles wearing a tall hat stands in the back. The Harper's Ferry Raid and Brown's trial caused intense excitement in Richmond, even prompting rumors of a slave insurrection.

Member of Company K, Virginia Rifles, ca. 1858–59. Sixth plate daguerreotype. Private Collection.

Richmond's German militia company formed in 1850 and regularly took part in national, state, and community celebrations. After their muster into Confederate service, however, the soldiers of the Virginia Rifles became increasingly disenchanted with the Southern cause. The company totally disbanded when the Confederate Congress exempted non-domiciled aliens from service in 1862.

Union banner, 1855. Painted banner on linen with silk and wool thread made by Rachel Simon Lewis, Richmond. Chicago Historical Society.

Rachel Simon Lewis made this banner for a fair in 1855 to celebrate Washington's victory at Yorktown. The day of the surrender (October 19) was a staple of the calender of militia companies. Like many militia flags, the banner combined state and national icons— Washington, a great Virginian and American, holds a United States flag aloft. Lewis flew the banner from her window to greet Union soldiers after the fall of Richmond on April 3, 1865.

Henry Page, ca. 1852. Sixth plate daguerreotype by Montgomery P. Simons, Richmond. Valentine Museum, Richmond, Virginia. X.53.1.66.

This unlabeled image is part of a group of Valentine family photographs and resembles the bust of Henry Page executed by Edward V. Valentine (*below*). Page's prominence in family lore further suggests that the man pictured is the patriarch of the Valentine's slave family. In 1856 Page replied to a letter from a son "whom he had never expected to hear from again," sending news of friends and family. Masters controlled the use of the mails by slaves, and such letters are exceedingly rare.

Uncle Henry, ancien régime, 1873. Marble bust by Edward V. Valentine. Valentine Museum, Richmond, Virginia.

Edward V. Valentine's bust of his family's former slave evoked the vision of content, happy servants held by many white Virginians.

Petit Jury Selected to Try Confederate President Jefferson Davis for Treason, 1867.
Photograph by the Cook Studio, Richmond. Valentine Museum, Richmond, Virginia.

The jury selected to try Jefferson Davis included noted Unionists John Van Lew
and Burnham Wardwell, political maverick Martin Meredith Lipscomb, and black
labor and political leaders Lewis Lindsay and Joseph Cox. Biracial alliances would
characterize late-nineteenth-century Richmond politics.

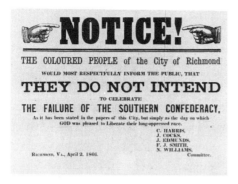

Notice! The Coloured People of the City of Richmond . . . Do not Intend to Celebrate the Failure of the Southern Confederacy . . . But Simply as the Day on Which God was Pleased to Liberate Their Long-Oppressed Race, April 2, 1865. Printed broadside. Virginia Historical Society, Richmond.

Emancipation Day, 1888. Photograph by the Cook Studio, Richmond. Valentine Museum, Richmond, Virginia.

Richmond's black community began celebrating Emancipation Day on April 3, 1866, the first anniversary of Richmond's capture by Union troops. African American organizations and militias paraded through the city's streets, and black homes and businesses displayed American flags and banners featuring popular icons, such as Abraham Lincoln. Despite white opposition, African Americans continued to commemorate the day until the early twentieth century.

CHAPTER SIX

Virginia and Union

We are Virginians. We owe allegiance to Virginia. Here are her coat of arms and her motto—"Virginia"—"Sic semper tyrannis."—where our Mother leads, we will follow. We have no fear that she will lead where her sons may not follow.

She is virtuous and prudent and wise, and when she plants her standard and unfurls her flag, ours will be planted by its side, and we shall be there to give it to the breeze and keep it afloat. But we are more than Virginians. We are citizens of the United States, citizens of this model republic. There are her stars and here her stripes. There is her Eagle with outstretched wing, extended over the ocean and the land, and underneath is the revered motto "The Union." The Union!

A union of lakes and lands,

A union none may sever;

A union of hearts, and a union of hands,

Oh, the flag of the Union forever.

GEORGE WYTHE MUNFORD, 1851

olonel George Wythe Munford proudly surveyed the new silk flag that he had just accepted on behalf of his old company, the Richmond Light Infantry Blues. Men in crisp blue uniforms and plumed shakos stood before him in rank and file on Capitol Square. Munford was in his element. Coming to the ceremony that November day in 1851, he might have remembered visiting his father for the first time in the Capitol, or his own installation as the clerk of the House of Delegates twenty-six years before. Perhaps he recalled recording the passionate speeches of delegates to the Virginia Constitutional Convention of 1829—

30 as secretary of that body. No doubt he also thought about the many parades he had led to Capitol Square at the head of his old company.

The forty-eight-year-old Munford's noble face and easy manner gave
him the look and air of a Roman patrician—a proper countenance for a
man who had spent much of his working life in the halls of Jefferson's classical temple on Shockoe Hill. But Munford understood that a new age of
democracy had come to the Old Dominion. That very year a new state constitution had been approved by the people, permitting universal white
manhood suffrage, and new faces crowded Richmond's streets. Despite his
own personal belief that Virginia was a sovereign member of a confederacy
of states, Munford understood that many of the men before him held different views. Munford's unifying invocation of Virginia and the Union in
describing the Blues' new flag would set well with the clerks, shopkeepers,
and artisans who stood in the ranks, no matter their political persuasion or
place of birth.

Richmonders shared in a national culture of public ceremony that integrated large numbers of citizens in a common experience and often emphasized the powerful symbols of America's Revolutionary heritage. The
main streets and public centers of cities served as the venues for these
events, which attracted a diverse group of participants and audience. In the
decades after the Revolution symbolic acts and public ceremony had acquired deep meaning for Americans. Public discourse, rhetoric, and ceremony conveyed information in a world of limited literacy; common people
understood the complex meanings in political and artistic performances
and events. The denizens of the Bowery did not attend Shakespeare simply
for its more bawdy or violent aspects but understood the subtle human
drama drawn out in the tales of treachery, kinship, and flawed character.
Likewise, parades and ceremonies on national holidays retold the American creation story and inspired patriotism through a common past.[1]

Virginia's political and militia leaders recognized the power of public
commemoration to meld heterogeneous bodies of white men. Joseph Reid
Anderson employed the familiar pageantry of labor parades and grand banquets to solidify his standing among his Tredegar workers; militia leaders
rallied their men through a culture of manly behavior and ritual brotherhood, reinforcing values of loyalty, conviviality, and patriotism the soldiers

shared with urban men in other East Coast cities during elaborately staged visits.[2]

The common values shared by urban artisans and clerks united militiamen, and so did Virginia's unique historical patrimony. Despite the intense sectionalism often expressed by Richmond's newspapers and States' Rights advocates, the public culture of Virginia's capital, like George Wythe Munford's speech, emphasized the reconciling of state and national identity. The militias celebrated Virginia's political heritage, best articulated through the figure of Washington, a nonpartisan and transcendent figure, a Virginian as well as the "father of his country." Militia toasts, flags, and parades honored the story of a glorious and powerful state—the "mother of Presidents"—and the ideal of the national Union.

Naturally, cracks in this facade of unity sometimes appeared. Officers sometimes revealed their States' Rights views, although these feelings were rarely displayed publicly before early 1861, and soldiers occasionally clashed along class or partisan lines. But militia events and organizations endured only infrequent disruptions because of the raising of sectional issues; soldiers and officers tried mightily and successfully to create a nonpartisan environment in a very partisan world. White, male Richmond may never have been more unified than in these celebrations, contributing to a persistent Unionism that endured until April 1861.

Militias in Virginia and America harked back to the citizen-soldiers of the American Revolution, state-level military organizations that at least theoretically included all male citizens of a certain age. Yearly musters were held to drill the state militia, although individuals could avoid these musters by paying a fine, a system that irked many men who were financially unable to do so. The line militia, those units made up of the general citizenry, were largely moribund for much of the antebellum period. Volunteer militias, companies raised by individuals in the community and having frequent drills and organization, were the most active part of the state militia system.

From their inception, the militia performed many duties. The most important was as a ready fighting force in case of a foreign or domestic threat. In 1807 the Richmond Light Infantry Blues offered their assistance in the aftermath of the *Leopard-Chesapeake* incident and were briefly mustered into service. The United States again called on the Blues during the War of 1812. The company served on active duty in Virginia in anticipation of a British attack on the state that never materialized.[3]

The city provided two companies for a Virginia regiment raised for service in the Mexican War. The Richmond Grays, formed just a few years before the conflict, had many members who, because of family and community obligations, were unable to meet the terms of extended service required by the U.S. government for that war. But the Grays did raise a company of men who were able to serve. Captain Robert G. Scott recruited in Richmond and surrounding counties to fill the company's ranks. Captain Edward C. Carrington raised another Richmond unit known as Carrington's Rangers, and both companies took part in the occupation of Mexico.[4]

Domestic threats outweighed national conflicts in the thinking of state leaders. The possibility of slave insurrection was foremost in the minds of Virginia's militia officials. Writing to Colonel William Ligon in 1832, John Rutherfoord acknowledged Ligon's communication regarding reform of the militia system. In keeping with his own views, however, he despaired of any reform: "For my own part, I have nearly abandoned all hope of ever seeing our militia properly instructed [and] Drilled, and were it not for our *slave population,* I w[ould]d be willing to dispense even with the few musters we have; which, *conducted as they are,* are of no service to either officers or men." In 1829, Rutherfoord had complained to Governor William Branch Giles that "having rcd orders to hold my company in readiness for service in consequence of the rumours which have been circulating respecting an insurrectionary spirit among the slaves, I feel it my duty to inform the Executive that the gun carriages and implements attached to the ordnance which have been placed under my command are at present unfit for service."[5]

The fears of insurrection were hardly imaginary. The Richmond Light Infantry Blues saw their first active service in the aftermath of the discovery of the slave Gabriel's well-planned 1800 plot, and rumors of insurrection kept the company vigilant. The years preceding and after the Nat Turner insurrection seem to have been especially tense. In 1831 the Blues announced that "whereas considerable commotion has been created among the citizens of Richmond and its vicinity by events which have recently transpired in the lower part of Virginia, The Richmond L. I. Blues believing it to be their duty to afford to their fellow citizens all the safety and protection in their power, will hold themselves constantly on the alert, and ready for action at a moments warning." Having heard that a "Camp meeting is to be held on Monday in the County of Chesterfield, between the city and the Coal Pitts and to which a military force will probably be ordered to ensure tranquility and quiet in the neighborhood," the Blues resolved that "the services of the company be tendered to the Executive for the purpose of repairing to the said Camp Meeting and there remaining until it is ended, providing such a measure shall be deemed necessary." [6]

In 1829, the Blues "proposed to try the expedient of raising a band of free colored men, and for this purpose have caused inquiries to be made, from which it appears by a list furnished and hereto attached that thirteen respectable men of the above class have signified their consent to serve the company two years for their instruction." A long tradition of blacks providing martial music stretching back to the American Revolution may have inspired this decision, as well as the service of some blacks in that struggle. Some of the wealthiest and most skilled free blacks in the city answered the Blues' call. The list included prominent free black barbers and artisans such as George W. Ruffin, Lomax B. Smith, and Benjamin W. Judah. Tied closely to white society and patronage, these men had the ironic task of providing patriotic airs for a company devoted to suppressing any signs of liberty and independence among slaves. The "Blues Band" was quickly retired, however; members occasionally attended events but provided no music for the company. Whites viewed their muted presence as affirmation of the benevolent state of race relations in the city and the loyalty of the black aristocracy. Like the band, Virginia's African-American population was largely excluded from the public commemorations of the Revolutionary past in the late antebellum era. Despite the black contribution to the struggle for freedom—well known to African Americans—most whites viewed blacks not as descendants of the Revolutionary generation but as a revolutionary threat requiring the vigilance of the state. [7]

The militias attended many events with a potential for public disorder to show the authority of the government. In April 1852 the Richmond Light Dragoons, Richmond Grays, Montgomery Guard, and Young Guard attended the hangings of Thomas Reed and Edward Clements for mutiny.

Just a month later, companies were called out to protect the governor from mobs of angry citizens outraged at the commutation of the death sentence of Jordan Hatcher, the young factory slave who had killed his overseer.[8]

In 1851, the Richmond volunteer companies formed the core of the First Regiment of Virginia Volunteers, and the city's citizen-soldiers remained in that organization until the Civil War.[9] By that time Richmond had a few volunteer companies that had celebrated several decades of service, but most companies were of relatively recent vintage, and the names of some units reflected the increasingly working-class and immigrant composition of the area's population, such as the Richmond German Rifles (soon renamed the Virginia Rifles), Caledonian Guard, and the Mechanic Guard. The Mechanic Guard, first organized in 1853, truly had officers from the mechanics' ranks, such as Leroy Barfoot, a tradesman who worked at several iron manufactories in the 1850s. Other companies represented growing "suburbs" with concentrations of immigrants, such as Union Hill, an area where many Germans settled. The Union Guard, formed in 1854, was defunct after a few years, as was the Mechanic Guard.[10]

The sight of mechanics and clerks executing military maneuvers on the city streets seemed incongruous to some. Jefferson Wallace, a veteran of the hardscrabble life of the California gold fields, observed the Richmond Light Infantry Blues marching down Main Street and found "their appearance . . . so ridiculous that I could hardly contain myself. It put me in mind of children playing soldiers with their little paper hats, tin swords and martial like strut, such things to me look childish." Wallace's derogatory comments were not typical of most observers' perceptions, but militia officers did struggle to keep their citizen-soldiers well drilled and uniformed.[11]

The volunteer companies typically purchased their own uniforms, and sometimes arms, and committed themselves to regular meetings, drills, rules, and dues. Maintaining enthusiasm for soldiering was difficult, and the cost of equipment and dues strained the resources of men of lesser means who increasingly made up the core of militias in the 1850s. One recently promoted clerk reported sardonically that "I have been to the expense of a sword to support the dignity of my 'sargeantship.' My military glory has cost me thus far about $35.50." He might well complain; his an-

nual salary amounted to only $400. Young men continued to join compa-
nies in large numbers despite the cost, although turnover was high.[12]

The Richmond Grays, formed in 1844, almost disbanded a few years after their formation because members were not attending drills and paying
dues, but recovered in the late 1850s. Even Richmond's oldest and most
venerable company, the Richmond Light Infantry Blues, felt the effects of
flagging interest. In 1854 the Blues' frustrated captain, John M. Patton Jr.,
offered his letter of resignation because "drill after drill and meeting after
meeting has been ordered, and though there has always been a small and
faithful band to respond to the summons, my heart has been discouraged
and my efforts have been crippled by the fact, that a large number of the
members have in many instances placed their duty to the company second
to any object of caprice or pleasure, and have been rarely in attendance."
Eventually the company flourished again, due in no small part to the enthusiasm generated by the company's trip to Philadelphia in 1855. The late
1850s brought a general revival of martial fervor among Richmond's young
men along with more frequent participation in public ceremonies and
parading by companies.[13]

The company rosters of the Richmond Light Infantry Blues and the
Richmond Grays during the 1850s provide an opportunity to examine the
composition of two established companies. Both companies were made up
of the broad middle of Richmond society, including clerks, artisans, and
merchants, and both had immigrant and Northern-born members, thus
giving new meaning to the constant references to militia men as ideal examples of Virginians.

The citizen-soldiers of the Richmond Light Infantry Blues who went
to Philadelphia in 1855 included a steamboat company agent, a watch-
maker, several carpenters, and the superintendent of a railroad. Of the
thirty-four men identified in sources (out of fifty-two men on the roster),
none was listed as a laborer, and John M. Patton Jr., the company's captain,
was the only lawyer. Four men were foreign-born, and four were born in
Pennsylvania. Of the twenty-six Virginians, at least two had one parent of
foreign birth, and four had at least one Northern-born parent. The devotion
to Virginia so evident in militia activities was apparently fostered in men
born well outside its borders.[14]

The *Richmond Daily Dispatch* perhaps exaggerated the middle-class standing and Virginian demeanor of the Richmond Grays who traveled to New York in 1859. Proclaiming them "fair types of citizen soldiers," the paper claimed that "all of them are business men in good standing—each one feels that he has the honor of his noble corps and beloved State to maintain—and none of them will so far forget their social positions at home, as to transcend, in a single instance, the bounds of strict propriety." Despite this observation, the Grays were a decidedly more working-class, Yankee, and ethnic outfit than the Blues. Out of a total of forty-three men identified from a roster of sixty-eight, eight were foreign-born, seven Northern-born. Of the twenty-eight Virginians identified, four had at least one foreign-born parent, and three had at least one Yankee parent. As with the enlisted men, some officers also hailed from the North; for example, two of the three lieutenants were born in New York. Artisans made up a larger percentage of the rank and file than in the Blues, including such occupations as carpenters and pattern-makers.[15]

The preservation of order and decorum in the companies hinged on muting partisan expressions and feelings among soldiers of widely different political persuasions and regional affiliations. The captain of the Grays was Wyatt M. Elliott. A native of Buckingham County, he graduated from the Virginia Military Institute in 1842 and studied law at the University of Virginia. In addition to his legal practice, Elliott was an editor of the *Richmond Whig* and a party stalwart. One of the privates in his company was John H. Askew, a New York–born printer at the Democratic *Richmond Enquirer*.[16]

For the artisans and petty shopkeepers of the companies, joining provided a way to make business connections and take part in manly camaraderie with friends and associates. Many men obviously joined at the same time, as shown by common workplaces, trades, residences, or family connections. For instance, Privates David McConochie and John Learmont, both carpenters of Scots birth, boarded together. Virginians Richard M. Crawford and Miles T. Phillips were partners in Phillips and Crawford, upholsterers and paperhangers. Private Louis F. Bossieux clerked at his father's confectionary shop, the elder man serving as a lieutenant. Jewish immigrant Philip Whitlock, a tailor, had only reached Richmond from Eastern Europe via Germany in 1854, and recalled that "I had no way of taking any exercise and thought that would be a good way of improving my health and getting in among men, and was quite a diversion from the daily toil." [17]

Other immigrants joined mainstream units for more ideological reasons. At the Blues' Fourth of July festivities at Slash Cottage (now Ashland) in 1855, Charles Bennett raised a toast to the "health and prosperity" of Private John Hartz, a former captain of the Virginia Rifles. Hartz responded by noting that "I could have joined other companies as some would think with fairer prospects" and proceeded to explain openly and forcefully his reasons for joining the enlisted men after enjoying the privileges of rank: "I had the promise of office, but what they thought would induce me to join them, was the very reason why I did not. I seek no office—I never sought it amongst my own countrymen, for I was elected captain of my old company, without asking any for the office. I accepted the trust only because I desired to serve my adopted company, should there be a call for my services." Hartz clearly valued his Washingtonian belief in service without regard to personal benefit or aggrandizement.[18]

In the end, Hartz felt he could not accomplish his patriotic goal in his all-German unit. He emphasized that he was captain "for two years and could have held it longer if *I had sold my principles for the sake of office.* Finding that I could serve my country no longer in that capacity I resigned my commission, and I am with you a private of the Blues, to accomplish that which I could not do as Captain—namely: to serve my country in case of need." Hartz, born in the German States, explained that America was "my country, for all my interests lie in America; my wife is American, my children are Americans. As for myself I have been so long in this country, that I believe if I was to go back to my 'Father Land' I would feel as a 'stranger in a strange land' and long to go back to the Land of my adoption." Hartz then toasted "*Our country's Flag* 'The star spangled banner, oh long may it wave, over the land of the free and the home of the brave,' " . . . to which Sergeant Davis "proposed '3 times 3' for Private Hartz which were given with a will." [19]

Aside from times of public crisis, slave revolts, and national wars, militias served as places for men to display fraternal feeling. Membership in a militia was in many ways similar to membership in a fraternal order or club. One common aspect was attendance at unit members' funerals. "In case of the death of any member of this corps," the citizen-soldiers in the

Montgomery Guard were required to "attend his funeral in complete uni-
form, with crape on the left arm, to confer military honors." This was
also a standard practice for fraternal orders. In 1854 a woman living in
Richmond "saw a funeral procession pass by of one of the Young Guards—
Mr. Britton—he was escorted to the grave by the masons, odd fellows &
Guards." The next spring Jefferson Wallace related to his brother Charles
Wallace the burial of another member of the Young Guard "with great
pomp," who had been tragically "shot at a Target firing." Some companies
even paid benefits in times of sickness or misfortune.[20]

"Manliness" and "brotherhood" were important concepts in militia
life. Target shooting, social drinking, and general conviviality emphasized
traditionally male behavior. The raucous nature of these events could try
even the owner of a lager beer saloon. Johann Gottfried Lange traveled
with his German company and other militias, and "through irregular
meals and a lot of drinking during these days I didn't feel so good and was
glad to sit in a corner of the train and take a little nap. But hardly had I
fallen asleep when a group of the [Baltimore] Law Greys came into our
compartment with glasses and champagne bottles in their hands. No one
dared to think of sleeping. Soldiers were running back and forth and it
seemed as if an extra wagon full of liqueur and wine had been hung onto
the locomotive."[21]

The festivities reported by Lange, with their frequent toasts and colla-
tions, were common to many militia events, but the German saloon-
keeper may have been less inhibited about reporting rowdy behavior than
official or press reports. Newspaper accounts of militia events made frequent references to the drinking of spirits, but the *Richmond Republican*
noted in 1852 that the Blues would not serve alcoholic drinks at any entertainments or dinners in the future. Perhaps fired by a recent Sons of
Temperance national meeting in Richmond, Corporal Charles Bennett offered a resolution at the Blues meeting on December 15, 1852, at Lafayette
Hall "as an amendment to the by laws 'that hereafter the Blues would not
use or have at any of their dinners or entertainments any wines or Liquors
as a company.'" The amendment "gave cause to quite an animated debate,
which was participated in by Messr. Paul C. Kimbrough and Martin M.
Lipscomb against the passage of the resolution, and by Corpl Bennet,

Sergt Trueman and others in favor of the passage of the resolution, when
the vote was taken which resulted in an unanimous adoption (except two)
of the resolution." [22]

In congratulating Bennett on the correctness of his position, the *Richmond Republican* emphasized the superior soldiering of sober men and felt
that "our merchant citizens will now feel that one *great objection* to permitting their young friends joining Volunteer Companies has been done
away with." As a druggist and merchant, Bennett would have no doubt
agreed with the *Republican*, but at least some working-class men in the
company did not, such as Martin Lipscomb, a bricklayer. Lipscomb was an
outspoken advocate of the "bone and sinew" of Richmond's population,
campaigning vigorously first for mayor and then successfully for the position of city sergeant while a member of the Blues. His campaigns transformed Richmond's politics from relatively predictable affairs between
gentlemen who rarely bothered to mount the hustings into classic American urban contests, fought out in saloons, militia halls, and the streets.
Lipscomb would be elected captain of the Mechanic Guard after his stunning upset of city sergeant John M. Fergusson in 1855.[23]

The "Blues bowl," which had been fraternally passed from man to man
at Blues events for many years, was not in retirement long. Eventually tradition and drinking won out, for the temperance resolution was repealed by
a vote of the company just four months later.[24] Replying to a toast at a
May 1853 celebration, George Wythe Munford quipped that the last time
he mingled with his "old comrades [he] was astonished beyond measure at
finding myself in the midst of a teetotal society, surrounded . . . by the
Governors aids, Lemonade and Promenade." He recounted the allusions
he had heard to "the well of science and the Pierian Spring and the limpid
stream, the refreshing Brooks, the cool & health giving draughts of the
water of life," then marveled that "every body gloried in wounding &
bruising and killing old John Barleycorn," for

> They took a plough & plough him down
> Put clods upon his head
> And they had sworn a solemn oath—John Barleycorn was
> dead.

"But it seems like a fulfilment of the prophesy to see what I see around me now," Munford exclaimed, again breaking into a verse of the ancient British folk song:

> But genial spring came trooping in
> And showers began to fall
> John Barleycorn got up again
> And so surprised them all.[25]

While old veterans of the militia like Munford often reacted with bemusement and surprise at soldiers' practicing temperance, many younger officers probably saw the reform as a means to preserve the military bearing and order of their companies as well as middle-class sensibilities about public restraint and decorum. Most in the rank and file felt that their version of manhood included fraternal imbibing. The companies never became as thoroughly middle class as Richmond's fraternal organizations and continued to indulge in boisterous activities that were being rooted out of national fraternal orders such as the Odd Fellows.[26]

Drinking as well as the discipline of the militias was part of a rite of passage for young men and even boys while removed from maternal influence. The age ranges of men in most companies were broad, and some units were specifically designed for younger soldiers, such as the Young Guard and the Junior Blues. One newspaper interpreted the formation in 1856 of the Junior Blues, a group of young men attached to the Richmond Light Infantry Blues, as a preparation for possible future conflict. In commending their organization, one paper stated, "The time is coming when the South may need all her military force to protect her rights, and for that reason we should like to see every boy in the land trained to the use of the sword, musket, and rifle." While some may have believed this was the case, membership in a company served the more basic purpose of initiating young men into military training and manly bearing.[27]

Militia rituals emphasized male roles as defenders of community and fireside. Women or young girls often took part in flag presentations. In a typical ceremony, "Georgia Virginia Patton, a sweet little Miss of only some five summers" presented the Young Guard with a flag. As the daughter of John M. Patton Jr., the captain of the Richmond Light Infantry Blues, this young girl represented both the most pure-hearted, innocent, and vulnerable members of the populace that the militia swore to defend as well as the dependence of children and females under patriarchy. Colonel Thomas P. August, the commander of the First Virginia Regiment, made the presentation to the Young Guard for Patton's daughter. August emphasized that the flag was as "pure and stainless as her own little heart" and that if one "could look into her little heart and see the feelings which have prompted this beautiful tribute to your gallant corps, you would behold a faithful daguerreotype of the wide-spread love and admiration in which the Young Guard are held by the whole people of the metropolis and the State." Offering an object lesson for both young girls and boys, August called the presentation "the offering of infant innocence to youthful valor." [28]

Militiamen in their more fanciful moments conceived of themselves as knights as well as protectors, and women were expected to play their role in this familiar fiction. In 1858 the Blues marched to the home of Ensign William O. Taylor at Ninth and Marshall Streets. After the company was "drawn up in front of the house . . . several ladies appeared on the balcony, among them was Mrs. Ro. A. E. Dabney through whom a beautiful new *Flag by Ensign Taylor* was to be *Presented.*" Colonel Cary stood "by the side of *Mrs. Dabney* and holding the Flag in his hands addressed the company in a brief and eloquent manner." Cary instructed the men in the symbolism of the ceremony, relating that "in olden time, in the days of ancient chivalry, woman with her own fair hands presented the guidon of merit to the brave." Cary "trusted that the presence of the fair being who presided over the presentation would inspire those to whom the Flag was presented." The men were solemnly charged as protectors and honorable men "to maintain it untarnished, ever to cluster round it manfully and devotedly, and if ever the day should come in which it should be unfurled on the Battle Field it would be seen in the thickest of the fight." In his speech accepting the flag, Captain William H. Fry wryly referred "to the well known fact that the Ladies were always on the side of the Blues." For the rank and file of the company, the admiration of women was expected and desired, a fair price for manly bearing, for upholding state and community honor.[29]

Many young Southern women, steeped in the romantic novels of Sir Walter Scott, firmly believed in the tenets of chivalry. Bessie Lacy, a North Carolinian attending school in Richmond in 1848, wrote her father in thrilled language about "a great parade day" in Richmond, when "all the companies are out celebrating the anniversary of Cornwallis surrender." Lacy's and her schoolmates' imaginations soared as "one man passed . . . in the full dress of a Mexican soldier. Of course we feminines, with our full stock of curiosity ran out to see him. He lowered his lance with so much chivalrous gallantry that I dreamed we were in England in the days of Coeur de Lion & that we were at a tilt or tournament." The martial music added to her flight of fancy. She loved "to watch them & hear the familiar sound of the fife & drum as much as a little child three years old. Here the troopers have trumpeters and when I hear the shrill warlike notes I think I am really on a sure enough battle field." When Bessie Lacy boldly proclaimed, "I do think soldiers are mighty pretty things," her father may have wished he was not so many miles away.[30]

White women were not mere appendages to militia events. Not only did they shape men's identity through gender, they also helped create the culture of the militias. The Continental Guard received both a flag and a short speech from Miss Mary S. Allen, the daughter of a lieutenant of the company. Speaking from the portico of the Allen residence on Leigh Street— the very act a symbolic gesture to the assembled "fireside protectors"— Mary Allen presented the "Stars and Stripes." She found it "impossible, on this occasion, to express my feelings," but "suffice it to say, though presented at an hour when peace and prosperity pervade our Union, there *may* be a time when our country will require our noblest energies in her behalf." When such an hour was at hand, she was sure that the company's "brave soldiers, clad in the uniform of our beloved Washington," would "stand forth and prove themselves true patriots." Mary Allen allowed the symbols of Union—the flag, uniforms, and Washington himself—to speak and unify, but, like many orators on such occasions, acknowledged the possibility of future struggle over the definition of patriotism.[31]

Wives and sisters often made the banners and flags that adorned militia events, reinforcing a strongly Unionist message. The *Richmond Daily Dispatch* reported that "the ladies of 'Union Hill,' with their characteristic liberality, have determined to present this company [the Union Guard] with a 'stand of colors,' as soon as they can be prepared, which will be in a short time." Women prepared for and attended events such as balls where many flags and banners adorned the room. A newspaperman attending a ball of the Young Guard at the appropriately named United States Hotel found the event "unique, picturesque and dazzling," attended by the "youth, beauty and manhood of the city." As he entered the ballroom, his "eyes were at once fixed upon a life-like portrait of the immortal WASHINGTON, dressed in a civilian's suit, shorts, long stockings, shoes and buckles, and wearing a masonic regalia." As he proceeded toward the portrait, he noticed banners on each side of the room commemorating battles of the American Revolution. The room was full of U.S. flags, and adorned with the colors of the Young Guard. The visitor concluded that the general effect was "not only picturesque but national." [32]

The role of Virginia's white women in militia activities mirrored their work as conciliators in the sectional controversy. Women created one of the first American heritage organizations with the founding of the Mount Vernon Ladies' Association in 1854. The association transcended its Virginia origins to become a truly national organization in the late antebellum era, with regents from across the Union. Moreover, the association skillfully used the image of Washington to raise funds for the preservation of the first president's estate. The Unionist and conciliatory activities of the male-dominated Richmond militias meshed well with the political and cultural roles carved out by Virginia's women activists in the 1840s and 1850s. [33]

Military companies had for many years tried to maintain a nonpartisan stance in the ranks. Older members remembered the rancor caused by earlier conflicts and sought to avoid such disruptions. During the intense political battles of the early 1800s, the Richmond Light Infantry Blues had split into opposing factions, resulting in a new company named the Republican Blues. Eventually the company of Jeffersonian soldiers folded. In the late 1820s a political dispute within the company that spilled over into the selection of officers prompted a resolution that "no division of party shall henceforth endanger the permanence of our ancient corps." The matter was resolved amicably and thereafter the soldiers kept a watchful eye out for further trouble. [34]

Militia leaders and soldiers denounced partisanship and sectional antagonism within their ranks in the decade before the Civil War, despite (or perhaps because of) the intensification of voter mobilization and vitriol in statewide political campaigns, which mirrored national trends. In fact, the culture of Richmond's militias reflected the state of city politics more than state or national contests. While voter turnout in the city increased and Richmonders witnessed heated partisan debates at state political conventions, most campaigns for city offices went forward with no reference to the party affiliation of candidates. The exception to the rule was the city elections of 1855 and 1856, when the rise of the American Party provoked candidates to announce their party allegiances. The general lack of clear partisan lines in city elections reflected the consensus on basic issues that unified most city dwellers regardless of party: advocacy of economic development and infrastructure, delivery of city services, and opposition to those in the General Assembly who thwarted these ambitions.[35]

Even as ever greater numbers of Richmonders marched in torchlight parades and to the polls, militia men maintained their commitment to a unified culture of Union. During the Blues' annual celebration of the Fourth of July at Buchanan's Spring in 1841, soldiers made regular toasts, including, "The States: Let their Union be harmonious as those mighty spheres whose changeless paths through Heaven's deep silence lie," followed by "Yankee Doodle," and "The North and the South: Touch not the apple of discord, whose mortal taste may desolate the Paradise of Liberty," followed by the playing of "Wind of the Wintry Night." Toasts called for an end to party discord, such as Private Macon's July 4th toast in 1855: "Party Spirit—The element of social strife as it is the bane of political integrity—De gustibus non est disputandum" (literally, "About taste there is no disputing"; in other words, "to each his own").[36]

As sectionalism intensified in the 1850s, the symbolism and language of Richmond's militias staunchly balanced state and national interests. At the "Celebration of the 80th Anniversary of the Independence of the United States," Colonel Thomas P. August of the First Virginia Regiment presented the Young Guard with a flag containing symbols of the state as well as elements of the national flag. August interpreted the flag for Captain Richardson and the corps: "The image of the Capitol and the coat of arms of your native State will remind you that you are the soldiers of a commonwealth whose gallantry and patriotism have been attested upon every battle field of the country, and have won for her . . . renown and glory; the stars and stripes will remind you that you are the soldiers of a republic whose career in peace and war has placed her upon a proud height, where she stands and will continue to stand, the pride and admiration of the civilized world." August, a lawyer, politician, and Mexican War veteran, balanced Southern rights and national interests in his public life as well as in his remarks to the Young Guard.[37]

George Wythe Munford's speech during the 1851 parade and flag presentation to the Richmond Light Infantry Blues on Capitol Square also emphasized the integration of state and national icons. Munford pointed out the state seal and motto, "Sic Semper Tyrannis," and the eagle and stars and stripes that represented the United States. Employing the male-centered language common in militias, Munford called the Union "the first born of our Fathers, nourished by their self-sacrificing virtue and wisdom and by their blood, the fruit of affection and love." [38]

The militia colonel knew well the art of rhetoric and persuasion, a skill honed in a long militia and political career. Munford, like many other officers, had a much more distinguished pedigree than the shopkeepers and artisans he commanded, but he had himself risen through the ranks to become an elected officer and eventually served two separate terms as captain of the Blues. A Richmond native and College of William and Mary graduate, he succeeded his father as clerk of the House of Delegates, serving for more than twenty-five years. Munford no doubt learned much about political compromise while laboring as secretary of the 1829–30 state constitutional convention. In 1853 he would become secretary of the commonwealth, serving in that post until the fall of Richmond in April 1865. In the late 1850s he worked closely with Democratic governor Henry A. Wise, who was known for his savvy politicking among working-class voters. Also skilled at addressing the common man, Munford expertly invoked sympathetic feelings for the Union but carefully qualified his vision of that Union for himself and his audience.[39]

Munford's America was "a Union of States, a union of sovereigns, a union of equals, a union of love, and not of force; a Union to protect life and liberty and property; a Union whose power is given, and power restrained, and power attained; a Union where each star shines with its own lustre, undimmed, unobscured by the others, with no difference between them except 'as one star differeth from another in glory'; a union like the milky way in the Heavens, whose light all nations may behold and enjoy, whose rays, while they proceed from independent worlds, yet send forth one harmonious, mellow and eternal stream of light." The confederacy model of Union invoked by Munford was calculated to satisfy Northerners and Southerners, Unionists and States Rights' men alike, although always maintaining a unified vision of the country.[40]

When Virginia officials commissioned a banner for the New York Crystal Palace Exposition in 1853, Munford oversaw its creation. Featured on one side was "the coat of arms of the State, enclosed in a wreath of oak leaves; a beautiful large star, with gilt rays, representing the State, whose name 'Virginia,' is inscribed below." On the other side was "the U.S. coat of arms, encircled by a wreath of laurel leaves; with thirty-one golden stars sown over the banner, and the word 'Union' inscribed below." The banner was painted by a Philadelphia artist under Munford's direction.[41]

Elites of various political persuasions held important militia posts, but all testified to their devotion to the Union. Munford's devotion to a Union of confederated states, a standard position for many adherents of the Democratic Party, was no less heartfelt than Richmond Grays' captain Wyatt M. Elliott's adherence to a strong federal Union. Elliott, a lifelong Whig, remained a strong Unionist until the Civil War, actively campaigning for John Bell and Edward Everett in 1860. Patriotism for state and country muted the partisan instincts of men like Munford and Elliott, and allowed them to lead men who were also buffeted by the partisan winds of the 1850s.[42]

The Revolutionary heritage of Virginia and its great icons were emphasized by militias in subtle ways, usually as a force for Unionism. In June 1855, the newly formed Liberty Guards elected officers, including John R. P. Crawford as captain, and decided on uniforms in the "Continental style." When next mentioned in the city press, the company had become the Continental Guard, after their "uniform of '76," which they first wore on parade with the Mechanic Guard and National Guard of Richmond. Dressed in "blue coat turned off with buff, white cross belts, buff vest, buff short-kneed pants, fair top boots and three-cornered hats," the company consciously imitated their Revolutionary predecessors of the Continental Line. Dr. E. C. Cole hoped that "as they imitate in peace the dress of the Patriots, who guarded the liberties of our glorious country in the times of the Revolution . . . So in war if the occasion require, may they imitate their example in sacrificing their life's blood upon the altar of our country." Presented with the "Stars and Stripes," Captain Crawford expressed the contradictory feelings of many Virginia militiamen when he stressed the importance of defending the Union, while recognizing the "dark, lowering cloud overshadowing our Northern and Northwestern horizon." [43]

Virginia's prominent place in national politics and iconography provided symbols that could be understood even by those not born on American shores. Richmond's German and Irish companies participated in citywide events, retaining distinctive elements of their ethnic heritage while also integrating American and Virginian elements. In February 1850 militia units from throughout Virginia paraded into Richmond to take part in the laying of the cornerstone for the Virginia Washington Monument in Capitol Square, and the German community was so impressed that "in all the German restaurants there was talk about forming a German Company." Later that year the Richmond German Rifles was formed, but the company quickly changed its name to the Virginia Rifles. The Virginia Rifles took part in celebrations and ceremonies with both German and American themes. They could be found celebrating the one hundredth anniversary of Schiller's birth as well as participating in the ceremonies surrounding the reburial of President James Monroe in Richmond's Hollywood Cemetery. Like other antebellum militia units, the company held balls, picnics, and other events, including a "Military and Civic Excursion" to Slash Cottage, a popular resort. The Virginia Rifles were well known for the imbibing and good spirits that attended all their gatherings. [44]

The Virginia Rifles served a protective as well as a social function in the German community, especially during the peak of the Know-Nothing agitation in the 1850s. The most serious affray occurred on June 20, 1853, when the German population attended a ceremonial flag presentation from the *Turnverein* (sports association) to the *Gesangverein* (singing society). During the event and festivities, which took place on the farm of German community leader August Schad just outside the city, ruffians provoked a fight and the flag disappeared. The "Germans marched back into the city under the protection of the Rifle Company," but rumors spread that the German population was going to rise up and take over the city. Further violence ensued as "American ruffians" attacked the procession, and eventually five prominent German citizens were arrested for assault. Because of the threat of violence, the Virginia Rifles guarded German picnics, social outings, ceremonies, and meetings and "displayed its martial strength by frequent parades."[45]

The Virginia Rifles was involved in another controversy that began in the summer of 1856 at the annual target shoot held by the company at a spot known as the Hermitage. A drunken bystander attacked a corporal of the company, who shot and killed the civilian. Richmond's city council reacted to the incident by stripping the company of a fifty-dollar annual allowance being made to the city's militia companies. The German community denounced the city council's decision at a mass meeting at St. John's Evangelical Lutheran Church, passing resolutions that appeared in the city's leading newspapers. The fears of German societies and their possible radical leanings long held by Richmond's elites appeared in news reports of the incident and of the subsequent controversy. These episodes tended to isolate the German element of the city, already distinctive in language, customs, and organizations, but they also strengthened the resolve of Germans to prove themselves faithful to the larger community, which they did by consistently taking part in the round of national holidays and celebrations that made up the militia calendar.[46]

Militias set specific days each month to muster, reflecting American, Southern, and ethnic traditions. The Montgomery Guard, a company of Irish soldiers, was required to "parade once in each month, to wit: On the 8th day of January; the 22nd of February; the 17th of March; General Muster in May; June 17th, Anniversary and Target practice; July 4th; October 19th; and the second Monday in every month not heretofore named, and at any other time at the option of the Commandant." Like other militia companies, it celebrated the anniversary of the unit's founding (June 17) and took part in the state's general militia muster every year. The company observed national celebrations such as Washington's Birthday (February 22) and the Fourth of July, as well as the Battles of New

Orleans (January 8) and Yorktown (October 19), parade days required of all companies by order of the First Virginia Regiment. Irish pride had its place on the calendar, notably the Feast Day of Saint Patrick (March 17). The company paraded in a uniform reflecting the integration of ethnic and national identity—green coats and hats featuring a brass shamrock and an American eagle.[47]

Just as a commemoration associated with Washington inspired the Virginia Rifles to form, the Irish citizen-soldiers of Richmond also focused on the most celebrated member of the Virginia Dynasty. At the Montgomery Guard's Fourth of July celebration at Griffin's Spring in 1855, the second toast was to "The memory of Washington—In the language of one of Erin's sons 'No people can claim, no country can appropriate him. The boon of Providence to the human race. His fame is eternal, his residence creation.' " The resonance of Washington as the supreme symbol of American liberty was not lost on men who only recently had been ruled by European nobility. Washington was not just a Virginian or an American icon but an international figure on the scale of Lafayette, familiar to the Irish and Germans alike.[48]

Washington's image was largely untarnished by partisan or sectional politics, making him a perfect object of adoration for militiamen seeking to sublimate such issues. Surprisingly, one of the few times a militia event in Richmond was disturbed by sectional issues occurred during a Washington's Birthday celebration. After the usual parades, the city's militia companies attended a meeting to raise interest in the plan of the ladies of the Central Mount Vernon Association to preserve Washington's home. John R. Thompson, the editor of the *Southern Literary Messenger,* spoke first, advocating that the funds be raised by the ladies privately rather than by legislative appropriation and that Mount Vernon then be given to the state of Virginia. Thompson then outlined his rationale for state ownership: "An effort had been made to secure it as a holiday grounds—as a place of speculation. He hoped this would never be done. Nor was it proper that the United States should own it, for then, in the event of a dissolution of the Union, which God forbid, it would be a humiliating sight to see a scramble among the divided States for the possession of the last resting place of the father of his country. As a soldier and statesman Virginia would divide her claims to Washington with her sisters of the confederacy; but as a christian and gentleman, she claimed him as her own, and must therefore have the power of guarding Mount Vernon to the end of time." No reaction to Thompson's speech was recorded by the newspaper, but Moses Drury Hoge, the popular minister of Second Presbyterian Church, "was continually interrupted by applause" during his address. Thompson's sentiments were unusual, if not inappropriate, to the national spirit that typically pervaded patriotic events attended by militias.[49]

German and Irish units also took part in ceremonial events with companies from other cities, simultaneously solidifying ethnic ties and celebrating national life. In his memoirs, Johann Gottfried Lange described the festivities surrounding the inauguration of President Franklin Pierce. The Law Greys, a Baltimore militia, came to Richmond on March 1, 1853, and were "received with open arms, put up in hotels and treated royally." Later, the Young Guard and the Virginia Rifles "accompanied them to Washington on the Fredericksburg Railroad." In Washington they were feted by a German unit known as the Washington Huntsmen (*Jagers*), and the "German women from Washington also did their part to treat us well. Besides us there were two more companies, one from Baltimore and one from Pennsylvania." The next day they paraded down Pennsylvania Avenue to the U.S. Capitol, where the newly elected president made an hour-long speech, sorely trying the spirit of the tired militiamen. Later they retired to more spirits and dinner.[50]

The Unionist message of the militias and statesmen, and especially their recourse to Virginia's political heritage and heroes, upset strongly pro-Southern Virginians like Mann Valentine Jr. The aspiring merchant viewed the political cult built around Washington, Jefferson, and other Virginians as a way to ignore the present. Writing to his brother Edward V. Valentine about his book, *The Mock Auction*, a parody built around the John Brown raid, Mann Valentine claimed, "I have not spared the Virginians, and more than the Yankees, I have thrust them at tender points—their dependance on the North, their love of tyro's pictures sold here at auction, their pride of departed heroes & statesmen, &c." Valentine felt that the glorification of the national creation story through the icons of Virginia's Revolutionary past created a false patriotism and masked the Southern sectional tradition, thus inhibiting the development of Southern nationalism.[51]

The artisans and clerks of the Richmond militias went well beyond toasts and flags in proclaiming their devotion to brotherhood, state, and Union. They visited Northern cities during the 1850s and entertained their Northern compatriots at celebrations of national holidays, battles, and birthdays. During the same period no evidence exists of any Richmond companies' visiting units or cities of the Southern states. During their reciprocal visits the men of the militia companies enjoyed the rituals and sentimental bonds of brotherhood common to urban men of the artisan and middle classes throughout America. In solemn ceremonies and dinner toasts their civic and military leaders explained those bonds as transcendent verities affirming the mutual ideals of patriotism and Union.

In 1854 the Blues hosted the Washington Greys of Philadelphia during the Washington's Birthday celebrations in Richmond, beginning several years of intercourse between the two cities. The Blues joined the Washington Greys at the Exchange Hotel and then marched with them through the principal streets to see the points of interest. After a return to the hotel, the two companies next went to the Virginia State Armory where they were entertained by fireworks. Their day concluded with a supper at the American Hotel, costing about three hundred dollars. "The members of the Washington Greys contributed largely in songs, tales &c to the entertainment of the company present." In recognition of their hospitality, the Greys later presented a goblet and ladle to the Blues. The event marked the beginning of a long relationship.[52]

The Blues decided to reciprocate by visiting Philadelphia for the Washington's Birthday events in 1855. The Richmond press took notice that this would be the first trip of a Richmond militia company north of the Mason-Dixon line. After they paraded at Lafayette Hall on February 20, the Blues prepared to depart and were given a "Fatherly Benediction" from George Wythe Munford. Munford implored the men to "Remember where you are going! Remember that you are Virginians! That a truly honorable man boasts not; The truly dignified man swaggers not. His steps are firm; you see that in his eye, and in his tread are determination. Be free to all—

open—frank—bland and courteous upon every subject *SAVE ONE*—upon that speak not, when others approach it turn the theme to a more pleasant thought—God be with you!" For Munford, slavery was beyond the pale of a civilized man's discourse.[53]

Munford's remarks illustrate the importance of manly bearing, which was tantamount to being a Virginian. State association transcended all other allegiances, and the Virginians raised the glorification of their state to a high level indeed. He implicitly recognized the dangers of citizen-soldiers from a slave state traveling to a Northern city where questions regarding the "peculiar institution" might be raised. Munford's fear that sectional discord might mar the event was not realized; by all accounts the Blues were well treated and grandly feted.[54]

Perhaps the pinnacle of the Blues' visit to Philadelphia was their entry into the holiest shrine to the American national creation story, Independence Hall. Captain John Patton respectfully intoned that "certainly there is no time or place more appropriate, than on this most interesting occasion, and within these venerable walls, to renew our fealty to the Union of the States." Responding to the "patriotic sentiments" of the mayor of Philadelphia, Patton laid out the rationale of the Blues' trip as an antidote to the development of a rift between North and South.[55]

Patton did not mince words regarding the growth of sectional passions. Like Munford, he knew personally the acrimony of party and sectional discord from his father's career as a Whig congressman, lieutenant governor, and acting governor. Noting that for "several years past, as has been well known to us all, the enemies of our peace out of the fold of the Union, and traitors within it, have engaged in the most determined and continued efforts to sow the seeds of jealousy and enmity between the different States," Patton concluded that "unhappily their efforts have been so successful, that distrust has to some extent sprung up between us." He clearly laid the blame for sectional discord at the feet of unseen "enemies" and "traitors," certainly not the honorable men assembled before him. He believed that "nothing is better calculated to counteract such evil influences than friendly communings and interchanges of military or civic kindnesses such as these." Reflecting the fraternal beliefs of the Pennsylvania and Virginia militiamen, Patton emphasized the personal bonding between men: "We meet together, and do not find each other the monsters in sentiment and principal which we had been taught to expect—we gaze into each other's eyes and each sees kindness beaming upon him—we seize each other's hands, and each receives a cordial grasp—we feel the warm pulsations of each other's hearts, and instead of being partial enemies, we become friends and brothers—sons of a common union, devotees of a common faith, worshippers at a common altar." [56]

The common faith Patton and other civic leaders wished to instill was patriotism and Unionism, and he was quick to emphasize this deeper meaning within the personal, fraternal bonds: "Let no one then tell us that these military visits have no deeper significance than that which springs from mere friendly intercourse or idle dissipation, for they exert an influence, however feeble, in increasing the sympathies and affection of the states (the only true basis of any lasting or desirable union) and so in strengthening the bonds of the Union itself. We should feel ourselves amply rewarded by our visit to Philadelphia—were it ten times as disagreeable as it has proved to be delightful—if we could contribute our mite, however small, to so glorious an object." Patton's speech neatly wedded belief in militia brotherhood and the civic religion of Union.[57]

Reports of the Blues' visit seemed to confirm Patton's hopes that a meeting of the citizen-soldiers of the North and South could produce fraternal goodwill and manly respect. A Richmond paper reported after the return of the Blues that "they speak in glowing terms of their Northern visit." They were entertained in Baltimore by the Law Greys and other military companies, escorted to the station by the Independent Grays, and met and entertained by other militias in Washington. The trip was "one continuous entertainment," and "Capt. Patton took occasion to compliment the members on their manly conduct and soldierly bearing during the trip."[58]

Some Philadelphia papers seem to have understood the results in a Unionist light. Noting the visit of the Blues a few months earlier, the *Philadelphia Sun* editorialized that "such interchanges of social feeling tend greatly to do away with sectional prejudices, and to create fraternity of sentiment which of itself would perpetuate the Union, if there were any danger of its disruption." The secretary of the Blues recorded this newspaper article in the Blues minute book, and he also noted other newspaper articles emphasizing the fraternal bond between Northern and Southern soldiers. On one such occasion, a Blues soldier hosted a visiting Washington Grey from Philadelphia, making arrangements to "show him the Elephant" while in Richmond, approvingly noted by the *Dispatch* and the minute-taker of the company. Later in 1855, the National Guard of Philadelphia presented a bronze musket to the Blues as a token of remembrance of their visit.[59]

Despite these feelings of goodwill, the sectional controversy still occasionally reared its head in militia meetings, although always couched within respectful deference to the ideal of the Union. The Blues chose Sergeant Robert L. Dickinson to present Patton with a ceremonial sword on the sixty-second anniversary of the company, in May 1855, and Patton addressed the company:

> I fear that your organ Sergt Dickinson has not greatly erred in contemplating the possibility of future violence. It is scarcely to be expected that in our time at least, the day will come when "swords shall be beaten into ploughshares and spears into pruning hooks." The violence of evil men and the intemperate rashness of the thoughtless will continue in the future, as in the past, to drive the peacibly disposed into extreme means, and so to delay the coming of that day when men "shall learn war no more." Let us, however as individuals and members of the community, whether State or sectional, endeavor, so far as we can exert an influence, to avoid a resort to extreme measures until the cup of forbearance and reconciliation has been drained, and if we do so, we may be enabled calmly to contemplate the consequences, concious that the blame is not upon us, but upon our adversaries.[60]

The next year Richmond was again visited by Philadelphia units, this time on the occasion of the sixty-third anniversary of the Blues' formation—May 9, 1856—at Buchanan Springs, a popular retreat on the outskirts of town. Fernando Wood, the mayor of New York, and Daniel E. Sickles, a New York state senator, were also in attendance. State pride and Union carried the day. Captain Patton of the Blues toasted "The Union—May the forked lightning of Heaven blister the tongue that would advocate its dissolution." The ninth toast honored "The Washington Grays and National Guard of Philadelphia—Virginia and Pennsylvania united into one—who can sunder them." Captain Perry of the Washington Greys of

Philadelphia replied, "The Flag of our Country—May no one star ever be dimmed or a stripe erased." Likewise, the eleventh toast was to "New York and Virginia—Twin sisters in the National Confederacy; bound together by the honor, glory and patriotism which established, and can alone maintain, the union of our common country." [61]

The *Richmond Daily Dispatch* reported that Sickles "promptly responded, and made a very happy speech, in which he paid a high compliment to the Blues, and spoke of the great delight he had derived from his social intercourse with them that day. He expressed his warm attachment to the Union, and assured all who heard him that New York was devoted to it—that although temporary indiscretions and the outpourings of fanaticism might occasionally give uneasiness, the *people* of New York were true to the Constitution and the Union, and would prove themselves so." As in Patton's speech in Philadelphia, Sickles saw the sectional controversy as the product of fringe radicals and the preservation of the Union safely in the hands of the great majority of Americans of goodwill. [62]

Militias further solidified Unionist ideas and ties to the founding fathers through attendance at monument dedications. Much to the chagrin of men like Mann Valentine Jr., Richmonders in the late 1850s were busily planning and erecting monuments to their grand political lineage. On February 22, 1858, thousands gathered in Capitol Square when the state unveiled the long-anticipated equestrian statue of Washington by Thomas Crawford. The Virginia Washington Monument was built to hold the body of Washington in its base, despite the stated intention of the family to let it remain at Mount Vernon. Undeterred, Richmonders enthusiastically planned the return of James Monroe's remains in July 1858. Monroe had died in 1831 at the New York home of his wife's family and was buried in a family plot. Negotiations with the family succeeded in moving the body in a series of ceremonies in 1858 that involved troops from the Empire State. [63]

The New York press and people seemed to agree that the return of the former president's remains was fitting. Several New York units asked to participate and contribute, including the Scott Life Guard and the Eighth and Seventh Regiments of the New York National Guard. One of the units requesting a part in the events, the Light Guard, was especially distinguished because "during an existence as a company of near thirty years, they have had none other than '*Virginia Captains*'—their late Capt Vincent is a Virginian from Norfolk, their present Captain Jno: R Garland is a Virginian & son of Maj James Garland and both he and the members of his company feel that there is a manifest propriety in their being called upon to furnish the escort upon an occasion in which Virginians are more interested than any other people." [64]

The membership of the Light Guard illustrated the fact that Virginians of distinction in finance, engineering, and other businesses naturally migrated to centers of commerce such as New York. The Light Guard's request was supported by those who knew its members in these fields of enterprise. N. H. Campbell, a New York banker in the firm of Peters, Campbell & Co., wrote Governor Wise that he believed the Virginia committee "should invite the New York Light Guard to detail a proper number of men & officers to take special charge of the 'remains' & accompany the same on the steamer Jamestown. I designate the above corps because from its earliest organization its principal officers have been & are still Virginians, and I know from personal communication with some of these gentlemen that such a request would be esteemed a peculiar honor to the Virginia officers with which they & their men would gladly comply." [65]

Ultimately, the Seventh Regiment of the New York National Guard was chosen to accompany the remains of James Monroe to Richmond for reburial in scenic Hollywood Cemetery. The well-drilled and -outfitted New York regiment greatly impressed Virginia's militia leaders, prompting Richmond's own regiment to adopt more consistent uniforms and organization. In a magnanimous gesture, the New York regiment "offered to take upon themselves the entire charge and expense of the removal." One newspaper felt that "this handsome offer cannot but give the Southerners a higher opinion than they are accustomed to expect of the liberality and fraternal feeling of the people of the North. We trust in future they will be disposed to accord to Northern chivalry a place in their vocabulary of compliment." [66]

Northerners had a right to wonder whether the Monroe reburial would elevate "Northern chivalry" in Southern eyes or increase sectional tensions. No one overtly couched the repatriation of this native son as an expression of Southern nationalism or as a rebuke to a hostile North, but such feelings lurked just below the surface. Monroe descendant Samuel L. Gouverneur tried to quash such ideas in a letter to Virginia governor Henry A. Wise, discounting the widely held belief that Northerners committed Monroe to a grave below his dignity. Gouverneur implored Wise, "Let not the people of Virginia believe, that his honored 'remains' were treated with neglect. In no 'public burying ground,' in no 'borrowed tomb,' do they lie. In a vault, originally, purchased by his daughters, in a beautiful private 'cemetery,' surrounded by some of the most respectable & virtuous of his day, they have awaited the call of his native state. Two sisters of his wife, one my own dear mother, and others of her family, have slept around him." [67]

Despite the potential for discord, the events surrounding the transfer of Monroe's remains followed the pattern of earlier militia events. Soldierly fraternalism and patriotic celebration were the watchwords. New Yorkers and Virginians sat down to a grand feast in the recently reconstructed War-wick and Barksdale (commonly known as Gallego) Mills, reputed to be the largest flour mill in the world. In that monument to material progress in the heart of the Old Dominion, Governor Henry A. Wise delivered a paean to the working classes that drew fire from some members of the Richmond press but certainly pleased most of his listeners.

Wise opened his address with a familiar litany of Virginia's accomplishments in the founding of the nation. He had been a prime mover in planning the Monroe ceremonies and the installation of the equestrian statue of Washington in Capitol Square. But Wise also looked to the future. He concluded his speech with an open challenge to those who claimed that Virginia was in decay. He asked the soldiers and assembled guests to

> go before you leave here, my friends from New York, and look at the iron factories that are growing up around this noble scenery. . . . Look at the iron factory here; look at the tobacco factory here—that factory which is every day stealing my life away with the very *weed* of luxury—(The Governor chews tobacco freely.) But it is worth some five or six millions now; and if you ask me where Virginia is to-day, I will tell you *where you are*—in Warwick & Barksdale's mill house, that grinds out . . . about five hundred thousand barrels of flour per year. (Applause).

During his tribute to Virginia's industrial progress, Wise paid homage to the nobility of workers at the expense of Virginia's traditional leadership. "I say that labor is not the 'mud sill' of society," he thundered, "and I thank

God that the old colonial aristocracy of Virginia, which despised mechanical and manual labor, is nearly run out. I thank God that we are beginning to see miners, mechanics and manufacturers who will help to raise what is left of that aristocracy up to the middle grade of respectability," a comment that provoked laughter and applause.[68]

Wise, a veteran stump speaker, rarely misjudged his audience. Mechanics and tradesmen—Virginians and New Yorkers—would easily laugh with gusto at Wise's clever barbs directed at the Virginia aristocracy. Wise's record also inspired some confidence from white working-class voters. Although often frustrated by the legislature while governor, he advocated free schools and pushed for white immigration into Virginia. Wise vigorously and consistently championed economic diversification through manufacturing and infrastructure development. He had, on occasion, openly agonized about Virginia's economic decay, but mainly to spur others to action. A man with national political ambitions, he also understood the necessity of speaking the language of workers, whether for local or national consumption.[69]

The men of the New York regiment clearly enjoyed the attentions of their Virginia hosts and wished to reciprocate the following year. Private Philip Whitlock of the Richmond Grays remembered that "after being in the company for several months the company received an invitation to New York City by the 7th Regiment of New York City to visit them which the company accepted and left this city for New York on August 12 1859." It took the Grays twenty-four hours to get to New York by rail, changing ten times, and they "were entertained by the 7th Regiment of New York for nearly a whole week. There were several prominent men along with us from Richmond among them was the Mayor Jos. Mayo—Col. Thom. August—Capt Dimock of the Public Guard and several others. We were shown great attention by the Citizens of New York as our company was considered one of the best drilled compan[ies] in the country." [70]

There was no doubt to the editor of the *Richmond Daily Dispatch* what the "effect of these soldierly visits" would be: "An interchange of sentiment, an awakening of patriotism, an arousing of love of country, should be the fruits of these visits, and result in making and keeping us one people, now and forever." "Patriotism" would be the great emotion and ideal to

bring together men of both sections, but it would also be a brotherly friendship born of familiarity and conviviality. The *Dispatch* editor asked rhetor-
ically whether the trips "will . . . not awaken a friendship between the
North and the South that will bind them more firmly together than hooks
of steel? Will not New York and Virginia know each other better in the future, and knowing, love each other as sisters of a great confederacy should?
Will not the sterling men of both parties be able to crush the spirit of mad
fanaticism in either section, and awaken a conservative spirit that will preserve from dissolution the glorious Union for which North and South alike
fought and bled?" Echoing John Patton's sentiments, reasonable men, the
broad middle of society, could unite to crush fanaticism on both sides.[71]

Whitlock had only recently returned from the Grays' trip to New York
when the news of John Brown's Raid electrified Richmond. He and his
fellow militiamen boarded trains to Washington, en route to Harper's
Ferry, but on arriving in the nation's capital they were told that the situation was under control, and the company made its return to Richmond.
The Virginia capital was in an uproar, with rumors of slave revolts circulating in the streets. On November 19, alarms awakened two New York–
born young men rooming together in Richmond. Robert Granniss watched
as his roommate Heman Baldwin prepared to join his militia company, the
Grays, called out to Charles Town, Virginia. Granniss wrote that at "about
6:30 Saturday night the bell rang the alarm and forthwith the whole city
was in confusion. Gov Wise had recd dispatches from Harpers Ferry (Col
Davis in command) that an attack from Abolitionists was anticipated to rescue Old Brown. The result was the ringing of the alarm. troops assembled
from all parts of the city. At 10 o'clk a train of 8 cars filled with 400 &
upwards armed men left for the scene of action." Richmond's "outskirts
were patrolled by detachments of the 'Lancers' as some of the citizens in
the suburbs had expressed fears of an insurrection among the negroes";
Granniss had "never before witnessed so much excitement."[72]

On November 28, the young clerk and several other men from his firm
enlisted in a militia company, Company B of the First Virginia Regiment,
responding to the widespread concern of citizens. He mused that "our company is drilling every night expecting to be called to go to Harper's Ferry.
I hardly think though that we shall be obliged to go." His friend Baldwin

was then in the Charles Town area with other Richmond militia units to guard against any rescue attempt to save John Brown. Baldwin, Whitlock, and John Wilkes Booth, who had accompanied the Grays to Charles Town, witnessed Brown's execution. We can only speculate what Baldwin and Whitlock, one a Yankee and the other an immigrant, felt during these tumultuous events.[73]

George Wythe Munford gave a speech to the Blues after their return to Richmond, vindicating Governor Wise's decision to send troops. His address was constantly interrupted by cheers from the troops. "Col. Munford remarked that if such an event as the Harper's Ferry raid should occur again, no Union would exist thereafter," although he also prayed that "while we remain in the Union, God grant that it may always be so—that you will have no enemy to meet, or have to maintain by force, the rights of Virginia."[74]

White Virginians would doggedly cling to the Union until April 1861. The difficulty that secessionists faced in turning Virginia southward began with the strong friendships formed in Richmond's militia halls. The late antebellum era in Richmond was a testament to the ability of average Americans to create a unified public culture in the face of heightened political conflict, economic contradictions, and inner prejudices. Caught vise-like between a Northern Republican president and an energized Southern confederacy, Unionists and emboldened secessionists would finally destroy the delicate compromises forged between white men in Richmond's hotels, workshops, parade fields, and counting houses.

PART THREE

Choosing Sides

CHAPTER SEVEN

The War Within

You have no idea how hateful the Word *Union* has become here, and Every
one who has been known to Entertain such sentiments is a *marked* man,
particularly if he hails from Philadelphia. . . . Write me soon again. We are all
well but very unhappy. We are as strangers and aliens here, and are afraid to
say a word—God bless you all.

JACOB BECHTEL to his brother in Philadelphia, April 24, 1861

*P*hiladelphian Jacob Bechtel reacted with dismay at the
change in his adopted home after Virginia's secession. For sixteen years Bechtel had happily resided in Richmond, working at
Adolphus Morris's bookstore and raising his family. Bechtel agreed with
his Southern neighbors on many points. He excoriated the Republicans
and Lincoln and believed that treatment of Southern slaves was far more
benevolent than the lot of Northern blacks. Despite these beliefs, he now
found himself unable to support the Confederacy and clinging to his Unionist principles in a hostile environment.

The coming of secession after Harper's Ferry and the experience of war
disrupted the cultural worlds of many Richmonders and laid bare divisions
that had lingered just below the surface of Richmond society throughout
the antebellum period. Newly confident secessionists among the civic and
political elite saw their opening, mobilizing pro-Southern sentiments in
the streets and legislative halls of Richmond. Richmond's urban leadership
defended the interests of plantation Virginia—a world to which merchants
and their families had long been tied by kinship, culture, and slavery. The

sons of the same commercial elite prepared to defend their state as Richmond mobilized for war.

But a Southern confederacy premised on the preservation of slavery did not fire the imaginations of all Richmonders. African Americans, workers, immigrants, and Unionists stood apart from and were often at odds with the civic elite. Political and military leaders became increasingly impatient with striking artisans, draft evaders, and Unionists. Prison, impressment, and public scorn greeted many as the war wore on. The elite cracked down on slaves and free blacks even as the Confederate government and its war effort became more dependent on African-American labor.

The shallow support Richmond gave the Confederacy has never been fully appreciated. Significant segments of Richmond's population undermined the new nation in both subtle and overt ways. Unable to express their Unionist views openly, many foreign- and Northern-born people simply voted with their feet, leaving the city in the intense months leading to secession. Those Unionists with deeper family, business, or community attachments to the city looked on stunned as secession rushed forward around them, but silently refused to bear arms for the Confederacy.

Many young men, especially recent immigrants from Germany and Ireland, initially rushed into the fray for Virginia and the South but quickly became disenchanted with a cause that ultimately was not theirs. When the Confederate Congress gave the foreign-born exemptions from military service in 1862, German and Irish soldiers quit the field in droves. For the rest of the war these former soldiers frustrated conscription officers with certificates of citizenship from the British and German consuls.

Working people also exhibited flagging interest in the Southern cause, struggling to survive under trying economic conditions. Strikes, defections through the lines, and, ultimately, the Richmond Bread Riot of 1863 showed that working people's allegiances often did not square with those of the elite.

African Americans stood in a particularly ironic position. With white men at war, black men and women were conscripted and mobilized in vital war industries and support roles. While white condemnations and suspicions of African Americans' loyalties increased, Richmond's black population exploited cracks in the system and their knowledge of the military and political situation. African Americans prayed for the victory of the Union armies or slipped silently through the lines when the opportunity presented itself.

A small group of the most devoted Union men and women decided to fight directly what they considered treason, banding together in a campaign of espionage and sabotage. The "enemy within," long feared by Richmond's elite, had showed its hand. While the machinations of Unionists and the disloyalty of outsiders most alarmed officials, the Confederate state suffered most from those who simply chose not to fight, work, or otherwise actively support the new government.

The Harper's Ferry raid mobilized Richmond's pro-Southern elements in every sector of Richmond's life. At least for a few months, supporters of States' Rights and secession held the political advantage in debates over the fate of the Union. Commercial men in Richmond renewed their call for Southern economic independence. Dry-goods merchant Daniel H. London chaired a meeting of the revived Central Southern Rights Association of Virginia on November 25, 1859, at Richmond's city hall. Reenergized by the events at Harper's Ferry, the association did not restrict its discussions to trade. The men in attendance unanimously passed a resolution offered by Edmund Ruffin that excoriated "Northern enemies, fanatics and conspirators," and called for Virginia to unite with the Southern States against Yankee aggression.

A committee of thirteen received the task of revising the association's 1851 memorial to the General Assembly in order to resubmit it for consideration. The presence of Southern partisans such as Ruffin on the committee ensured that the memorial contained a strong dose of States' Rights rhetoric that went well beyond trade issues. After the memorial was submitted, London spoke before the House of Delegates, presenting the association's political perspective as well as a catalog of the economic injustices suffered by the South, including unfair rates of exchange, navigation laws, and tariffs. London, as he had many years earlier, fell back on the mantra of direct trade with Europe as the only way to redress those grievances.[1]

In January 1860 a larger group of Richmond merchants also submitted a printed memorial to the Virginia General Assembly to make Virginia "independent of the Northern and Eastern States of this Confederacy."

Citing the "evident hostility of the Free-Soil States to the South" and "their plain determination to subject the Slave States to the despotism of a sectional majority," the memorial's signers proposed a number of economic reforms, including taxing the imports and manufactures of the "Free-Soil States." To promote direct trade, they asked the state to provide a bonus for direct foreign imports and tonnage bounties to build up the state's commercial marine; the legislature was asked to reform banking and inspection laws considered injurious to Virginia interests. More a call for Southern economic independence than a secessionist screed, the memorial still contained strongly sectional language.[2]

A broad cross-section of Richmond's commercial elite—even some Unionists, such as Horace Kent—endorsed the memorial. Signers represented the major manufacturing sectors, including Joseph Reid Anderson of the Tredegar Iron Works, tobacco manufacturer James H. Grant, and the flour company of Dunlop, Moncure and Company, as well as many of the largest importers and dry-goods merchants. Some Northern-born men and Unionists ignored the petition, however, notably shoe merchants William H. Hubbard and James H. Gardner, dry-goods merchant Samuel P. Lathrop, and hardware vendor John Van Lew.

While merchants issued memorials and made speeches, Richmond's women launched a grassroots campaign against Northern goods. One Richmonder, commenting on the intensification of Southern feeling after John Brown's Raid, remembered that "the ladies determined to manifest their condemnation of the cowardly proceedings by discarding at their social gatherings the product of looms and factories of our Northern neighbors and arranging their charms only in articles of Southern manufacture." Merchants probably had mixed feelings about these activities. Ideologically, the women concurred with the public utterances of a majority of the city's merchants; practically, the Northern goods that already stocked store shelves might go unpurchased.[3]

Military mobilization surged following Harper's Ferry. Scores of new volunteer companies organized across the state, eventually doubling the number of units from the time of John Brown's Raid to secession. Jacob Bechtel noted in November 1859 that "the military spirit seems to have received quite an impetus here lately, and it is expected that very stringent laws will be passed by our legislature this winter, in regard to the enrollment and equipment of every able bodied citizen capable of serving, with very heavy penalty for disobediance or neglect. So much has been gained anyhow toward converting a peaceable orderly community into a vast entrenched camp of soldiery." Bemoaning the lack of conservative sentiment in the North, he added, "And who can wonder! When such ruffians as Brown are applauded by those who should know better."[4]

The Howitzer Company, an artillery unit, began organizing on November 9, 1859, under the command of George Wythe Randolph, a secessionist who would later serve in the 1861 convention and as the Confederate secretary of war. Amid the confusion of the nineteenth, when rumors of plots to rescue Brown were widespread, the Howitzers, "although without uniforms, were quickly armed by the state and sent to Charles Town with other Richmond Companies." Dry-goods clerk Thomas J. Macon, the son of a Hanover County planter, was among the eager young Southern recruits that enlisted in the artillery company. The Howitzers were soon joined by three new Richmond militia units organized in the aftermath of Harper's Ferry and the trial of John Brown.[5]

Recruiting for existing companies was invigorated. Peter Helms Mayo, the son of a tobacco manufacturer, joined the Governor's Mounted Guard on February 20, 1860, a unit commanded by Joseph Reid Anderson, a West Point graduate and owner of the Tredegar Iron Works. Mayo remembered that "each member furnished his own horse and uniform which at the time was the fatigue uniform of the United States cavalry, and each gave bond to Captain Anderson for 'one sword and one pistol and holster, of the value of $41.00.'"[6]

Despite these martial preparations, the mood of Virginia cooled considerably as 1860 wore on. Mann Valentine Jr. wrote in frustration to his brother: "The truth is John Brown my hero is dead, & the feeling against our northern enemies is buried, preparatory to our being buried in 1861 by the Republican president—who will doubtless be elected, & we will like good citizens of our country take him to our bosom, lick the cloven foot, & yield ourselves up Indian like to the encroachments of the civilized

Yankee. . . . Heaven preserve this Union, civil war were better than civil wrong." Valentine's pessimistic assessment of the possibilities for disunion in 1860 reflected the remarkable calm that prevailed a year after John Brown's Raid. Wary of the coming storm clouds, some Richmonders prepared for war, economically and militarily, but most remained aloof from the sectional struggle. Virginia maintained its independent stance within the Union."[7]

Life went on as usual for many, even recently transplanted Yankees. In the time between Harper's Ferry and Lincoln's election a lull set in and some aspects of life returned to a semblance of order. Henry Lafayette Pelouze, a type founder from Brooklyn, traveled to many cities in the antebellum era, arriving in Richmond in 1860. His sister Harriet wrote to him from Boston soon after his arrival, concluding her letter with the prescient statement, "I heard you had started a type foundry in Richmond this is a bad time to move South." Still, Pelouze's letters continued to report his business progress and activities, including mounting a display at the 1860 state fair.[8]

Northerner Robert Granniss continued to serve in his militia company, attending the dedication of the Henry Clay statue in Capitol Square on April 12, 1860, and receiving a promotion from fourth to third Sergeant. The dedication, held on the eighty-third anniversary of Clay's birth, brought to fruition the efforts of Whig women from across the state. Twenty thousand men and women turned out for the unveiling of the statue of the Great Pacificator, reaffirming hopes that sectional conflict might yet be avoided.[9]

Despite the apparent return of calm, some Northerners became increasingly frightened by the reaction to John Brown and the apparent inability of the North to comprehend the danger. Jacob Bechtel told his brother that "we are in a state of painful concern at the manner in which the recent invasion on Harpers Ferry is received at the North. It's very plain that the general wish there is that he had succeeded in his piratical undertaking. How else can we account for the apathy that prevails in the midst of the clamor raised by the fanatics in his behalf." Bechtel could not understand the failure of "the Conservative portion of the North" to "cry out with one voice in condemnation of a man who has endeavored to excite the negroes here to rise in insurrection and came provided with bloody weapons to cut our throats." He had seen "one of those pikes and more hellish instrument to put in the hands of brutal ignorant wretches like *slaves* can scarcely be conceived." Chilled by the thought of slave insurrection, he marveled at Brown's defenders: "And then to think that such a wretch should find apologists among a Civilized Community calling themselves Christians— Ah me! I see a dreadful day coming, and woe betide those who shall live to see it." [10]

The 1860 presidential election both reaffirmed the strength of Unionism in Virginia and fueled secessionist efforts. The Constitutional Union ticket of John Bell and Edward Everett easily carried the state and Richmond. Stephen Douglas also ran well as a Democratic, Unionist alternative to John C. Breckinridge. Douglas garnered considerable support in Richmond, especially among workers. Published lists of the candidates' vigilance committees showed that Joseph Reid Anderson supported Breckinridge, while eight of eleven Tredegar workers on the lists went for Douglas. Aversion to former Know Nothings and elites in the Bell camp, combined with fear of disunion, may have influenced immigrants and workers to vote for Douglas. Workers were increasingly forging their own political identity, and fears of economic change and development might also have played a role in their decision not to climb on the Bell-Everett bandwagon. [11]

Commercial men came under considerable economic pressure after Lincoln's election and the secession of Deep South states. As the possibility of Virginia's secession intensified, Northern commercial houses were increasingly reluctant to extend credit. In November 1860, Henry Pelouze wrote his wife that "I know from this sesession feeling that money will be very hard to get in New York for that reason I am working night & day to get out the order I have here so that I can come home with funds." [12]

Clerk Jacob Bechtel also felt the insecurity of the wilting economy during the usually busy springtime of 1861. At Adolphus Morris's bookstore, he noted, "This is or ought to be our active season and in ordinary times, we are at it from early to late, selling and packing Goods for our Country Merchants, but just now all is silent as the grave, and we stand about the store, staring at each other, or sucking our fingers like so many statues. A continuance of this state of things cannot but be disastrous to every body, whether clerks or merchants, and I am expecting to receive notice every day that my services will be no longer required after July next." [13]

Northern merchants, hardly uninterested in the political outcome, pleaded with their Richmond customers to oppose secession. In January 1861, New York merchant Alexander T. Stewart informed dry-goods entrepreneur Thomas R. Price of his "intention to leave for Washington tomorrow (Tuesday evg) in company with Judge Hilton, Mr. Wiley & perhaps Judge Ingraham, expecting to reach Washington in the course of Wednesday, and remaining the balance of the week or if pleasant, longer." Inviting Price to meet his party at the Willard Hotel, Stewart wrote that "it is a time when all who possess weight and have the right spirit, should use all their exertions to save our institutions and that failing—which heaven prevent—keep us from the calamity of Civil War." [14]

Three weeks later, Stewart, "although much engaged," replied quickly to a letter from Price, "for the time is precious and I would say a few words to stay if possible the rapid changes which are occurring." Stewart called on Price's sense of history to stem the secession sentiment, arguing that "your noble state has a past too great and too secure to make it necessary to depart now or ever from the example of the solid men who formed the government, and who needed no such demonstration of ireverent haste as has been presented in the action of the extreme South, to convince the world of the justice of their cause, or the spirit and determination of those who espoused it." Stewart also recalled the glories of American civilization, "blessings which millions on the earth do not know," and hoped "a stand will be made by Virginia in behalf of these great blessings." By March, Stewart became even more direct: "Be firm in resisting Secession, & let us have the happiness to see you immediately." [15]

Some Northern Unionists living in Richmond during the secession crisis sympathized with the widespread hatred of Lincoln but rejected disunion. Jacob Bechtel staunchly maintained his Unionist principles, yet agreed with the Southern fear of Lincoln, stating "much as we love the Union the detestation of Black Republican Rule far Exceeds it." Just before the elections for the secession convention, Bechtel wrote his brother that he intended "to Vote the Enclosed ticket which if it fails will perhaps require of me to take up my bed and remove to a cooler atmosphere, as the secession-ists have vowed to set a mark upon any and every man who refuses to go with them head long. So don't be surprised if you see a wandering Exile among you about the first of July, with a retinue of six small children—for I am determined not to insult the flag of my Country, nor tamely see it in-sulted; Hence my free speech, and loyalty to the Union will I fear make the atmosphere uncongenial with my health, and constitution." [16]

The safest policy was to keep quiet. In March 1861, Henry Pelouze wrote his wife that "the secessionists here are gaining ground. . . . I do not mix with either party not having a vote I could not do any good and might in-jure myself." Despite his apathy towards any involvement in the political debate raging in Richmond, he was concerned about his business. He re-vealed to his wife a week later what he thought the crux of the secession de-bate was truly about, writing that he did "not see any settlement of the Negro question yet and Business never will be good untill it is setled." [17]

Lincoln's election also brought a new wave of militia organizing. From December 1860 to March 1861, six new Richmond companies were formed.[18] Some companies began to evince a much more prosecessionist stance. Witnesses to events in Richmond charged that several militia com-panies of Richmond volunteers and secessionist mobs had been infiltrated by leaders of the extralegal Southern Rights Convention and stood ready to assist secessionists if the state convention failed to carry Virginia out of the Union.[19]

The records of the Richmond Light Infantry Blues reveal how this transformation took place within one company. On January 21, 1861, members of the Blues elected O. Jennings Wise, the son of former governor and Southern rights leader Henry A. Wise, captain of the Richmond Light Infantry Blues. A noted duelist and the publisher of the *Richmond En-quirer*, a leading secessionist paper, Wise had never been a member of the Blues, and the election occurred under suspicious circumstances. The min-utes record that "a special meeting was called for the election of Captain and for the transaction of other business," with "Lieut Scott and a quorum of the company" present. George Wythe Munford, a close ally of Wise's fa-ther, presented the report of a "committee of Ex-Captains" that had met "on Saturday last, and unanimously agreed to present to the 'Blues,' a gentleman every way qualified for the post to which they recommended him." A rump of Blues members voted, giving Wise a unanimous tally by twenty-nine members of the company as well as seventeen honorary members on a highly unusual visit. The committee of former captains then sent for Wise, who accompanied his new comrades to the Columbian Hotel in order to "partake of the Hospitalities extended by Ensign Luck." [20]

Only two of the active soldiers voting for Wise were with the company when it traveled to Philadelphia in 1855, and fifteen of the twenty-nine men had joined since 1859. While Wise certainly did not influence all of these men to join, the intensification of sectional differences favored younger recruits with less commitment to the Union. Also, twelve men resigned on January 18, 1861, the Friday before the Monday election. [21]

Wise moved quickly to consolidate his hold on the company. A curious entry in the company's minutes records that on March 12, 1861, nineteen men "were recommended for active membership 'under the peculiar circumstances' of March 11th 1861," two of whom voted for Wise on January 21. On March 27 the *Richmond Daily Dispatch* commented positively on Wise's leadership and the changes in the company, asserting that the "ranks are being augmented by the addition of the right sort of material and . . . the members could soon put themselves on a war footing." On April 15 the bylaws were suspended to elect men as active members with a single vote, and seven were accepted, during a time of enormous public turmoil in the streets of Richmond. [22]

O. Jennings Wise and other secessionists also sought to harness working-class activism for their cause, but workers viewed the world very differently from the Southern elite. Early in 1861 Virginians mobilized for an election to choose representatives to the state convention charged with deciding the secession issue. Workingmen assembled on January 23 at First African Baptist Church to debate the issues and possibly nominate candidates to represent Richmond.

Thomas H. Wynne, a secessionist, was called to the chair and appointed a committee of fifteen to "prepare business for the meeting." While the committee deliberated, the proceedings became contentious. Calls for O. Jennings Wise to speak were heard, but when he attempted to address the men "there was an evident desire to hear a speech from some practical working man, and Mr. Wise yielded the floor." James H. May, a carpenter, then "called attention to the fact that this was a working men's meeting, and neither lawyers nor doctors ought to be allowed to speak." May also won a motion to appoint a committee to wait on Unionist John Minor Botts. Soon the committee appointed by Wynne returned and read a decidedly secessionist set of resolutions. Unionist John Minor Botts then entered the hall to cheers, and another set of resolutions of a much more conciliatory tone were read. When Botts attempted to speak, however, the meeting dissolved into chaos as objections to a nonworkingman speaking were again heard. The assembled men finally voted adjournment for the purpose of holding a "Union meeting." The confusion was so great, however, that after several attempts to open a new meeting (including the clearing of the church because of someone turning the gaslights off), the men decided to assemble again at a later date. Richmond's workingmen obviously valued their own judgment on the issues of the day and objected to professional politicians of either faction attempting to control their deliberations.[23]

A second meeting soon followed, this time controlled from the outset by Richmond's workingmen. Among the speakers before the large, orderly assembly were Martin Meredith Lipscomb and conditional Unionist candidate Marmaduke Johnson. A committee charged with drafting a resolution returned two reports. The authors of both the majority and minority reports urged the passage of a compromise plan to reconcile the national government and the seceding states, specifically touting the Crittenden plan. The authors of the majority report, however, decreed that when no hope of a peaceful settlement existed, Virginia should leave the Union and that, in case of war, "the non-slaveholding working men of Richmond, will stand by our slaveholding brethren and make their cause our cause, believing our interests to be the same."

The men presenting the minority report saw the preservation of the Union as key to economic prosperity and urged every effort to maintain it. While also pledging support to the South if all attempts at compromise failed, the authors of the minority report said nothing about defending slavery. The workers adopted the minority report. Amid calls for preservation of the Union, workers selected representatives to a national convention of workingmen in Philadelphia. Class-based concerns, including the dreary economic situation, shaped the perspective of urban workers, who no longer simply followed the lead of Virginia's elites.[24]

German citizens also held a mass meeting during this time of great tumult to consider the issues of the day. Hermann L. Wiegand, a devout Unionist and *Turnverein* leader, chaired the meeting at Steinlein's Monticello Hall, where German radicals had once met. O. Jennings Wise, a former Göttingen law student and attaché at the American legation in Berlin, addressed the assembled Germans in their native tongue, no doubt urging the cause of secession. The meeting came to no definite conclusion; the Germans proceeded cautiously, simply asserting their support for whatever course the majority in their adopted state took.[25]

The men who had once stood before both working-class and foreign-born citizen-soldiers and proclaimed their undying devotion to the Union now publicly called for another course. On January 28, an assembly of Richmond citizens "in favor of resistance to Black Republican rule and aggression, and in favor of prompt and decided action on the part of Virginia," crowded into First African Baptist Church to nominate men to the secession convention. John M. Patton Jr. set the tone of the meeting by stating that "the object of the meeting was to nominate men who were prepared to say on the floor of the Convention that Virginia should withdraw from the Confederacy before the 4th of March, unless satisfactory guarantees were speedily given for the protection of Southern rights." Patton, George Wythe Munford, and Thomas P. August all were nominated as candidates to the convention, but the meeting settled on George Wythe Randolph, John O. Steger, and John Robertson out of a crowded field.[26]

Virginia Unionists dealt secession forces a stunning defeat in the convention election of February 4, 1861. Despite the popular perception of a rising tide of pro-Southern fervor following Lincoln's election, Unionists captured more than two-thirds of the seats in the convention. Conditional Unionists William H. Mcfarland and Marmaduke Johnson received the largest numbers of votes in Richmond, each capturing approximately 19 percent of the vote (voters selected three names from a field of seven). Secessionist George Wythe Randolph, a grandson of Thomas Jefferson and a former city councilman, finished third with 17 percent of the ballots. John

Minor Botts, an uncompromising Unionist, received 14 percent of the vote, finishing fifth.[27]

The debacle in the February elections only increased the resolve of secessionists. The Southern rights cause found willing allies in newly formed or transformed militia companies and also established a mutual relationship with a group of commercial men intensely interested in the outcome of the secession convention. The slave traders of Richmond actively aided secessionists, pouring money into the coffers of the Southern rights movement. Fearing the election of Lincoln as a signal of the eventual extinction of slavery, they, more than any other commercial group in Richmond, saw their considerable economic power in jeopardy.[28]

Many elite white women became active in the secession movement, continuing their long-standing pro-Southern and anti-Northern sentiment. The women in the Valentine family were all intensely prosecession, just as they had been anti-Northern before the war. Ann Maria Gray Valentine wrote her brother-in-law William Winston Valentine, then studying in Paris, in January 1861, speculating that William and his brother Edward V. Valentine "must be intensely excited about your own dear Country. It is natural, and as for my part it seems as if I were a man I would do a great deal. Business is dull, every body talks about the times and you hear the people inquiring constantly what was the last telegraph from Washington or South Carolina." She excoriated the Virginia legislature, "now in session, but for what they are doing, they might better be at home, smoking or eating for that is all they do in the Capitol." For her part, Ann Maria Gray Valentine claimed to be "a real secessionist and wear constantly the blue Cockade," which apparently was the family consensus. She teased William Valentine that "I know you all would enjoy hearing Mary Martha, Nettie, cousin Fred and myself discussing politics, every night. We all agree exactly, therefore, it is not as interesting as if there were some one oposed to us. We talk so loud and are so excited you can scarcely hear a word." Despite their apparent enthusiasm for secession, the Valentine family urged both William and Edward V. Valentine, William's brother and a budding sculptor, to stay in Europe in case of hostilities.[29]

Other Richmond women held a less enthusiastic and more studied view of the secession controversy. Women who had promoted sectional conciliation now slowly turned to support for sectional independence. American nationalism gave way to Southern nationalism, as Southerners prepared to defend their homes. While the public debate dragged on into March, Ellen Mordecai wrote a niece that "the convention is still going on & speakers on opposite sides use strong arguments which if they have no other effect keep *lady* politicians in a state of indecision." Women went to hear the positions presented in the convention, where "the room is generally crowded." Mordecai "went on Thursday with Emma & our next neighbour Mrs. Robertson who sent to ask some of us to accompany her to hear the last half of Mr. Holcomb's speech on secession it was very interesting & well delivered. Mr. Baldwin is replying to him on the Union side & said to be equally powerful." Grasping fully the gravity of the situation, Mordecai hoped that "they all speak from honest principles and that an overruling Providence may decide the all important result."[30]

The moment of conversion for Caroline Mordecai probably was the same as for many Richmonders—when the first news of Lincoln's call for troops was heard. Emma Mordecai reported that her sister Caroline, "after a day of fasting and sorrow following Lincoln's proclamation, sorrow which amounted to sickness," had "arisen a strong warm southern rights woman—She seems born anew."[31] Even after the secession ordinance was finally passed, Emma Mordecai reported the somber power of the moment, noting that "when our convention passed the ordinance the scene was most solemn and affecting and there were tears on all mens faces in that assembly. Even those most anxious for the event could not unmoved break the ties which bound them to the dear old Union." In contrast, she pointed to her sister, who was "practicing the Marsellaise at this moment," and who had "been a strong secessionist from the beginning.[32]

Northerners and foreign-born Richmonders held their breath throughout the secession crisis, unsure until the last of the eventual outcome. Robert Granniss, the Brooklyn-born dry-goods clerk, cautiously assessed the situation in early April, recording that "politically, matters remain much the same. The Southern Confederacy is in full blast and Va still remains in the Union." Although he believed that the "secessionists are gaining ground here," he felt it was "impossible to tell the ultimate result. Trade continues fearfully dull for this season."[33]

As late as March 8, 1861, Henry L. Pelouze matter-of-factly reported to his wife that "I think I shall have plenty of Business down here if we don't have Civil War. The people here are about equally divided between Union & Sesession. I don't know which will come out ahead." He told his wife that "I think you would like the people down here Maggie likes them. She says she likes them much better than she espected she would." [34]

Jacob Bechtel gauged public sentiment by popular street activity and the standards flying over the city. Washington as a unifying symbol probably went through his mind as he wrote, "This is the 22nd of February, and the streets are filled with soldiery, and the national flag is waving from the roof of the Capitol, and every other public building as well as from the windows of the hall, where is now assembled the Convention, upon whose decision is to rest the solution of the question—shall we go with the North, or shall we join with the South? The course of Mr. Lincoln and his Cabinet will soon decide the question." Feeling helpless, he told his brother: "As for you or me, or what we may say or think, matters but little—We can only look on, and prepare to swim with the masses around us, either North or South." [35]

On the first of April, Bechtel noted a distinct change in the city's skyline: "If the increase of secession flags is any indication, I think that side is gradually increasing; to which every effort is being made by vaporizing demagogues who have been suddenly thrown out of public employment and are seeking to advance themselves by precipitating us all into revolution." Joseph Reid Anderson and other members of the Southern Rights Convention had learned the art of street theater well. Anderson and other leaders led a procession through the streets of Richmond in support of secession. Arriving at the Tredegar Iron Works, they hoisted the secession flag above the spike mill. [36]

Northerners living in the Virginia capital clearly understood the consequences of Lincoln's actions. On April 15 Robert Granniss noted in his diary that "Mr. Lincoln's policy is coercive and Va will secede from the Union." Granniss anticipated a "grand torchlight procession tomorrow night" and went so far as to "confess that since last Sunday my feelings and opinions have undergone a radical change and I see no course but secession." [37]

Descriptions of the crescendo of the secession movement in mid-April 1861 reveal the wide gulf between the perceptions of Northerners and Southerners. Emma Mordecai described a willful but restrained atmosphere in Richmond, finding "no disorder of any kind no noisy exultation—every countenance looked serious—anxious—determined—even among the young volunteers the same calm determined spirit is manifest." Mordecai witnessed a rally from an elevated bridge connecting the Ballard and Exchange Hotels, "looking down on a sea of faces thronging the whole space between the two buildings—Hundreds of ladies among them—everything quiet and orderly. The only noise being the calling out of different speakers and the hearty responses of the men to such sentiments as pleased them—or such determinations as they endorsed such as 'We will drive Lincoln from that chair.'—A voice 'we will do it.'"[38]

On April 18, 1861, New Yorker Robert Granniss made his last entry in the Richmond diary that he had kept since 1858. Noting that the ordinance of secession had passed the day before, Granniss ruefully recorded that "the excitement is intense. The wildest joy seems to prevail. All is war and bloodshed in the way of talk." His young Southern friends no doubt openly boasted about what they would do in the coming struggle. The clerk felt himself "to be very singularly situated," and like hundreds of other young men in Richmond, he realized that "I cannot be expected to bear arms against home and kindred." Anticipating business "very dull and it will be worse," and that the "mails will probably be stopped in a day or two," Granniss began planning his removal from Richmond. Two days later, he and a fellow Yankee clerk boarded a northbound train and left for home.[39]

For urban workers, Northerners, and immigrants, Richmond had been transformed from an American city to a Southern place practically overnight. No longer comfortable in their adopted home, many joined Granniss in his exodus from the city; even more would follow him in the years ahead. This was especially true for those with no property or family ties in Richmond. Pelouze related to his wife that most of his associates in the city "are single men or men whose wifes are at the north. There has quite a number of my former acqiantices left here for there homes." German Johann Gottfried Lange remembered that upon the outbreak of the war "many foreigners who did reside in Richmond but were not citizens sold all their belongings and left the city," and those who stayed often did so "because work was easy to find and paid well." [40]

In the week leading to secession, the *Richmond Daily Dispatch* had complained that the "most respectable and influential citizens" of the state might leave for "some more congenial latitude"—the states that had already seceded—if the convention did not act decisively to protect their property by taking Virginia out of the Union. But the newspaper failed to mention the workers who were leaving daily, thus depriving the Southern confederacy of a critical asset: skilled labor. The Tredegar Iron Works lost experienced artisans in the months leading to Virginia's secession. Robert S. Archer, a manager at the Armory rolling mills, complained to an associate on April 11 that J. M. McCarty, a manager at the ironworks, had "left us, he went off the day after Mr. Anderson left. . . . He has acted badly, will tell you all about it when you return. He is employed at St. Louis and took back with him some 5 or 6 of our Irish Puddlers." [41]

Tredegar advertised for skilled workers in March and April. The company requested R. J. Capron of Baltimore "to have the annexed advertisement inserted in the Balt Sun or some other paper that reaches the working class in your City." Tredegar wanted "first class Black Smiths . . . none but good workmen need apply." Anderson's reliance on skilled workers from the North and Europe was now a serious liability. During the war the ironworks would become more dependent on black workers than ever before as workers left for the North while a crush of Confederate contracts strained the capacity of the mills. In at least one case, workers were discharged for disloyalty to the Confederacy. [42]

Those that stayed in the Confederate capital eyed the daily happenings carefully and thought about sending relatives out of danger. Jacob Bechtel told his brother that "as soon as travelling can be resumed, I will send Sarah home, and regulate my own movements here by the course of events," but it soon became apparent that escape might be impossible for some time. Just a few days later he reported that "as to going North at present it is entirely impracticable, all direct communication with Washington being cut off by the blockade, and seizure of the Potomac Boats by Lincoln, and to send them around by the way of Chambersburg & Harrisburg Harpers Ferry & Winchester, would cost too much, besides being at great risk. I therefore prefer staying here until the direct route through Washington, shall be resumed." [43]

Bechtel agonized about his decision because he had strong attachments to Richmond and the South. He could not "forget that I have eaten and drank at the hospitable boards, and sat by the peaceful fireside of the South for sixteen years, if I am Northern by birth.—Here three of my children were born, and here the ashes of one repose. I cannot raise my hand against them; even at the expense, as you say, of the sympathy of you all." Despite these feelings, Bechtel, like Robert Granniss, could not bear arms against his homeland, telling his brother in Philadelphia that "I have not joined any military company for I cannot bear to turn against the Old Flag." [44]

Secession brought a heightened awareness of possible internal enemies and the possibility of recriminations against any dissenters from the Confederate cause. With emotions in Richmond running high, Bechtel cautioned his brother that "I received your letter yesterday and read it with *great Caution.* The sentiments therein expressed were so foreign to those at present in vogue here that I deemed it prudent to commit it to the flames, . . . lest by dropping out of my pocket, it might put my neck in danger of a hempen collar." Bechtel ruefully noted that he had been "particularly free in my speech up to recently, while the question was a debatable one, but since the War Proclamation of that stupid ass at Washington, all such ideas have been abandoned and those known to have entertained them must put their hands upon their mouths, or *quit.*" [45]

The opening of letters from the North had been practiced before the war, but only those addressed to slaves. Now a government supposedly founded on the fear of centralized power opened the mail of white men. Bechtel warned his brother that "a strict surveillance is being exercised here, and a number of instances have occurred recently of letters having been opened, previously to being delivered. This particularly with letters coming to any who are suspected of Northern proclivities." In the face of these new realities, Bechtel tried to assure himself and his brother that "I have been so long here, and am so well known, that I am regarded in a great measure as being *one of them,* so that with the exception of the pain at hearing the unstinted abuse poured upon the land of my birth, and Philadelphia in particular, I experience no inconvenience whatsoever. The children go to school and no one molests them; because I suppose they are as ready to sing Dixie, and wear secession cockades, as the best of them." Yet a month later, he again cautioned, "Dont write me any thing about politics, all letters are scrutinized, and any strong expressions might involve me in trouble, as a traitor & holding traitrous correspondence." [46]

Men with families and strong Union feelings held back or openly resisted joining the military, but many others filled the ranks of companies in the flush of secession fever. Richmond's commercial men, who had largely sided with the advocates of Southern rights, now saw their Southern-born junior partners, clerks, and sons march off to war. William Ludwell Sheppard, a former clerk at John H. Claiborne's commission house, returned from his artistic studies in New York and joined the Howitzer Company as a private. When the unit was expanded into a battalion, Sheppard received a commission as a second lieutenant in the Howitzer's second company. Dry-goods magnate Thomas R. Price watched his son Richard Channing Price leave the city and join the Howitzers at Yorktown in July. Gustavus A. Wallace, the brother and partner of Jefferson Wallace in the commission business that their father had established, enlisted on July 20 as the captain of the Richmond Light Guard, which became part of the Wise Legion.[47]

Some Tredegar workmen preferred wielding weapons to making them, and these defections cooled Joseph R. Anderson's usual zeal for the Southern cause. Anderson wrote Governor John Letcher on April 27 seeking the discharge of Lewis Ogden, a blacksmith who had joined an artillery company, noting Ogden's importance in "getting out the iron work for gun carriages." Anderson also asked for the services of John McDonald, the first Sergeant of the all-Irish Montgomery Guard, "one of the most important men engaged in furnishing cannon in our employment." John McGill, the Catholic bishop of Richmond, blessed the pikes wielded by the company "in a solemn celebration in the basement of Saint Peter's Cathedral" only a city block from Capitol Square. The unit became Company C of the First Virginia Infantry Regiment.[48]

The German militia companies of Richmond also responded enthusiastically to the call for troops. On April 21, 1861, the Virginia Rifles enrolled for active service as Company K of the First Regiment Virginia Infantry.

That same month another German company, the Marion Rifles, were organized and brought into state service in May, eventually forming Company K of the Fifteenth Regiment Virginia Infantry.[49]

Private Charles August Hennighausen expressed the near-universal sentiment of Confederate and Union soldiers at the beginning of the Civil War that the war would be over quickly: "My idea at the beginning of this war was that it would come to two or three battles at the most and in three months everything would be over. On the 26th of May 1861 I marched with Company K (Marion Rifles) . . . with bands playing and flags flying, cheered by thousands through Richmond to the steamboat landing where we embarked and rode to Williamsburg." For Hennighausen and his comrades, this was a time to glory in the sounds and sights of martial display. "Our company was the finest of the Regiment," he proclaimed, "We had grey hunting jackets and trousers with black rifles and cutlasses." This war was not to end with a quick victory, however, and the experience of ethnic soldiers as the war wore on demonstrated their marginal allegiance to the Confederacy.[50]

The Marion Rifles and Virginia Rifles drew on established leaders from the German community for their officers. Albert Lybrock, the captain of the Marion Rifles, had previously served as captain of the Virginia Rifles and was an architect of some renown. He had been superintendent of the construction of the U.S. Customs House in Richmond a few years earlier. Located just below Jefferson's State Capitol, the building now housed Confederate government offices. Another officer of the Marion Rifles, August Schad, was also well known to the Virginia Rifles and the German community but not as a soldier. The company and many German organizations met at Schad's Hall, and Schad had been arrested in the nativist troubles of 1853. He had also been a charter member of Saint John's Evangelical-Lutheran Church and served as its president in 1853. Prominent Catholics also served as officers. The Virginia Rifles elected Florence Miller, a member of Saint Mary's German Catholic Church, captain of the company on May 30, 1859, and he served until the end of 1861. Catholics and Protestants also served together in the enlisted ranks.[51]

The men of the Virginia Rifles and Marion Rifles mirrored the religious and class composition of their community. The Virginia Rifles were almost all artisans, a collection of shoemakers, butchers, and other tradesmen and skilled workers. The Marion Rifles were somewhat more middle class than the Virginia Rifles, with a higher representation of shopkeepers, clerks, salesmen, and professionals, but of fifty-six men of the Marion Rifles whose profession could be identified thirty-seven were artisans and tradesmen.[52] Skill was a distinct advantage, for it often led to special duty, quite often in Richmond, the home city for most of the men. The Virginia state government, the Confederate Ordnance and Quartermaster Departments, and other government and military agencies detailed men from these companies.[53]

Despite their ability to gain preferred duty, the men of both companies eventually decided to leave the service after their initial one-year enlistment, even if it meant being considered deserters or traitors by the Confederate army and government. On taking command of the Fifteenth Virginia Regiment, E. M. Morrison wrote to the adjutant general of the Army of Northern Virginia decrying the disorganized state of the Fifteenth:

> I was informed that two compys F & K the one composed entirely of Irish & the other of German claimed exemption from service under the clause of the Conscript Act approved 16th April 62 discharging from service *non domiciled residents* [and] had refused to reorganize. Their officers had left their commands without permission in this disorganized condition & such of the enlisted men as had not deserted were temporarily placed under the command of officers of other companies. A short while afterwards by special order from the then Secy of War (Genl. Randolph) the number and date of which were not then preserved and are not now remembered, these two companies were disbanded.[54]

Another Confederate officer clarified just how many men were left after this mass exodus from the field, writing that "nine or ten" remained, "the last of whom deserted at Hagerstown Md" on September 10, 1862. Initial charges of desertion and being absent without leave landed a few members in custody. Confederate authorities confined the second wartime captain of the Virginia Rifles, Frederick W. Hagemeyer, and three other members of the company in Castle Godwin and the guard-house.[55] The men of the

German companies did not, of course, consider themselves deserters but cited General Orders No. 30, issued by the Confederate War Department and Adjutant and Inspector General's Office, based on an act passed by the Confederate Congress on April 16, 1862, and further clarified by General Orders No. 37, which exempted certain classes of people from military service, including "foreigners who have not acquired domicile in the Confederate States." [56]

For Hennighausen and his fellow German soldiers it was never a fight for the "fatherland," and the hardships became difficult to endure. "We soon found out that military service in southern America is no child's play and we had to sweat for having bound ourselves to it for a year," Hennighausen stated in his memoir. "Old German soldiers in our company would rather have had five years of German service than one year here." Eventually, the constant marching and lack of adequate shelter, rations, and tobacco cooled the martial spirit among the men, and they reentered their adopted home, the city of Richmond, in a far different frame of mind than when they left. "Approaching Richmond our year had come to an end and since we were foreigners they could not hold us longer; since the staff officers made difficulties we all tore away one night and found our [right?] and got our Honorable Discharge sometime later in Richmond. From this time on I went about my business with constant complaints with the conscript officer." [57] It was not only the men of Companies F and K of the Fifteenth that took advantage of the exemption. Men in the Irish components of the First Virginia Regiment also used it to end their service, as did foreign soldiers in units with no ethnic identification.

Foreign-born soldiers used their exemption to prevent their later conscription by the Confederate government, which was desperate for men to send into the field. An affidavit in the file of Bernhard Bergmeyer of the Virginia Rifles gives a good sense of what foreigners thought nondomiciled meant, and the difficulty of proving that status. The notary public took Bergmeyer's statement under oath that he "is a native of Prussia and came to America about five and a half years ago, to visit the Country, and seek employment." Bergmeyer claimed he intended to return to "his Native Country" and had never "voted, has no property, never took any steps towards being naturalized, or in any manner attempted to exercise the rights of citizenship in this Country, and has never reenlisted or received Bounty." Bergmeyer's affidavit was supported by a document from the Consul of the Free City of Bremen in Richmond, which also stated that "he has never taken the oath of Allegiance to the United States of America or the Confederate States of America or to any other foreign nation." [58]

Similar documents appear in numerous service records of soldiers in Richmond companies. William Buckley of the Montgomery Guard submitted an affidavit, along with a letter from the British Consulate, as did Henry Boucher, an Irishman in Company B, known as the City Guard. Many men who were discharged as part of the companywide special orders issued by the War Department did not fall under the strictest definition of "non domiciled." For instance, Charles Haase, a cap manufacturer and a member of the Marion Rifles, certainly owned property and probably intended to stay in America. Charles Hennighausen owned and ran a store during the Civil War. Such cases probably heightened the ill will toward foreign-born residents of the city who refused to fight. Hennighausen recalled that "for some time these certificates were respected by the Confederate police and military authorities . . . but they also intensified the ill-feeling towards the foreigners." [59]

As the war wore on and the conscription officers became more insistent, some Germans joined home-defense units within the city. Others fled through the Union lines. The provost marshal in Washington, D.C., interviewed several former members of the German home guard from Richmond in 1864. He also interrogated a number of Richmond civilians of German birth who felt that they had worn out their welcome in Richmond, although some were longtime residents. [60]

There were also other ways of avoiding service, even for those who were naturalized. Philip Whitlock, a recent immigrant, had belonged to the Richmond Grays for a number of years, reporting for duty during the John Brown episode. He later recalled the conflicting emotions he had during his Civil War years. After being mustered into service, the Grays marched to Norfolk, and Whitlock remembered feeling "very patriotic and loved the country of my adoption. Being a full fledged citizen I was ready to fight for its rights. Especially when I was of the Jewish Faith I thought that if I am negligent in my duty as a Citizen of this country it would unfavorably reflect on the whole Jewish race and religion." [61]

While Whitlock initially felt patriotism, he soon realized that he lacked a commitment for actual combat. "As far as I was concerned," he related, "I was not very anxious to go to the front as they called it. While I realized the fact that I then was a 'soldier' whose business was to fight—if that was his profession—but I knew that that was not mine. While I was willing to do my duty to the country of which I had the good fortune to be a citizen and I was very proud of it, and no doubt would fight as well as anyone, but I was not one of these that [was] *Spoiling* for a *Fight.*" [62]

Finally, Whitlock resolved to quit the service. Soldier "life did not suit" him, and he rationalized that "The Confederate cause was getting weaker and weaker every day," although only about a year had passed and many Confederate victories lay ahead. Whitlock preferred to leave "Honorably if possible," and he wrote his brother to acquire a substitute as others in his company had done. Unfortunately, the cost of buying a replacement was too high.[63]

Eventually, events conspired to help Whitlock out of his dilemma. A series of illnesses landed him in Richmond's Chimborazo Hospital and eventually relegated him to civilian duty. Whitlock made sure to stay out of uniform. Mandatory physical examinations every thirty days meant that he "was liable to be sent to the *Front* (as they called it) at any time but by being friendly with the Dr. this was mannaged so then I got extension every time." Whitlock even managed to receive a month's furlough in March 1863 and spent it running the Union blockade, spending almost a week in New York purchasing goods to sell upon his return to Richmond. This entrepreneurial activity received a setback when Whitlock was arrested trying to cross back into Richmond through Confederate lines and lost about half of his goods when the soldiers rifled through his bags.[64]

The lack of loyalty to the Confederacy shown by foreign-born soldiers should not be surprising; most had no roots in Virginia or the South. Despite their youth, only one soldier in the two German companies was born in America, meaning that almost all of the soldiers had come to America in the twenty years before the Civil War. The many men who filed affidavits of nondomiciled status claimed to have come even more recently, most within three or four years of the war. Indeed, the bulk of the mid-nineteenth-century immigration from Germany to America occurred in the 1850s, peaking in 1854. The larger patterns of German immigration also supports the men's contention that they came to America seeking economic opportunity. Most German immigrants came not because of religious and political persecution but because of agricultural and economic displacement. This was clearly also the case with Irish soldiers. The Irish in Richmond were generally unskilled, and most had made their way to Richmond in the great famine migrations of the late antebellum years.[65]

Richmond's German and Irish community had very little economic power besides their skills and were only loosely tied to the Southern economy. Most had probably not acquired a large amount of property, if any at all, and had little interest or connection with the institution of slavery. Being largely a group of mechanics, artisans, and laborers, most had little interest in the ideologies supporting the use of slave labor. All these factors made their commitment to the Confederacy tenuous at best. The difficulties and losses of war soon overcame them, and they turned to defend their community and homes. Looking back on the battles of 1861 and 1862 one German veteran exclaimed, "Would to God they [the north] had won then."[66]

The flagging interest in the war by foreign-born troops was not the only sign that support for the Confederacy was weakening. Sallie Putnam recalled that early in 1862 city residents, much to their surprise, "became conscious of the remains of Union sentiment in Richmond." Union men and women expressed themselves on walls throughout the city, proclaiming "Union Men to the Rescue!"; "Now is the time to rally around the Old Flag"; and "God bless the Stars and Stripes." Defeats in the west and at Roanoke Island provoked jibes such as "What has become of Providence?" Putnam and other Confederate supporters became "convinced we had traitors among us."[67]

The approach of the massive Army of the Potomac under George McClellan emboldened Unionists and fueled the fears of pro-Southern citizens and Confederate officials. The *New York Herald* gleefully reported what Sallie Putnam had observed, that "the streets of Richmond are plac-

arded with calls upon Union men to watch and wait, that the day is dawn-
ing, and proclaiming 'the Union forever.'" The *Herald* also accurately announced to New Yorkers that the Confederate government had declared
Richmond under martial law and that Unionist John Minor Botts and
others had been arrested "on charges of being connected with a Union
conspiracy."[68]

In the heart of "secessia," *Charleston Mercury* readers learned of another round of arrests from their reporter in Richmond, who melodramat-
ically announced that "a few minutes ago two detectives passed down Bank
Street, on their way to 'Castle Godwin,' the jail for traitors, having in custody CHARLES PALMER, a prominent citizen, a great friend of BOTTS."
A. Judson Crane attempted to see Botts as his counsel, but the Old Whigs
were not allowed to meet.[69]

Foreign-born citizens came under heightened scrutiny as well. The
Herald delighted in reporting the detainment of "a number of Germans
belonging to the Turnverein . . . in consequence of a Union flag being dis-
played in the meeting hall." Many Germans became residents of Castle
Godwin and Castle Thunder, Richmond's political prisons, including
Hermann L. Wiegand, a well-known German citizen who had opposed se-
cession, and Frederick William E. Lohman, a former lieutenant in the
Virginia Rifles.[70]

Obviously the Confederate government took the threat of "Fifth Columnists" quite seriously, but many who later wrote about these events,
including Sallie Putnam, often discounted the strength or seriousness of
opposition activity in the Confederacy. Others attacked the notion of a
Unionist underground movement by ascribing profit as the primary motive
for any disloyal acts.

Johann Gottfried Lange, a naturalized, pro-Southern German writing
after the war, used the case of F. W. E. Lohman to show "how a German can
become a bad character." Lange recalled that "F. W. E. Lohman had served
as lieutenant of the German Huntsman Company [the Virginia Rifles] in
the First Volunteer Regiment on July 21, 1861 in the Battle of Mannassas.
Now, after the company had been dissolved he began the dirty business to
secretly transport men across the border who did not want to serve in the
army which earned him a lot of money."[71]

In fact, Lohman traveled within a secret world of Union sympathizers, spies, saboteurs, and speculators in Richmond. Many of his colleagues also came from foreign lands, but native-born Union men and women, black and white, also collaborated in fifth-column activities. The coordination of these diverse groups into a single network is suggested by the events surrounding the smuggling of the body of Union officer Ulric Dahlgren through the Confederate lines in 1864. Dahlgren led a daring but foolhardy raid on Richmond, purportedly to free Union prisoners, destroy property, and assassinate members of the Confederate government. He was killed and his body interred in Oakwood Cemetery. Fearing abuse of the body by rabid Confederates, Elizabeth Van Lew enlisted Lohman to find the body, believing him "willing to run the risk of its removal." Lohman convinced Martin M. Lipscomb, the overseer of military burials in the city, to assist him. Christopher Taylor, a free black who worked with Thomas McNevin, had observed the burial, and told Lipscomb the location. Lohman, his brother, and an African-American man, possibly Taylor, removed the corpse.[72]

According to later newspaper accounts, the body was then "taken to the house of a German, near by Chelsea Hill," north of the head of Shockoe Valley. Van Lew and "three or four Union men of Richmond" met there to attend to the corpse and make plans.[73] The house was the home of William L. Rawley, who, according to Van Lew, "drove Dalgren's body through the rebel lines," although the postwar newspaper accounts credited Lohman with this deed. Van Lew also praised Rawley for harboring deserters and spies during the war to aid the Union cause. These descriptions of Unionist activities suggest an organized cell of activists that included a number of members of the German community.[74] Johann Gottfried Lange clearly believed that Lohman's motivation for his activities was financial. Like all underground, illegal movements, the Richmond Union network attracted those who would take risks for a price as well as true believers, and Lohman could have been a little of both.

The personal histories of several of the better-known characters in the wartime drama suggest that many held serious antislavery and Unionist convictions. Thomas McNiven left Glasgow, Scotland, in 1853 with his two brothers, settling in Brooklyn, New York. According to a memoir, he left his homeland to escape "English domination," and he began his career on behalf of those dominated by slavery when he was barely twenty years old. McNiven traveled to Richmond in 1855 sponsored by the Waldense Society, a Scottish group opposed to slavery. He joined with fellow countrymen in conducting underground railroad activities in Virginia. During the Civil War he ran a bakery at 811 North Fifth Street, using it as a front for spying activities under the code name "Quaker." Although he had already been naturalized in New York, McNiven used his old British citizenship papers to effect while moving through the Confederate lines. He worked closely with Christopher Taylor, the free black who helped with the removal of Dahlgren's body and who carried messages for Richmond's fifth columnists.[75]

Merchant Charles Palmer devoted both money and information to the Union cause. He gave a large sum of cash that was distributed to needy Union families and contributed to the aid of prisoners of war in Richmond. He also provided information on Confederate troop strengths and positions around Richmond for Major General Benjamin F. Butler's aborted raid on the capital, planned for early February 1864. Palmer believed strongly in the Union. A long-time critic of the States' Rights doctrine, he had expressed his belief in gradual abolition many years before in a private letter to his son, Dr. William Price Palmer, who joined the Richmond Howitzers in 1859 and rose to the rank of captain, later serving as a regimental surgeon. Charles Palmer despised the cause for which his son fought, and his sentiments and activities landed him in Castle Godwin, a former jail in Richmond's slave-trading district that had been converted into a political prison. Palmer joined the more famous Unionists Franklin Stearns and John Minor Botts in the same cells that had once held African Americans bound for sale.[76]

Accounts of Union activity during the Civil War often stress the Northern and immigrant background of many fifth columnists, but Palmer was born and bred in Virginia and was a member of the business community. Other Virginia-born men aided Union activities. Martin M. Lipscomb became well known after the Civil War as a participant in the recovery of Union officer Ulric Dahlgren's body. Lipscomb touted his working-class

origins while campaigning for office before, during, and after the Civil War and was a strong advocate of African-American rights during the early years of Reconstruction. Ironically, Lipscomb had been a member of the Richmond Light Infantry Blues during the company's 1855 trip to Philadelphia.[77]

Elizabeth Van Lew, the key figure in Richmond's spy network, had been raised in Virginia and made no secret of her abolitionist and Unionist beliefs. Unionists often paid a heavy cost for their disloyal activities in Confederate Richmond. Van Lew and her brother John Van Lew spent a great deal of their own money in Unionist activities, including aiding Yankee prisoners, and "when their convertible property, or a good portion of it, was gone, they used in the same way the receipts of the brothers [John's] hardware store, until he (having steadily refused to bear arms even for local defense) was seized and put in the ranks, when he immediately made his way to our lines near Cold Harbor in 1864 with valuable information. This of course closed his store and nearly took away the means of subsistence of the family."[78]

Other women joined Elizabeth Van Lew in her fight against the Confederate government. Although very little is known about her, Mary Elizabeth Bowser directly aided Van Lew's spying activities. Apparently freed before the war by Van Lew, and possibly educated in Philadelphia, the former slave entered the household of Jefferson Davis and, according to McNiven, provided valuable information to the Union spy ring. Bowser and free black Christopher Taylor actively participated in the campaign for Union victory, yet few details of their activities are known.[79]

Thomas McNiven acknowledged two women in particular for their work in the Union underground. Johannah Hoffman, a native of Bavaria, came to Virginia sometime in the decade before the Civil War. A widow in her early twenties with at least two daughters when the war began, Hoffman carried messages through the lines and participated in the reburial of Ulric Dahlgren's body at Scotsman Robert Orrock's farm near Hungary Station in Henrico County, an important way station on the espionage network. Louisa Delarue also assisted in the reburial of Dahlgren at Orrock's farm. Delarue was born in Virginia, probably of French and/or

German descent. Like Hoffman, she used her skill as a seamstress to conceal messages in her clothing and her language skills to move through the lines and deliver intelligence.[80]

Some traitors to the Confederacy held positions of great confidence and responsibility, most notably on Richmond's railroads. Samuel Ruth, the superintendent of the Richmond, Fredericksburg, and Potomac Railroad, hailed from Pennsylvania, and testified to his anti-Confederate activities in petitions to the federal government after the war. Information passed through the lines by Ruth gave Grant intelligence about Lee's movements at Fort Stedman in 1864, with devastating results. Government agents arrested Ruth in 1865 for helping men desert to the Union lines. He languished in Castle Thunder with F. W. E. Lohman, a fellow conspirator, but the court released Ruth within a few weeks. Ruth again passed information to the Union army regarding the defenses of his own railroad. In light of these acts against the Confederacy, Ruth's record as superintendent of the Richmond, Fredericksburg, and Potomac seems especially suspicious. His railroad seemed especially inept during times of greatest military need. Troop movements were delayed despite the availability of railroad cars, private baggage occupied cars needed for critical shipments of foodstuffs to the front, and vital bridges went unrepaired.[81]

Hard-core Unionists acted positively to undermine the Confederacy, but the vicissitudes of war and the actions of government officials prompted others to express the limits of their loyalty in less overt ways. Despite the mobilization for the war effort, workers tried to maintain their independence from employers in the workplace. Irish foundry workers struck at Tredegar in September 1861, threatening to go to the nearby Richmond Armory (housed in the former Virginia State Armory, originally the Virginia Manufactory of Arms) where higher pay could be had. This work action prompted Tredegar's management to increase wages for a variety of classes of skilled workers. Competition for the dwindling number of ironworkers in the Confederate capital gave these skilled men considerable leverage over employers. In March 1863 a group of Tredegar workers struck again, complaining that their pay was not competitive with the government-run shops. Josiah Gorgas, the Confederate chief of ordnance, was forced to freeze wages and centralize control of pay increases.[82]

Industrialists and the Ordnance Department indulged ironworkers because these men were absolutely essential to the making of the instruments of war. Government officials and pro-Confederate newspapers branded strikers in less crucial industries as traitors to the cause. When journeymen lithographers struck in April 1862 in response to the use of apprentices in the printing of Confederate currency, Provost Marshall John H. Winder had them jailed until the workers consented to abandon their activism.[83]

Workingmen also took positions on the issues of the day that reinforced their view of themselves as citizen-workers first and foremost, not Confederate citizens. In September 1863 a workingmen's mass meeting asked the General Assembly to adopt a price-fixing bill that was then under consideration. After state senator George W. Randolph stated that he would oppose the bill unless the electorate declared its will otherwise, workingmen reconvened in October and passed resolutions in favor of the bill. Workers posed their appeal in starkly class terms that anticipated the rhetoric of the Knights of Labor, contrasting workers with the moneyed class that "consumes all and produces nothing." Newspapers railed against the workers as threats to property and public order, considering them "candidates for the penitentiary." [84]

Hundreds of ironworkers expressed overt disloyalty to the cause by fleeing into the Union lines. In 1862 Joseph Reid Anderson pressed the Confederate government to have the Tredegar workforce enrolled into service so that they could be detailed back to the works. Anderson hoped that this would stem the tide of defections through the lines, but when the men were finally enrolled as conscripts in early 1863 the order had exactly the opposite effect. Tredegar managers now had to "report that many of the men, of foreign birth, employed at these works, are leaving to go beyond our lines." The Ironmaker to the Confederacy assembled just enough puddlers to fire five furnaces, well below the ironwork's capacity.[85]

During Grant's campaigns in 1864, even more disastrous losses occurred. Pressed into the trenches to defend Richmond, workers from Tredegar Iron Works and the government ordnance shops deserted in massive numbers. From May to October, Josiah Gorgas, the head of the Confederate Ordnance Department, reported the defection of 264 mechanics, and the losses of men from Tredegar were also very high. The inflation of government currency drove down real wages, increasing the pressure on working families. With increasingly little economic incentive to stay and much to lose, including life and limb, workers sought the relative safety of Northern soil.[86]

Worker activism also caused conflict across racial lines. When white gravediggers at Shockoe Cemetery went on strike in August 1864, city authorities replaced them with blacks. The whites returned and assaulted the African-American replacements, reclaiming their positions. Black workers entered (usually peacefully) many new fields during the war, replacing whites at the city gasworks, doing hospital work, and providing teamsters and laborers to assist the armies in the field.[87]

Despite the crucial role of slave and free-black workers in the war effort, Confederate leaders believed blacks to be increasingly restive and defiant. Jefferson Davis warned the Confederate Congress in 1864 that he feared plots by Union officials to foment a servile insurrection in the city. Davis's perspective no doubt was shaped by the loss of numerous house servants who ran away and the attempt by another to burn the Confederate president's home.[88]

The impressment of large numbers of African Americans to work on the city's fortifications provided opportunities for slaves to flee into the Union lines. In 1862 almost two hundred slaves escaped through the lines while working on the defenses of Richmond. The Tredegar Iron Works lost enslaved workers Alfred, Monroe, Turner, Toney, and Edorn on New Year's Eve 1863. Slaves were often recaptured while trying to make their escape and found themselves imprisoned in Richmond until their owners reclaimed them.[89]

Fears of slave insurrection and spying contributed to the passing of new restrictive city ordinances that further limited the activities and movements of free blacks and slaves in Richmond. Conservatives pointed to familiar targets as the cause of unrest among the slave population. When the Reverend J. L. Reynolds of South Carolina attacked black church congregations and their white ministers in print, Robert Ryland, the white minister of First African Baptist Church in Richmond, replied, asserting the orderliness and conservatism of black churchgoers.[90]

Black flight and acts of defiance probably increased during the war, but several factors also limited overt conflict between whites and blacks in the city. Although the war produced a certain amount of social disruption and confusion that sometimes aided escape, mobilization also turned Richmond into a vast armed camp of Southern white men. Open rebellion would have been extremely hazardous. In addition, many in Richmond's African-American community may have anticipated a Union victory that would soon offer new opportunities. Richmond tobacco worker Thomas Johnson led Bible classes during the war, and his group especially enjoyed reading Daniel 11, which prophesied that "the king of the north shall come, and cast up a mount, and take the most fenced cities: and the arms of the south shall not withstand, neither his chosen people, neither *shall there be any* strength to withstand." The possibility of victory by the Northern armies might have easily influenced many blacks to watch and wait.[91]

Rebelliousness in wartime Richmond was not restricted to the black population. Food shortages and high prices fueled a violent breakdown of public order in the city that involved a wide range of white citizens. The Bread Riot of April 2, 1863, was the most visible sign of the social disruption that the Civil War visited on Richmond. Probably a planned protest that went awry, the riot involved women from various neighborhoods and from outside the city. The women gathered at Capitol Square and demanded food. When their request was denied, they swarmed down several adjacent commercial streets, especially Main, Cary and Franklin, breaking into shops along with men who joined in the looting. The Public Guard eventually scattered the rioters. Food was in short supply and thus sold at high prices because of a combination of factors, including impressment of foodstuffs by military authorities, the disruption of agricultural production owing to the constant military campaigns in Virginia, and bad weather, which broke down transportation to the city. News of earlier riots in other Southern cities and towns had probably reached Richmond and may have inspired the mob's leaders. Crime was already rife in the city, and the women and men who participated in the riot were only doing on a larger scale what was a daily phenomenon in the Confederate city.[92]

The Bread Riot was just a symptom of larger social and economic problems that afflicted the wartime city. The city's population swelled to approximately three times its antebellum size with the influx of soldiers and their inevitable retainers and hangers-on. This rapid growth strained pub-

lic services to the breaking point and promoted the further development of
the city's already thriving seamier side. Richmond, the capital of an overwhelmingly rural country supposedly based on conservative social values,
became the epitome of urban disorder and immorality to Southerners. In
August 1862 Dr. Benjamin Fleet referred to Richmond as "that *Hog
hole.* . . . I never supposed I could ever have been so thoroughly disgusted
with any place this side of Yankeedom." Fleet and many others recoiled at
the brothels, faro banks, and saloons that lined the city's streets, and elites
and government leaders looked down on and feared the many thousands
of new people that filled these establishments: rough soldiers, camp followers, deserters, criminals, and other unsavory characters. They were
just as disgusted at the workers, African Americans, and immigrants who,
they believed, showed little or no loyalty to their new nation. In their
eyes, Richmond had fulfilled its antebellum destiny and truly become a
Yankee city.[93]

Attacks on outsiders that remained largely confined to private opinion
in the antebellum era now found their way into the public presses and
sometimes prompted actions as well, such as the arrest of immigrants for
suspected disloyalty. For instance, most contemporary accounts of the
Bread Riot focused on the leadership and participation of working-class
and foreign-born women, who were usually denounced as the dregs of society. Yet middle-class, native-born women also joined the protest, and the
foreign-born were both participants and victims. Rioters broke into the
shop of a widowed Jewish merchant, Minna Schweitzer, which was located
in a "German and Jewish quarter reputed to be a center for profiteers, or
'speculators.'"[94]

The looting of Jewish businesses during the Bread Riot was part of a rise
in anti-Semitic and anti-immigrant feeling in the city during the Civil
War. Jewish leaders in the Confederate government, such as Judah P.
Benjamin, and usually unnamed Jewish merchants and speculators were
subjected to anti-Semitic attacks and stereotypes in *Southern Punch* and
other Richmond publications, although foreigners in general also drew the
fire of editors. Describing the plague of "Yankees" who had swarmed into
Richmond since the beginning of the war, *Southern Punch* stated, "we have

the Jew-Yankee, the Dutch-Yankee, French, Irish—in fact all breeds, who like the wild locusts of Egypt are devouring the substance of the land, oppressing the poor, and striking an indirect, though deadly blow at the independence of our country." Special criticism was heaped on "the dirty greasy Jew pedlar." Jewish involvement in Richmond's retail and wholesale trades and in the Confederacy's military procurement system was the excuse used by critics to accuse Jews of usury and extortion when prices inevitably rose, or when government contracts went over budget.[95]

These unwarranted attacks must have been particularly galling to Jewish leaders, many of whom had enthusiastically supported the Confederacy. Rabbi George Jacobs of Beth Shalome "was an ardent Southern patriot," and Rabbi Maximillian Michelbacher of Beth Ahabah "was second to none in loyalty to the Confederate cause."[96] As leaders of the two major synagogues in Richmond, they represented the views of a Jewish community that could claim roots in Richmond as far back as the 1780s. Significantly, German Jews generally did not join the all-German military units, preferring the more established organizations such as the Richmond Light Infantry Blues and Richmond Grays. Jewish soldiers fought with these units to the very end of the war. The allegiances of the Richmond Jewish community reflected their long residence in Richmond. Jewish families generally accepted Southern norms of slaveholding, and they were far more financially successful and integrated into the economy of Richmond than more recent immigrants, owning numerous dry-goods stores and other establishments. Given their economic status and ties, it is not surprising that most Jewish citizens supported the Confederacy.[97]

While the Jews who fought for Dixie were being reviled by Southern newspapers, little was said of the Fire-eaters who failed to shoulder a musket when the shooting started. None of Mann Valentine Sr.'s sons, for example, served in the Confederate army. Edward and William waited out the war in Europe. Mann Valentine Jr. remained in the world of goods rather than the world of the battlefield, working as "agent of the Marshall Cotton-Mills . . . which partially supplied the Confederate Government with cloths." Personal politics sometimes outweighed abstract allegiances to a cause.[98]

The fate of a few of Richmond's native-born soldiers reveals the human toll of war among loyal Southerners. Richard Channing Price rose to the rank of major and joined the staff of Major General J. E. B. Stuart on April 23, 1863. Eight days later Price was killed at Chancellorsville. Like thousands of other Confederates, he was buried at Hollywood Cemetery. Former clerk and aspiring artist William Ludwell Sheppard quit the Richmond Howitzers in 1862 and served the rest of the war as an assistant engineer in the Topographical Department of the Army of Northern Virginia. Dry-goods clerk Thomas J. Macon fell ill and was eventually discharged from General Hospital No. 9 in August 1864 and returned to civilian life. Merchant Gustavus A. Wallace, who was captured in the debacle at Roanoke Island, North Carolina, in 1862 and later exchanged, resigned his commission in early 1864 (his brothers Jefferson and Charles Wallace apparently did no active service). War-weariness affected many native-born men as the fighting seemed more and more hopeless in the final stages of the conflict.[99]

When the end came on April 2–3, 1865, Richmonders of all stations would face a world that looked radically different from the one Virginia had left in April 1861. With slavery swept away and a new political order emerging, the capital braced for one of the most-contested periods in its history. Wartime conflict turned on the question of loyalty to the Confederate nation. In the postwar world, the meaning of freedom—political, economic, and social—and citizenship would be the central issues, and working people and African Americans would set much of the agenda.

The Antebellum Legacy

*D*uring the Civil War the latent tensions inherent in antebellum Richmond became manifest. Postwar Richmond witnessed even greater struggles along the fissures of race and class, revealing conflicts that had simmered just below the surface of the prewar city. The absence of the Confederate government and army, the lifting of martial law, the freeing of thousands of African Americans, and the reestablishment of contact with the larger world all created a fluid situation ripe with possibilities.

Some aspects of city life returned quickly to their familiar rhythms after Appomattox. Merchants again plied their goods and traded with Northern associates; ironworkers rekindled the fires of the Tredegar Iron Works' furnaces; members of First African Baptist Church continued the church's role as a center of black life. But Emancipation and Union victory opened opportunities for greater liberty and independence that, precisely because of their broad understanding of their world in the antebellum period, African Americans and workers were well prepared to grasp.

A worldly African-American community drew on its antebellum experiences by organizing for politics, extending fraternal bonds, and promoting the community's full liberation through education and the reconstruction of the family. Likewise, Richmond's working class fully comprehended the political and economic power it had begun to establish in the antebellum era, although its wartime experience also enlightened workers as to the limits of cooperation with elites. Unionists and the foreign-born understood all too well the repression possible at the hands of city and state lead-ers, and both groups contributed key leadership to the Republican Party.

Blocking the political and social aspirations of blacks and working-class whites was Richmond's dispirited, but hardly beaten, conservative elite. Eulogizing their dead as well as an idealized prewar way of life, most city leaders continued on the same path they trod before the Civil War. The leadership combined probusiness, city-building boosterism with conserva-tive views on politics, race, and class. But they now faced an unprecedented political struggle that would not be resolved decisively in their favor until the advent of Jim Crow at the end of the nineteenth century and passage of a retrogressive state constitution in 1902.

Richmond's almost four-year reign as the capital of the Confederate States of America ended on the night of April 2, 1865. Grant's army finally broke the lines at Petersburg and threatened to encircle the Confederate army un-der Lee. With the Army of Northern Virginia retreating westward, the gates of Richmond stood open. Confederate officials prepared to withdraw from the city, calling for the destruction of military stores and tobacco. As nightfall came, the flames set by the fleeing Confederates rose throughout the heart of the city, and strong winds carried the conflagration throughout the business district. The great evacuation fire left a large portion of the downtown burning. The Union army and city residents would finally bring it under control the next day.[1]

As Union troops entered the city, they were greeted by a young woman displaying a flag from a window along East Main Street. Stitched for a fair in 1855, the banner commemorated the Battle of Yorktown. The flag showed George Washington triumphant on horseback, holding an American flag as his horse trampled the British colors. Hidden behind a mirror for four long years, the brightly colored standard now proclaimed Union victory to Yankee soldiers.[2]

A similar scene played out on the Capitol grounds. A seventeen-year-old African-American man named Richard Gill Forrester awoke on April 3, 1865, to find the city burning and the evacuation under way. He returned to his bed and removed a hidden United States flag that had flown over the Capitol before the passage of the Ordinance of Secession. Making his way through the chaos of the still-smoldering city, Forrester returned the banner to the flagpole atop Jefferson's classical edifice.[3]

The end of the war began a process of negotiation to reintegrate Virginia into the Union as well as a slow resumption of trade. Despite four years of isolation from Northern markets, trade largely fell back into the familiar patterns of antebellum commerce. New York merchant William Paton wrote Thomas Price only a week after the fall of Richmond to reestablish a relationship of nearly a "quarter of a Century." Paton reassured Price that "I have often deeply sympathized with you thro the various trials and afflictions you have been called upon to pass thro." Price had indeed faced many trials, not the least the death of his son Richard Channing Price at the Battle of Chancellorsville. Paton hoped that "there is no *cloud* between us" and offered Price any personal or business assistance he could provide. By April 26 another Broadway firm had advanced Price five hundred dollars to aid in the recovery of his fortunes. Richmond merchants would quickly erect a new commercial district in the Shockoe Slip area—fine iron-front buildings featured columns made in the North and others cast by the revived Tredegar Iron Works.[4]

The dynamic growth of the city in the post-Civil War era aided those who had at best tepidly embraced the South's cause. Philip Whitlock became a prosperous tobacco manufacturer, producing cheroots and cigars in his Richmond factory. Henry Lafayette Pelouze flourished in the typefounding and printing business in his adopted home. Mann Valentine Jr. would eventually recoup the family fortunes through worldwide sales of Valentine's Meat Juice, a patent medicine. Entrepreneurial success trumped any stain derived from standing on the sidelines during the war. Richmond, at least until the 1880s, remained a city on the make.[5]

Joseph Reid Anderson armed his men to guard against mobs that attempted to burn the Tredegar Iron Works and then enlisted the aid of the Union army in stopping the flames of the evacuation fire just before they reached his ironworks. The conflagration left the contiguous Richmond Armory (the former Virginia State Armory) a burned-out shell, prompting many later historians to assume erroneously that Anderson's facilities had also been destroyed in the conflagration. A small party of Richmond men, including Anderson, met with Lincoln on his visit to the fallen capital on

April 4, just a day after the fire was extinguished. The ardent Southern nationalist now used his considerable diplomatic skills to argue for a liberal peace with the least disruption of the Virginia status quo. Lee's surrender, however, rendered these negotiations moot.[6]

While Virginia's elite reestablished many of the same economic ties that existed before the war, it also retreated into memorialization of slain leaders and nostalgic views of prewar race relations. The young sculptor Edward V. Valentine returned to his native city from Europe and began working on several busts of Confederate martyrs. His plaster bust of J. E. B. Stuart adorned the cavalry leader's grave at Hollywood Cemetery in 1866. Valentine's *Recumbent Lee,* a sarcophagus for Lee's final resting place at Washington College (now Washington and Lee University), firmly established Valentine's reputation, and he would execute many other busts of Confederate heroes, as well as the Jefferson Davis statue on Monument Avenue. Edward V. Valentine's sister, Sarah Benetta Valentine, also aided the development of the Lost Cause through sentimental poetry written for Southern newspapers and periodicals such as the *Dispatch,* the *Old Dominion,* and the *Landmark.* Among her compositions were "The Death of Stuart," "Marse Robert Asleep," and "The Soldier's Grave." [7]

Richmond's elite white women poured their considerable organizational skills—finely honed in antebellum reform movements and politics—into Confederate memorial associations and activities. The Hollywood Memorial Association of the Ladies of Richmond formed on May 3, 1866, to care for the graves of the Confederate dead, and quickly set about raising money to honor the fallen soldiers. The solemn ceremonies held at the cemetery later that year marked a decisive moment in Hollywood's transformation from a classic example of the American urban cemetery movement into a sacred Southern shrine. Virginia's elite and middle-class white women continued to be arbiters of culture, working in reform movements begun before the war and creating organizations in fields as diverse as health care and Baptist missions. But these same women also fostered the development of the Lost Cause movement and defended the legacy of an antebellum Southern culture firmly based on white supremacy. After the Civil War, Virginia's memorial builders erected statues of fallen Confederate heroes, not national politicians and leaders.[8]

The racial attitudes of white elites changed very little. In 1873, Edward V. Valentine produced one of his three genre sculptures of African Americans, a smiling, cheerful representation of his family's former slave Henry Page, titling the work *Uncle Henry, ancien régime.* Like the sentimental novelists of the postwar era, Valentine romanticized his former servant as a perfect example of the loyal, happy slaves of antebellum Virginia. The local press understood perfectly Valentine's intentions, reporting that Henry Page's marble likeness "tells its own story at a glance. . . . It is not the suggestion of African stupidity, but of the colored aristocratic servant of the brass-button standing-collar, and ruffle-shirt school whose courtliness was hardly exceeded by his master's." Indeed, the aged Henry Page became quite a local celebrity in the 1880s and was interviewed several times regarding olden days in Richmond. Page recounted the aftermath of the discovery of the slave Gabriel's aborted rebellion in 1800 and the visit of the Marquis de Lafayette in 1824. At his funeral in 1886, two of Mann Valentine Jr.'s sons served as pallbearers, bearing the casket alongside former Valentine slaves Simon Winston and John Harris.[9]

Many white Virginians contrasted the docile slaves of the ancien régime with the newly freed slaves of the Reconstruction era. Former Richmond clerk William Ludwell Sheppard, now a popular illustrator, drew such a comparison in the pages of *Appleton's Journal of Popular Literature, Science and Art* in 1870. A contented, simply dressed slave named "Sam" becomes transformed into "Samuel Harris, Esq. (colored)" in the postemancipation era. Harris has "removed to town, and become a prominent member of an association known as the 'Rising Sons of Ham,' whose banner displays a rising sun on one side, and a ham of bacon on the other." Now nattily attired, politically active, and "smoking a domestic cigar in the depot, in disregard of rule," Samuel Harris was meant to evoke laughter from white readers. But Harris was also a threatening figure to those who sought to regain control of Southern society.[10]

Organizations like the Sons and Daughters of Ham had existed under slavery, but most whites were unable to comprehend, or unwilling to recognize, the level of sophistication reached by Richmond's antebellum black community. Whites also denigrated the abilities of postbellum blacks to conduct their own affairs, yet the freedmen's subtle understanding of, and full participation in, Reconstruction belied white beliefs. African-Americans' petitions to Congress and President Andrew Johnson reflected their mastery of the pressing issues of the day and a clear comprehension of their rights. First African Baptist Church continued to be the scene of political speeches and conventions, but now African Americans participated in the debates on the floor and influenced the proceedings by their substantial presence in the galleries.[11]

First African Baptist Church recognized new leadership nurtured in the antebellum church. Robert Ryland submitted his resignation in May 1865, but members were split on whether to retain him. Ryland again tendered his resignation in June, and the church temporarily hired a white anti-slavery preacher from the North. In 1867 congregants elected James H. Holmes, already an assistant pastor, who became the first black minister of the city's largest African-American congregation.[12]

Holmes's remarkable life traversed the paths of liberty and slavery that characterized the world of black Richmond. Born a slave in King and Queen County in 1826, he was hired out at an early age to Samuel S. Myers's tobacco factory. Holmes was baptized in First African Baptist Church in 1842 and also married his first wife around that same time. In 1848 he was sold by his master, Judge James M. Jeffries, to New Orleans, possibly as punishment for aiding the escape of his wife or wife's family to the North. Holmes's departure from Richmond occurred suspiciously close to the mail incident at First African Baptist Church that brought Robert Ryland under intense recrimination and suspicion over a slave escape.[13]

While in New Orleans, Holmes worked as a dockhand and received serious injuries in an explosion on a boat. He recovered, although he was left unfit for the heavy labor of the New Orleans wharfs. In a strange turn of events, his master committed suicide and he and his new wife were purchased by a former Richmond resident. When the master's business in New Orleans failed, James and Rebecca Holmes returned to Richmond with their new owner in 1853. Holmes again spent time laboring in a tobacco factory and then worked in his master's store. Despite his earlier troubles, he served as a deacon of First African Baptist Church from 1855 until the end of the war. During Reconstruction, Holmes used the organizational knowledge developed under slavery as the secretary of four church-based secret societies, which now flourished in the postemancipation world.[14]

African-American women also drew on a long history of leadership in church, reform, and fraternal activities. Lucy Brooks had been a faithful member of First African Baptist Church before the war. In 1867 she led the Ladies Sewing Circle for Charitable Work, providing clothing and other necessities to impoverished members of Richmond's African-American population. A few years later, Brooks approached the Society of Friends for resources to establish the Friends Asylum for Colored Orphans, which was incorporated in 1872.[15]

Women were prominent in the early history of the United Order of True Reformers, which was founded as a temperance organization. Among these women was "Mrs. Eliza Allen, one of the Charter Members of the Order, a Director and Grand Worthy Governess of the Rosebud Department." But no organization was as deeply influenced by the perspective of black women as the Independent Order of Saint Luke. Founded in Baltimore by Mary Prout as a women's death benefit society, the Order quickly moved its headquarters to Richmond and began admitting men in the 1880s. In 1899 Maggie Lena Walker became grand secretary, extending the Order's business enterprises and stressing family, community, and race consciousness. Women were at the center of the Order, making up a high percentage of the officers. These Richmond-based organizations eventually grew into national orders spanning scores of states.[16]

African Americans used their new freedom to reconstruct families dispersed in the antebellum black diaspora. Stephen H. Boles, formerly a slave in the Valentine household, wrote from Louisiana requesting information on his brothers and other relatives. Boles, his mother Sally Boles Gladman, and three other siblings had been purchased by Mann S. Valentine in 1831 from the estate of Valentine's father-in-law, Benjamin Mosby. Stephen Boles sent his "love to all inquiring friends and to my brother James Boles and Henry Boles, Mrs. Nancy Harris." Boles asked if members of Benjamin Mosby's family "live yet" and reported that he had three sons and two daughters, although his wife had left him at the "comencement of the war." The letter, addressed to Mrs. Mann S. Valentine, reached a household that had lost its white patriarch only a year before.[17]

Black militias protected the African-American community and served as another way to enter the public discourse on citizenship. African-American militias marched to Capitol Square on the first Emancipation Day in 1866, held on April 3 — the day Richmond fell to Union forces with regiments of the United States Colored Troops in the vanguard. Well aware of the symbolic importance of Capitol Square, from which they had been excluded by antebellum law, black citizens and soldiers carried their celebration into the symbolic heart of the Virginia capital.[18]

While African Americans energetically built their community, they also participated in class-based activism and interracial efforts in politics. Labor organizations sprang up throughout Richmond in both the white and black communities. Black labor leaders in the city quickly developed substantial followings after the Civil War. Joseph Cox and Lewis Lindsay served on the jury assembled to try Jefferson Davis for treason, and both represented Richmond in the Virginia Constitutional Convention of 1867–68. During the convention Cox declared himself "in favor of disenfranchising all rebels except poor whites" and championed public schools from a class perspective.[19] Both labor leaders and black militia captains were involved in Republican and later Readjuster politics. Lindsay, Cox, and militia captains Robert Austin Paul and Josiah Crump all received federal patronage at various times, reflecting their long-term alliance with white politicians at the state and local levels. Black leaders were well aware of national movements, sending delegates to meetings of the Colored National Labor Union, which "melded race and class awareness." [20]

White workers continued their antebellum organizing. Building on prewar unions of typographers, stonecutters, and cordwainers, Richmond's labor movement extended into the iron industry and many other sectors of the economy. Eventually white and black workers would unite under the banner of the Knights of Labor in the 1880s, building the most vibrant labor movement that had ever existed in the American South.[21]

The war emboldened elements of the Richmond community to express views on Union, slavery, and race that did not comport with the old stereotypes. Immigrants now came forward in a more vigorous way into politics, many in the Republican Party. A large block of the local Republican leadership in Richmond after the Civil War was made up of men born in Germany. A Reconstruction-era broadside imploring Richmond's "German Adoptive Citizens" (*deutchen Adoptiv-Bürger*) to vote the Conservative ticket noted that "the emancipation of the slaves generated the sympathy of immigrants, namely the Germans," but denounced the Republican Party for its ruthless use of black votes.[22] Ignoring the advice of older leaders such as Johann Gottfried Lange, the generation of Germans who had arrived during the Know-Nothing era and struggled in the harsh conditions of the Civil War now began to find their own way in a new political and social world fraught with opportunities and dangers.

Veterans of the struggle during the Civil War now turned to Republican politics. Republicans rewarded Elizabeth Van Lew for her wartime loyalty with the sinecure of postmaster of Richmond, much to the chagrin of the city's old elite. Burnham Wardwell, an ice merchant in antebellum Richmond who had been arrested for Unionist activities during the war, now became an important Republican leader in the early years of Reconstruction. Martin Meredith Lipscomb also dabbled in Reconstruction politics in the Republican Party.[23]

In Jackson Ward, the gerrymandered, black-majority ward of post-1870 Richmond, blacks patronized and voted for white saloonkeepers and grocers in strong biracial alliances, reflecting the mixed population of the district. The ward encompassed the old neighborhood of Navy Hill and the areas of free-black settlement around Ebenezer Baptist Church. Jackson Ward politics made strange bedfellows, such as the strong alliance between James Bahen, an Irish grocer and ward heeler, and John Mitchell Jr., the black editor of the *Richmond Planet*.[24]

Despite all the efforts of workers and African Americans to create a new Richmond, the dream would end after several decades of struggle. By the 1890s most African Americans had been driven from office through fraud, gerrymandering, and intimidation; the labor movement of the 1880s had been shattered by racial divisions in the ranks and concerted attacks from elites; and the political challenge of the Readjuster Party and the Knights of Labor had been destroyed by internal struggles and the focused hostility of the Republican and Democratic Parties. The 1902 state constitution loomed in the offing, which would disenfranchise most blacks and many working-class whites. One-party control by white conservative Democrats only required formalization through a racist constitution.

Historians have usually viewed the rise of Jim Crow and white supremacy as the inevitable conclusion of the late nineteenth century in the

South. In retrospect, the lack of any substantial late-nineteenth-century immigration, the decline of skills among black workers, and the ability of elites to play the race card with an increasingly assimilated white working class all spelled trouble for continued activism. But we must also ask how those who resisted racism and elite control endured as long as they did and why they struggled. The answers may reside in the experiences of Richmonders in the antebellum era and during the Civil War.

NOTES

Introduction

1. Two key books establish the position of Richmond in national and state urban networks during this period: Allan Pred, *Urban Growth and City-Systems in the United States, 1840–1860* (Cambridge, Mass.: Harvard University Press, 1980), and David R. Goldfield, *Urban Growth in the Age of Sectionalism: Virginia, 1847–1861* (Baton Rouge: Louisiana State University Press, 1977). On the problem of "essentializing" regions and their people in the study of American history, see Edward L. Ayers et al., *All Over the Map: Rethinking American Regions* (Baltimore: Johns Hopkins University Press, 1996).

2. William G. Shade's recent book fills a major void in the literature on Virginia politics. *Democratizing the Old Dominion: Virginia and the Second Party System, 1824–1861* (Charlottesville: University Press of Virginia, 1996).

3. Pred, *Urban Growth and City-Systems in the United States*, emphasizes the lack of a true "city system" in the South. William W. Freehling graphically demonstrates the poor development of Southern inter-urban transportation and communication by tracing an arduous trip from New Orleans to Charleston, and then describes the ease of travel between Baltimore and Saint Louis. *The Road to Disunion* (New York: Oxford University Press, 1990), 25–36. He also highlights the existence of many different "Souths" in the area later covered by the Confederacy.

4. Like the Chicago region described by William Cronon, in central Virginia "city and country shared a common past, and had fundamentally reshaped each other. Neither was as 'natural' or 'unnatural' as it appeared." Cronon, *Nature's Metropolis: Chicago and the Great West* (New York: W. W. Norton, 1991), 7–8.

5. David Goldfield outlined the major connections between city and country in Virginia—railroads, markets, and the reliance on slave labor—many years ago. I hope to explain these connections further, especially slave hiring, as well as integrate new literature, such as Kenneth Noe's fine book on the Virginia and Tennessee Railroad. See David R. Goldfield, "Urban-Rural Relations in the Old South: The Example of Virginia," *Journal of Urban History* 2 (Feb. 1976): 146–68. Kenneth W.

Noe, *Southwest Virginia's Railroad: Modernization and the Sectional Crisis* (Urbana: University of Illinois Press, 1994).

6. David Goldfield, in his later work, asserts that the countryside and its values shaped the identity of Southern cities, seemingly contradicting his earlier position that "the striking feature of urban-rural cooperation in Virginia was its similarity to, rather than difference from, the rest of nineteenth century America," in "Urban-Rural Relations in the Old South: The Example of Virginia," 163. This article, and his most important subsequent essays, are now available in David R. Goldfield, *Region, Race, and Cities: Interpreting the Urban South* (Baton Rouge: Louisiana State University Press, 1997). In this work Goldfield explains the apparent contradiction by arguing that "southern cities are similar in some respects to cities elsewhere yet are different in others, and that such differences derive from the South's distinctiveness" (p. 8). I generally agree with this notion, and I hope to show both the sameness of American urban culture for many people of the middle and working classes and the distinctly "Southern" ideas that most elite Richmonders held. A considerable body of recent work places nineteenth-century Virginia either in the mainstream of national trends or at least on "the Edge of the South." See Shade, *Democratizing the Old Dominion*; Edward L. Ayers, "Virginia History as Southern History: The Nineteenth Century," *Virginia Magazine of History and Biography* 104, no. 1 (Winter 1996): 129–30; Edward L. Ayers and John C. Willis, eds., *The Edge of the South: Life in Nineteenth-Century Virginia* (Charlottesville: University Press of Virginia, 1991).

7. Works on slavery in Southern cities often emphasize differences between rural and urban slavery, while writers on industrial slavery sometimes point out the continuity between rural and urban industrial work. See Robert S. Starobin, *Industrial Slavery in the Old South* (New York: Oxford University Press, 1970); Ronald L. Lewis, *Coal, Iron, and Slaves: Industrial Slavery in Maryland and Virginia, 1775–1865* (Westport, Conn.: Greenwood Press, 1979); Charles B. Dew, *Bond of Iron: Master and Slave at Buffalo Forge* (New York: W. W. Norton, 1994); Suzanne Gehring Schnittman, "Slavery in Virginia's Urban Tobacco Industry, 1840–1860" (Ph.D. diss., University of Rochester, 1987); Richard Wade, *Slavery in the Cities: The South, 1820–1860* (New York: Oxford University Press, 1964); and Claudia Dale Goldin, *Urban Slavery in the American South: A Quantitative Analysis* (Chicago: University of Chicago Press, 1976). Tracey M. Weis points out the fundamental, but often ignored, dominance of domestic slavery as the paradigm for race relations even in a commercial city like Richmond. "Negotiating Freedom: Domestic Service and the Landscape of Labor and Household Relations in Richmond, Virginia, 1850–1880" (Ph.D. diss., Rutgers, The State University of New Jersey–New Brunswick, 1994).

8. Elizabeth Fox-Genovese criticizes Suzanne Lebsock and other historians for imposing urban, bourgeois values on all Southern women based on studies of Southern cities. She sees the South generally as lacking a system of cities that controlled the po-

litical economy and culture of the region, and points to the persistence of slavery in city and country, concluding that "Cities did not dominate southerners' perceptions of proper relations between women and men, masters and servants, rich and poor." Elizabeth Fox-Genovese, *Within the Plantation Household: Black and White Women of the Old South* (Chapel Hill: University of North Carolina Press, 1988), 70–81.

9. The classic study of Southerners traveling in the North is John Hope Franklin, *A Southern Odyssey: Travelers in the Antebellum North* (Baton Rouge: Louisiana State University Press, 1976).

10. Daniel R. Hundley, *Social Relations in Our Southern States*, ed. with an introduction by William J. Cooper Jr. (1860; reprint, Baton Rouge: Louisiana State University Press, 1979).

11. The overemphasis on industrial slavery has led several recent authors to inflate the power of industrialists as members of the city's elite. For example, see Schnittman, "Slavery in Virginia's Urban Tobacco Industry, 1840–1860," and McLeod, "Free Labor in a Slave Society: Richmond, Virginia, 1820–1860." Goldfield's ranking of city activists in *Urban Growth in the Age of Sectionalism* clearly shows that merchants were far more important than industrialists as city leaders.

12. My findings support Eugene Genovese's and Elizabeth Fox-Genovese's contention that merchant capital had a remarkable ability to adapt to a variety of social systems, and the view that Southern urban elites, while accepting many of the trappings of Northern bourgeois culture, shared Southern concepts of social order. Eugene D. Genovese, *The World the Slaveholders Made: Two Essays in Interpretation* (New York: Pantheon, 1969); Elizabeth Fox-Genovese and Eugene D. Genovese, *Fruits of Merchant Capital: Slavery and Bourgeois Property in the Rise and Expansion of Capitalism* (New York: Oxford University Press, 1983).

13. Explanations of the persistence of Southern culture in the face of today's mass society often emphasize the role of well-traveled Southerners in preserving their heritage. See especially John Shelton Reed, *The Enduring South: Subcultural Persistence in Mass Society* (Lexington, Mass.: Heath, 1972). I believe many in Richmond's elite had a similar reaction to the encroachment of an industrial, commercial society in the 1850s. However, Richard L. Leonard also portrays Northern merchants as conservative on the issue of slavery, despite the perceptions of Southern merchants, perhaps pointing to a more general conservatism among any entrenched class against radical change. See *Gentlemen of Property and Standing: Anti-Abolition Mobs in Jacksonian America* (New York: Oxford University Press, 1970).

14. James O. Horton, *Free People of Color: Inside the African American Community* (Washington: Smithsonian Institution Press, 1993). On connections among African Americans in post-Revolutionary Richmond, see James Sidbury, *Ploughshares into Swords: Race, Rebellion, and Identity in Gabriel's Virginia, 1730–1810* (Cambridge, Eng.: Cambridge University Press, 1997), and Douglas R. Egerton, *Gabriel's Rebellion:*

The Virginia Slave Conspiracies of 1800 and 1802 (Chapel Hill: University of North Carolina Press, 1993). See also Paul Gilroy, *The Black Atlantic* (Cambridge, Mass.: Harvard University Press, 1992).

15. On the growth and composition of Richmond's male working class, see Ira Berlin and Herbert G. Gutman, "Natives and Immigrants, Free Men and Slaves: Urban Workingmen in the Antebellum American South," *American Historical Review* 88 (Dec. 1983): 1175–2000.

16. For accounts of the strike, see Charles B. Dew, *Ironmaker to the Confederacy: Joseph R. Anderson and the Tredegar Iron Works* (New Haven: Yale University Press, 1966), 23–26; Kathleen Bruce, *Virginia Iron Manufacture in the Slave Era* (New York: Century Company, 1931), 224–27; and Patricia A. Schechter, "Free and Slave Labor in the Old South: The Tredegar Ironworkers' Strike of 1847," *Labor History* 35 (1995): 165–86. On the worldview of the nineteenth-century ironworker, see David Montgomery, *The Fall of the House of Labor: The Workplace, the State, and American Labor Activism, 1865–1925* (Cambridge, Eng.: Cambridge University Press, 1989), 9–57, 171–213.

17. Craig M. Simpson, *A Good Southerner: The Life of Henry A. Wise of Virginia* (Chapel Hill: University of North Carolina Press, 1985).

18. On the development of the public memory and commemoration of the American Revolution, see Michael Kammen, *A Season of Youth: The American Revolution and the Historical Imagination* (New York: Alfred A. Knopf, 1978), and Barry Schwartz, *George Washington: The Making of an American Symbol* (New York: Free Press, 1987).

19. These encounters fit well with John Bodnar's explanation of the formation of public memory, which "emerges from the intersection of official and vernacular cultural expressions." John Bodnar, *Remaking America: Public Memory, Commemoration, and Patriotism in the Twentieth Century* (Princeton, N.J.: Princeton University Press, 1991), 13–14.

20. For an articulation of these views, see Gerald F. Linderman, *Embattled Courage: The Experience of Combat in the American Civil War* (New York: Free Press, 1987).

CHAPTER 1. Capital and Commercial City

1. Bessie Lacy, Richmond, to her father Drury Lacy, 18 Oct. 1848, Drury Lacy Papers, Southern Historical Collection, Wilson Library, University of North Carolina at Chapel Hill.

2. *Richmond Enquirer*, Sept. 7, 1838.

3. Bessie Lacy to Drury Lacy, Oct. 18, 1848, Drury Lacy Papers.

4. *Richmond Business Directory*, 146.

5. Fiske Kimball, *The Capitol of Virginia: A Landmark in American Architecture,* ed. by Jon Kukla (Richmond: Virginia State Library and Archives, 1989), 7, quote on 13; Robert L. Alexander, *The Architecture of Maximilian Godefroy,* The Johns Hopkins Studies in Nineteenth-Century Architecture (Baltimore: Johns Hopkins University Press, 1974), 120–30.

6. "The Narrative of Thomas Rutherfoord, 1766–1852," 102–4, typescript, Valentine Museum, Richmond.

7. Michael Kammen, *A Season of Youth: The American Revolution and the Historical Imagination* (New York: Alfred A. Knopf, 1978), 85; Barry Schwartz, *George Washington: The Making of an American Symbol* (New York: Free Press, 1987), 125.

8. Kammen, *Season of Youth,* 103; Thomas B. Brumbaugh, "The Evolution of Crawford's 'Washington,'" *Virginia Magazine of History and Biography* 70, no. 1 (Jan. 1962): 3–29; Lauretta Dimmick, "'An Altar Erected to Heroic Virtue Itself': Thomas Crawford and His *Virginia Washington Monument,*" *American Art Journal* 23, no. 2 (1991): 4–73; Richmond Light Infantry Blues Minutes, vol. 1, Feb. 22, 1858, p. 443, Personal Papers, Library of Virginia, Richmond.

9. Schwartz, *George Washington,* 41–89, argues that although some important figures, such as Thomas Paine, were fearful of Washington, he remained immensely popular among the general population throughout the 1780s and 1790s; John Bodnar, *Remaking America: Public Memory, Commemoration, and Patriotism in the Twentieth Century* (Princeton: Princeton University Press, 1991), 23; Louis H. Manarin and Lee A. Wallace Jr., *Richmond Volunteers: The Volunteer Companies of the City of Richmond and Henrico County, Virginia, 1861–1865,* Official Publication No. 26, Richmond Civil War Centennial Committee (Richmond: Westover Press, 1969), 89.

10. Petition of James, New Kent County, Nov. 31, 1786, Legislative Petitions, General Assembly (Record Group 78), State Records, Library of Virginia, Richmond; John Salmon, "'A Mission of the most secret and important kind': James Lafayette and American Espionage in 1781," *Virginia Cavalcade* 31 (1981): 78–85; James E. Heath, *Edge-Hill, or The Family of the Fitzroyals, A Novel* (Richmond: W. T. White, 1828), 2:72–84, 223–24; *Richmond Enquirer,* Oct. 29, 1824; Douglas R. Egerton, *Gabriel's Rebellion: The Virginia Slave Conspiracies of 1800 and 1802* (Chapel Hill: University of North Carolina Press, 1993); James Sidbury, *Ploughshares into Swords: Race, Rebellion, and Identity in Gabriel's Virginia, 1730–1810* (Cambridge: Cambridge University Press, 1997).

11. John B. Danforth, Richmond, to Col. John Rutherfoord, White Sulphur Springs, Aug. 24, 1855, Letter Book, 1854–64, p. 32, John B. Danforth Papers, Rare Book, Manuscript, and Special Collections Library, Duke University, Durham, North Carolina.

12. William P. Palmer to Charles Palmer, New Orleans, Feb. 3, 1851, Palmer Family Papers, Virginia Historical Society, Richmond.

13. *Biographical Directory of the United States Congress, 1774–1989, Bicentennial Edition* (Washington, D.C.: Government Printing Office, 1989), 47.

14. David Hackett Fischer and James C. Kelly, *Away, I'm Bound Away: Virginia and the Westward Movement* (Richmond: Virginia Historical Society, 1993), 66–67.

15. William G. Shade, *Democratizing the Old Dominion: Virginia and the Second Party System, 1824–1861* (Charlottesville: University Press of Virginia, 1996), 107–10.

16. Ibid., 121–22.

17. Charles Palmer, New Orleans, to William P. Palmer, Richmond, Apr. 5, 1849, Palmer Family Papers.

18. Bessie Lacy, Richmond, to Drury Lacy, Nov. 24, 1848, Drury Lacy Papers.

19. Jefferson Wallace, Richmond, to Charles Wallace, Apr. 15, 1855, Clopton Family Papers, Rare Book, Manuscript, and Special Collections Library, Duke University, Durham, North Carolina; Subscription Book, Virginia Association of Ladies for Erecting a Statue to Henry Clay, Virginia Historical Society, Richmond; Elizabeth R. Varon, *We Mean to Be Counted: White Women and Politics in Antebellum Virginia* (Chapel Hill: University of North Carolina Press, 1998), 71–102.

20. Michael Douglas Naragon, "Ballots, Bullets, and Blood: The Political Transformation of Virginia, 1850–1874." (Ph.D. diss., University of Pittsburgh, 1996), 163–68.

21. John T. O'Brien, " 'The People's Favorite': The Rise and Fall of Martin Meredith Lipscomb," *Virginia Cavalcade* 31, no. 4 (Spring 1982): 216–23, quote on p. 217.

22. Naragon, "Ballots, Bullets, and Blood," 154–226; Jefferson Wallace, Richmond, to Charles Wallace, Apr. 1 and 15, 1855, Clopton Family Papers.

23. Jefferson Wallace, Richmond, to Charles Wallace, May 26, 1855, Clopton Family Papers; Musician's diary, Nov. 4, 1856, recorded in *Daily Pocket Diary for 1856: for the Use of Private families and Persons of Business* (New York: Higgins & Kellogg, 1856), Personal Papers, Library of Virginia, Richmond.

24. Jefferson Wallace, Richmond, to Charles Wallace, May 26, 1855, Clopton Family Papers.

25. Charles Dew, *Ironmaker to the Confederacy: Joseph R. Anderson and the Tredegar Iron Works* (New Haven: Yale University, 1966), 40–42.

26. Robert A. Granniss diary, Nov. 20, 1858, p. 26, Virginia Historical Society, Richmond. On the Wise-Clemens duel, see Charles Henry Ambler, *Sectionalism in Virginia from 1776 to 1861* (Chicago: University of Chicago Press, 1910), 321–23. Wise badly wounded Clemens, from western Virginia, during the campaign.

27. Granniss diary, May 27, 1859, p. 54.

28. Dew, *Ironmaker to the Confederacy*, 40–42.

29. Jefferson Wallace, Richmond, to Charles Wallace, Mar. 27, Apr. 1, 1855, Clopton Family Papers.

30. Jefferson Wallace, Richmond, to Charles Blair, Nov. 27, 1854, Clopton Family

Papers; *Richmond Business Directory,* 154; Thomas S. Berry, "The Rise of Flour Milling in Richmond," *Virginia Magazine of History and Biography* 78, no. 4 (Oct. 1970): 387.

31. *Statistics of the United States . . . in 1860; Compiled from the Original Returns and Being the Final Exhibit of the Eighth Census* (Washington, D.C.: Government Printing Office, 1866), xviii.

32. Information on the value of tobacco and other exports are from Peter V. Bergstrom, "Markets and Merchants: Economic Diversification in Colonial Virginia, 1700–1775" (Ph.D. diss., University of New Hampshire, 1980), 149–52; quote in James O'Mara, *An Historical Geography of Urban System Development: Tidewater Virginia in the Eighteenth Century* Geographical Monographs, no. 13 (Downsview, Ont.: Department of Geography, Atkinson College, York University, 1983), 88.

33. John Spencer Bassett, ed., *The Writings of "Colonel William Byrd, of Westover in Virginia, Esqr."* (New York: Doubleday, Page, 1901), 292.

34. Carville Earle and Ronald Hoffman, "Staple Crops and Urban Development in the Eighteenth Century South," *Perspectives in American History* 10 (1976): 66; Berry, "Rise of Flour Milling in Richmond," 387–408.

35. Miriam Jane Smith, "Forgotten Virginian—From British Merchant to Prominent Citizen: Thomas Rutherford, 1766–1852," *West Virginia History* 36, no. 1 (Fall 1974): 50.

36. Jefferson Wallace, Richmond, to Charles Wallace, California, Apr. 15, 1855, Clopton Family Papers.

37. Germain Bréant, Larue, France, to Charles Palmer, Richmond, July 26, 1860, Palmer Family Papers. Bréant's comments reflect the French penchant for hydraulic power and transportation systems, not surprising in a country practically devoid of coal but with extensive rivers.

38. Joseph Reid Anderson to James S. Woods, Buchanan, Jan. 8, 1850, Letter Book, Out, May 14, 1849–Mar. 20, 1851, pp. 272–73, Tredegar Iron Company Records, Business Records, Library of Virginia, Richmond.

39. Henry L. Cathell diary, Feb. 26–27, 1856, Southern Historical Collection, Wilson Library, University of North Carolina at Chapel Hill.

40. Edward V. Valentine, Rockbridge Alum Springs, to Mann S. Valentine, Sept. 30, 1856, Valentine Family Papers, Valentine Museum, Richmond.

41. William Ludwell Sheppard diary, Mar. 7, 1854, Personal Papers, negative photostat, Library of Virginia, Richmond; Elizabeth Ann Valentine Gray, Rockbridge Alum Springs, to her husband, William Gray, Sept. 20, 1856, Valentine Family Papers.

42. Ann Webster Gordon Christian Diary, Jan. 2, Mar. 2, 1860, Virginia Historical Society, Richmond.

43. *Statistics of the United States . . . in 1860,* 327–28, 333.

44. Dew, *Ironmaker to the Confederacy,* 27–28.

45. Information on locomotives produced is from Kathleen Bruce, *Virginia Iron Manufacture in the Slave Era* (New York: Century Company, 1931), 285–86.

46. Gregg L. Michel, "From Slavery to Freedom: Hickory Hill, 1850–1880," in *The Edge of the South: Life in Nineteenth-Century Virginia*, ed. Edward L. Ayers and John C. Willis (Charlottesville: University Press of Virginia, 1991).

47. Lynda J. Morgan, *Emancipation in Virginia's Tobacco Belt, 1850–1870* (Athens: University of Georgia Press, 1992), 6.

48. Joseph C. Robert, *Tobacco Kingdom: Plantation, Market, and Factory in Virginia and North Carolina, 1800–1860* (Durham: Duke University Press, 1938), 187–88, 222–24; *Hunt's Merchant Magazine and Commercial Review* 40, no. 1 (Jan. 1859): 55. The numbers reported in *Hunt's* may have included the town of Manchester, directly across the James from Richmond.

49. Kenneth W. Noe, *Southwest Virginia's Railroad: Modernization and the Sectional Crisis* (Urbana: University of Illinois Press, 1994), 8–9.

50. David R. Goldfield, *Urban Growth in the Age of Sectionalism: Virginia, 1847–1861* (Baton Rouge: Louisiana State University Press, 1977), 236.

51. Memorials of "Planters and Farmers of Albemarle," "Planters of Tobacco," and "Planters commission merchants and Buyers of Tobacco," 1852, Executive Papers (Record Group 3), Governor Joseph Johnson, 1852–56, State Records, Library of Virginia, Richmond.

52. T. J. Macon, *Life Gleanings* (Richmond: W. H. Adams, 1913), 24. The printer misspelled the dry goods firm's name in the beginning of this work, but corrected the error later on p. 40.

53. Jonathan Pitts to Thomas and Charles Ellis, Jan. 2, 1850, Ellis-Allan Records, Library of Congress, Washington, D.C.

54. *Richmond Times,* Apr. 1, 1851.

55. Goldfield, *Urban Growth in the Age of Sectionalism*, chap. 3; Bruce, *Virginia Iron Manufacture in the Slave Era*, 317–19; John B. Danforth, Richmond, to Thomas S. Simms, New York, Nov. 6, 1854, Letter Book, 1854–64, p. 14, John B. Danforth Papers.

56. Charles W. Dabney, quoted in Goldfield, *Urban Growth in the Age of Sectionalism*, 223; second and third quote, William Ludwell Sheppard diary, Nov. 1, 2, 1853.

57. Philip Whitlock's Recollections, 1843–1913, pp. 60–61, Virginia Historical Society, Richmond; Granniss diary, Oct. 28, 1858, p. 22; Anderson, Delaney & Co. To Dr. M. M. Harrison, Summit Depot, near Gaston, Northampton County, N.C., Dec. 26, 1854, and Jan. 11, 1855, Letter Book, Out, Dec. 1854–Mar. 29, 1855, pp. 124–25, 187–88, Tredegar Iron Company Records.

58. Jefferson Wallace, Richmond, to Charles Wallace, Calif., July 15, 1855, Clopton Family Papers.

59. WPA interview with Mr. William I. Johnson Jr., May 28, 1937, transcribed in

Charles L. Perdue Jr., Thomas E. Barden, and Robert K. Phillips, eds., *Weevils in the Wheat: Interviews with Ex-Slaves* (Charlottesville: University Press of Virginia, 1976), 165–70.

60. Charles Emery Stevens, *Anthony Burns: A History* (Boston: John P. Jewett and Company, 1856), 170–71.

61. Perdue, Barden, and Phillips, *Weevils in the Wheat*, 165–70.

62. Based on a statistical analysis of members received, First African Baptist Church Minute Book, 1841–59, microfilm, Church Records, Library of Virginia, Richmond.

63. Ibid.

64. William P. Palmer, Richmond, to Charles Palmer, New Orleans, Dec. 26, 1849, Palmer Family Papers.

65. John Gault, Richmond, to Samuel Gault, Boston, Dec. 31, 1853, Virginia Historical Society, Richmond; see also John Gault, Richmond, to Samuel Gault, Boston, Dec. 25, 1853, letter completed on Dec. 27, Special Collections Department, University of Virginia Library, Charlottesville.

66. "The Hiring Business," *Richmond Enquirer*, Jan. 3, 1855; "Servants for Hire," *Richmond Enquirer*, Jan. 18, 1855.

67. "Servants for Hire," *Richmond Enquirer*, Jan. 18, 1855.

68. Richard Wade, *Slavery in the Cities: The South, 1820–1860* (New York: Oxford University Press, 1964); Claudia Dale Goldin, *Urban Slavery in the American South: A Quantitative Analysis* (Chicago: University of Chicago Press, 1976); Michael B. Chesson, *Richmond After the War, 1865–1890* (Richmond: Virginia State Library, 1981), 12, 119–20; *Population of the United States in 1860; Compiled from the Original Returns of the Eighth Census* (Washington, D.C.: Government Printing Office, 1864), xxxi–xxxii. The percentages of foreign-born in the respective cities was, New Orleans, 38.31; Louisville, 33.73; Memphis, 30.66; Boston, 35.88; Philadelphia, 28.93; and Providence, 24.80.

69. Randall M. Miller, "The Enemy Within: Some Effects of Foreign Immigrants on Antebellum Southern Cities," *Southern Studies* 24 (Spring 1985): 33–34; Randall M. Miller, "Immigrants in the Old South," *Immigration History Newsletter* 10 (Nov. 1978): 8–9; Ira Berlin and Herbert G. Gutman, "Natives and Immigrants, Free Men and Slaves: Urban Workingmen in the Antebellum American South," *American Historical Review* 88 (Dec. 1983): 1191, table 13.

70. A summary of the literature on working-class relations in Richmond is contained in Gregg D. Kimball, "The Working People of Richmond: Life and Labor in an Industrial City, 1865–1920," *Labor's Heritage* 3, no. 2 (Apr. 1991): 42–65.

71. Berlin and Gutman, "Natives and Immigrants, Free Men and Slaves," 1186; Norman C. McLeod Jr., "Not Forgetting the Land We Left: The Irish in Antebellum Richmond," *Virginia Cavalcade* 47, no. 1 (Winter 1998): 36–47; Chesson, *Richmond*

After the War, 120; Tracey M. Weis, "Negotiating Freedom: Domestic Service and the Landscape of Labor and Household Relations in Richmond, Virginia, 1850–1880" (Ph.D. diss., Rutgers, The State University of New Jersey—New Brunswick, 1994), 29.

72. Macon, *Life Gleanings,* 21.

73. Granniss diary, Mar. 18, 26, 1859, pp. 52–53.

74. William Ludwell Sheppard diary, Sept. 15, 20, 1853. Sheppard became a well-known illustrator and artist after the Civil War. See *William Ludwell Sheppard: A Retrospective Exhibition of His Works, December, 1969* (Richmond: Valentine Museum, 1969).

75. "A List of Young Men in my employ since I began business in 1810," Valentine Family Papers, Valentine Museum, Richmond; John Y. Megginson to Thomas and Charles Ellis, Jan. 7, 1850, Ellis-Allan Records; Benjamin Wilkes to James Thomas Jr., Jan. 4, 1858, Correspondence, James Thomas Jr. Papers, 1850–79, Rare Book, Manuscript, and Special Collections Library, Duke University, Durham, North Carolina.

76. Granniss diary, Dec. 23, 1858; Berlin and Gutman, "Natives and Immigrants, Free Men and Slaves," 1192, n. 21.

77. *Hunt's Merchant Magazine,* 63.

78. James Rawlings to William H. Allen and Thomas R. Blair, Aug. 5, 1827, Mutual Assurance Society of Virginia Records, Business Records, Library of Virginia, Richmond; Goldfield, *Urban Growth in the Age of Sectionalism,* 242–45.

79. *Montague's Richmond Directory and Business Advertiser* (1850–51), 114.

80. Wirt Armistead Cate, "History of Richmond, Virginia," unpublished typescript, 401, Valentine Museum, Richmond; William P. Palmer to Charles Palmer, Dec. 26, 1849, Palmer Family Papers. The national telegraphic system is described in Allan Pred, *Urban Growth and City-Systems in the United States, 1840–1860* (Cambridge, Massachusetts: Harvard University Press, 1980), 151–56.

81. Olmsted, *A Journey in the Seaboard Slave States, with Remarks on Their Economy* (New York: Dix & Edwards, 1856), 55. Michael Tadman also comments on the increasing use of modern transportation to transport slaves in *Speculators and Slaves: Masters, Traders, and Slaves in the Old South* (Madison: University of Wisconsin Press, 1989), 77–79.

82. Chesson, *Richmond After the War,* 12.

CHAPTER 2. American City in a Southern Place

1. Frederika Bremer, *The Homes of the New World: Impressions of America* (New York: Harper & Brothers, 1853), 2:535.

2. Donald B. Dodd and Wynelle S. Dodd, *Historical Statistics of the South, 1790–1970* (University, Ala., 1973), 58–59; 1840 to 1860 percentages are calculated in

David R. Goldfield, *Urban Growth in the Age of Sectionalism: Virginia, 1847–1861* (Baton Rouge: Louisiana State University Press, 1977), xii, from the Dodds' statistics. These numbers exclude western Virginia. Virginia is often pointed to as an exception in terms of Southern cities. Elizabeth Fox-Genovese writes that Virginia "most closely resembled the North in its urban development," in *Within the Plantation Household: Black and White Women of the Old South* (Chapel Hill: University of North Carolina Press, 1988), 70–81.

3. Launcelot Minor Blackford diary, Apr. 10, 1855, pp. 132–33, Southern Historical Collection, Wilson Library, University of North Carolina at Chapel Hill; "Launcelot Minor Blackford" in John T. Kneebone et al., *Dictionary of Virginia Biography: Vol. 1, Aaroe-Blanchfield* (Richmond: Library of Virginia, 1998), 521–23.

4. M. Ellyson, *Map of the City of Richmond, Henrico County, Virginia*, originally bound into *The Richmond Directory and Business Advertiser for 1856* (Richmond: H. K. Ellyson, 1856). The quote is in the preface. The best study of the city's neighborhoods remains Mary Wingfield Scott, *Old Richmond Neighborhoods* (Richmond: Whittet & Shepperson, 1950).

5. Hess, Richmond, Feb. 1, 1849, to "Dearest Empie," Wilmington, North Carolina, Wooster Family Papers, Southern Historical Collection, Wilson Library, University of North Carolina at Chapel Hill.

6. Bessie Lacy to Drury Lacy, Oct. 18, 1848, Drury Lacy Papers, Southern Historical Collection, Wilson Library, University of North Carolina at Chapel Hill; Blackford diary, Aug. 1, 1855, p. 178.

7. Lewis H. Blair, "Random Sketches of Old Richmond," *Richmond Times-Dispatch*, Sept. 2, 1916; "Death of Mr. John P. Ballard," typescript of *Richmond Daily Dispatch* article, May 29, 1878, in Vertical File—Biography—B, Valentine Museum, Richmond.

8. Gregg D. Kimball and Nancy Jawish Rives, "'To live in hearts we leave behind is not to die': The Barton Heights Cemeteries of Richmond," *Virginia Cavalcade* 46, no. 3 (Winter 1997): 119–20; Marie Tyler-McGraw and Gregg D. Kimball, *In Bondage and Freedom: Antebellum Black Life in Richmond, Virginia* (Richmond: Valentine Museum, 1988), 28–30.

9. Patricia Click, *The Spirit of the Times: Amusements in Nineteenth-Century Baltimore, Norfolk and Richmond* (Charlottesville: University Press of Virginia, 1989).

10. Mary (Bowen) Funsten, Miradore, Albemarle County, to Charles Palmer, June 17, 1853, Palmer Family Papers, Virginia Historical Society, Richmond; Hess, Richmond, to "Dearest Empie," Wilmington, North Carolina, Feb. 1, 1849, Wooster Family Papers.

11. Blackford diary, 89. The entry dated Jan. 1, 1855, recounts the entire Christmas season; Frederick Law Olmsted, *A Journey in the Seaboard Slave States, With Remarks on Their Economy* (New York: Dix & Edwards, 1856), 50.

12. First African Baptist Church Minute Book, 1841–59, Feb. 6, 1842, p. 13, microfilm, Church Records, Library of Virginia, Richmond.

13. First African Baptist Church Minutes, Feb. 4, 1844, p. 60, June 6, 1852, p. 201; *Marion Harland's Autobiography: The Story of a Long Life* (New York: Harper & Brothers, 1910), 227. The speaker who offended the members of First African Baptist Church was probably Judge John Belton O'Neall, who was a Baptist promoter of slave missions and, ironically, a supporter of slave literacy. See Janet Duitsman Cornelius, *"When I Can Read My Title Clear": Literacy, Slavery, and Religion in the Antebellum South* (Columbia: University of South Carolina Press, 1991), 54.

14. Granniss diary, Feb. 11, 1859, p. 46; First African Baptist Church Minutes, Oct. 5, 1851, p. 191, Aug. 6, 1848, p. 133; Click, *Spirit of the Times,* 38.

15. T. J. Macon, *Life Gleanings* (Richmond: W. H. Adams, 1913), 37.

16. Draft report of a "committee appointed by the citizens of Richmond at their meeting held on the twenty eighth day of October 1833, to devise means for suppressing the vice of gambling in this city"; H. Maxwell, New York, to the Committee, Nov. 20, 1833. Both in Conway Robinson Papers, Rare Book, Manuscript, and Special Collections Library, Duke University, Durham, North Carolina.

17. Macon, *Life Gleanings,* 25.

18. Jefferson Wallace, Richmond, to Charles Wallace, Apr. 1, 1855, Clopton Family Papers, Rare Book, Manuscript, and Special Collections Library, Duke University, Durham, North Carolina.

19. Jefferson Wallace, Richmond, to Charles Wallace, Jan. 2, Apr. 29, May 26, 1855, Clopton Family Papers.

20. Joseph Reid Anderson (hereafter JRA) to George Whittimore, Boston, May 19, 1846, Letter Book, Out, Dec. 3, 1845–May 1, 1847, p. 157, and JRA to David Jones, Roller, June 3, 1848, Letter Book, Out, Sept. 30, 1847–May 14, 1849, p. 245, Tredegar Iron Company Records, Business Records, Library of Virginia, Richmond; Patricia A. Schechter, "Free and Slave Labor in the Old South: The Tredegar Ironworkers' Strike of 1847," *Labor History* 35 (Spring 1994): 169; Click, *Spirit of the Times,* 81.

21. Jacob Bechtel, Richmond, to George Bechtel, Philadelphia, Mar. 1, 1858, Clements Library, University of Michigan, Ann Arbor.

22. *The Charters and Ordinances of the City of Richmond . . .* (Richmond: Ellyson's Steam Presses, 1859), 195, 197; *Richmond Daily Dispatch,* Aug. 27, 1853, Aug. 29, 1855, June 28, 1856.

23. Granniss diary, Jan. 24, 1861, p. 206.

24. "ISW" to Bob, May 22, 1845, Clopton Family Papers.

25. Bessie Lacy, Richmond, to Drury Lacy, Nov. 2, 1848, Drury Lacy Papers; Granniss diary, Sept. 27, 1858, p. 13.

26. Blackford diary, 90–91; on Cummins, see Minor T. Weisiger, Donald R. Traser, and E. Randolph Trice, *Not Hearers Only: A History of St. James's Episcopal Church,*

Richmond, Virginia, 1835–1985 (Richmond: St. James Episcopal Church, 1986), 19–21; on Hoge, see Wyndham Bolling Blanton, *The Making of a Downtown Church: The History of the Second Presbyterian Church, Richmond, Virginia, 1845–1945* (Richmond: John Knox Press, 1945).

27. William Ludwell Sheppard diary, Sept. 25, 1853, Jan. 30, 1854, negative photostat, Personal Papers, Library of Virginia, Richmond.

28. *Marion Harland's Autobiography*, 230; James Redpath, *The Roving Editor, or Talks with Slaves in the Southern States*, ed. John R. McKivigan (1859; rev. ed., University Park: Pennsylvania State University Press, 1996), 32–33; Tyler-McGraw and Kimball, *In Bondage and Freedom*, 37–40; "Joseph Abrams," *Dictionary of Virginia Biography*, 1:13.

29. On Richmond's German organizations and churches, see Herrmann Schuricht, *History of the German Element in Virginia* (Baltimore: T. Kroh & Sons, printers, 1898–1900), and Klaus G. Wust, "German Immigrants and Nativism in Virginia, 1840–1860" in *Twenty-ninth Report. Society for the History of the Germans in Maryland* (Baltimore, 1956), 31–50. On the various religious congregations, see *Celebration of the Ninetieth Anniversary of St. John's Evangelical-Lutheran Church* (Richmond: Deitz Printing Co., 1933); Ignatius Remke, *Historical Sketch of St. Mary's Church, Richmond, Virginia, 1843–1935* (Richmond, 1935); Herbert T. Ezekiel and Gaston Lichtenstein, *The History of the Jews in Richmond from 1769 to 1917* (Richmond: H. T. Ezekiel, 1915); Myron Berman, *Richmond's Jewry: Shabbat in Shockoe, 1769–1976* (Charlottesville: University Press of Virginia, 1979); Claire Millhiser Rosenbaum, *Universal and Particular Obligations: Beth Shalome-Beth Ahabah, 1789–1989* (Richmond: Beth Ahabah Museum and Archives Trust, 1988).

30. Locations based on listing in W. Eugene Ferslew, comp., *Second Annual Directory for the City of Richmond, to which is added a Business Directory for 1860* (Richmond: W. Eugene Ferslew, 1860), appendix, 46.

31. Mary Jane Corry, "The Role of German Singing Societies in Nineteenth-century America," in *Germans in America: Aspects of German-American Relations in the Nineteenth Century*, ed. E. Allen McCormick (New York: Brooklyn College Press, 1983), 155–68; Marion L. Huffines, "Language-Maintenance Efforts Among German Immigrants and Their Descendants in the United States," in *America and the Germans: An Assessment of a Three-Hundred Year History. Volume 1: Immigration, Language, Ethnicity*, ed. Frank Trommler and Joseph McVeigh (Philadelphia: University of Pennsylvania Press, 1985), 241; *Deutsches A-B-C und erstes Lese-buch* (Richmond: *Richmonder Anzeiger*, 1863); Charles August Hennighausen, Richmond, to Maria Schulz Hennighausen and Wilhelm Hennighausen, Apr. 24, 1865, translation of original letter, p. 3, Virginia Historical Society, Richmond.

32. Johann Gottfried Lange, "Der veraenderte Nahme, oder der Schumacher in der alten und der neuen Welt. 30 Jahre in Europa und 30 Jahre in Amerika" [The

Changed Name, or the Shoemaker in the Old and the New World. 30 Years in Europe and 30 Years in America], typescript translation of manuscript memoir, 77 (original, 121), Virginia Historical Society, Richmond.

33. Berman, *Richmond's Jewry,* 125.

34. Lange, "Changed Name," 98 (original, 152–53); Schuricht, *History of the German Element in Virginia,* 2:33–36; Wust, "German Immigrants and Nativism in Virginia," 40–43.

35. *Wanderbuch nach der allerhöchsten Verordnung vom 20. November 1809 . . . für Thomas Ruppert,* printed book with manuscript entries in the possession of Mary Geschwind, Greensboro, N.C.; Order of the Richmond City Hustings Court, Apr. 21, 1851, regarding Thomas Ruppert, in Charles August Hennighausen Papers, Virginia Historical Society, Richmond.

36. Musician's diary, Jan. 16, Feb. 10, Mar. 21, Oct. 30, 1856, recorded in *Daily Pocket Diary for 1856: for the Use of Private families and Persons of Business* (New York: Higgins & Kellogg, 1856), Personal Papers, Library of Virginia, Richmond. The probable author of this diary is George H. Kundyman, whose son George Henry's birth is recorded both in the diary and in Richmond City births, p. 27, microfilm, Division of Vital Records and Health Statistics, Department of Health (Record Group 36), State Records, Library of Virginia, Richmond. His wife is listed as Mary. No record of Kundyman could be found in the census.

37. Musician's diary, Feb. 3, Mar. 25, Mar. 30, May 28, June 22, Sept. 15, Sept. 19, 1856.

38. Ibid., Feb. 26, Mar. 6, Mar. 8, Mar. 10, Oct. 17, 1856.

39. Norman C. McLeod Jr., "Not Forgetting the Land We Left: The Irish in Antebellum Richmond," *Virginia Cavalcade* 47, no. 1 (Winter 1998): 36–47.

40. Philip Whitlock's Recollections, 1843–1913, pp. 52–55, Virginia Historical Society, Richmond; U.S. Census, 1850, Richmond City, p. 421, microfilm, Library of Virginia, Richmond.

41. Granniss diary, July 5, 1859, pp. 61–64.

42. Musician's diary, May 12, June 18, 1856.

43. Mary H. Mitchell, *Hollywood Cemetery: The History of a Southern Shrine* (Richmond: Virginia State Library, 1985), 3–45. On the development of Mount Auburn, see Thomas Bender, *Toward an Urban Vision: Ideas and Institutions in Nineteenth Century America* (Baltimore: Johns Hopkins University Press, 1975), 80–87.

44. Mitchell, *Hollywood Cemetery,* 3–45.

45. Ann Webster Gordon Christian diary, Friday, Feb. 9, 1860, Virginia Historical Society, Richmond.

46. Maria Watts Gwathmey diary, Aug. 17, 1853, Gwathmey Family Papers, Virginia Historical Society, Richmond.

47. Samuella Hart Curd diary, May 7, 1860, p. 1, typescript, Virginia Historical Society, Richmond; Maria Watts Gwathmey diary, Aug. 18, 1853.

48. Charles Dickens, *American Notes for General Circulation* (1842; reprint ed. New York: D. Appleton & Company, 1868), 57–59.

49. Ibid.

50. David Goldfield studied slave ownership among "city-builders" across Virginia in *Urban Growth in the Age of Sectionalism*, 38–40. Berlin and Gutman identified the percentage of slaves owned or hired by city residents in five cities. They defined merchants, planters, professionals, and politicians as a group, and I added this number to the total for manufacturers. Ira Berlin and Herbert G. Gutman, "Natives and Immigrants, Free Men and Slaves: Urban Workingmen in the Antebellum American South," *American Historical Review* 88 (Dec. 1983), table 8, p. 1184.

51. Kathleen Bruce, *Virginia Iron Manufacture in the Slave Era* (New York: Century Company, 1931), 262.

52. Norman C. McLeod Jr., "Free Labor in a Slave Society: Richmond, Virginia, 1820–1860" (Ph.D. diss., Howard University, 1991), 15–20.

53. Mary Wingfield Scott, *Houses of Old Richmond* (Richmond: Valentine Museum, 1951), 43–45; *Richmond Portraits in an Exhibition of Makers of Richmond, 1737–1860* (Richmond: Valentine Museum, 1949), 132–33.

54. Musician's diary, June 6, 11, July 9–Sept. 12, 1856.

55. Granniss diary, Saturday, June 4, 1859, p. 56; Kent's will is quoted in Scott, *Houses of Old Richmond*, 235.

56. *Marion Harland's Autobiography*, 24–56, 143–44; Karen Manners Smith, "Half My Heart in Dixie: Southern Identity and the Civil War in the Writings of Mary Virginia Terhune," in *Beyond Image and Convention: Explorations in Southern Women's History*, ed. Janet L. Coryell et al. (Columbia: University of Missouri Press, 1998), 119–37.

57. *Marion Harland's Autobiography*, 196; sketch of the Hawes House in Scott, *Houses of Old Richmond*, 125–27; Hawes's mother lived with the family according to *Richmond City and Henrico County, Virginia: 1850 United States Census* (Virginia Genealogical Society, Special Publication No. 6, 1977), 183; ownership of five slaves in Personal Property Tax List, Richmond City, 1850, Auditor of Public Accounts, microfilm, Library of Virginia, Richmond.

58. *Marion Harland's Autobiography*, 162, 187.

59. Ibid., 1–8.

60. Fredericka H. Trapnell, *Virginia Tucker-Henry L. Brooke Correspondence: Richmond, Virginia, 1831–1869* (Frederica H. Trapnell, 1978), xv, 40–41, 67–68.

61. Virginia S. Brooke, Washington, to her mother, Mrs. Anne E. Tucker, Winchester, postmarked Nov. 18, 1851, in Trapnell, *Virginia Tucker-Henry L. Brooke Correspondence*, 40.

62. Virginia S. Brooke, Washington, to her mother, Mrs. Anne E. Tucker, Winchester, Nov. 1, 1852 in Trapnell, *Virginia Tucker-Henry L. Brooke Correspondence*, xvi, 69.

63. Elizabeth Ann Valentine Gray, Rockbridge Alum Springs, to William Gray, Sept. 26, 1856, Valentine Family Papers.

64. Ibid. The painting, by Christian Mayr, is owned by the North Carolina Museum of Art, Raleigh, and is reproduced in Kym S. Rice and Edward D. C. Campbell Jr., *Before Freedom Came: African-American Life in the Antebellum South* (Charlottesville: Museum of the Confederacy and the University Press of Virginia, 1991), 65.

65. Elizabeth Ann Valentine Gray, Rockbridge Alum Springs, to William Gray, Sept. 29, 1856, Valentine Family Papers.

66. Elizabeth Ann Valentine Gray, Rockbridge Alum Springs, to William Gray, undated, Valentine Family Papers.

67. Samuel Mordecai, *Virginia, Especially Richmond, in By-Gone Days*, 2d ed. (Richmond: West & Johnston, 1860), 356.

68. On slave housing in Richmond, see Gregg D. Kimball, "African-Virginians and the Vernacular Building Tradition in Richmond City, 1790–1860," in *Perspectives in Vernacular Architecture, VI,* ed. Thomas Carter and Bernard L. Herman (Columbia and London: University of Missouri Press for the Vernacular Architecture Forum, 1991), 121–29.

69. Tracey M. Weis, "Negotiating Freedom: Domestic Service and the Landscape of Labor and Household Relations in Richmond, Virginia, 1850–1880" (Ph.D. diss., Rutgers, The State University of New Jersey—New Brunswick, 1994), 26, 57–59.

70. Virginia S. Brooke, Washington, to her mother, Mrs. Anne E. Tucker, Winchester, Dec. 29, 1851, in Trapnell, *Virginia Tucker-Henry L. Brooke Correspondence*, 44.

71. Virginia S. Brooke, Washington, to her mother, Mrs. Anne E. Tucker, Winchester, Nov. 4, 1852, in Trapnell, *Virginia Tucker-Henry L. Brooke Correspondence*, 71.

72. Sarah Benetta Valentine to Mann S. Valentine Jr., July 25, 1852, Valentine Family Papers.

73. Ibid.; Mary Virginia Hawes Terhune, Richmond, to a friend, July 20, 1852, and Mary Virginia Hawes Terhune, Richmond, to Virginia Eppes Dance, June 8, 1847, Mary Virginia Hawes Terhune Papers, Rare Book, Manuscript, and Special Collections Library, Duke University, Durham, North Carolina; *Marion Harland's Autobiography*, 186–87.

74. William A. Link, "The Jordan Hatcher Case: Politics and 'A Spirit of Insubordination' in Antebellum Virgina," *Journal of Southern History* 64, no. 4 (Nov. 1998): 644–46; Robert Ryland, "Reminiscences of the First African Baptist Church, Richmond, VA., by the Pastor, No. 3," *American Baptist Memorial* 14 (Nov. 1855): 324–27.

75. For a good overview of benevolent activity among Virginia women, see Elizabeth R. Varon, *We Mean to Be Counted: White Women and Politics in Antebellum Virginia* (Chapel Hill: University of North Carolina Press, 1998), 10–40.

76. Ann Webster Gordon Christian diary; Sarah Benetta Valentine to Edward V. Valentine, Mar. 9, 1860, Valentine Family Papers. "Mr. Dashiel" was probably the Reverend T. G. Dashiell, listed in 1866 as rector of Saint Philip's African Church (Episcopal) on 4th Street south of Leigh. S. Dow Mills & H. W. Starke, comp., *The City of Richmond Business Directory and City Guide* (Richmond: Gary & Clemmitt, printers, 1866).

77. Charles F. Irons, "And All These Things Shall Be Added Unto You: The First African Baptist Church, Richmond, 1841–1865," *Virginia Cavalcade* 47, no. 1 (Winter 1998): 28–29; Robert Ryland, *The Scriptural Catechism, for Coloured People* (Richmond: Harrold and Murray, 1848).

78. Edmund Berkeley Jr., "Prophet Without Honor: Christopher McPherson, Free Person of Color," *Virginia Magazine of History and Biography* 77, no. 2 (Apr. 1969): 180–90; Luther Porter Jackson, *Free Negro Labor and Property Holding in Virginia* (New York: Appleton, 1942), 24–25, 154.

79. Cornelius, *"When I Can Read My Title Clear,"* 32–34, 79–80. The other states with legal bars on literacy from the 1830s to 1865 were North Carolina, South Carolina, and Georgia. Alabama and Louisiana approved literacy restrictions in the 1830s, but these laws were not maintained in later state codes.

80. *Butters' Richmond Directory for 1855* (Richmond: H. K. Ellyson, 1855), 168; *Southern Planter, Devoted to Agriculture, Horticulture, and the Household Arts* 17, no. 3 (Mar. 1857): 8 (advertising sheet).

81. The history of the Richmond Female Institute is from a "Historical Sketch by Maude H. Woodfin," Feb. 12, 1937, read at the dedication of the Richmond Female Institute-Woman's College Alumnae Room, Keller Hall, Westhampton College, University of Richmond, in Richmond Female Institute Records, Virginia Historical Society, Richmond. The quote is from *Report to the Stockholders of the Richmond Female Institute, Together with the Catalogue for 1856* (Richmond: H. K. Ellyson, 1856), 18, in Vertical File—Education—Richmond Female Institute, Valentine Museum, Richmond.

82. *Report to the Stockholders of the Richmond Female Institute, Together with the Catalogue for 1856*, 35.

83. On the problem of control, see Richard Wade, *Slavery in the Cities: The South, 1820–1860* (New York: Oxford University Press, 1964). On the church and burial societies, see John O'Brien, "Factory, Church, and Community: Blacks in Antebellum Richmond," *Journal of Southern History* 44, no. 4 (Nov 1978): 509–36; Tyler-McGraw and Kimball, *In Bondage and Freedom*, 35–44; and Kimball and Rives, " 'To live in hearts we leave behind is not to die,' " 118–31.

84. My numbers are derived from a study of the First African Baptist Church Minute Book, 1841–59, described in detail in chapter 4. The initial number of church members is from Robert Ryland, "Reminiscences of the First African Baptist Church, Richmond, Va., by the Pastor, No. 1," *American Baptist Memorial* 14 (Sept. 1855): 264.

85. First African Baptist Church Minutes, Jan. 5, 1851, Sept. 6, 1855.

86. *Richmond Daily Dispatch,* June 22, 1858.

87. *The Charters and Ordinances of the City of Richmond,* 193–200.

88. Claudia Dale Goldin, *Urban Slavery in the American South: A Quantitative Analysis* (Chicago: University of Chicago Press, 1976), 38–42.

89. Entries for William, Feb. 28, Mar. 16, 1846, Register, Mar. 13, 1841–May 8, 1851, Richmond City Sergeant's Papers, Virginia Historical Society, Richmond; Richmond Police Day Book, 1834–43, Jan. 5, 1841, Apr. 4, 1842, July 20, 1843, Special Collections Department, University of Virginia Library, Charlottesville.

90. Richmond Police Day Book, 1834–43, June 5, 1843.

91. Petition of Henry Mason, Richmond City, Dec. 22, 1847, Legislative Petitions, General Assembly (Record Group 78), State Records, Library of Virginia, Richmond.

92. Entries for Jacob Pittman, Sept. 9, 23, 1843, Register, Mar. 13, 1841–May 8, 1851, Richmond City Sergeant's Papers.

93. William Scott and Lucy Scott, Richmond, to their children, New Kent County, Aug. 26, 1849, and Peter Lennard, Richmond, to Eliza Pearman, New Kent County, June 28, 1843, Scott and Pearman Family letters, 1852–69, Norvell W. Wilson Papers, Southern Historical Collection, Wilson Library, University of North Carolina at Chapel Hill; Free Negro Register, Henrico County, 1831–44, p. 42, microfilm, Library of Virginia, Richmond; *Richmond City and Henrico County, Virginia: 1850 United States Census,* 12, 125. There are two entries for the same family grouping taken by different census takers, with only minor differences in ages.

94. Mary J. Bratton, ed., "Fields's Observations: The Slave Narrative of a Nineteenth-Century Virginian," *Virginia Magazine of History and Biography* 88, no. 1 (Jan. 1980): 75–93.

95. On African-American housing, see Kimball, "African-Virginians and the Vernacular Building Tradition in Richmond City, 1790–1860," 121–29. For a map showing residential patterns of free blacks, see Gregg D. Kimball and Elsa Barkley Brown, "Mapping the Terrain of Black Richmond," *Journal of Urban History* 21, no. 3 (Mar. 1995): 296–346.

96. See Gregg D. Kimball, "The Working People of Richmond: Life and Labor in an Industrial City, 1865–1920," *Labor's Heritage* 3, no. 2 (Apr. 1991): 42–65.

97. Whitlock, Recollections, 76–77.

98. Ibid., 62–63.

99. Ibid., 63.

100. Granniss diary, Oct. 28, 1858, pp. 21–22.

101. Lange, "Changed Name," 87 (original, 139).

102. Jacob Bechtel, Richmond, to George Bechtel, Philadelphia, Dec. 12, 1860, Bechtel Papers.

103. Charles Emery Stevens, *Anthony Burns: A History* (Boston: John P. Jewett and Company, 1856), 194–95.

104. Eyre Crowe, *With Thackeray in America* (New York: Charles Scribner's Sons, 1893), 131–36.

105. *Illustrated London News*, Sept. 27, 1856.

CHAPTER 3. The World of Goods

1. I am indebted to my former colleague Jane Webb Smith for helping me understand Mann S. Valentine Jr.'s views on being a Southern merchant in a Northern world of goods and for spurring my interest in this entire subject. See her "Creating History: The Valentine Family and Museum," typescript essay distributed by the Valentine Museum, May 1996.

2. *Richmond City and Henrico County, Virginia: 1850 United States Census* (Virginia Genealogical Society, Special Publication No. 6, 1977), 97; advertisements for Wallace & Sons, *Elliott & Nye's Virginia Directory, and Business Directory for 1852* (Richmond: Elliott & Nye, 1852), 42 of Richmond advertisements.

3. David R. Goldfield, *Urban Growth in the Age of Sectionalism: Virginia, 1847–1861* (Baton Rouge: Louisiana State University Press, 1977); Daniel R. Hundley, *Social Relations in Our Southern States*, ed. William J. Cooper (Baton Rouge: Louisiana State University Press, 1979).

4. This analysis is based on Richmond advertisements in *Elliott & Nye's Virginia Directory*, cross-referenced with *Richmond City and Henrico County, Virginia: 1850 United States Census*.

5. On Hubbard and Gardner, see *Richmond Portraits in an Exhibition of Makers of Richmond, 1737–1860* (Richmond: Valentine Museum, 1949), 76–77, 96–97. For a summary of the early history of H. M. Smith and Co., see typescript "The Cardwell Machine Company," in History File, Cardwell Machine Company Records, 1868–1960, Valentine Museum, Richmond.

6. Samuel Mordecai, *Virginia, Especially Richmond, in By-Gone Days.* 2d ed. (Richmond: West and Johnston, 1860), 58; Biography of Horace L. Kent in Vertical File, Valentine Museum, Richmond; *Richmond Daily Dispatch*, June 7, 14, 1854; ownership of six slaves in Personal Property Tax List, Richmond, 1850, Auditor of Public Accounts, microfilm, Library of Virginia, Richmond; identified as a "moderate activist" among Richmond's urban leaders in Goldfield, *Urban Growth in the Age of Sectionalism*, appendix B; Charles Palmer, New Orleans, to Dr. William P. Palmer, Dec. 17, 1848, William P. Palmer Papers, Rare Book, Manuscript, and Special Collections Library, Duke University, Durham, North Carolina; Mann S. Valentine, New York, to Sarah Benetta Valentine, Mar. 2, 1851, Valentine Family Papers, Valentine Museum, Richmond.

7. Thomas R. Price, New York, to his wife, Christian Elizabeth Price, Mar. 7, 1851, Price Family Papers, Virginia Historical Society, Richmond.

8. *The Edward Pleasants Valentine Papers* (Richmond: Valentine Museum, n.d.),

4:2329–30, 2346–48, quote on 2330; Norman C. McLeod Jr., "Mann Satterwhite Valentine: Patriarch of a Richmond, Virginia, Merchant Family" (Master's thesis, Virginia State University, 1982).

9. Mann S. Valentine's accounts and receipts file, Valentine Family Papers, especially receipt for sale of "Sally, and her four children," to Mann S. Valentine from estate of Benjamin Mosby, Feb. 26, 1831; Personal Property Tax Lists, Richmond City, 1840–50, Auditor of Public Accounts, microfilm, State Records, Library of Virginia, Richmond.

10. Mann S. Valentine, New York, to Elizabeth Mosby Valentine, Aug. 19, 1850, Valentine Family Papers.

11. Mann S. Valentine, New York, to Elizabeth Ann Valentine Gray, Aug. 15, 1839, Valentine Family Papers.

12. Mann S. Valentine, New York, to Elizabeth Ann Valentine Gray, Mar. 15, 1842, Valentine Family Papers.

13. Mann S. Valentine, New York, to Mann S. Valentine Jr., Aug. 5, 1851, Valentine Family Papers.

14. Mann S. Valentine, New York, to his son William Winston Valentine, Aug. 22, 185[torn], Valentine Family Papers; see also Mann S. Valentine, New York, to Elizabeth Ann Valentine Gray, Mar. 15, 1842: "We have a large number of Richmd gentlemen here to wit Binford, Brooks, Drewry Ellis & the eloquent gentleman."

15. Mann S. Valentine Jr., New York, to Ann Maria Gray Valentine, Feb. 29, 1856, Valentine Family Papers.

16. Ann Maria Gray Valentine, Richmond, to Mann S. Valentine Jr., New York, Mar. 7, 1856, Valentine Family Papers.

17. Louis Luhan, New York, to Charles Wallace, care of William Wallace, Jan. 17, 1848, Clopton Family Papers, Rare Book, Manuscript, and Special Collections Library, Duke University, Durham, North Carolina.

18. James S. Kent, New York, to Elizabeth Ann Valentine Gray, Mar. 14, 1846, Valentine Family Papers; U.S. Census, 1860, Richmond City, Second Ward, p. 441; ownership of a slave in Personal Property Tax Lists, Richmond City, 1842–49, Auditor of Public Accounts, microfilm, State Records, Library of Virginia, Richmond; listed as belonging to the firm of Kent, Paine and Kent in *Elliott & Nye's Virginia Directory*.

19. Mann S. Valentine Jr., New York, to Ann Maria Gray Valentine, Feb. 26, 1857, Valentine Family Papers.

20. Ibid.

21. Charles M. Wallace, New York, to Isabella Wallace, Sept. 17, 1845, Clopton Family Papers.

22. Ibid.

23. Mann S. Valentine Jr., New York, to Ann Maria Gray Valentine, Aug. 30, 1856, Valentine Family Papers.

24. Ibid.

25. George D. Fisher, Richmond, to James H. Stanard, Philadelphia, Nov. 13, 1857, James Stanard Papers, Virginia Historical Society, Richmond; dismissal of Stanard, Oct. 3, 1847, p. 121, First African Baptist Church Minute Books, microfilm, Church Records, Library of Virginia, Richmond.

26. McIntosh's reaction is discussed in Elizabeth Moss, *Domestic Novelists in the Old South: Defenders of Southern Culture* (Baton Rouge: Louisiana State University Press, 1992), 120–25; Evelyn L. Pugh, "Women and Slavery: Julia Gardiner Tyler and the Duchess of Sutherland," *Virginia Magazine of History and Biography* 88, no. 2 (Apr. 1980): 186–202; William Wallace, Richmond, to Mrs. Captn B. Donald, Jan. 9, 1853, Clopton Family Papers.

27. William Wallace, Richmond, to Mrs. Captn B. Donald, Jan. 9, 1853, Clopton Family Papers.

28. Chapter 4 of *Bleak House* is entitled "Telescopic Philanthropy." The quote is from Charles Dickens, *Bleak House* (London: Thomas Nelson and Sons, 1912), 40.

29. Mann S. Valentine Jr., Richmond, to his brother Edward Virginius Valentine, Aug. 9, 1860, Valentine Family Papers.

30. Sarah Benetta Valentine, Richmond, to Edward Virginius Valentine, Mar. 9, 1860, Valentine Family Papers.

31. Ann Maria Gray Valentine, Richmond, to William Winston Valentine, directed to Paris, Jan. 21, 1861.

32. *Notes on Travel and Life, by Two Young Ladies—Misses Mendell and Hosmer* (New York, 1853), 168.

33. *Marion Harland's Autobiography: The Story of a Long Life* (New York: Harper & Brothers, 1910), 111–13.

34. See the summary of Terhune's domestic fiction in Moss, *Domestic Novelists in the Old South. Moss-side* is discussed in depth on pp. 143–53. Karen Manners Smith argues that Terhune's fiction was largely without sectional prejudice and that she liked the North and Northerners. I find Moss's analysis of *Moss-Side* convincing, especially in light of Terhune's antebellum letters, some of which are cited below and in earlier chapters. (Smith did, however, have access to a privately held diary not available to me.) In any event, Smith acknowledges Terhune's adherence to a typically Southern view of domestic relations and African Americans. See "Half My Heart in Dixie: Southern Identity and the Civil War in the Writings of Mary Virginia Terhune," in *Beyond Image and Convention: Explorations in Southern Women's History,* ed. Janet L. Coryell et. al. (Columbia: University of Missouri Press, 1998).

35. Mary Virginia Hawes Terhune, Brookline, Mass., to a friend, July 1851, Mary Virginia Hawes Terhune Papers, Rare Book, Manuscript, and Special Collections Library, Duke University, Durham, North Carolina.

36. Mary Virginia Hawes Terhune, New York, to a friend, Oct. 18, 1855, Mary Virginia Hawes Terhune Papers.

37. For an overall treatment of Southern tourists in the North, see John Hope Franklin, *A Southern Odyssey: Travelers in the Antebellum North* (Baton Rouge: Louisiana State University Press, 1976).

38. Samuella Hart Curd diary, May 8, 11, 1860, pp. 1–2, typescript, Virginia Historical Society, Richmond.

39. Ibid., May 10, 1860, p. 1.

40. Richmond Light Infantry Blues Minute Book, Feb. 22, 1855, pp. 309–10, Personal Papers, Library of Virginia, Richmond.

41. *Richmond Daily Dispatch*, Aug. 18, 1859.

42. Goldfield identifies Dimmock as a "moderate activist" among Richmond's urban leaders in *Urban Growth in the Age of Sectionalism*, appendix B. His nativity is from *Richmond City and Henrico County, Virginia: 1850 United States Census*, 43. Biographical information is from Biographical Vertical File, Valentine Museum, Richmond, and Kathleen Bruce, *Virginia Iron Manufacture in the Slave Era* (New York: Century Company, 1931), 214.

43. Accounts of the organization's deliberations ran in a number of newspapers. See *Richmond Enquirer*, Dec. 10, 1850. See also the Record Book of the Central Southern Rights Association of Virginia, 1850–60, pp. 1–4, Virginia Historical Society, Richmond. For an overview of the organization, see Michael Douglas Naragon, "Ballots, Bullets, and Blood: The Political Transformation of Virginia, 1850–1874." (Ph.D. diss., University of Pittsburgh, 1996), 217–25.

44. *Richmond Enquirer*, Dec. 10, 1850; Record Book of the Central Southern Rights Association, 3–4.

45. The *Richmond Enquirer* incorrectly attributed these resolutions to Richmond mayor Joseph Mayo. See Record Book of the Central Southern Rights Association for the correct attribution, 7–8.

46. *Richmond Enquirer*, Dec. 13, 1850; Record Book of the Central Southern Rights Association, 7–13.

47. *Richmond Enquirer*, Dec. 17, 1850; Record Book of the Central Southern Rights Association, 17–20.

48. *Richmond Enquirer*, Dec. 21, 1850. The final constitution is found in Record Book of the Central Southern Rights Association, 21–24, and was published in *The Proceedings and Address of the Central Southern Rights Association of Virginia . . .* (Richmond: Ritchie and Dunnavant, 1851), 4–5. At least two other dry-goods merchants, Irishman Hugh Raleigh and Virginian Thomas U. Dudley, attended.

49. Franklin, *Southern Odyssey*, 99–100, 107–8.

50. Daniel H. London, New York, to Robert L. Walker, Aug. 6, 1851; unidentified correspondent, Amsterdam, to D. H. London, Richmond, Oct. 21, 1851; and Daniel H. London, Richmond, to W. Mcfarland, of Mcfarland & Stapley, London, Sept. 11, 1851,

all in Daniel H. London Papers, Virginia Historical Society, Richmond; Record Book of the Central Southern Rights Association, 54–56, 117–21. The organization claimed more than 300 members late in Jan. 1851.

51. Charles Palmer, Richmond, to William P. Palmer, Elk Hill, Amelia County, Virginia, Sept. 16, 1850, Palmer Family Papers, Virginia Historical Society, Richmond.

52. Jefferson Wallace, Richmond, to Charles Blair, Calif., Feb. 2, 1855, Clopton Family Papers.

53. *Marion Harland's Autobiography*, 84–85, 246–48.

54. Thomas R. Price, New York, to his wife, Christian Elizabeth Price, May 7, 1858, Price Family Papers. The marriage date is from Richmond City marriages, 1858, p. 91, Division of Vital Records and Health Statistics, Department of Health (Record Group 36), State Records, Library of Virginia, Richmond. The couple are listed in U.S. Census, 1860, Richmond City, Ward 3, p. 349, microfilm, Library of Virginia, Richmond.

55. Maria Watts Gwathmey diary, Aug. 17, 1853, Gwathmey Family Papers, Virginia Historical Society, Richmond.

56. Curd diary, May 10, 1860, p. 2.

57. Anne Eliza Pleasants Gordon diary, 4, typescript, Virginia Historical Society, Richmond.

58. Elizabeth Ann Valentine, Astor House, New York, to her brother, William Winston Valentine, May 9, [1850], Valentine Family Papers.

59. "Trousseau given me by my father and mother bought at 'Stewart's' store when we were in New York together," May 1850, Valentine Family Papers.

60. Gwathmey diary, Sept. 10, 12, 1853.

61. Franklin, *Southern Odyssey*, 34–35.

62. Frederick Law Olmsted, *A Journey in the Seaboard Slave States, With Remarks on Their Economy* (New York: Dix & Edwards, 1856), 50.

63. *Notes on Travel and Life, by Two Young Ladies*, 162.

64. Mann S. Valentine, New York, to Elizabeth Ann Valentine Gray, Aug. 15, 1839, Valentine Family Papers. On minstrel shows and characters, see Annemarie Bean, James V. Hatch, and Brooks McNamara, ed., *Inside the Minstrel Mask: Readings in Nineteenth-Century Blackface Minstrelsy* (Hanover, N.H.: University Press of New England for Wesleyan University Press, 1996). On the Broadway Swell and other urban types, see John F. Kasson, *Rudeness and Civility: Manners in Nineteenth-Century Urban America* (New York: Hill and Wang, 1990).

65. Olmsted, *Journey in the Seaboard Slave States*, 28.

66. *Notes on Travel and Life, by Two Young Ladies*, 161.

67. Jefferson Wallace, Richmond, to Charles Wallace, California, Nov. 27, 1854, Clopton Family Papers.

68. Ibid.

69. Jefferson Wallace, Richmond, to Charles Blair, California, Feb. 2, 1855, Clopton Family Papers.

70. Jefferson Wallace, Richmond, to Charles Wallace, California, Dec. 17, 1854, Jan. 2, 1855, Clopton Family Papers.

71. *Report of a Committee Appointed by the Board of Directors to the Annual Meeting of the Board of Trade, held in the City of Richmond, May, 1857* (Richmond: Whig Book and Job Office, 1857), 5.

72. Maury Bros., New York, to Samuel Mordecai, Richmond, May 4, 1857, Mordecai Family Papers, Southern Historical Collection, Wilson Library, University of North Carolina at Chapel Hill.

73. Michael Tadman, *Speculators and Slaves: Masters, Traders, and Slaves in the Old South* (Madison: University of Wisconsin Press, 1989), 183.

74. Charles Palmer, New Orleans, to William P. Palmer, Richmond, Mar. 3, 1851, Palmer Family Papers; *Montague's Richmond Directory and Business Advertiser* (1850–51); Louis H. Manarin, *Richmond at War: The Minutes of the City Council*, Official Publication No. 17, Richmond Civil War Centennial Committee (Chapel Hill: University of North Carolina Press, 1966), 631.

75. Charles Palmer, New Orleans, to William P. Palmer, Richmond, Apr. 14, 1849, and Mar. 3, 1851, Palmer Family Papers.

76. Notes on Samuel Mordecai made by Edward Virginius Valentine from his diaries, in Samuel Mordecai biography folder, Vertical File, Valentine Museum, Richmond.

77. Mordecai, *Virginia, Especially Richmond, in By-Gone Days*, 355.

78. William Ludwell Sheppard diary, Oct. 26, 1853, negative photostat, Personal Papers, Library of Virginia, Richmond; Philip J. Schwarz, *Slave Laws in Virginia* (Athens: University of Georgia Press, 1996), 140–41.

79. "Petition of P. M. Tabb and Others to change law concerning runaways," Richmond City, Dec. 14, 1850, Legislative Petitions, General Assembly (Record Group 78), State Records, Library of Virginia, Richmond.

80. Tracey M. Weis gives the percentages of domestic workers in Richmond as 91 percent slave, 6 percent free black, and 3 percent white. "Negotiating Freedom: Domestic Service and the Landscape of Labor and Household Relations in Richmond, Virginia, 1850–1880" (Ph.D. diss., Rutgers, The State University of New Jersey—New Brunswick, 1994), 27, 75, 159–66.

81. James Rawlings, Boston, to William H. Allen and Thomas R. Blair, Aug. 5, 1827, Mutual Assurance Society Records, Business Records, Library of Virginia, Richmond; Charles Palmer, New Orleans, to William P. Palmer, Jan. 12, 1850, William P. Palmer Papers.

82. Lewis E. Atherton, *The Southern Country Store, 1800–1860* (Baton Rouge:

Louisiana State University Press, 1949), 140; Mann S. Valentine, New York, to Elizabeth Ann Valentine Gray, Mar. 7, 1851, Valentine Family Papers; in a letter from New York on Mar. 2, 1851, Mann S. Valentine told his daughter "Netty" (Sarah Benetta Valentine), "we have a number of Richmond merchants in N.Y. Captn Nimmo, Price, Grey, Barksdale, the Prophet, H. Kent, Lathrop Dt Dt." Valentine Family Papers.

83. George F. Adams, *A Brief Sketch of the Life and Character of the Late William Crane of Baltimore* (Baltimore: John F. Weishampel Jr., 1868), 11.

84. Ibid., 12–29. Clipping "Colonization Society of Virginia," facing entry for Feb. 23, 1849, Minutes of the Virginia Branch, American Colonization Society, Nov. 4, 1823–Feb. 5, 1859, Virginia Historical Society, Richmond.

85. Adams, *Brief Sketch of the Life and Character of the Late William Crane of Baltimore,* 30.

86. "Miss Van Lew Now Very Ill," *Evening Leader* (Richmond and Manchester), July 27, 1900, and "Miss Van Lew Dead," clippings in Vertical File, "Confederate States of America—Spies—Elizabeth Van Lew," Valentine Museum, Richmond.

87. Newspaper clipping, Elizabeth Van Lew Papers, misc. microfilm, reel No. 14, Library of Virginia, Richmond, originals in the Manuscript and Archives Division, New York Public Library, Astor, Lenox, and Tilden Foundation; Frederika Bremer, *The Homes of the New World: Impressions of America* (New York: Harper and Brothers, 1853), 2:509–10.

88. Annual meeting of society in Hall of Delegates, with Governor Floyd presiding as president, Feb. 13, 1851, Virginia Branch, American Colonization Society Minutes.

89. Ibid; Anne Sarah Rubin, "Between Union and Chaos: The Political Life of John Janney," *Virginia Magazine of History and Biography* 102, no. 3 (July 1994): 381–416.

90. Harrison M. Ethridge, "The Jordan Hatcher Affair of 1852: Cold Justice and Warm Compassion," *Virginia Magazine of History and Biography* 84, no. 4 (Oct. 1976): 446–63; William A. Link, "The Jordan Hatcher Case: Politics and 'A Spirit of Insubordination' in Antebellum Virgina," *Journal of Southern History* 64, no. 4 (Nov. 1998): 615–48.

91. Ethridge, "Jordan Hatcher Affair of 1852," 454.

92. Mann S. Valentine Jr., Stevens Hotel, New York, to Ann Maria Gray Valentine, Aug. 27, 1856, Valentine Family Papers.

93. Sawyer, Wallace & Co., New York, to William Gray, Dec. 5, 1859, Correspondence, William Gray & Company Papers, Virginia Historical Society, Richmond.

94. *Richmond Daily Dispatch,* June 19, 1858. Newspaper accounts and most of the Valentine papers give the slave's name simply as "Washington." The only document bearing Washington's last name is a receipt, Sednum Grady to Mann Valentine, Dec. 24, 1858, Valentine Family Papers.

95. *Richmond Daily Dispatch,* June 19, 1858; Mann S. Valentine memorandum, June 22, 1858, Valentine Family Papers.

96. *Richmond Daily Dispatch,* June 22, 1858; Mann S. Valentine memorandum, July 11, 1858, Valentine Family Papers.

97. Mann S. Valentine memorandum, July 11, 1858, Valentine Family Papers. The relationship of China to Washington Winston is set out in Henry Page, Richmond, to his son, Nov. 20, 1856, Valentine Family Papers.

98. Sednum Grady to Mann Valentine, Dec. 24, 1858, Valentine Family Papers.

CHAPTER 4. Liberty and Slavery

1. First African Baptist Church Minute Book, 1841–59, Oct. 1, 1848, p. 134, microfilm, Church Records, Library of Virginia, Richmond.

2. "Petition of a number of persons of colour residing in the City of Richmond," Richmond City, Dec. 23, 1823, Legislative Petitions, General Assembly (Record Group 78), State Records, Library of Virginia, Richmond; Robert Ryland, "Reminiscences of the First African Baptist Church, Richmond, VA., by the Pastor, No. 1," *American Baptist Memorial* 14 (Sept. 1855): 262–63.

3. *Richmond Portraits in an Exhibition of Makers of Richmond, 1737–1860* (Richmond: Valentine Museum, 1949), 184.

4. Ryland, "Reminiscences of the First African Baptist Church, No. 1," 263.

5. First African Baptist Church Minutes, 192.

6. The database used to derive these statistics was composed of members received and dismissed in the First African Baptist Church Minute Book, 1841–1859. It contains the church and place where the member came from or went to, the name, status (slave, free, unrecorded, or unknown), date of entry, and the slave owner's name, if given. I did not record received and dismissed members to and from other Richmond churches in the database, because these do not show geographic movement. Not all entries in the minute book are complete, and many lack the place to or from which members were dismissed. (Entries for received members are more complete than dismissals to other places.) I recorded all free black entries, but restricted slave entries to those listing a church or location. Likewise, a relatively small number of entries—about 103—lack or question the member's status (i.e. slave or free).

7. William C. and Lucy P. Scott, Brantford, Canada West, to "My Dear Children," Oct. 29, 1854, Norvell W. Wilson Papers, Southern Historical Collection, Wilson Library, University of North Carolina at Chapel Hill.

8. First African Baptist Church Minutes, Nov. 7, 1852, p. 210; Nov. 14, 1855, p. 263. Emmanuel Quivers's story is told in Kathleen Bruce, *Virginia Iron Manufacture in the Slave Era* (New York: Century Company, 1931), 239–42. The First African Baptist Church Minutes record twelve dismissals to New York.

9. Leonard P. Curry, *The Free Black in Urban America, 1800–1850: The Shadow of the Dream* (Chicago: University of Chicago Press, 1981), 249; James O. Horton, *Free People of Color: Inside the African American Community* (Washington: Smithsonian

Institution Press, 1993), 53−78; Luther Porter Jackson, *Free Negro Labor and Property Holding in Virginia* (New York: Appleton, 1942), 24−25, 154.

10. Census figures calculated from Michael Chesson, *Richmond After the War, 1865−1890* (Richmond: Virginia State Library, 1981), table 1, p. 12.

11. Petition of the Society of Friends, Richmond City, Dec. 31, 1844, Legislative Petitions.

12. James Redpath, *The Roving Editor, or Talks with Slaves in the Southern States,* ed. John R. McKivigan (1859; rpt., University Park: Pennsylvania State University Press, 1996), 28−30. The collected city codes related to free blacks and slaves can be found in *The Charters and Ordinances of the City of Richmond*... (Richmond: Ellyson's Steam Presses, 1859), 193−200.

13. Redpath, *Roving Editor,* 28−30.

14. First African Baptist Church Minutes: William Scott was dismissed on July 16, 1854, p. 242. The Prices were dismissed on Mar. 5, 1854, p. 234. On June 25, 1854, p. 239, the following were dismissed with no destination: Isham Ellis (deacon), Nancy Ellis, Mary Madden, Maria Ellis, Virginia Madden, Eliza Ellis, Lucy Logan, Martha Ann Warren, Mary Harris, William Harris, James Ellis, Claiborne Garnett, Stepney Laughton. On Oct. 14, 1855, p. 262, John Kinney was dismissed and James Oliver on May 24, 1857, p. 295. Isham and James Ellis are listed as shoemakers in a section entitled "Free Colored Housekeepers" in William L. Montague, *The Richmond Directory and Business Advertiser for 1852* (Baltimore: J. W. Woods, printer, 1852), 141.

15. Ira Berlin downplays the role of self-purchase in emancipation, particularly in the period from 1820 to 1860, although he admits that it was more common in the urban setting. See *Slaves without Masters: The Free Negro in the Antebellum South* (New York: Pantheon Books, 1974), 153−57. Luther Porter Jackson emphasizes self-purchase as a cause of slave emancipations in *Free Negro Labor and Property Holding in Virginia,* 174, 181.

16. Joseph R. Anderson to Henry Harrison, Berkeley, Dec. 13, 1845, Letter Book, Out, Dec. 3, 1845−May 1, 1847, p. 9, Tredegar Iron Company Records, Business Records, Library of Virginia, Richmond. Much of the information on Quivers is from Kathleen Bruce, "Slave Labor in the Virginia Iron Industry," *William and Mary Quarterly* 7, no. 1 (Jan. 1927): 21−23.

17. Bruce, "Slave Labor in the Virginia Iron Industry," 22.

18. Ibid.

19. Joseph Reid Anderson to Henry L. Brooke, June 27, 1850, Letter Book, Out, May 14, 1849−Mar. 20, 1851, pp. 444−45, Tredegar Iron Company Records; Bruce, *Virginia Iron Manufacture in the Slave Era,* 239−42.

20. Joseph Reid Anderson to John J. Werth, Stockton, California, Mar. 7, 1851, Apr. 21, 1851, Letter Book, Out, Mar. 20, 1851−Dec. 7, 1852, pp. 10−12, 51−53, Tredegar Iron Company Records.

21. Bruce, *Virginia Iron Manufacture in the Slave Era*, 239–42; Jackson, *Free Negro Labor and Property Holding in Virginia*, 184–85; First African Baptist Church Minutes, Nov. 7, 1852, Nov. 14, 1855, pp. 210, 263; Richmond Hustings Court Deed Book, No. 63, 1852–53, p. 126, microfilm, Library of Virginia, Richmond; *Richmond City and Henrico County, Virginia: 1850 United States Census* (Virginia Genealogical Society, Special Publication No. 6, 1977), 45.

22. Newspaper obituary, Apr. 2, 1917, quoted in Bruce, *Virginia Iron Manufacture in the Slave Era*, 23.

23. A recent work on slavery in tobacco factories is Suzanne Gehring Schnittman, "Slavery in Virginia's Urban Tobacco Industry, 1840–1860" (Ph.D. diss., University of Rochester, 1987). Also useful on hiring systems and overwork are Robert Starobin, *Industrial Slavery in the Old South* (New York: Oxford University Press, 1970); Richard Wade, *Slavery in the Cities: The South, 1820–1860* (New York: Oxford University Press, 1964); Claudia Dale Goldin, *Urban Slavery in the American South: A Quantitative Analysis* (Chicago: University of Chicago Press, 1976); and John O'Brien, "Factory, Church and Community: Blacks in Antebellum Richmond," *Journal of Southern History* 44, no. 4 (Nov. 1978): 509–36.

24. Jackson, *Free Negro Labor and Property Holding in Virginia*, 192.

25. Ibid., 184–85, 188–89; First African Baptist Church Minutes, May 9, 1847, p. 115, July 20, 1851, p. 189, Feb. 6, 1853, p. 216.

26. Jackson, *Free Negro Labor and Property Holding in Virginia*, 198.

27. Free Negro Register, Henrico County, 1844–52, p. 20, microfilm, Library of Virginia, Richmond; *Richmond City and Henrico County, Virginia: 1850 United States Census*, 317.

28. *Richmond City and Henrico County, Virginia: 1850 United States Census*, 317; William C. and Lucy P. Scott, Brantford, Canada West, to "My Dear Children," Oct. 29, 1854, Norvell W. Wilson Papers. There is some variation in the spelling of "Pearman" and other names in the records. I have generally standardized to avoid confusion, or in some cases put the name in quotes.

29. William C. Scott, Brantford, Canada West, to "My Dear Children," Apr. 25, 1859, Norvell W. Wilson Papers.

30. Mary J. Bratton, ed., "Fields's Observations: The Slave Narrative of a Nineteenth-Century Virginian," *Virginia Magazine of History and Biography* 88, no. 1 (Jan. 1980): 92–93.

31. Janet Duitsman Cornelius, *"When I Can Read My Title Clear": Literacy, Slavery, and Religion in the Antebellum South* (Columbia: University of South Carolina Press, 1991), 59–61.

32. William C. and Lucy P. Scott, Brantford, Canada West, to "My Dear Children," Oct. 29, 1854, Norvell W. Wilson Papers.

33. Petition of Peter Strange, Richmond City, Jan. 25, 1844, Legislative Petitions.

34. Petition of Clara Robinson, Richmond City, Dec. 20, 1848, Legislative Petitions.

35. *Richmond Daily Dispatch*, Oct. 24, 1854.

36. First African Baptist Church Minutes, Feb. 1, 1846, p. 89; Richmond Hustings Court Will Book No. 14, May 4, 1852, pp. 381–82, microfilm, Local Records, Library of Virginia, Richmond.

37. *Richmond Daily Dispatch*, Nov. 17, 1856.

38. Robert Ryland, "Reminiscences of the First African Baptist Church, Richmond, VA., by the Pastor, No. 4," *American Baptist Memorial* 14 (Dec. 1855): 353.

39. William Still, *The Underground Railroad* (1871; rpt., Chicago: Johnson Publishing Company, 1970), 154.

40. Ibid., 143.

41. Redpath, *Roving Editor*, 35.

42. For a full account of the repression suffered by Northern blacks, see Lean F. Litwack, *North of Slavery: The Negro in the Free States, 1790–1860* (Chicago: University of Chicago Press, 1961), and Curry, *Free Black in Urban America.*

43. Susie Sharper, Oct. 31, 1941, to the Virginia Historical Society, with the James Stanard Papers, Virginia Historical Society, Richmond; P. J. Staudenraus, *The African Colonization Movement, 1816–1865* (New York: Columbia University Press, 1961), 244–45.

44. Bell I. Wiley, *Slaves No More: Letters from Liberia, 1833–1869* (Lexington: University Press of Kentucky, 1980), 2; Randall M. Miller, ed., *"Dear Master": Letters of a Slave Family* (Ithaca: Cornell University Press, 1978), 46–47; Marie Tyler-McGraw, "Richmond Free Blacks and African Colonization, 1816–1832," *Journal of American Studies* 21 (1987): 220–21.

45. "Petition of a number of persons of colour residing in the City of Richmond," Richmond City, Dec. 23, 1823, Legislative Petitions.

46. Philip Barrett, *Gilbert Hunt, the City Blacksmith* (Richmond: James Woodhouse and Company, 1859); numerous entries in the First African Baptist Church Minutes, 1841–59; Marie Tyler-McGraw and Gregg D. Kimball, *In Bondage and Freedom: Antebellum Black Life in Richmond, Virginia* (Richmond: Valentine Museum, 1988), 54–58; Tyler-McGraw, "Richmond Free Blacks and African Colonization," 220–21.

47. Annual meeting of the society in Hall of Delegates, with Governor Floyd presiding as president, Feb. 13, 1851, Minutes of the Virginia Branch, American Colonization Society, Nov. 4, 1823–Feb. 5, 1859, Virginia Historical Society, Richmond.

48. Alison Goodyear Freehling, *Drift Toward Dissolution: The Virginia Slavery Debate of 1831–1832* (Baton Rouge: Louisiana State University Press, 1982), 288; Staudenraus, *African Colonization Movement, 1816–1865*, 244, 251.

49. Virginia Branch, American Colonization Society Account, Nov. 13, 1855;

Staudenraus, *African Colonization Movement, 1816–1865*, 251; Statistical analysis of dismissals from First African Baptist Church Minutes.

50. Freehling overstates this point in *Drift Toward Dissolution*, 288.

51. First African Baptist Church Minutes, Mar. 5, 1843, p. 47.

52. Ibid.

53. Ibid., Apr. 6, 1845, p. 77.

54. Ibid., May 30, 1847, p. 115; June 6, 1847, p. 115.

55. "Miss Van Lew Now Very Ill," *Evening Leader* (Richmond and Manchester), July 27, 1900; Newspaper clipping, Elizabeth Van Lew Papers, misc. microfilm, reel 14, Library of Virginia, Richmond, originals in the Manuscript and Archives Division, New York Public Library, Astor, Lenox, and Tilden Foundation.

56. *African Repository* Subscription Book, vol. 32, series 5: Business Papers, American Colonization Society Records, microfilm reel 297, Library of Congress, Washington, D.C. William Ballandine is listed as a barber in a section entitled "Free Colored Housekeepers" in Montague, *Richmond Directory and Business Advertiser for 1852*, 139.

57. Virginia Branch, American Colonization Society Minutes, Nov. 4, 1823–Feb. 5, 1859.

58. Elizabeth Van Lew, Richmond, to Rev. William McLain, ACS Secretary, Dec. 2, 1858, and Samuel P. Lathrop, Richmond, to McLain, Jan. 4, 1859, Domestic Letters, Incoming Correspondence, American Colonization Society Records, microfilm reel 85, Library of Congress, Washington, D.C.

59. First African Baptist Church Minutes, Dec. 31, 1852, p. 213, Mar. 6, 1853, p. 218, Jan. 7, 1855, p. 251; George F. Adams, *A Brief Sketch of the Life and Character of the Late William Crane of Baltimore* (Baltimore: John F. Weishampel Jr., 1868).

60. First African Baptist Church Minutes record contributions to: Buxton Church, Apr. 3, 1853, p. 220; Detroit Church, Apr. 5, 1857, p. 290, May 24, 1857, p. 295; Washington Church, May 1, 1853, p. 221; Shiloh Church, Philadelphia, July 3, 1853, p. 222, Nov. 4, 1853, p. 230, Dec. 6, 1853, p. 231; and decline to contribute to Baptist Church, Clayashland, Liberia, Apr. 4, 1858, p. 306.

61. This incident is ably documented in John Thomas O'Brien Jr., *From Bondage to Citizenship: The Richmond Black Community, 1865–1867*, Studies in Nineteenth-Century American Political and Social History (New York: Garland Publishing, Inc., 1990), 69–70. The original source for this and O'Brien's account is Robert Ryland, "Reminiscences of the First African Baptist Church, Richmond, VA., by the Pastor, No. 3," *American Baptist Memorial* 14 (Nov. 1855): 323–24. O'Brien guessed that the incident happened "in the early 1850's." Jeremiah B. Jeter's defense of Ryland in the *Richmond Religious Herald* of Sept. 14, 1848, clarifies the correct year. I would like to thank Beth Schweiger for bringing this source to my attention.

62. Ryland, "Reminiscences of the First African Baptist Church, No. 3," 323–24.

63. *Richmond Religious Herald*, Sept. 14, 1848.

64. Charles Emery Stevens, *Anthony Burns: A History* (Boston: John P. Jewett and Company, 1856), 180, 194.

65. Ibid., 193–94.

66. Ibid., 176–79; First African Baptist Church Minutes, Feb. 6, 1853, p. 217.

67. Still, *Underground Railroad*, 37, 136, 192, 567.

68. The Society for the Prevention of the Absconding and Abduction of Slaves, Richmond, Minutes of director's meetings, 1833–49, Apr. 11, 1834.

69. Ibid., May 7, 1834; Dec. 22, 1834.

70. Philip J. Schwarz, *Slave Laws in Virginia*, Studies in the Legal History of the South, ed. Paul Finkelman and Kermit L. Hall (Athens: University of Georgia Press, 1996), 120–21, 140–45.

71. Charles Stearns, *Narrative of Henry Box Brown* . . . Afro-American History Series, Rhistoric Publications No. 205 (1849; rpt., Philadelphia: Rhistoric Publications, 1969), 59.

72. Ibid., 59–62.

73. To come up with an approximate number of slaves dismissed to places outside Richmond, I totaled minister Robert Ryland's yearly tabulations of dismissals recorded in the minute book, resulting in 908. I subtracted the 218 members dismissed to Second African Baptist Church in 1847 and Third African Baptist Church (renamed Ebenezer) in 1858–1859 when those churches were founded. I then subtracted the 269 free blacks dismissed and the 103 dismissed members of undetermined status (i.e., recorded as neither free nor slave), resulting in 318, my rough total for slaves dismissed to places outside Richmond.

74. First African Baptist Church Minutes, July 6, 1851, p. 186.

75. Ibid., May 4, 1851, p. 182; Feb. 4, 1855, p. 252, Jan. 2, 1858, p. 302.

76. Ibid., July 9, 1848, p. 131. On Andrew C. Marshall, see First African Baptist Church Minutes, Nov. 16, 1856, p. 286, and Jan. 4, 1857, p. 288; Whittington B. Johnson, "Andrew C. Marshall: A Black Religious Leader in Antebellum Savannah," *Georgia Historical Quarterly* 69, no. 2 (Summer 1985): 173–92.

77. Henry Page, Richmond, to his son, Nov. 20, 1856, Valentine Family Papers, Valentine Museum, Richmond. The 1870 census taker recorded Page as unable to read and write. The seventy-one-year-old Page lived with his wife, Maria, a fifty-six-year-old washerwoman. U.S. Census, 1870, Richmond City, Clay Ward, p. 353, microfilm, Library of Virginia, Richmond. However, Page's obituaries in 1886 gave his age as 101. *State*, Dec. 13, 1886; *Richmond Dispatch*, Dec. 12, 1886.

78. Henry Page, Richmond, to his son, Nov. 20, 1856, Valentine Family Papers; *The Edward Pleasants Valentine Papers* (Richmond: Valentine Museum, n.d.), 4:2330; receipt for "Sally, and her four children," to Mann S. Valentine from estate of Benjamin Mosby, Feb. 26, 1831, Valentine Family Papers.

79. Henry Page, Richmond, to his son, Nov. 20, 1856, Valentine Family Papers.

80. Michael Tadman, *Speculators and Slaves: Masters, Traders, and Slaves in the Old*

South (Madison: University of Wisconsin Press, 1989), 57–64, and table A6.3, "Slave prices according to trade circulars and reports, 1846–61," 289–90.

81. Silas and R. H. Omohundro Ledger, 1857–63, Special Collections Department, University of Virginia Library, Charlottesville. See also Silas Omohundro Business and Estate Records, 1842–82, Business Records, Library of Virginia, Richmond.

82. WPA interview with Mrs. Patience Avery, Mar. 19, 1937, original in the Library of Virginia, transcribed in Charles L. Perdue Jr., Thomas E. Barden, and Robert K. Phillips, *Weevils in the Wheat: Interviews with Ex-Slaves* (Charlottesville: University Press of Virginia, 1976), 14–18.

83. Stearns, *Narrative of Henry Box Brown*, 50–51.

84. Ibid., 55.

CHAPTER 5. Strangers, Slaves, and Southern Iron

1. *Richmond Daily Dispatch*, July 13, 1853.

2. Anderson's Southern contemporaries viewed him as the winner, as have most later historians. Charles B. Dew, *in Ironmaker to the Confederacy: Joseph R. Anderson and the Tredegar Iron Works* (New Haven: Yale University Press, 1966), says that "Anderson won a total victory in his battle with the strikers," 26. Kathleen Bruce, *Virginia Iron Manufacture in the Slave Era* (New York: Century Company, 1931), claims that "like most hasty, ill considered actions which spring from ignorance, the strike of 1847 returned like a boomerang upon the perpetrators," 227. Patricia A. Schechter takes a more studied view in "Free and Slave Labor in the Old South: The Tredegar Ironworkers' Strike of 1847," *Labor History* 35 (1995): 165–86, noting some ambivalence in Anderson's actions after the strike. It is precisely these actions I hope to illuminate.

3. Patricia Schechter follows Kathleen Bruce in misidentifying Rhys Davies as Reev Davis in "Free and Slave Labor in the Old South: The Tredegar Ironworkers' Strike of 1847," 170. Bruce cites an 1890 address by Joseph Reid Anderson, but also the *Richmond Compiler*, Feb. 6, 1838, which gives his name as Reese Davies, a logical, if incorrect, spelling of his first name. His death notice in the *Richmond Enquirer*, Sept. 14, 1838, gives his name as Rhys Davies, the correct spelling of the Welsh name. General treatments of the founding of Tredegar are given in Bruce, *Virginia Iron Manufacture in the Slave Era*, 149–53, and in Dew, *Ironmaker to the Confederacy*, 1–9.

4. I will use the name "Tredegar Iron Works" to discuss the operations, as did most nineteenth-century observers. Numerous partnerships actually ran different parts of the works in the antebellum period. For instance, for a number of years Dr. Robert Archer, Anderson's father-in-law, operated the contiguous Armory rolling mill as a separate company, at least on paper, while as a practical matter the operations were coordinated with the rest of the works.

5. Joshua Reid Anderson to B. F. De Bow, Office, Commercial Review, New Orleans, July 1, 1848. Letter Book, Out, Sept. 30, 1847–May 14, 1849, p. 287, Tredegar Iron Company Records, Business Records, Library of Virginia, Richmond; Dew, *Ironmaker to the Confederacy*, 9, 40.

6. JRA to Colonel James Gadsden, Charleston, S.C., Sept. 9, 1850, Letter Book, Out, May 14, 1849–Mar. 20, 1851, pp. 529–30, Tredegar Iron Company Records.

7. *Richmond Daily Dispatch*, Aug. 23, 1852.

8. JRA, by John F. Tanner, to J. W. Lapsley, Selma, Ala., Sept. 11, 1850, Letter Book, Out, May 14, 1849–Mar. 20, 1851, p. 531, Tredegar Iron Company Records.

9. JRA to S. Cochran, Forsythe, Monroe Co., Ga., July 7, 1848, Letter Book, Out, Sept. 30, 1847–May 14, 1849, pp. 293–94, Tredegar Iron Company Records.

10. *Richmond Daily Dispatch*, July 13, 1853; Dew, *Ironmaker to the Confederacy*, 36–37.

11. JRA to Judge L. Baker, Franklin, La., Jan. 14, 1846, Letter Book, Out, Dec. 3, 1845–May 1, 1847, p. 32, Tredegar Iron Company Records.

12. JRA to Dr. C. S. Duncan, Natchez, Miss., Apr. 27, 1850, Letter Book, Out, May 14, 1849–Mar. 20, 1851, pp. 388–89, Tredegar Iron Company Records; Dew, *Ironmaker to the Confederacy*, 35.

13. JRA to Dr. William C. Daniell, Savannah, Dec. 13, 1849, and Feb. 15, 1850, Letter Book, Out, May 14, 1849–Mar. 20, 1851, pp. 311–12, 334, Tredegar Iron Company Records.

14. JRA to Major Mark A. Cooper, Etowah Works, Carr County, Ga., Dec. 15, 1851, Letter Book, Out, Mar. 20, 1851–Dec. 7, 1852, pp. 394–95; JRA to Harrison Row, Fall River, Mass., Jan. 3, 1848, Letter Book, Out, Sept. 30, 1847–May 14, 1849, pp. 98–99, Tredegar Iron Company Records.

15. JRA to Judge Joshua Baker, Centerville, La., June 12, 1849, and John F. Tanner to Judge Joshua Baker, July 11, 1849, Letter Book, Out, May 14, 1849–Mar. 20, 1851, pp. 27–28, 65–66, Tredegar Iron Company Records.

16. JRA to Judge Joshua Baker, Centreville, La., June 12, 1849, and John F. Tanner to Judge Joshua Baker, Franklin, La., Aug. 23, 1849, Letter Book, Out, May 14, 1849–Mar. 20, 1851, pp. 27–28, 133, Tredegar Iron Company Records.

17. JRA to George Taylor, Richmond, Feb. 7, 1847, Letter Book, Out, Dec. 3, 1845–May 1, 1847, p. 610, Tredegar Iron Company Records.

18. Richmond Police Day Book, 1834–43, Nov. 1, 1841, Special Collections Department, University of Virginia Library, Charlottesville.

19. John F. Tanner to P. H. Price, Verdon P.O., Hanover County, May 31, 1848, Letter Book, Out, Sept. 30, 1847–May 14, 1849, p. 241, Tredegar Iron Company Records.

20. Patricia A. Shechter claims that workers were given five-year contracts, citing an article by Kathleen Bruce. Bruce, however, only states that Anderson proposed this to the Tredegar directors in 1842, not that the plan was carried out. Bruce and the Tredegar correspondence cited here show that Anderson eventually fixed on a some-

what different plan. Shechter, "Free and Slave Labor in the Old South," 171; Bruce, "Slave Labor in the Virginian Iron Industry," *William and Mary Quarterly,* ser. 2, vol. 6, no. 4 (Oct. 1926): 289–302; JRA to S. H. Hartman, Pittsburgh, Nov. 18, 1845, Letter Book, Out, May 1, 1844–Nov. 1845, pp. 463–64, Tredegar Iron Company Records.

21. JRA to Evan Hopkins, Saugerties, N.Y., Jan. 22, 1847, Letter Book, Out, Dec. 3, 1845–May 1, 1847, p. 584, Tredegar Iron Company Records.

22. For an overview of the work culture of mid-nineteenth-century ironworkers, see David Montgomery, *The Fall of the House of Labor: The Workplace, the State, and American Labor Activism, 1865–1925* (Cambridge: Cambridge University Press, 1989), 9–57, 171–213.

23. JRA to John Y. Mason, Dec. 19, 1844, Letter Book, Out, May 1, 1844–Nov. 1845, Tredegar Iron Company Records.

24. On the strike, see Schechter, "Free and Slave Labor in the Old South," 165–86; Dew, *Ironmaker to the Confederacy,* 23–26; and Bruce, *Virginia Iron Manufacture in the Slave Era,* 224–27.

25. Anderson's address to his workers was published in several Richmond newspapers and was transcribed in its entirety in Bruce, *Virginia Iron Manufacture in the Slave Era,* 225–26.

26. JRA to Harrison Row, Fall River, Mass., Jan. 3, 1848, Letter Book, Out, Sept. 30, 1847–May 14, 1849, pp. 98–99, Tredegar Iron Company Records; Patricia Schechter, "Free and Slave Labor in the Old South," 170, n. 30.

27. J. F. Tanner to Crenshaw, Bagby and Carter, Lynchburg, Oct. 18, 1847, Letter Book, Out, Sept. 30, 1847–May 14, 1849, p. 14, Tredegar Iron Company Records.

28. Typescript of Tredegar record, ca. 1867, in Box 6, Copies and Original Documents, 1846–1936, *Chesapeake & Ohio Railroad Company v. Tredegar Company* Suit Papers, Tredegar Iron Company Records.

29. Dew, *Ironmaker to the Confederacy,* 14; Bruce, *Virginia Iron Manufacture in the Slave Era,* 227–28; typescript of Tredegar record, ca. 1867, in Box 6, Copies and Original Documents, 1846–1936, *Chesapeake & Ohio Railroad Company v. Tredegar Company* Suit Papers, Tredegar Iron Company Records.

30. Morriss & Tanner to Lewis Scofield, Trenton, N.J., Apr. 12, 1855, Letter Book, Out, Nov. 3, 1854–May 1855, pp. 333–34, Tredegar Iron Company Records.

31. Schechter, "Free and Slave Labor in the Old South," 177–78; Dew, *Ironmaker to the Confederacy,* 25.

32. JRA to Harrison Row, Fall River, Mass., Jan. 3, 1848, Letter Book, Out, Sept. 30, 1847–May 14, 1849, pp. 98–99, Tredegar Iron Company Records. This letter is quoted extensively by Bruce, "Slave Labor in the Virginian Iron Industry," 300, and in her book, *Virginia Iron Manufacture in the Slave Era,* 237–38, in regard to Anderson's labor plan but not regarding the difficulty he had implementing it. Schechter, "Free and Slave Labor in the Old South," cites this letter several times, misdating it on p. 176.

33. J. F. Tanner to Michael Lynch, Peekskill, N.Y., Oct. 9, 1847, Letter Book, Out, Sept. 30, 1847–May 14, 1849, p. 7, Tredegar Iron Company Records.

34. JRA to George Whittimore, Boston, June 7, 1848; JRA to William Dove, Ellicotts Rolling Mill, City Block, Baltimore, June 14, 1848, Letter Book, Out, Sept. 30, 1847–May 14, 1849, pp. 251, 264; John F. Tanner to Jno Hays, Safe Harbour, Lancaster City, Pa., Aug. 2, 1849, Letter Book, Out, May 14, 1849–Mar. 20, 1851, p. 101. Also see John F. Tanner to Thomas Gandy, Windsor Lock, Conn., July 30, 1851, Letter Book, Out, Mar. 20, 1851–Dec. 7, 1852, pp. 207–8, all in Tredegar Iron Company Records.

35. JRA to James W. Churchill, Tredegar Iron Works, Mar. 15, 1848; JRA to N. L. Shearwood, Tredegar Works, Oct. 7, 1847, Letter Book, Out, Sept. 30, 1847–May 14, 1849, pp. 5, 155, Tredegar Iron Company Records.

36. JRA to James M. Sublett, Columbian Hotel, Jan. 3, 1848, Letter Book, Out, Sept. 30, 1847–May 14, 1849, p. 97, Tredegar Iron Company Records.

37. JRA to John Morgan, June 2, 1849, Letter Book, Out, May 14, 1849–Mar. 20, 1851, p. 18, Tredegar Iron Company Records.

38. Kathleen Bruce notes that Francis Deane, in an early president's report in 1839, requested expansion of the workers' quarters, and that a fence be built around the property, *Virginia Iron Manufacture in the Slave Era*, 156. The earliest insurance records for these buildings are: declaration 11694, dated Feb. 26, 1844; declaration 12633, dated Mar. 19, 1844; and declaration 12634, dated Mar. 19, 1844, Mutual Assurance Society of Virginia Records, Business Records, Library of Virginia, Richmond.

39. Bruce, *Virginia Iron Manufacture in the Slave Era*, 252, states that the bell rang at half past six every morning, based on the "Rules of Yard" for Anderson's shipyard, but ignores the fact that various operations had distinctly different work schedules. See JRA to Mr. Clayton, June 29, 1849, Letter Book, Out, May 14, 1849–Mar. 20, 1851, p. 51, Tredegar Iron Company Records.

40. A survey of Oregon Hill properties in the Mary Wingfield Scott Collection at the Valentine Museum in Richmond suggests this chronology, rather than the one that Schechter describes, with Oregon Hill a full-blown community by the time of the Tredegar strike, p. 169. The Scott Collection consists of geographically arranged files of antebellum houses in Richmond, documenting their date of construction and history through Mutual Assurance Society records, deed and land books, and city directories. On the Tredegar free school, see the *Richmond Daily Dispatch*, June 3 and Oct. 11, 1852.

41. JRA to John Lindsay, Old Point, May 2, 1848, Letter Book, Out, Sept. 30, 1847–May 14, 1849, p. 206, Tredegar Iron Company Records.

42. JRA to Rev. M. L. Chevers, Old Point, Oct. 5, 1850, Letter Book, Out, May 14, 1849–Mar. 20, 1851, p. 556; JRA to N. M. Martin, Richmond, July 14, 1851, Letter Book, Out, Mar. 20, 1851–Dec. 7, 1852, p. 183, Tredegar Iron Company Records.

43. JRA to H. D. Bird, Petersburg, Mar. 16, 1848, Letter Book, Out, Sept. 30, 1847–May 14, 1849, p. 160, Tredegar Iron Company Records.

44. Dew, *Ironmaker to the Confederacy*, 28–29.

45. Ibid., 29–30.

46. JRA to Dr. W. C. Daniell, Savannah, Oct. 28, 1850, Letter Book, Out, May 14, 1849–Mar. 20, 1851, p. 574, Tredegar Iron Company Records; Dew, *Ironmaker to the Confederacy*, 19, describes the Tredegar rolling mill in 1858 as having nine puddling furnaces, seven heating furnaces, and three trains of rolls, and also notes that the mill already had nine puddling furnaces by 1850. See JRA to furnace builder Job. Hatch, Wareham, Mass., Nov. 23, 1847, Letter Book, Out, Sept. 30, 1847–May 14, 1849, pp. 56–57, Tredegar Iron Company Records. In such an operation, we can estimate the number of workers thus: at least two roughers, three hookers, a roller and a catcher for each train of rolls, plus at least nine puddlers and seven heaters. We then double this figure, because rolling mills operated a day and night turn, giving a total of forty-six for peak production. I have not included other workers that would also be required, such as men to run the squeezers and shears, helpers, and hotbed workers.

47. JRA to Morriss & Tanner, Jan. 1855, p. 171, Letter Book, Out, Dec. 1854–Mar. 29, 1855, Tredegar Iron Company Records.

48. Total numbers for slaves employed in the Tredegar and Armory rolling mill are from Dew, *Ironmaker to the Confederacy*, 27. In 1861 R. S. Archer complained that the Armory rolling mill's superintendent had "left us . . . and took back with him some 5 or 6 of our Irish Puddlers." R. S. Archer to unknown correspondent, Apr. 11, 1861, Letter Book Out, Jan. 16, 1861–May 1, 1861, Tredegar Iron Company Records.

49. *Richmond Daily Dispatch*, Aug. 23, 1852.

50. For a good summary of these partnerships, see Michael S. Raber, Patrick M. Malone, and Robert B. Gordon, "Historical and Archaeological Assessment, Tredegar Iron Works Site, Richmond, Virginia," report submitted to the Valentine Museum and the Ethyl Corporation, 1992, copies at the Valentine Museum.

51. Valentine Museum Vertical Files—Biography—Matthew Delaney; Dew, *Ironmaker to the Confederacy*, 15–16; U.S. Census, 1850, Richmond City, p. 389, microfilm, Library of Virginia, Richmond.

52. *Richmond Daily Dispatch*, Jan. 1, 1853.

53. Ibid. Samuel D. Denoon is listed as a minimum activist in David Goldfield's compilation of city leaders in *Urban Growth in the Age of Sectionalism: Virginia, 1847–1861* (Baton Rouge: Louisiana State University Press, 1977), Appendix B. See also the biographical sketch in Louis H. Manarin, *Richmond at War: The Minutes of the City Council*, Official Publication No. 17, Richmond Civil War Centennial Committee (Chapel Hill: University of North Carolina Press, 1966), 628, and the profile in Norman C. McLeod Jr., "Free Labor in a Slave Society: Richmond, Virginia, 1820–1860" (Ph.D. diss., Howard University, 1991), 109–10.

54. *Richmond Daily Dispatch*, Jan. 1, 1853. Both Anderson and William H. McFarland are listed as maximum activists in Goldfield, *Urban Growth in the Age of*

Sectionalism, appendix B. In the months before this event, A. Judson Crane was under attack for being a "Jordan Hatcher Whig," and he resigned his seat during the 1852–53 session. See *Richmond Daily Dispatch*, Oct.–Dec. 1852. Membership in the legislature is from Cynthia Miller Leanard, comp., *The General Assembly of Virginia, July 30, 1619–January 11, 1978: A Bicentennial Register of Members* (Richmond: Virginia State Library for the General Assembly of Virginia, 1978), 448–63.

55. *Richmond Daily Dispatch*, Jan. 1, 1853.

56. *Richmond Daily Dispatch*, Dec. 28, 1853. Joshua Carey lived between First and Broad Streets according to William L. Montague, comp., *Richmond Directory and Business Advertiser for 1852* (Richmond: J. W. Woods, printer, Baltimore, 1852).

57. *Richmond Daily Dispatch*, Dec. 28, 1853. James A. Cowardin is listed as a maximum activist in Goldfield, *Urban Growth in the Age of Sectionalism*, appendix B.

58. Dew, *Ironmaker to the Confederacy*, 39.

59. Harrison M. Ethridge, "The Jordan Hatcher Affair of 1852: Cold Justice and Warm Compassion," *Virginia Magazine of History and Biography* 84, no. 4 (Oct. 1976): 446–63; William A. Link, "The Jordan Hatcher Case: Politics and 'A Spirit of Insubordination' in Antebellum Virgina," *Journal of Southern History* 64, no. 4 (Nov. 1998): 615–48.

60. *Richmond Daily Dispatch*, Dec. 14, 15, 16, 1854; McLeod, "Free Labor in a Slave Society," 294–96. McLeod views the resolution of this strike and the various events held by workers and Anderson as an indication that "important bonds existed between white laborers and their employers, that they could communicate with each other, and that Richmond's slaveholding ruling class had the upper hand when it came to dealing with white mechanics," 296. I obviously disagree about who had the upper hand.

61. "James Andrew Cowardin," in Lyon Gardiner Tyler, ed., *Encyclopedia of Virginia Biography* (New York: Lewis Historical Publishing Company, 1915), 2:333–34.

62. McLeod, "Free Labor in a Slave Society," 289–93.

63. Michael Douglas Naragon, "Ballots, Bullets, and Blood: The Political Transformation of Richmond, Virginia, 1850–1874" (Ph.D. diss., University of Pittsburgh, 1996), 56–58. Naragon also discusses the other instances of workplace activism mentioned in McLeod.

64. McLeod, "Free Labor in a Slave Society," 293–94; *Constitution, By-Laws, and Bill of Prices of the Association of Journeyman Stone-Cutters of the City of Richmond, Established 1845* (Richmond, 1850).

65. The seminal work in the study of the racial consciousness among whites in the North and its connection to popular culture is David R. Roediger, *The Wages of Whiteness: Race and the Making of the American Working Class* (New York: Verso, 1991).

66. Leon F. Litwack, *North of Slavery: The Negro in the Free States, 1790–1860* (Chicago: University of Chicago Press, 1961), 100–2; Bruce Laurie, *Artisans into*

Workers: Labor in Nineteenth-Century America, American Century Series (New York: Noonday Press, 1989), 91, 108–9; Randall M. Miller, "The Enemy Within: Some Effects of Foreign Immigrants on Antebellum Southern Cities," *Southern Studies* 24 (Spring 1985): 33–40; Michael P. Johnson and James L. Roark, *No Chariot Let Down: Charleston's Free People of Color on the Eve of the Civil War* (Chapel Hill: University of North Carolina Press, 1984), 10–14.

67. *Richmond Enquirer*, Aug. 27, 1857, quoted in Claudia Dale Goldin, *Urban Slavery in the American South, 1820–1860: A Quantitative Analysis* (Chicago: University of Chicago Press, 1976), 31; Ira Berlin and Herbert G. Gutman, "Natives and Immigrants, Free Men and Slaves: Urban Workingmen in the Antebellum American South," *American Historical Review* 88 (Dec. 1983): 1194–97; Philip J. Schwarz, *Slave Laws in Virginia*, Studies in the Legal History of the South, ed. Paul Finkelman and Kermit L. Hall (Athens: University of Georgia Press, 1996), 137, 145.

68. For descriptions of labor activism, see McLeod, "Free Labor in a Slave Society," 289–94.

CHAPTER 6. Virginia and Union

1. Lawrence Levine, *High Brow/Low Brow: The Emergence of Cultural Hierarchy in America* (Cambridge: Harvard University Press, 1988); Susan G. Davis, *Parades and Power: Street Theatre in Nineteenth-Century Philadelphia* (Philadelphia: Temple University Press, 1986).

2. For a comparison of membership with fraternal orders, see Mary Ann Clawson, *Constructing Brotherhood: Class, Gender, and Fraternalism* (Princeton, N.J.: Princeton University Press, 1989). My research generally supports Clawson's findings regarding the composition of antebellum white fraternal orders. While individual lodges (or in my case companies) may have had a defined ethnic or class identity, most organizations and many lodges reflected a cross-section of the white, male population.

3. John A. Cutchins, *A Famous Command: The Richmond Light Infantry Blues* (Richmond: Garrett and Massie, 1934), 16–21.

4. Lee A. Wallace Jr., "The First Regiment of Virginia Volunteers, 1846–1848," *Virginia Magazine of History and Biography* 77, no. 1 (Jan. 1969): 46–77; *Richmond Daily Dispatch*, Aug. 12, 1859.

5. John Rutherfoord to William Ligon, July 27, 1829, and Feb. 1832, Rutherfoord Letter Book, 1825–37, Rare Book, Manuscript, and Special Collections Library, Duke University, Durham, North Carolina.

6. Cutchin, *Famous Command*, 15–16, 22, 38–45, notes the Gabriel episode and the constant fear of insurrection, especially leading up to the Southampton insurrection; Richmond Light Infantry Blues Records, Vol. 1, Minutes, Aug. 26, 1831, p. 96, Personal Papers, Library of Virginia, Richmond.

7. Richmond Light Infantry Blues Minutes, Aug. 5, 1829, p. 76, and Jan. 29, 1833, p. 102, Personal Papers, Library of Virginia, Richmond; "A Patriotic Barber," Clipping File, Valentine Museum; Ervin L. Jordan Jr., *Black Confederates and Afro-Yankees in Civil War Virginia* (Charlottesville: University Press of Virginia), 219; Cutchins, *Famous Command*, 172; A. A. Taylor, "The Negro in Reconstruction Virginia," *Journal of Negro History* 11 (Apr. 1926): part 1, p. 247.

8. *Richmond Daily Dispatch*, Apr. 24, 1852; *Richmond Republican*, May 11, 1852.

9. For a history of the First Regiment and many of its companies see Lee A. Wallace Jr. and Detmar H. Finke, "Virginia Military Forces, 1858–1861," *Military Collector & Historian* 10 (Fall 1958): 61–73.

10. *Richmond Daily Dispatch*, June 14, July 6, 1853, Apr. 21, 1854. Barfoot (often spelled Barefoot) is listed in 1852 as a blacksmith at the Samson & Pae ironworks and in 1856 as a carpenter at the Armory Iron Works, residing on Oregon Hill. William L. Montague, *The Richmond Directory and Business Advertiser for 1852* (J. W. Woods, printer, Baltimore, 1852); Moses Ellyson, *The Richmond Directory and Business Advertiser for 1856* (Richmond: H. K. Ellyson, 1856).

11. Jefferson Wallace, Richmond, to Charles Blair, California, Feb. 2, 1855, Clopton Family Papers, Rare Book, Manuscript, and Special Collections Library, Duke University, Durham, North Carolina.

12. Robert A. Granniss diary, Dec. 13, 1859, p. 110, Virginia Historical Society, Richmond. Granniss reported his salary on Jan. 1, 1859, p. 37, when he received a raise from his employer, Horace Kent.

13. Cutchins, *Famous Command;* Richmond Light Infantry Blues Minutes, Oct. 25, 1854, p. 300; the resignation is accepted on Nov. 8, p. 301; Patton is reelected on Jan. 24, 1855, p. 304; on Feb. 17, 1855, p. 306, the minutes quote the *Dispatch* on the company's earlier troubles and rejuvenation.

14. A roster of the members of the Richmond Blues who visited Philadelphia in 1855 was found in the *Richmond Daily Dispatch*, Feb. 21, 1855. Occupations of Blues' members was taken from the 1860 census and *Butters' Richmond Directory for 1855* (Richmond: H. K. Ellyson's Steam Press, 1855). Nativity was derived from the 1850 and 1860 censuses.

15. *Richmond Daily Dispatch*, Aug. 13, 1859. A roster of the members of the Richmond Grays who visited New York in 1859 appears in Philip Whitlock's Recollections, 1843–1913, Virginia Historical Society, Richmond, and is essentially the same list that appeared in the *Richmond Daily Dispatch*, Aug. 2, 1859. Occupations of the Grays were taken from the 1860 census and W. Eugene Ferslew, *First Annual Directory for the City of Richmond, to Which is Added a Business Directory for 1859* (Richmond: George M. West, 1859). Nativity was derived from both the 1850 and 1860 census.

16. Information on Elliott is from Louis H. Manarin and Lee A. Wallace Jr.,

Richmond Volunteers: The Volunteer Companies of the City of Richmond and Henrico County, Virginia, 1861–1865, Official Publication No. 26, Richmond Civil War Centennial Committee (Richmond: Westover Press, 1969), 248.

17. Whitlock, Recollections, 80.

18. Richmond Light Infantry Blues Minutes, July 4, 1855, p. 335.

19. Ibid.

20. *By-laws of the Montgomery Guard, Second Company, First Regiment Virginia Volunteers, Adopted July 17th, 1850. Revised May 1858* (Richmond: McFarlane & Fergusson, 1858), 14, "Article IX. Funeral Honors"; anonymous woman's diary, Dec. 31, [1854], David Bullock Harris Papers, Rare Book, Manuscript, and Special Collections Library, Duke University, Durham, North Carolina; Jefferson Wallace to Charles Wallace, May 17, 1855, Clopton Family Papers. The Grays gave such benefits starting in 1855, see *Richmond Daily Dispatch,* Jan. 25, 1855.

21. Johann Gottfried Lange, "Der veraenderte Nahme, oder der Schumacher in der alten und der neuen Welt. 30 Jahre in Europa und 30 Jahre in Amerika" [The Changed Name, or the Shoemaker in the Old and the New World. 30 Years in Europe and 30 Years in America], typescript translation of manuscript memoir, 121, Virginia Historical Society, Richmond, 106–7 (original, 162).

22. Richmond Light Infantry Blues Minutes, Dec. 15, 1852, p. 274.

23. *Richmond Republican,* Dec. 17, 1852; John T. O'Brien, " 'The People's Favorite': The Rise and Fall of Martin Meredith Lipscomb," *Virginia Cavalcade* 31, no. 4 (Spring 1982): 216–23.

24. Charles Bennett is listed as a merchant with Bennett & Beers, Druggists, in *Butters' Directory for 1855.* Martin M. Lipscomb is listed as a bricklayer in the U.S. Census, 1860, Richmond City, Ward 3, p. 492, microfilm, Library of Virginia, Richmond. The repeal is in the Richmond Light Infantry Blues Minutes, p. 280, Apr. 20, 1853, p. 280.

25. "Reply to a toast at a 'Blues' celebration—May 1853—by G. W. Munford," Munford-Ellis Family Papers, Rare Book, Manuscript, and Special Collections Library, Duke University, Durham, North Carolina.

26. On the middle-class composition of Richmond fraternal orders, see Patricia Click, *The Spirit of the Times: Amusements in Nineteenth-Century Baltimore, Norfolk and Richmond* (Charlottesville: University Press of Virginia, 1989), 77. On the evolution of the Odd Fellows, and on the temperance issue in nineteenth-century fraternal orders in general, see Clawson, *Constructing Brotherhood,* 118–23, 155–64.

27. Richmond Light Infantry Blues Records, Richmond Junior Blues, 1856–58, vol. 3, p. 1. This is listed as vol. 3 in the guide, but as 29873 (6) in the collection. Captain Dimmock of the Public Guard was to instruct boys in military tactics, *Richmond Daily Dispatch,* Sept. 18, 1857.

28. "Celebration of the 80th Anniversary of the Independence of the United States,

by the Young Guard—Presentation of a Flag &c.," *Richmond Daily Dispatch*, July 6, 1855.

29. Richmond Light Infantry Blues Minutes, "65th Anniversary of Company," May 10, 1858, p. 447.

30. Bessie Lacy, Richmond, to her father, Drury Lacy, Oct. 18, 1848, Southern Historical Collection, Wilson Library, University of North Carolina at Chapel Hill. In a letter to her father on Dec. 29, 1848, Lacy reported reading Scott's "Waverly novels" and proclaimed that she would prefer to be the author of a few words of Scott than "all the fashionable trash that loads the tables of the would be literary — or crams the book stores of the public."

31. *Richmond Daily Dispatch*, Dec. 18, 1855.

32. *Richmond Daily Dispatch*, Apr. 21, 1854, Feb. 23, 1854.

33. Elizabeth R. Varon, *We Mean to be Counted: White Women and Politics in Antebellum Virginia* (Chapel Hill: University of North Carolina Press, 1998), 71–136.

34. Cutchins, *Famous Command*, 14–15, 33–35.

35. Michael Douglas Naragon, "Ballots, Bullets, and Blood: The Political Transformation of Virginia, 1850–1874" (Ph.D. diss., University of Pittsburgh, 1996), 154–226.

36. William G. Shade, *Democratizing the Old Dominion: Virginia and the Second Party System, 1824–1861* (Charlottesville: University Press of Virginia, 1996); Richmond Light Infantry Blues Minutes, July 5, 1841, p. 153, July 4, 1855, p. 335.

37. "Celebration of the 80th Anniversary of the Independence of the United States, by the Young Guard—Presentation of a Flag &c.," *Richmond Daily Dispatch*, July 6, 1855; "Thomas Pearson August" in John T. Kneebone, et. al., *Dictionary of Virginia Biography: Vol 1, Aaroe–Blanchfield* (Richmond: Library of Virginia, 1998), 246–47.

38. Richmond Light Infantry Blues Minutes, Nov. 26, 1851, pp. 262–63.

39. "George Wythe Munford" in Lyon Gardiner Tyler, ed., *Encyclopedia of Virginia Biography* (New York: Lewis Historical Publishing Company, 1915), 2:221–22; Cutchins, *Famous Command*, 54–55, 308.

40. Richmond Light Infantry Blues Minutes, Nov. 26, 1851, pp. 262–63.

41. "State Banner," in *Richmond Daily Dispatch*, Sept. 2, 1853.

42. Naragon, "Ballots, Bullets, and Blood," 261; obituary of Elliott in *Lynchburg News*, Feb. 26, 1897.

43. *Richmond Penny Post*, June 22, 28, 1855; *Richmond Daily Dispatch*, Aug. 21, Oct. 23, 1855, Dec. 18, 1855.

44. Lange, "Changed Name," 104 (original, 159); Manarin and Wallace, *Richmond Volunteers*, 188; Klaus G. Wust, "German Immigrants and Nativism in Virginia, 1840–1860" in *Twenty-ninth Report. Society for the History of the Germans in Maryland* (Baltimore, 1956), 37.

45. This incident is recounted in Wust, "German Immigrants and Nativism in Virginia," 39–40, quotes on 40.

46. Herrmann Schuricht, *History of the German Element in Virginia* (Baltimore: T. Kroh & Sons, printers, 1898–1900), 2:37–39.

47. *By-laws of the Montgomery Guard,* 11, "Article V. Parades"; Norman C. McLeod Jr., "Free Labor in a Slave Society: Richmond, Virginia, 1820–1860" (Ph.D. diss., Howard University, 1991), 220.

48. "The Montgomery Guard," *Richmond Daily Dispatch,* July 6, 1855.

49. *Richmond Daily Dispatch,* Feb. 23, 1855.

50. Lange, "Changed Name," 106–8 (original, 162–64); *Richmond Times,* Mar. 7, 1853.

51. Mann S. Valentine Jr. to Edward V. Valentine, Apr. 25, 1860, Valentine Family Papers, Valentine Museum, Richmond; Mann S. Valentine, *The Mock Auction: Ossawatomie Sold, a Mock Heroic Poem . . .* (Richmond: J. W. Randolph, 1860).

52. Richmond Light Infantry Blues Minutes, Feb. 24, 1854, pp. 290–91; May 16, 1854, p. 296.

53. *Richmond Daily Dispatch,* Feb. 15, 1855; Richmond Light Infantry Blues Minutes, 307.

54. Richmond Light Infantry Blues Minutes, 308.

55. Ibid., Feb. 22, 1855, p. 312.

56. Ibid; Patton's father's career is presented in Tyler, *Encyclopedia of Virginia Biography* 2:53.

57. Richmond Light Infantry Blues Minutes, Feb. 22, 1855, p. 312.

58. *Richmond Daily Dispatch,* Feb. 26, 1855.

59. Excerpt from the *Philadelphia Sun,* July 27, 1855, in the Richmond Light Infantry Blues Minutes, 338; *Richmond Daily Dispatch,* May 17, 1855.

60. Richmond Light Infantry Blues Minutes, May 10, 1855, p. 323.

61. "Sixty-Third Anniversary of the Richmond Light Infantry Blues," *Richmond Daily Dispatch,* May 10, 1856; Richmond Light Infantry Blues Minutes, 374–75.

62. *Richmond Daily Dispatch,* May 10, 1856.

63. For an account of the Monroe reburial, see Mary H. Mitchell, *Hollywood Cemetery: The History of a Southern Shrine* (Richmond: Virginia State Library, 1985), 35–45.

64. Dexter Otey, New York City, No. 50 Wall Street, to Henry A. Wise, June 17, 1858, Executive Papers (Record Group 3), Governor Henry A. Wise, 1856–60, State Records, Library of Virginia, Richmond.

65. N. H. Campbell, No. 50 [52 changed in mss to 50] Wall Street, to Henry A. Wise, June 17, 1858, Executive Papers, Governor Henry A. Wise.

66. Undated clipping from a New York newspaper, noting plans for "transferring the remains of President Monroe to Virginia," Executive Papers, Governor Henry A. Wise.

67. Samuel L. Gouverneur to Henry A. Wise, June 15, 1858, Executive Papers, Governor Henry A. Wise.

68. *Richmond Daily Dispatch,* July 7, 1858.

69. On Wise's politics, see Craig M. Simpson, *A Good Southerner: The Life of Henry A. Wise of Virginia* (Chapel Hill: University of North Carolina Press, 1985).

70. Whitlock, Recollections, 80−81.

71. *Richmond Daily Dispatch,* Aug. 20, 1859.

72. Whitlock, Recollections, 84−87; Granniss diary, Nov. 21, 1859, p. 100.

73. Granniss diary, Nov. 30, 1859, p. 102; Whitlock, Recollections, 84−87; Richmond Light Infantry Blues Minutes, 497−501.

74. Richmond Light Infantry Blues Minutes, 500.

CHAPTER 7. The War Within

1. Record Book of the Central Southern Rights Association of Virginia, 1850−60, pp. 132−67, Virginia Historical Society, Richmond; Central Southern Rights Association of Virginia, *Memorial of the Central Southern Rights Association of Virginia, Being a Statement of Grievances and Suggestion of Remedies Therof* (Richmond: 1859); "Mr. London's Speech," *Richmond Enquirer,* Jan. 12, 1860; Michael Douglas Naragon, "Ballots, Bullets, and Blood: The Political Transformation of Virginia, 1850−1874" (Ph.D. diss., University of Pittsburgh, 1996), 241−43.

2. Memorial to the General Assembly of Virginia from "Merchants of Richmond City," Richmond City, Jan. 11, 1860, Legislative Petitions, General Assembly (Record Group 78), State Records, Library of Virginia.

3. Peter H. Mayo Recollections, section entitled "Memories of Strawberry Cottage from a MSS of Col. John D. H. Ross of Lexington, VA," 105−6, typescript on microfilm, Southern Historical Collection, Wilson Library, University of North Carolina at Chapel Hill; Elizabeth R. Varon, *We Mean to Be Counted: White Women and Politics in Antebellum Virginia* (Chapel Hill: University of North Carolina Press, 1998), 142−44.

4. Jacob Bechtel, Richmond, to George Bechtel, Philadelphia, Nov. 5, 1859, Bechtel Papers, Clements Library, University of Michigan, Ann Arbor.

5. T. J. Macon, *Life Gleanings* (Richmond: W. H. Adams, 1913), 21; Lee A. Wallace Jr., *The Richmond Howitzers* (Lynchburg: H. E. Howard, 1993), 1−3; Louis H. Manarin and Lee A. Wallace Jr., *Richmond Volunteers: The Volunteer Companies of the City of Richmond and Henrico County, Virginia, 1861−1865,* Official Publication No. 26, Richmond Civil War Centennial Committee (Richmond: Westover Press, 1969), 116, 183, 211, 222, quote on p. 3. The other companies were Co. I, First Virginia Regiment, on Nov. 19, 1859; the Henrico Grays in Dec. 1859; and the Southern Guard about Jan. 1860. On George Wythe Randolph, see George Green Schackelford, *George Wythe Randolph and the Confederate Elite* (Athens: University of Georgia Press, 1988).

6. Peter H. Mayo Recollections, 29. The Governor's Mounted Guard organized on Sept. 3, 1859. On May 8, 1861 the company was mustered into state service becoming Co. I, Fourth Virginia Cavalry.

7. Mann S. Valentine Jr. to Edward Virginius Valentine, Apr. 25, 1860, Valentine Family Papers, Valentine Museum, Richmond.

8. Harriett Pelouze Hartshorne, Boston, to Henry L. Pelouze, Richmond, Oct. 28, 1860, and Henry L. Pelouze, Richmond, to his wife, Oct. 31, 1860, Henry Lafayette Pelouze Papers, Rare Book, Manuscript, and Special Collections Library, Duke University, Durham, North Carolina.

9. Robert A. Granniss diary, Apr. 15, June 6, 1860, pp. 132–35, 140, Virginia Historical Society, Richmond; Elizabeth R. Varon, "'The Ladies Are Whigs': Lucy Barbour, Henry Clay, and Nineteenth-Century Virginia Politics," *Virginia Cavalcade* 42, no. 2 (Autumn 1992): 72–83.

10. Jacob Bechtel, Richmond, to George Bechtel, Philadelphia, Nov. 5, 1859, Bechtel Papers.

11. Naragon, "Bullets, Ballots, and Blood," 256–60; Daniel W. Crofts, *Reluctant Confederates: Upper South Unionists in the Secession Crisis* (Chapel Hill: University of North Carolina Press, 1989), 46–47, 77.

12. Henry L. Pelouze, Richmond, to his wife, Brooklyn, Nov. 18, 1860, Pelouze Papers.

13. Jacob Bechtel, Richmond, to George Bechtel, Philadelphia, Apr. 1, 1861, Bechtel Papers.

14. Alex. T. Stewart, New York, to Thomas R. Price, Jan. 14, 1861, Price Family Papers, Virginia Historical Society, Richmond.

15. Alex. T. Stewart, New York, to Thomas R. Price, Richmond, Feb. 9, 1861, and A. T. Stewart, New York, to Thomas R. Price, Richmond, Mar. 1, 1861, Price Family Papers.

16. Jacob Bechtel, Richmond, to George Bechtel, Philadelphia, Feb. 2, 1861, Bechtel Papers.

17. Henry L. Pelouze, Richmond, to his wife, Mar. 17, 24, 1861, Pelouze Papers.

18. These units included the Richmond City Guard, organized Dec. 1860; the Henrico Grays, Dec. 1860; the Virginia Life Guards, Jan. 1861; the Henrico Guard, Jan. 1861; the Henrico Mounted Rangers, 31 Jan. 1861, and the Old Dominion Guard, Mar. 1861. Manarin and Wallace, *Richmond Volunteers,* 164, 211, 214, 217, 142, 173.

19. Crofts, *Reluctant Confederates,* 317–20. Crofts cites Robert Young Conrad to his wife, Apr. 14, 1861, Conrad Papers, Virginia Historical Society, Richmond.

20. Manarin and Wallace, *Richmond Volunteers,* 265; Richmond Light Infantry Blues Records, Vol. 1, Minutes, Jan. 21, 1861, pp. 527–28, Personal Papers, Library of Virginia, Richmond.

21. The dates of service for soldiers in the Blues was taken from Richmond Light Infantry Blues Records, Vol. 2, Register of the 50th Anniversary of the Corps, May 10,

1843. Despite its title, this volume is an alphabetical listing of soldiers who served, noting when elected, when resigned, and remarks, especially the circumstances of resignation or expulsion.

22. Richmond Light Infantry Blues Records, Vol. 1, Minutes, Mar. 12, Apr. 15, 1861, p. 531; *Richmond Daily Dispatch*, Mar. 27, 1861.

23. *Richmond Daily Dispatch*, Jan. 25, 1861; May is listed in W. Eugene Ferslew, *Second Annual Directory for the City of Richmond, to which is added a Business Directory for 1860* (Richmond: W. Eugene Ferslew, 1860).

24. *Richmond Daily Dispatch*, Jan. 31, 1861.

25. Herrmann Schuricht, *History of the German Element in Virginia* (Baltimore: T. Kroh & Sons, printers, 1898–1900), 2:69–70; Klaus Wust, *The Virginia Germans* (Charlottseville: University Press of Virginia, 1979), 220.

26. *Richmond Daily Dispatch*, Jan. 30, 1861.

27. Crofts, *Reluctant Confederates*, 140–41; Naragon, "Ballots, Bullets, and Blood," 288, gives the following Richmond totals and percentages (voters selected three names from the seven on the ballot): Marmaduke Johnson, 2,114 (19 percent); William Macfarland, 2,109 (19 percent); George Randolph, 1,891 (17 percent); John Robertson (secessionist), 1672 (15 percent); John Minor Botts, 1,600 (15 percent); John O. Steger (secessionist), 1,517 (13 percent); and John H. Gilmer (Douglas Democrat), 343 (3 percent).

28. Crofts, *Reluctant Confederates*, 315–16.

29. Ann Maria Gray Valentine, Richmond, to William Winston Valentine, directed to Paris, Jan. 21, 1861, Valentine Family Papers.

30. Aunt Ellen Mordecai, Richmond, to Ellen Mordecai, Mar. 23, 1861, Mordecai Family Papers, Southern Historical Collection, Wilson Library, University of North Carolina at Chapel Hill; Varon, *We Mean to Be Counted*, 137–68.

31. Emma Mordecai, Richmond, to Nell, Apr. 21, 1861, Mordecai Family Papers.

32. Emma Mordecai, Richmond, to Nell, Apr. 26, 1861, Mordecai Family Papers.

33. Robert Granniss diary, Apr. 2, 1861, pp. 209–10.

34. Henry L. Pelouze, Richmond, to his wife, Mar. 8, 1861, Pelouze Papers.

35. Jacob Bechtel, Richmond, to George Bechtel, Philadelphia, Feb. 22, 1861, Bechtel Papers.

36. Jacob Bechtel, Richmond, to George Bechtel, Philadelphia, Apr. 1, 1861, Bechtel Papers; *Richmond Enquirer*, Apr. 16, 1861; Charles B. Dew, *Ironmaker to the Confederacy: Joseph R. Anderson and the Tredegar Iron Works* (New Haven: Yale University Press, 1966), 34.

37. Robert Granniss diary, Apr. 15, 17, 1861, p. 215.

38. Emma Mordecai, Richmond, to Nell, Apr. 21, 1861, Mordecai Family Papers.

39. Granniss diary, Apr. 18, 1861, p. 215.

40. Henry L. Pelouze, Richmond, to his wife, Mar. 28, 1861, Pelouze Papers; Johann Gottfried Lange, "Der veraenderte Nahme, oder der Schumacher in der alten und der

neuen Welt. 30 Jahre in Europa und 30 Jahre in Amerika" [The Changed Name, or
the Shoemaker in the Old and the New World. 30 Years in Europe and 30 Years in
America], typescript translation of manuscript memoir, 142 (translation 204–5),
Virginia Historical Society, Richmond.

41. *Richmond Daily Dispatch,* Apr. 12, 1861; R. S. Archer to unknown correspondent, Apr. 11, 1861, Letter Book Out, Jan. 16, 1861–May 1, 1861, Tredegar Iron
Company Records, Business Records, Library of Virginia, Richmond.

42. J. R. Anderson and Co. to R. J. Capron, Apr. 16, 1861, Letter Book, Out, Jan. 16,
1861–May 1, 1861, Tredegar Iron Company Records; Dew, *Ironmaker to the Confederacy,* 90–91.

43. Jacob Bechtel, Richmond, to George Bechtel, Philadelphia, May 7, 11, 1861,
Bechtel Papers.

44. Jacob Bechtel, Richmond, to George Bechtel, Philadelphia, Apr. 24, May 7,
1861, Bechtel Papers.

45. Jacob Bechtel, Richmond, to George Bechtel, Philadelphia, Apr. 24, 1861,
Bechtel Papers.

46. Jacob Bechtel, Richmond, to George Bechtel, Philadelphia, May 17, June 10,
1861, Bechtel Papers.

47. Wallace, *Richmond Howitzers,* 146, 156; G. L. Sherwood and Jeffrey C. Weaver,
59th Virginia Infantry (Lynchburg: H. E. Howard, 1994), 10, 201.

48. Joseph Reid Anderson to Governor John Letcher, Apr. 27, 1861, Letter Book,
Out, Jan. 18, 1861–May 1, 1861, Tredegar Iron Company Records; James Henry Bailey
II, *A History of the Diocese of Richmond: The Formative Years* (Richmond: Chancery
Office, Diocese of Richmond, 1956), 145.

49. Basic overviews of these companies are contained in Manarin and Wallace,
Richmond Volunteers, 188–92, 228–30. Compiled Service Records of Confederate
Soldiers who served in Organizations from the State of Virginia, microfilm, Library of
Virginia, Richmond, described in National Archives Microfilm Publication, Microcopy
No. 324, *Compiled Service Records of Confederate Soldiers Who Served in Organiza-
tions from the State of Virginia* (Washington, D.C., 1961).

50. Charles August Hennighausen, Richmond, to Maria Schulz Hennighausen and
Wilhelm Hennighausen, Apr. 24, 1865, translation of original letter, pp. 2–3, Virginia
Historical Society, Richmond.

51. Although the religion of half of the officers was found, a fairly low percentage
of enlisted members were found in denominational records. Among the enlisted in the
Virginia Rifles, 7 were identified in Saint John's records, and 8 from Saint Mary's, out
of a total of 110 enlisted men. In the Marion Rifles, 9 enlisted men were identified in
Saint John's, and 3 from Saint Mary's, out of a total of 79 enlisted men. Some may have
been in Bethlehem Lutheran Church, although the church history implies that no
men from the church saw active service. I have excluded from my calculations one man
who was an Irish-born substitute, and three officers listed in Manarin and Wallace as

members of the Virginia Rifles who clearly were members of the Floyd Guards. The religion of soldiers was determined from congregational records, including Saint Mary's German Catholic Church, Richmond, Birth Register, 1848–1908 (in German and Latin), misc. microfilm, reel 352; Saint John's Church (United Church of Christ), Richmond, Death and Marriage Register, 1865–1907 (in German), photostat; Congregation Beth Ahabah, Richmond, Records, 1841–1903 (in German), photostat, all in Church Records, Library of Virginia, Richmond.

52. The professions of soldiers in the companies was determined by information in the Compiled Service Records and from the 1860 Richmond city directory. The composition of the companies generally fit the profile of skill given in Ira Berlin and Herbert G. Gutman, "Natives and Immigrants, Free Men and Slaves: Urban Workingmen in the Antebellum American South," *American Historical Review* 88 (Dec. 1983): 1175–1200.

53. Letter, CSA Quartermaster's Office, Richmond, Nov. 26, 1961, in CSR of Henry Dubel, Co. K, First Regiment Virginia Infantry; Compiled Service Records of Henry Bockelman and Philipp Brill, Company K, Fifteenth Regiment Virginia Infantry; letter, CSA Ordinance Department, Richmond, Oct. 4, 1861, in Compiled Service Record of George Gersdorfer, Company K, First Regiment Virginia Infantry.

54. E. M. Morrison to W. H. Taylor, n.d., Compiled Service Record, Roll 558.

55. Note on Quartermaster record by B. F. Howard, July 18, 1863, in Compiled Service Record of Thomas Richter, Company K, First Virginia Regiment Infantry; Wust, *Virginia Germans,* 220.

56. For the text of these orders see *The War of the Rebellion: A Compilation of the Official Records of the Union and Confederate Armies,* ser. 4, vol. 1 (Washington: Government Printing Office, 1900), 1094–1100, 1123–24, quote on 1123.

57. Charles August Hennighausen, Richmond, to Maria Schulz Hennighausen and Wilhelm Hennighausen, Apr. 24, 1865, translation of original letter, pp. 2–7.

58. Affidavit of Berhard Bergmeyer, taken and witnessed by George A. Freeman, Oct. 10, 1862, and affidavit of Edward W. De Voss, Consul of the Free City of Bremen, Richmond, June 17, 1862, in the Compiled Service Record of Bernhard Bergmeyer, Company K, First Regiment Virginia Infantry.

59. Charles August Hennighausen, Richmond, to Maria Schulz Hennighausen and Wilhelm Hennighausen, Apr. 24, 1865, translation of original letter, pp. 7–8; Schuricht, *History of the German Element in Virginia,* 2:91.

60. Second lieutenant's commission of Charles August Hennighausen, Nineteenth Regiment, Second Brigade, Fourth Division, Virginia Militia, July 11, 1864, and roster of Company H, German Home Guard, in Charles August Hennighausen Papers, Virginia Historical Society, Richmond; Wust, *Virginia Germans,* 222.

61. Philip Whitlock's Recollections, 1843–1913, pp. 92–93, Virginia Historical Society, Richmond.

62. Ibid., 105.

63. Ibid., 107–8

64. Ibid., 111–21.

65. See Gunter Moltmann, "The Pattern of German Emigration to the United States in the Nineteenth Century," in *America and the Germans: An Assessment of a Three-Hundred-Year History. Volume One: Immigration, Language, Ethnicity,* ed. Frank Trommler and Joseph McVeigh (Philadelphia: University of Pennsylvania Press, 1985), 15.

66. Charles August Hennighausen, Richmond, to Maria Schulz Hennighausen and Wilhelm Hennighausen, Apr. 24, 1865, translation of original letter, p. 3.

67. Sallie A. Putnam, *Richmond During the War: Four Years of Personal Observation, by a Richmond Lady* (New York: G. W. Carleton & Co., 1867), 101–2.

68. *New York Herald,* Mar. 6, 1862.

69. *Charleston Mercury,* Mar. 8, 1862.

70. Schuricht, *History of the German Element in Virginia,* 2:96–97.

71. Lange, "Changed Name," 226–27 (original, 291).

72. The quote is from an account of the Dahlgren episode in the Elizabeth Van Lew Papers, misc. microfilm, reel 14, Library of Virginia, Richmond, originals in the Manuscript and Archives Division, New York Public Library, Astor, Lenox, and Tilden Foundation. The best source for the entire Dahlgren episode is Meriwether Stuart, "Colonel Ulric Dahlgren and Richmond's Union Underground, April, 1864," *Virginia Magazine of History and Biography* 72, no. 2 (Apr. 1964): 152–204.

73. "Miss Van Lew Now Very Ill," *Evening Leader* (Richmond and Manchester), July 27, 1900, and "Miss Van Lew Dead," in Vertical File—Confederate States of America—Spies—Elizabeth Van Lew, Valentine Museum, Richmond.

74. Elizabeth Van Lew to U. S. Grant, Oct. 3, 1869, Elizabeth Van Lew Papers.

75. "Recollections of Thomas McNiven and His Activities in Richmond During the American Civil War," photocopy of transcription, Personal Papers, Library of Virginia, Richmond. Although this recollection is a transcription, the details given fit remarkably well with other existing material, including the Van Lew Papers and Meriwether Stuart's article on Richmond's Union underground. For instance, it contradicts newspaper accounts of the exhumation of Ulric Dahlgren's body given in the Richmond press many years later, while squaring with Stuart's findings and the Van Lew Papers that an African-American man, not Martin Lipscomb, reported where the body was buried.

76. Charles Palmer, New Orleans, to Doctor William P. Palmer, Jan. 12, 1850, William P. Palmer Papers; Stuart, "Colonel Ulric Dahlgren and Richmond's Union Underground," 180, 187–89; Wallace, *Richmond Howitzers,* 131; Ernest B. Furguson, *Ashes of Glory: Richmond at War* (New York: Alfred A. Knopf, 1996), 113.

77. John T. O'Brien, "'The People's Favorite': The Rise and Fall of Martin Meredith Lipscomb," *Virginia Cavalcade* 31, no. 4 (Spring 1982): 216–23.

78. Gen. George H. Sharpe, Ulster County, N.Y., to Gen. C. R. Comstock, Headquarters, Armies of the United States, Jan. 1867, Elizabeth Van Lew Papers.

79. A standard account of Bowser's activity's is "Miss Van Lew Now Very Ill," *Evening Leader* (Richmond and Manchester), July 27, 1900.

80. "Recollections of Thomas McNiven." Johannah Hoffman is listed in the U.S. Census, 1880, Richmond City, enumeration district 95, p. 22, as living just two doors down from McNiven, microfilm, Library of Virginia, Richmond. Louisa Delarue appears in the U.S. Census, 1870, Richmond City, p. 64. On Orrock, see Stuart, "Colonel Ulric Dahlgren and Richmond's Union Underground," 195–96; Elizabeth Van Lew and Mrs. S. J. Wardwell testified after the war that "two faithful German women" helped bury Ulric Dahlgren's body at Orrock's farm. Merriweather Stuart speculates that these women may have been a neighbor, Augusta Bolton, and Mrs. Orrock, who was not German. McNiven identifies them as Johannah Hoffman and Louisa Delarue. Stuart, "Colonel Ulric Dahlgren and Richmond's Union Underground," 196–97.

81. Meriwether Stuart, "Samuel Ruth and General R. E. Lee: Disloyalty and the Line of Supply to Fredericksburg, 1862–1863," *Virginia Magazine of History and Biography* 71, no. 1 (Jan. 1963): 35–109.

82. Dew, *Ironmaker to the Confederacy*, 91, 129, 239–40.

83. Naragon, "Ballots, Bullets, and Blood," 319.

84. Emory M. Thomas, *The Confederate State of Richmond: A Biography of the Capital* (Austin: University of Texas Press, 1971), 148–49.

85. Anderson & Co. to Josiah Gorgas, Mar. 7, 1863, quoted in Dew, *Ironmaker to the Confederacy*, 245.

86. Dew, *Ironmaker to the Confederacy*, 246–47.

87. Thomas, *Confederate State of Richmond*, 156.

88. Ibid., 155–56; Ervin L. Jordan Jr., *Black Confederates and Afro-Yankees in Civil War Virginia* (Charlottesville: University Press of Virginia, 1995), 71–72, 79–80.

89. Midori Takagi, "Slavery in Richmond, Virginia, 1782–1865" (Ph.D. diss., Columbia University, 1994), 282; Jordan, *Black Confederates and Afro-Yankees in Civil War Virginia*, 79–80.

90. Thomas, *Confederate State of Richmond*, 156; Jordan, *Black Confederates and Afro-Yankees in Civil War Virginia*, 57–58, 116.

91. Janet Duitsman Cornelius, *"When I Can Read My Title Clear": Literacy, Slavery, and Religion in the Antebellum South* (Columbia: University of South Carolina Press, 1991), 59–61; Dan. 11:15 AV.

92. Michael B. Chesson, "Harlots or Heroines? A New Look at the Richmond Bread Riot," *Virginia Magazine of History and Biography* 92, no. 2 (Apr. 1984): 131–75.

93. Michael B. Chesson, *Richmond After the War, 1865–1890* (Richmond: Virginia State Library, 1981), 48.

94. Ibid., 146, 160, 169, 175.

95. *Southern Punch*, Oct. 17, 1863, quoted in Myron Berman, *Richmond's Jewry: Shabbat in Shockoe, 1769–1976* (Charlottesville: University Press of Virginia, 1979), 185.

96. Berman, *Richmond's Jewry*, 177–78.

97. Schuricht, *History of the German Element in Virginia*, 2:60–66, 93; Berman, *Richmond's Jewry*, 170–203.

98. *The Edward Pleasants Valentine Papers* (Richmond: Valentine Museum, n.d.), 4:2356.

99. Wallace, *Richmond Howitzers*, 129, 146, 156; Sherwood and Weaver, *59th Virginia Infantry*, 10, 201.

Epilogue. The Antebellum Legacy

1. Michael B. Chesson, *Richmond After the War, 1865–1890* (Richmond: Virginia State Library, 1981), 57–61.

2. The Washington banner is owned by the Chicago Historical Society and reproduced in Olivia Mahoney and Eric Foner, *America's Reconstruction: People and Politics After the Civil War* (New York: HarperCollins, 1995), color illustration between pages 62 and 63.

3. Theresa M. Guzman-Stokes, "A Flag and a Family: Richard Gill Forrester, 1847–1906," *Virginia Cavalcade* 47, no. 2 (Spring 1998): 52–63.

4. William Paton to Thomas R. Price, Apr. 10, 1865; C. P. and T. Cochran to Thomas R. Price, Apr. 26, 1865, Palmer Family Papers, Virginia Historical Society, Richmond.

5. *Richmond, Virginia, and the New South* (Richmond and Chicago: George W. Englehardt & Company, 1888), 97; Philip Whitlock's Recollections, Virginia Historical Society, Richmond; H. L. Pelouze and Son, *The Richmond Type Foundry: Typographic Specimens* (Richmond: H. L. Pelouze & Son, 1888); *The Edward Pleasants Valentine Papers* (Richmond: Valentine Museum, n.d.), 4:2357; Jane Webb Smith, "Creating History: The Valentine Family and Museum," typescript essay, May 1996, Valentine Museum, Richmond.

6. Charles B. Dew, *Ironmaker to the Confederacy: Joseph R. Anderson and the Tredegar Iron Works* (New Haven: Yale University Press, 1966), 291–93; Chesson, *Richmond After the War*, 60.

7. Elizabeth Valentine Huntley, *Dawn to Twilight: Work of Edward V. Valentine* (Richmond: William Byrd Press, 1929); "J. E. B. Stuart" in Works file, Edward V. Valentine, Valentine Family Papers, Valentine Museum, Richmond; *Edward Pleasants Valentine Papers*, 4:2331, 2350–51.

8. Mary H. Mitchell, *Hollywood Cemetery: The History of a Southern Shrine*

(Richmond: Virginia State Library, 1985), 63–81; Elizabeth R. Varon, *We Mean to Be Counted: White Women and Politics in Antebellum Virginia* (Chapel Hill: University of North Carolina Press, 1998), 169–77.

9. *Richmond Enquirer,* Dec. 7, 1873; *Richmond State,* Dec. 27, 1885, Dec. 13, 1886; *Richmond Dispatch,* Dec. 12, 1886.

10. "Uncle Henry" in Works file, Edward V. Valentine, Valentine Family Papers; Gregg D. Kimball, " 'The South As It Was': Social Order, Slavery, and Illustrators in Virginia, 1830–1877," in *Graphic Arts and the South: Proceedings of the 1990 North American Print Conference,* ed. Judy L. Larson (Fayetteville: University of Arkansas Press, 1993), 146–50.

11. John T. O'Brien, *From Bondage to Citizenship: The Richmond Black Community, 1865–1867,* Studies in Nineteenth-Century American Political and Social History (New York: Garland Publishing, Inc., 1990), 172–80.

12. Ibid., 96–97.

13. Charlotte K. Brooks and Joseph K. Brooks, with Walter H. Brooks, *The Brooks Chronicles: The Life and Times of an Afro-American Family* (Washington, D.C., 1989), 85, states that Holmes "had been implicated in the escape of his wife, also a slave, from Richmond. He spent several months in jail and was afterward sold south to New Orleans, where he lived until the war ended." A short biography published in the *Richmond Planet,* Jan. 31, 1885, and bound into the First African Baptist Church Minute Book II, pp. 270–71, microfilm, Library of Virginia, Richmond, states that he was sold away from his wife but that "the mother and father of his wife, who had escaped to Massachusetts by the Underground Railroad, succeeded in having their daughters and two children purchased by some interested abolitionists." Holmes received a letter of dismissal from First African Baptist on Dec. 2, 1849.

14. *Richmond Planet,* Jan. 31, 1885; First African Baptist Church Minutes, Apr. 10, 1853; *Inventory of the Church Archives of Virginia: Negro Baptist Churches in Richmond* (Richmond: Historical Records Survey of Virginia, 1940); Peter J. Rachleff, *Black Labor in the South: Richmond, Virginia, 1865–1890* (Philadelphia: Temple University Press, 1984), 57.

15. Brooks and Brooks, *Brooks Chronicles,* 91–102, quote on page 94.

16. D. Webster Davis, *The Life and Public Services of Rev. Wm. Washington Browne . . .* (Philadelphia: Mrs. Mary A. Browne, printed by the A. M. E. Book Concern, 1910), caption under portrait between pages 68 and 69; James D. Watkinson, "William Washington Browne and the True Reformers of Richmond, Virginia," *Virginia Magazine of History and Biography* 97, no. 3 (July 1989): 376–80; Elsa Barkley Brown, "Womanist Consciousness: Maggie Lena Walker and the Independent Order of Saint Luke," *Signs* 14, no. 3 (Spring 1989): 616–21.

17. Stephen H. Boles, Wilmsburough, Franklin Parish, La., to Mrs. Mann S.

Valentine, Apr. 1, 1866, Valentine Family Papers; *Edward Pleasants Valentine Papers,* 4:2330; receipt for "Sally, and her four children," to Mann S. Valentine from estate of Benjamin Mosby, Feb. 26, 1831, Valentine Family Papers.

18. Elsa Barkley Brown and Gregg D. Kimball, "Mapping the Terrain of Black Richmond," *Journal of Urban History* 21, no. 3 (Mar. 1995): 304–6.

19. Rachleff, *Black Labor in the South,* 46.

20. Ibid, 46, 56–61; Daniel Barclay Williams, *A Sketch of the Life and Times of Capt. R. A. Paul* (Richmond: Johns and Goolsby, 1885); obituary of Josiah Crump, in the *Richmond Planet,* Feb. 22, 1890.

21. Gregg D. Kimball, "The Working People of Richmond: Life and Labor in an Industrial City, 1865–1920," *Labor's Heritage* 3, no. 2 (Apr. 1991): 42–65.

22. Michael Chesson found that one-sixth of all scalawag leaders whom he could identify were born in Germany. Chesson defines "scalawags" as men "who were born in Richmond, or in Virginia or other southern states, or had lived in Richmond before and during the war." *Richmond After the War,* 107; *Aufruf an die deutschen Adoptiv-Bürger der Stadt Richmond* (Richmond: Offices of the *Täglicher Anzeiger,* ca. 1870).

23. Chesson, *Richmond After the War,* 110–11.

24. "James Bahen," in *Dictionary of Virginia Biography: Vol. 1, Aaroe-Blanchfield,* ed. John T. Kneebone et al. (Richmond: Library of Virginia, 1998), 282–83.

BIBLIOGRAPHY

MANUSCRIPT AND ARCHIVAL SOURCES

Clements Library, University of Michigan, Ann Arbor
  Jacob Bechtel Papers, 1858–62
Rare Book, Manuscript, and Special Collections Library, Duke University, Durham,
  North Carolina
  Clopton Family Papers
  John B. Danforth Papers. Letter Book, 1854–64
  George W. Munford Correspondence, 1849–62. Munford-Ellis Family Papers
  William P. Palmer Papers, 1847–51
  Henry Lafayette Pelouze Papers, 1841–89
  Conway Robinson Papers, 1830–33
  John Rutherfoord Papers. Letterbook, 1825–37
  Mary Virginia Hawes Terhune Papers, 1843–1920
  James Thomas Jr. Papers, 1850–79
  Unidentified woman's diary, 1854–55. David Bullock Harris Papers
Archives Research Services, Library of Virginia, Richmond
  Business Records
    Mutual Assurance Society of Virginia Papers. Declarations and Revaluations of
      Assurance, 1796–1867, accession 30117
    Silas Omohundro Business and Estate Records, Richmond, 1842–82, accession
      29642
    Tredegar Iron Company Records, 1836–1957, accessions 23881 and 24808
  Church Records
    First African Baptist Church, Richmond, Minute Book, 1841–59, accession
      28225 (misc. microfilm reel 494)
    Congregation Beth Ahabah, Richmond, Records, 1841–77, accession 26038
    Saint Mary's German Catholic Church, Richmond, Birth and Marriage Records,
      1848–1908, accession 29802 (misc. microfilm reel 352)

Saint John's Church (United Church of Christ), Richmond, Register, 1865–1907,
    accession 29365a (photostat)
Local Records
    Henrico County, Free Negro Registers, 1831–63 (microfilm)
    Richmond City, Hustings Court Deed Books, 1840–60 (microfilm)
    Richmond City, Hustings Court Will Books, 1840–60 (microfilm)
State Records
    Department of Health (Record Group 36), Division of Vital Records and Health
        Statistics, Richmond Births, Deaths, and Marriages (microfilm)
    Auditor of Public Accounts, Personal Property Tax Lists, Richmond City, 1836–
        50 (microfilm reel 365)
    Executive Papers (Record Group 3), Governor Joseph Johnson, 1852–56
    Executive Papers (Record Group 3), Governor Henry A. Wise, 1856–60
    General Assembly (Record Group 78), Legislative Petitions, Richmond City,
        1840–61
Personal Papers
    "Recollections of Thomas McNiven and His Activities in Richmond During the
        American Civil War," accession 33673 (photocopy of transcription)
    Richmond Light Infantry Blues Records, 1794–1933, accession 29873
    William Ludwell Sheppard diary, 1853–54, accession 24772 (negative photostat)
    Musician's diary, 1 Jan.–19 Dec. 1856, accession 22671
Federal Records
    Compiled Service Records of Confederate Soldiers from Virginia (microfilm)
    U.S. Census, 1850–70, Richmond City (microfilm)
Other
    Elizabeth Van Lew Papers, 1862–1901 (misc. microfilm reel 14, originals in
        Manuscript and Archives Division, New York Public Library, Astor, Lenox,
        and Tilden Foundation)
Library of Congress, Washington, D.C.
    American Colonization Society Records, 1792–1964
    Ellis-Allan Records
Southern Historical Collection, Wilson Library, University of North Carolina at
    Chapel Hill
    Launcelot Minor Blackford diary
    Henry L. Cathell diary
    Bessie Lacy letters, 1848. Drury Lacy Papers
    Peter H. Mayo Recollections (typescript on microfilm)
    Mordecai Family Papers
    Scott and Pearman Family Letters, 1852–69. Norvell W. Wilson Papers
    Wooster Family Papers

Valentine Museum, Richmond

"The Narrative of Thomas Rutherfoord, 1766–1852" (typescript)

Richmond History Vertical Files

Mary Wingfield Scott Papers, 1935–53

Valentine Family Papers, 1786–1920

Special Collections Department, University of Virginia Library, Charlottesville

John Gault Letter, 25 December 1853 (mss 9683-E)

Silas and R. H. Omohundro Ledger, 1857–63 (mss 4122)

Richmond Police Day Book, 1834–43 (mss 1481)

Virginia Historical Society, Richmond

Central Southern Rights Association of Virginia, Record Book, 1850–60

Ann Webster Gordon Christian diary, 1860–67

Claiborne Family Papers

Samuella Hart Curd diary (typescript), 1860–63

John Gault Letter, 31 December 1853

Anne Eliza Pleasants Gordon diary (typescript), 1857

Robert A. Granniss diary, 1858–61

William Gray and Company Papers

Gwathmey Family Papers. Maria Watts Gwathmey diary, 1853

Charles August Hennighausen Letters, 24 April and 25 May 1865, translation of original letters

Charles August Hennighausen Papers

Johann Gottfried Lange, "Der veraenderte Nahme, oder der Schumacher in der alten und der neuen Welt. 30 Jahre in Europa und 30 Jahre in Amerika," [The Changed Name, or the Shoemaker in the Old and the New World. 30 Years in Europe and 30 Years in America], manuscript memoir

Daniel H. London Papers

Palmer Family Papers

Price Family Papers, 1794–1973

Richmond City Sergeant's Papers, 1841–51

Richmond Female Institute Records

Society for the Prevention of the Absconding and Abduction of Slaves, Richmond, Minutes of director's meetings, 1833–49 (photocopy, original in Miscellaneous Manuscripts, New-York Historical Society)

James Stanard Papers

Virginia Association of Ladies for Erecting a Statue to Henry Clay Subscription Book

Virginia Branch, American Colonization Society Records, Minutes, 1823–59

Philip Whitlock, Recollections, 1843–1913

PUBLISHED SOURCES

Adams, George F. *A Brief Sketch of the Life and Character of the Late William Crane of Baltimore.* Baltimore: John F. Weishampel Jr., 1868.

Ambler, Charles Henry. *Sectionalism in Virginia from 1776 to 1861.* Chicago: University of Chicago Press, 1910.

Atherton, Lewis E. *The Southern Country Store, 1800–1860.* Baton Rouge: Louisiana State University Press, 1949.

Barrett, Philip. *Gilbert Hunt, the City Blacksmith.* Richmond: James Woodhouse and Company, 1859.

Bender, Thomas. *Toward an Urban Vision: Ideas and Institutions in Nineteenth Century America.* Baltimore: Johns Hopkins University Press, 1975.

Bergstrom, Peter V. "Markets and Merchants: Economic Diversification in Colonial Virginia, 1700–1775." Ph.D. diss., University of New Hampshire, 1980.

Berlin, Ira. *Slaves without Masters: The Free Negro in the Antebellum South.* New York: Pantheon Books, 1974.

———, and Herbert G. Gutman, "Natives and Immigrants, Free Men and Slaves: Urban Workingmen in the Antebellum American South." *American Historical Review* 88 (Dec. 1983): 1175–2000.

Berman, Myron. *Richmond's Jewry: Shabbat in Shockoe, 1769–1976.* Charlottesville: University Press of Virginia, 1979.

Berry, Thomas S. "The Rise of Flour Milling in Richmond." *Virginia Magazine of History and Biography* 78, no. 4 (Oct. 1970): 387–408.

Blanton, Wyndham Bolling. *The Making of a Downtown Church: The History of the Second Presbyterian Church, Richmond, Virginia, 1845–1945.* Richmond: John Knox Press, 1945.

Bodnar, John. *Remaking America: Public Memory, Commemoration, and Patriotism in the Twentieth Century.* Princeton: Princeton University Press, 1991.

Bratton, Mary Jo, ed. "Fields's Observations: The Slave Narrative of a Nineteenth-Century Virginian." *Virginia Magazine of History and Biography* 88, no. 1 (Jan. 1980): 75–93.

Bremer, Frederika. *The Homes of the New World: Impressions of America.* 2 vols. New York: Harper & Brothers, 1853.

Brooks, Charlotte K., and Joseph K. Brooks, with Walter H. Brooks. *The Brooks Chronicles: The Life and Times of an Afro-American Family.* Washington, D.C., 1989.

Brown, Elsa Barkley. "Womanist Consciousness: Maggie Lena Walker and the Independent Order of Saint Luke." *Signs* 14, no. 3 (Spring 1989): 610–33.

———, and Gregg D. Kimball. "Mapping the Terrain of Black Richmond." *Journal of Urban History* 21, no. 3 (Mar. 1995): 296–346.

Bruce, Kathleen. "Slave Labor in the Virginia Iron Industry." *William and Mary Quarterly* ser. 2, vol. 6, no. 4 (Oct. 1926): 289–302; vol. 7, no. 1 (Jan. 1927): 21–31.

————. *Virginia Iron Manufacture in the Slave Era.* New York: Century Company, 1931.

Brumbaugh, Thomas B. "The Evolution of Crawford's 'Washington.'" *Virginia Magazine of History and Biography* 70, no. 1 (Jan. 1962): 3–29.

Butter's Richmond Directory for 1855. Richmond: H. K. Ellyson, 1855.

By-laws of the Montgomery Guard, Second Company, First Regiment Virginia Volunteers, Adopted July 17th, 1850. Revised May 1858. Richmond: McFarlane & Fergusson, 1858.

Cate, Wirt Armistead. "History of Richmond, Virginia." Unpublished typescript. Valentine Museum, Richmond.

Central Southern Rights Association of Virginia. *Memorial of the Central Southern Rights Association of Virginia, Being a Statement of Grievances and Suggestion of Remedies Thereof.* Richmond: n.p., 1859.

————. *The Proceedings and Address of the Central Southern Rights Association of Virginia . . .* Richmond: Ritchie and Dunnavant, 1851.

The Charters and Ordinances of the City of Richmond . . . Richmond: Ellyson's Steam Presses, 1859.

Chesson, Michael B. "Harlots or Heroines? A New Look at the Richmond Bread Riot." *Virginia Magazine of History and Biography* 92, no. 2 (Apr. 1984): 131–75.

————. *Richmond After the War, 1865–1890.* Richmond: Virginia State Library, 1981.

Clawson, Mary Ann. *Constructing Brotherhood: Class, Gender, and Fraternalism.* Princeton, N.J.: Princeton University Press, 1989.

Click, Patricia. *The Spirit of the Times: Amusements in Nineteenth-Century Baltimore, Norfolk, and Richmond.* Charlottesville: University Press of Virginia, 1989.

Coffield, E. M., & Co., comp. *Richmond Business Directory, and Merchants and Manufacturers' Advertiser.* Richmond: John W. Randolph, 1858.

"Commercial and Industrial Cities of the United States. Number LX. Richmond, Virginia." *Hunt's Merchant Magazine and Commercial Review* 40, no. 1 (Jan. 1859): 54–66.

Constitution, By-Laws, and Bill of Prices of the Association of Journeyman Stone-Cutters of the City of Richmond, Established 1845. Richmond: n.p., 1850.

Cornelius, Janet Duitsman. *When I Can Read My Title Clear: Literacy, Slavery, and Religion in the Antebellum South.* Columbia: University of South Carolina Press, 1991.

Crofts, Daniel W. *Reluctant Confederates: Upper South Unionists in the Secession Crisis.* Chapel Hill: University of North Carolina Press, 1989.

Cronon, William. *Nature's Metropolis: Chicago and the Great West.* New York: W. W. Norton, 1991.

Crowe, Eyre. *With Thackeray in America.* New York: Charles Scribner's Sons, 1893.

Curry, Leonard P. *The Free Black in Urban America, 1800–1850: The Shadow of the Dream.* Chicago: University of Chicago Press, 1981.

Cutchins, John A. *A Famous Command: The Richmond Light Infantry Blues.* Richmond: Garrett and Massie, 1934.

Davis, Susan G. *Parades and Power: Street Theatre in Nineteenth-Century Philadelphia.* Philadelphia: Temple University Press, 1986.

Dew, Charles B. *Ironmaker to the Confederacy: Joseph R. Anderson and the Tredegar Iron Works.* New Haven: Yale University, 1966.

Dickens, Charles. *American Notes for General Circulation.* 1842. New York: D. Appleton & Company, 1868.

Earle, Carville, and Ronald Hoffman. "Staple Crops and Urban Development in the Eighteenth Century South." *Perspectives in American History* 10 (1976): 7–78.

Egerton, Douglas R. *Gabriel's Rebellion: The Virginia Slave Conspiracies of 1800 and 1802.* Chapel Hill: University of North Carolina Press, 1993.

Elliott & Nye's Virginia Directory, and Business Directory for 1852. Richmond: Elliott & Nye, 1852.

Ellyson, Moses. *The Richmond Directory and Business Advertiser for 1856.* Richmond: H. K. Ellyson, 1856.

Ethridge, Harrison M. "The Jordan Hatcher Affair of 1852: Cold Justice and Warm Compassion." *Virginia Magazine of History and Biography* 84, no. 4 (Oct. 1976): 446–63.

Ezekiel, Herbert T., and Gaston Lichtenstein. *The History of the Jews in Richmond from 1769 to 1917.* Richmond: H. T. Ezekiel, 1915.

Ferslew, W. Eugene. *First Annual Directory for the City of Richmond, to Which is Added a Business Directory for 1859.* Richmond: George M. West, 1859.

———. *Second Annual Directory for the City of Richmond, to which is added a Business Directory for 1860.* Richmond: W. Eugene Ferslew, 1860.

Fischer, David Hackett, and James C. Kelly. *Away, I'm Bound Away: Virginia and the Westward Movement.* Richmond: Virginia Historical Society, 1993.

Fox-Genovese, Elizabeth. *Within the Plantation Household: Black and White Women of the Old South.* Chapel Hill: University of North Carolina Press, 1988.

Franklin, John Hope. *A Southern Odyssey: Travelers in the Antebellum North.* Baton Rouge: Louisiana State University Press, 1976.

Freehling, Alison Goodyear. *Drift Toward Dissolution: The Virginia Slavery Debate of 1831–1832.* Baton Rouge: Louisiana State University Press, 1982.

Furguson, Ernest B. *Ashes of Glory: Richmond at War.* New York: Alfred A. Knopf, 1996.

Gilroy, Paul, *The Black Atlantic: Modernity and Double Consciousness* (Cambridge, Mass.: Harvard University Press, 1992).

Goldfield, David R. *Region, Race, and Cities: Interpreting the Urban South.* Baton Rouge: Louisiana State University Press, 1997.

————. *Urban Growth in the Age of Sectionalism: Virginia, 1847–1861.* Baton Rouge: Louisiana State University Press, 1977.

————. "Urban-Rural Relations in the Old South: The Example of Virginia." *Journal of Urban History* 2 (Feb. 1976): 146–68.

Goldin, Claudia Dale. *Urban Slavery in the American South: A Quantitative Analysis.* Chicago: University of Chicago Press, 1976.

Horton, James O. *Free People of Color: Inside the African American Community.* Washington, D.C.: Smithsonian Institution Press, 1993.

Hundley, Daniel R. *Social Relations in Our Southern States.* Introduction by William J. Cooper. 1860. Baton Rouge: Louisiana State University Press, 1979.

Huntley, Elizabeth Valentine. *Dawn to Twilight: Work of Edward V. Valentine.* Richmond: William Byrd Press, 1929.

Inventory of the Church Archives of Virginia. Negro Baptist Churches in Richmond. Richmond: The Historical Records Survey of Virginia, 1940.

Irons, Charles F. "And All These Things Shall Be Added Unto You: The First African Baptist Church, Richmond, 1841–1865." *Virginia Cavalcade* 47, no. 1 (Winter 1998): 26–35.

Jackson, Luther Porter. *Free Negro Labor and Property Holding in Virginia.* New York: Appleton, 1942.

Johnson, Michael P., and James L. Roark. *No Chariot Let Down: Charleston's Free People of Color on the Eve of the Civil War.* Chapel Hill: University of North Carolina Press, 1984.

Johnson, Whittington B. "Andrew C. Marshall: A Black Religious Leader in Antebellum Savannah," *Georgia Historical Quarterly* 69, no. 2 (Summer 1985): 173–92.

Jordan, Ervin L., Jr. *Black Confederates and Afro-Yankees in Civil War Virginia.* Charlottesville: University Press of Virginia, 1995.

Kammen, Michael. *A Season of Youth: The American Revolution and the Historical Imagination.* New York: Alfred A. Knopf, 1978.

Kimball, Gregg D. "African-Virginians and the Vernacular Building Tradition in Richmond City, 1790–1860." In *Perspectives in Vernacular Architecture, vol. 6,* edited by Thomas Carter and Bernard L. Herman. Columbia and London: University of Missouri Press for the Vernacular Architecture Forum, 1991.

————. " 'The South as it Was': Social Order, Slavery, and Illustrators in Virginia, 1830–1877." In *Graphic Arts & the South: Proceedings of the 1990 North American Print Conference,* edited by Judy L. Larson. Fayetteville: University of Arkansas Press, 1993.

————. "The Working People of Richmond: Life and Labor in an Industrial City, 1865–1920." *Labor's Heritage* 3, no. 2 (Apr. 1991): 42–65.

Kimball, Gregg D., and Nancy Jawish Rives, "'To live in hearts we leave behind is not to die': The Barton Heights Cemeteries of Richmond," *Virginia Cavalcade* 46, no. 3 (Winter 1997): 118–31.

Kneebone, John T., et al. *Dictionary of Virginia Biography: Vol. 1, Aaroe-Blanchfield.* Richmond: Library of Virginia, 1998.

Levine, Lawrence. *High Brow/Low Brow: The Emergence of Cultural Hierarchy in America.* Cambridge: Harvard University Press, 1988.

Linderman, Gerald F. *Embattled Courage: The Experience of Combat in the American Civil War.* New York: The Free Press, 1987.

Link, William A. "The Jordan Hatcher Case: Politics and 'A Spirit of Insubordination' in Antebellum Virginia." *Journal of Southern History* 64, no. 4 (Nov. 1998): 615–48.

Litwack, Leon F. *North of Slavery: The Negro in the Free States, 1790–1860.* Chicago: University of Chicago Press, 1961.

Macon, T. J. *Life Gleanings.* Richmond: W. H. Adams, 1913.

Mahoney, Olivia and Eric Foner. *America's Reconstruction: People and Politics after the Civil War.* New York: HarperCollins, 1995.

Manarin, Louis H. *Richmond at War: The Minutes of the City Council.* Official Publication No. 17, Richmond Civil War Centennial Committee. Chapel Hill: University of North Carolina Press, 1966.

Manarin, Louis H., and Lee A. Wallace Jr. *Richmond Volunteers: The Volunteer Companies of the City of Richmond and Henrico County, Virginia, 1861–1865.* Official Publication No. 26, Richmond Civil War Centennial Committee. Richmond: Westover Press, 1969.

Marion Harland's Autobiography: The Story of a Long Life. New York: Harper & Brothers, 1910.

McLeod, Norman C., Jr. "Free Labor in a Slave Society: Richmond, Virginia, 1820–1860." Ph.D. diss., Howard University, 1991.

———. "Mann Satterwhite Valentine: Patriarch of a Richmond, Virginia, Merchant Family." Master's thesis, Virginia State University, 1982.

———. "Not Forgetting the Land We Left: The Irish in Antebellum Richmond." *Virginia Cavalcade* 47, no. 1 (Winter 1998): 36–47.

Michel, Gregg L. "From Slavery to Freedom: Hickory Hill, 1850–1880." In *The Edge of the South: Life in Nineteenth-Century Virginia,* edited by Edward L. Ayers and John C. Willis. Charlottesville: University Press of Virginia, 1991.

Miller, Randall M. "The Enemy Within: Some Effects of Foreign Immigrants on Antebellum Southern Cities." *Southern Studies* 24 (Spring 1985): 30–53.

———. "Immigrants in the Old South." *Immigration History Newsletter* 10 (Nov. 1978): 8–14.

Mills & Starke, comp. *The City of Richmond Business Directory and City Guide.* Richmond: Gary & Clemmitt, printers, 1866.

Mitchell, Mary H. *Hollywood Cemetery: The History of a Southern Shrine*. Richmond: Virginia State Library, 1985.

Moltmann, Gunter. "The Pattern of German Emigration to the United States in the Nineteenth Century." In *America and the Germans: An Assessment of a Three-Hundred-Year History. Volume 1: Immigration, Language, Ethnicity*, ed. Frank Trommler and Joseph McVeigh. Philadelphia: University of Pennsylvania Press, 1985.

Montague, William L. *The Richmond Directory and Business Advertiser for 1852*. Baltimore: J. W. Woods, Printer, 1852.

Montague's Richmond Directory and Business Advertiser. 1850–51.

Montgomery, David. *The Fall of the House of Labor: The Workplace, the State, and American Labor Activism, 1865–1925*. Cambridge: Cambridge University Press, 1989.

Mordecai, Samuel. *Virginia, Especially Richmond, in By-Gone Days*. 2d ed. Richmond: West & Johnston, 1860.

Morgan, Lynda J. *Emancipation in Virginia's Tobacco Belt, 1850–1870*. Athens: University of Georgia Press, 1992.

Moss, Elizabeth. *Domestic Novelists in the Old South: Defenders of Southern Culture*. Baton Rouge: Louisiana State University Press, 1992.

Naragon, Michael Douglas. "Ballots, Bullets, and Blood: The Political Transformation of Virginia, 1850–1874." Ph.D. diss., University of Pittsburgh, 1996.

Noe, Kenneth W. *Southwest Virginia's Railroad: Modernization and the Sectional Crisis*. Urbana: University of Illinois Press, 1994.

Notes on Travel and Life, by Two Young Ladies—Misses Mendell and Hosmer. New York: n.p., 1853.

O'Brien, John T. "Factory, Church, and Community: Blacks in Antebellum Richmond." *Journal of Southern History* 44, no. 4 (Nov. 1978): 509–36.

———. *From Bondage to Citizenship: The Richmond Black Community, 1865–1867*. Studies in Nineteenth-Century American Political and Social History. New York: Garland Publishing, 1990.

———. "'The People's Favorite': The Rise and Fall of Martin Meredith Lipscomb." *Virginia Cavalcade* 31, no. 4 (Spring 1982): 216–23.

Olmsted, Frederick Law. *A Journey in the Seaboard Slave States, with Remarks on Their Economy*. New York: Dix & Edwards, 1856.

O'Mara, James. *An Historical Geography of Urban System Development: Tidewater Virginia in the Eighteenth Century*. Geographical Monographs, no. 13. Downsview, Ont.: Department of Geography, Atkinson College, York University, 1983.

Pelouze, H. L. & Son. *The Richmond Type Foundry. Typographic Specimens*. Richmond: H. L. Pelouze & Son, 1888.

Perdue, Charles L., Jr., Thomas E. Barden, and Robert K. Phillips. *Weevils in the*

Wheat: Interviews with Ex-Slaves. Charlottesville: University Press of Virginia, 1976.

Population of the United States in 1860; Compiled from the Original Returns of the Eighth Census. Washington, D.C.: Government Printing Office, 1864.

Pred, Allan. *Urban Growth and City-Systems in the United States, 1840–1860.* Cambridge, Mass.: Harvard University Press, 1980.

Pugh, Evelyn L. "Women and Slavery: Julia Gardiner Tyler and the Duchess of Sutherland." *Virginia Magazine of History and Biography* 88, no. 2 (Apr. 1980): 186–202.

Putnam, Sallie A. *Richmond During the War: Four Years of Personal Observation, by a Richmond Lady.* New York: G. W. Carleton & Co., 1867.

Raber, Michael S., Patrick M. Malone, and Robert B. Gordon. "Historical and Archaeological Assessment, Tredegar Iron Works Site, Richmond, Virginia." Report submitted to the Valentine Museum and the Ethyl Corporation, 1992.

Rachleff, Peter J. *Black Labor in the South: Richmond, Virginia, 1865–1890.* Philadelphia: Temple University Press, 1984.

Redpath, James. *The Roving Editor, or Talks with Slaves in the Southern States.* Edited by John R. McKivigan. 1859. University Park: Pennsylvania State University Press, 1996.

Remke, Ignatius. *Historical Sketch of St. Mary's Church, Richmond, Virginia, 1843–1935.* Richmond: n.p., 1935.

Report of a Committee Appointed by the Board of Directors to the Annual Meeting of the Board of Trade, held in the City of Richmond, May, 1857. Richmond: Whig Book and Job Office, 1857.

Report to the Stockholders of the Richmond Female Institute, Together with the Catalogue for 1856. Richmond: H. K. Ellyson, 1856.

Richmond City and Henrico County, Virginia, 1850 United States Census. Virginia Genealogical Society, Special Publication No. 6, 1977.

Richmond Portraits in an Exhibition of Makers of Richmond, 1737–1860. Richmond: Valentine Museum, 1949.

Robert, Joseph C. *Tobacco Kingdom: Plantation, Market, and Factory in Virginia and North Carolina, 1800–1860.* Durham: Duke University Press, 1938.

Roediger, David R. *The Wages of Whiteness: Race and the Making of the American Working Class.* New York: Verso, 1991.

Rosenbaum, Claire Millhiser. *Universal and Particular Obligations: Beth Shalome-Beth Ahabah, 1789–1989.* Richmond: Beth Ahabah Museum and Archives Trust, 1988.

Ryland, Robert. "Reminiscences of the First African Baptist Church, Richmond, Va., by the Pastor." Nos. 1–4, *American Baptist Memorial* (Sept.–Dec. 1855).

———. *The Scriptural Catechism, for Coloured People.* Richmond: Harrold and Murray, 1848.

Salmon, John. "'A Mission of the most secret and important kind': James Lafayette and American Espionage in 1781," *Virginia Cavalcade* 31 (1981): 78–85.

Schechter, Patricia A. "Free and Slave Labor in the Old South: The Tredegar Ironworkers' Strike of 1847." *Labor History* 35 (Spring 1994): 165–86.

Schnittman, Suzanne Gehring. "Slavery in Virginia's Urban Tobacco Industry, 1840–1860." Ph.D. diss., University of Rochester, 1987.

Schuricht, Herrmann. *History of the German Element in Virginia.* Baltimore: T. Kroh & Sons, Printers, 1898–1900.

Schwartz, Barry. *George Washington: The Making of an American Symbol.* New York: Free Press, 1987.

Schwarz, Philip J. *Slave Laws in Virginia.* Studies in the Legal History of the South, edited by Paul Finkelman and Kermit L. Hall. Athens: University of Georgia Press, 1996.

Scott, Mary Wingfield. *Houses of Old Richmond.* Richmond: Valentine Museum, 1951.
———. *Old Richmond Neighborhoods.* Richmond: Whittet & Shepperson, 1950.

Shade, William G. *Democratizing the Old Dominion: Virginia and the Second Party System, 1824–1861.* Charlottesville: University Press of Virginia, 1996.

William Ludwell Sheppard: A Retrospective Exhibition of His Works, December, 1969. Richmond: Valentine Museum, 1969.

Sherwood, G. L., and Jeffrey C. Weaver. *59ᵗʰ Virginia Infantry.* Lynchburg: H. E. Howard, 1994.

Sidbury, James. *Ploughshares into Swords: Race, Rebellion, and Identity in Gabriel's Virginia, 1730–1810.* Cambridge: Cambridge University Press, 1997.

Simpson, Craig M. *A Good Southerner: The Life of Henry A. Wise of Virginia.* Chapel Hill: University of North Carolina Press, 1985.

Smith, Jane Webb. "Creating History: The Valentine Family and Museum." Typescript essay, Valentine Museum, ca. 1994.

Smith, Karen Manners. "Half My Heart in Dixie: Southern Identity and the Civil War in the Writings of Mary Virginia Terhune." In *Beyond Image and Convention: Explorations in Southern Women's History*, edited by Janet L. Coryell et al. Columbia: University of Missouri Press, 1998.

Smith, Miriam Jane. "Forgotten Virginian—From British Merchant to Prominent Citizen: Thomas Rutherford, 1766–1852." *West Virginia History* 36, no. 1 (Oct. 1974): 50–62.

Starobin, Robert. *Industrial Slavery in the Old South.* New York: Oxford University Press, 1970.

Statistics of the United States . . . in 1860; Compiled from the Original Returns and Being the Final Exhibit of the Eighth Census. Washington, D.C.: Government Printing Office, 1866.

Staudenraus, P. J. *The African Colonization Movement, 1816–1865.* New York:

Columbia University Press, 1961.

Stearns, Charles. *Narrative of Henry Box Brown. . . .* Boston: Brown and Stearns, 1849. Afro-American History Series, Rhistoric Publications No. 205. Philadelphia: Rhistoric Publications, 1969.

Stevens, Charles Emery. *Anthony Burns: A History.* Boston: John P. Jewett and Company, 1856.

Still, William. *The Underground Railroad.* 1871. Reprint, Chicago: Johnson Publishing Company, 1970.

Stuart, Meriwether. "Colonel Ulric Dahlgren and Richmond's Union Underground, April 1864." *Virginia Magazine of History and Biography* 72, 2 (Apr. 1964): 152–204.

———. "Samuel Ruth and General R. E. Lee: Disloyalty and the Line of Supply to Fredericksburg, 1862–1863." *Virginia Magazine of History and Biography* 71, no. 1 (Jan. 1963): 35–109.

Tadman, Michael. *Speculators and Slaves: Masters, Traders, and Slaves in the Old South.* Madison: University of Wisconsin Press, 1989.

Takagi, Midori. "Slavery in Richmond, Virginia, 1782–1865." Ph.D. diss., Columbia University, 1994.

Thomas, Emory M. *The Confederate State of Richmond: A Biography of the Capital.* Austin: University of Texas Press, 1971.

Trapnell, Frederica H. *Virginia Tucker-Henry L. Brooke Correspondence: Richmond, Virginia, 1831–1869.* N.p.: Frederica H. Trapnell, 1978.

Tyler, Lyon Gardiner, ed. *Encyclopedia of Virginia Biography.* Vol. 2. New York: Lewis Historical Publishing Company, 1915.

Tyler-McGraw, Marie. "Richmond Free Blacks and African Colonization, 1816–1832." *Journal of American Studies* 21 (1987): 220–21.

———. *At the Falls: Richmond, Virginia, and Its People.* Chapel Hill: University of North Carolina Press, 1994.

Tyler-McGraw, Marie, and Gregg D. Kimball. *In Bondage and Freedom: Antebellum Black Life in Richmond, Virginia.* Richmond: Valentine Museum, 1988.

The Edward Pleasants Valentine Papers. Richmond: Valentine Museum, n.d.

Varon, Elizabeth R. " 'The Ladies Are Whigs': Lucy Barbour, Henry Clay, and Nineteenth-Century Virginia Politics." *Virginia Cavalcade* 42, no. 2 (Autumn 1992): 72–83.

———. *We Mean to Be Counted: White Women and Politics in Antebellum Virginia.* Chapel Hill: University of North Carolina Press, 1998.

Virginia Geographic Alliance. *An Atlas of Virginia.* Dubuque, Iowa: Kendall/Hunt, 1989.

Wade, Richard. *Slavery in the Cities: The South, 1820–1860.* New York: Oxford University Press, 1964.

Wallace, Lee A., Jr. "The First Regiment of Virginia Volunteers, 1846–1848." *Virginia Magazine of History and Biography* 77, no. 1 (Jan. 1969): 46–77.

———. *The Richmond Howitzers.* Lynchburg: H. E. Howard, 1993.

Wallace, Lee A., Jr., and Detmar H. Finke. "Virginia Military Forces, 1858–1861." *Military Collector and Historian* 10 (Fall 1958): 61–73.

The War of the Rebellion: A Compilation of the Official Records of the Union and Confederate Armies. Ser. 4, vol. 1. Washington: Government Printing Office, 1900.

Watkinson, James D. "William Washington Browne and the True Reformers of Richmond, Virginia." *Virginia Magazine of History and Biography* 97, no. 3 (July 1989): 375–98.

Weis, Tracey M. "Negotiating Freedom: Domestic Service and the Landscape of Labor and Household Relations in Richmond, Virginia, 1850–1880." Ph.D. diss., Rutgers, The State University of New Jersey—New Brunswick, 1994.

Weisiger, Minor T., Donald R. Traser, and E. Randolph Trice. *Not Hearers Only: A History of St. James's Episcopal Church, Richmond, Virginia, 1835–1985.* Richmond: St. James Episcopal Church, 1986.

Wust, Klaus G. "German Immigrants and Nativism in Virginia, 1840–1860." *Twenty-ninth Report. Society for the History of the Germans in Maryland.* Baltimore, 1956.

———. *The Virginia Germans.* Charlottesville: University Press of Virginia, 1979.

INDEX